# *Assessing Behavior:*

## READINGS IN EDUCATIONAL AND PSYCHOLOGICAL MEASUREMENT

*Edited by*
JOHN T. FLYNN and HERBERT GARBER
*University of Connecticut*

ADDISON-WESLEY
PUBLISHING COMPANY
READING, MASSACHUSETTS · PALO ALTO · LONDON · DON MILLS, ONTARIO

This book is in the
ADDISON-WESLEY SERIES IN EDUCATION

*Preface*

The articles and excerpts presented in this anthology are intended to fulfill a need experienced by nearly every graduate and undergraduate student beginning the study of educational and psychological measurement and evaluation. That need is for a wider, deeper acquaintance with the history, problems, and strategies of psychological measurement. In one or two ordinary semesters, it is impossible for the teacher to provide directly for personal experiences which will bring about the required appreciations and other necessary noncognitive changes in the student.

Even the best-written major textbook, while it is concerned primarily with imparting concepts and principles and a "feel" for the field, represents the condensation and reinterpretation of countless individual contributions. One consequence of such transformation is that a particular set of emphases is transmitted which reflects the particular preferences of the writer; this goes a long way to increasing the understanding of some concepts but leaves others less well-mastered or neglected entirely. As an example, the differences between the psychometric and the impressionistic orientations present a difficult task for a single writer to handle. If he is effective in presenting the affect associated with one viewpoint he is certain to be accused of "bias." If he is cold and objective in his treatment, the student is unmoved and hence neglects to formulate a rational or even not so rational position with respect to an important issue.

One way experienced teachers have found to both deepen and widen student understanding is to require evidence that some collateral, outside reading has been done. It is an ancient story requiring no extended explanation here that control over such student reading by the teacher is close to the vanishing point. It is our hope that this book may somewhat restore a degree of such needed direction.

The selections gathered here were chosen if they met one or both of two principal criteria: concrete illustrations of important applied measurement technique and nonesoteric presentations of measurement theory. We have tried to include within each chapter a balance between the two criteria. It is left to the critical reader, if he so desires, to identify the articles which belong under each of the two rubrics. To aid both instructor and student, a chart correlating the readings with chapters in popular measurement texts has been provided at the end of the book.

Finally, this collection in itself represents the biases, condensations, interpretations and other idiosyncrasies of the editors as they judged along many intangible dimensions the merit of many readings, most of which were discarded. For the glaring omissions we are to blame. For the glorious inclusions we are loath to take credit. The original writers and good counsel of supporting colleagues deserve any approbrium due this book.

We are indeed grateful to the authors and publishers of the selections contained in this collection for permission to reprint their materials. We also wish to acknowledge our thanks to Mr. Daniel Turro for his excellent and reliable assistance in the development of the book. In the final preparation of the manuscript we received invaluable assistance from Donald Marcotte, Vera Smith, and Orba Washburn under the effective supervision of Louise Patros.

*Storrs, Connecticut*                                    John T. Flynn
*December 1966*                                      Herbert Garber

# Contents

CHAPTER 1. PURPOSES AND HISTORY

1.1 Dingle, H. *Basic Problems of Measurement* . . . . . 1
1.2 Dyer, H. *On the Assessment of Academic Achievement* . . 7
1.3 Chauncey, H. *Report of the President 1960–1961, Educational Testing Service* . . . . . . . . . . . . . 21
1.4 Adkins, Dorothy. *Measurement in Relation to the Educational Process* . . . . . . . . . . . . . . . . 35

CHAPTER 2. ESSENTIALS OF A USEFUL TEST

2.1 Wesman, A. G. *Reliability and Confidence* . . . . . . 54
2.2 Knauft, E. B. *Test Validity Over a Seventeen-Year Period* . 65
2.3 Ebel, R. L. *Measurement and the Teacher* . . . . . . 67

CHAPTER 3. RELIABILITY AND VALIDITY

3.1 Doppelt, J. E. *The Correction for Guessing* . . . . . . 77
3.2 Lambert, Nadine. *The Present Status of the Culture-Fair Testing Movement* . . . . . . . . . . . . . 83
3.3 Lennon, R. T. *The Stability of Achievement Test Results from Grade to Grade* . . . . . . . . . . . 103
3.4 Joint Committee on Standards for Educational and Psychological Tests and Manuals. *Validity and Reliability Defined* . . . . . . . . . . . . . . . . . 111

CHAPTER 4. TEST SCORE INTERPRETATIONS

4.1 Anastasi, Anne. *The Concept of Validity in the Interpretation of Test Scores* . . . . . . . . . . . . 120
4.2 Dunnette, M. D. *Critics of Psychological Tests: Basic Assumptions: How Good?* . . . . . . . . . . . 132
4.3 Lister, J. L. *When Are Test Scores Different?* . . . . . 141
4.4 Seashore, H. G. and Ricks, J. H., Jr. *Norms Must Be Relevant* . . . . . . . . . . . . . . . . . 147

CHAPTER 5. MEASURING COGNITIVE VARIABLES

5.1 Good, W. R. *Misconceptions About Intelligence Testing* . 156

5.2 Brim, O. G., Jr. *American Attitudes toward Intelligence Tests* . . . . . . . . . . . . . . . . . . . 160
5.3 Loretan, J. O. *Alternatives to Intelligence Testing* . . . . 171

CHAPTER 6. MEASURING NONCOGNITIVE VARIABLES

6.1 Krathwohl, D. R., et. al. *How and Why to Classify Affective Educational Objectives* . . . . . . . . . . . 183
6.2 Ruff, G. E. and Levy, E. Z. *Psychiatric Evaluation of Candidates for Space Flight* . . . . . . . . . . . 202
6.3 Cronbach, L. J. *The Unique Functions of Assessment Procedures* . . . . . . . . . . . . . . . . . . 214
6.4 Darling, D. W. *Why a Taxonomy of Affective Learning?* . 221

CHAPTER 7. DECISION-MAKING AND PREDICTION

7.1 Thorndike, R. L. *Educational Decisions and Human Assessment* . . . . . . . . . . . . . . . . . . 227
7.2 Thorndike, R. L. *The Prediction of Vocational Success* . . 240
7.3 Cronbach, L. J. and Gleser, Goldine C. *The Tester and Decision Theory* . . . . . . . . . . . . . . . . 255

CHAPTER 8. TEACHER-MADE TESTS

8.1 Ebel, R. L. *Improving the Competence of Teachers in Educational Measurement* . . . . . . . . . . . . 263
8.2 Diederich, P. B. *Making and Using Tests* . . . . . . 269
8.3 Laidlaw, W. J. *Teacher-made Tests: Models to Serve Specific Needs* . . . . . . . . . . . . . . . . . . 278
8.4 Stanley, J. C. *The ABC's of Test Construction* . . . . . 284

CHAPTER 9. SCHOOL TESTING PROGRAMS

9.1 Womer, F. B. *Testing Programs—Misconception, Misuse, Overuse* . . . . . . . . . . . . . . . . . . 292
9.2 Lefever, D. W. *The Teacher's Role in Evaluating Pupil Achievement* . . . . . . . . . . . . . . . . . 301
9.3 Lennon, R. T. *Testing: Bond or Barrier between Pupil and Teacher?* . . . . . . . . . . . . . . . . . . 309

CHAPTER 10. MEASUREMENT IN RESEARCH

10.1 Brownell, W. A. *The Evaluation of Learning under Differing Systems of Instruction* . . . . . . . . . . . . 316
10.2 Allport, G. W. *Traits Revisited* . . . . . . . . . 328
10.3 Comrey, A. L. *Mental Testing and the Logic of Measurement* 348
10.4 Stoddard, G. D. *On the Meaning of Intelligence* . . . . 358
10.5 Garber, H. *The Digital Computer Simulates Human Rating Behavior* . . . . . . . . . . . . . . . . . . 367
10.6 Flynn, J. T. *The Adjective Check List, a Device to Assess Perceived Self* . . . . . . . . . . . . . . . . 374

CORRELATION CHART OF READINGS AND POPULAR
MEASUREMENT TEXTS 376

# 1  Purposes and History

## 1.1  Basic Problems of Measurement

*Herbert Dingle*

This distinguished physicist-astronomer presents in this condensed book review the scientist's philosophy of measurement. It may be somewhat disturbing to some readers to discover that even the physical scientist does not necessarily believe he is measuring a *real thing* when he makes his precise weighings, sightings, and length measurements. Since proof is often lacking that some underlying trait has been tapped, what value do you feel tests have in providing evidence for educational judgments about children?

To understand what measurement means we must turn to the physical sciences as the field affording the potentialities of measurement their widest scope; there alone are all the known processes of measurement exemplified. Consequently a true conception of measurement must cover physical measurements in their widest generality. Such a conception shows that measurement is a self-contained process, a process that implies nothing beyond that of which it gives a numerical estimation.

It is perfectly legitimate to ask an astronomer to measure the area in the sky of the constellation Orion as defined by the International Astronomical Union. But what is the "something" that he measures? We no longer think in terms of a "sky" and from another viewpoint the constellation ceases to exist. There is no "something," but beyond question there is a measurement.

Pursuing the matter, we see not only that all physical measurements are of this kind, but also that, far from starting with a something and then measuring it, we start with a measure and then try to find something to which we can attach it. We measure the weight, $W$, of a body, and its height, $h$, above the ground, and form the product $Wh$. This we regard as significant because it is equal to the kinetic energy with which the body, having been released, reaches the ground. We therefore invent something that $Wh$ measures and call it the potential energy of the body. When the body falls, and $h$ becomes O, it loses its potential energy. We are delighted, and think we have "discovered" potential energy. But we are now forced to say that when a body moves toward or away from the sun, it similarly loses or gains potential energy. Suppose, then, that our body falls to the earth when the sun is directly overhead. Has it gained or lost potential energy? We can take our choice, which means that potential energy is not "something to be measured," but a quantity devised after the measurement has shown its importance. In its devising we are free to exercise our choice among various possibilities; and, if we do not devise it at all, the measurement has exactly the same status it had before.

Take another example. We make a measurement with a diffraction grating and call the result the "wave length" of light. But we do not first perceive the waves and then measure their length; we make a measurement and then invent "wave length" to attach to it. The invention is just as arbitrary as that of potential energy, and at present it is even less satisfactory. Another observer, moving away from us in the direction of the light, gets a different value. It is the same light. Which observer determines the "right" wave length? Clearly, at least one of our measurements does not imply a "wave length to be measured." But if the something is not wave length, what is it? We do not know though there can be no doubt that this measurement is important.

So we could continue. For this reason I some years ago proposed the rudiments of a theory in which measurement was defined as "any precisely specified operation that yields a number"; that is, measurement is related to the operation performed and not to the hypothetical "something" on which it is supposed to be performed. This theory appeared in *The British Journal for the Philosophy of Science* (Vol. 1, page 5) and as it seems not to have been noticed by any of the contributors to the present volume, I shall take the liberty of outlining its basic idea. But first of all I think it will be useful to take a step still further back and see how measurement came to be practiced at all. This point is not touched upon in the volume, yet it is of some relevance and is indeed essential if we are to understand fully what measurement signifies. The contributors to the volume take measurement for granted and then discuss—often admirably—what it is, but they do not ask why it must be taken for granted. They tacitly assume the strategy of the campaign and concentrate on the tactics. Let us see why the strategy commits us to measurement.

The fundamental problem of philosophy is that of making sense of our experience. We are originally aware of a haphazard succession of experiences. After a while some regularities force themselves on our attention—night and day alternate, falling is followed by a pain, and so on. The first philosopher is the man who first conceives the possibility that other—perhaps all—experiences are related; that is, experiences form a rational system. Given a knowledge of some experiences, therefore, other experiences that seem quite independent can be predicted.

The earliest philosophers accepted the obvious relations and tried to supplement them—the alternation of night and day was associated with alternations of heat and cold, falling on grass hurt less than falling on stone—until in such a system as that of Aristotle, with its generalizations in terms of matter and form, a considerable area of experience became organized into a rational system. Two things characterized this approach: first, it was concerned entirely with involuntary experience; and second, progress in it was painfully slow.

By the 17th century the patience of philosophers was exhausted (I am of course describing not what consciously went on in their minds, but what we, knowing the outcome of their actions, can see to be the truest rationalization of them), and they said: "Look here; we aren't getting anywhere with ordinary experience; it is too difficult. Let us make some artificial experiences and find relations between them. Then perhaps ordinary experiences will fit in later." So instead of studying the natural motions of birds and smoke and rivers, they made artificial motions—balls rolling down carefully prepared grooves. Thus was born scientific experiment: the deliberate production of artificial experiences more simply related to one another than those that come naturally.

The aspect of the artificial experiences that was examined was the metrical aspect. The rolling ball did not pass from potentiality to actuality; it merely gave readings on a measuring scale and a form of clock, readings represented by numbers. What was the advantage of this? Simply that, since rational relations were required, it brought into operation the most highly developed form of reasoning known: pure mathematics. The artificial experiences were reduced to experiences of numbers, and then metrical science was born. Thus the original aim of relating all natural experience was transformed to that of relating the numbers yielded by contrived operations.

But this was not at all understood. It was thought that each measurement represented a property of something in the "external world." The object of philosophy was conceived to be the study of this external world. Our experience—which is ultimately all that is of any importance to anybody—was simply a trivial effect of the casual impinging of the "world" on our bodies; the "world" would be exactly the same if this had never occurred. This idea could persist because there happened to be a pretty close correspondence between the other "things" that were thought to be measured and the "things" that we actually experience, but in fact this correspondence is illusory. Take mass, for instance. This is the name given to something conceived to be responsible for the recordings of certain measuring instruments. But mass was imagined to be "the quantity of matter in a body," and this was plausible, because when the instrument recorded a big number, a large body was usually seen. Hence it was believed that Newton's law of gravitation described the path of a planet around the sun. In reality it describes the path of a mass-point in a gravitational field, and both mass-point and gravitational field belong to an invented world that only in part corresponds to the common-sense world of material objects. If the earth should explode to smithereens through internal stresses, the mass-point (the "center of gravity") would continue on its orbit undisturbed, but there would be no matter where it was situated.

Every symbol in every physical equation stands for the result of a measurement or a combination of such results, and fundamentally for nothing else. In a simple case like that of mass, the correspondence between symbol and some element of ordinary experience is fairly close; usually matters are more complex. Take, for example, Avogadro's number, N—the number of molecules in a cubic centimeter of gas in a certain state. N actually stands for a combination of measurements with thermometers, pressure gauges, balances and so on. (There are various combinations that give the same result; that is why the "number" is important.) But we describe N as "a number of molecules"—the name given to the result of the operation of counting. And we think of it as such. But in fact the operation of counting molecules is impossible. We can delude ourselves into believing that the operation of weighing is a discovery of the mass of a body, but no honest man can claim that when he is finding N he is counting anything. Yet such is our faith that each measurement is a measurement of "something" that we are ready to make such a claim in order to maintain that faith. Nor is that the worst. We even analyze the intricate concept that we call "the momentum of an electron" as though we had a particle of matter before us and were applying the process for measuring momentum to it; and then we imagine that we are learning something about the world of experience. God help us!

The whole world of physics is a set of relations between concepts that represent combinations of the results of measurements, i.e., of artificially created experiences. Nothing that this world contains would ever have happened if we had not made it happen. To verify any of the relations you must adjust the conditions with the greatest care; let experience come naturally, and their supposed requirements are always violated. Go on dropping an object to the ground, and it will come to rest at a different place every time. Go out one day, and you feel warm; do the same the next day, and you feel cold. The laws of falling bodies and of heat are obeyed only in laboratories. Physics tells us a tremendous amount about the world, but it is not the natural world; it is a world of our own making.

How is it, then, that we have turned the results of physical research to such significant account in ordinary life? Simply because of a purely empirical relation between the natural and the artificial worlds. Over a large part of experience they maintain a close parallelism. When a balance gives a big number, we usually do see a big object (but we have seen that a large value of M does not always mean that). When the thermometer has a high reading, we usually feel hot (but in outer space we should probably die instantly of cold, although astronomers tell us that the temperature there can be over 1,000 degrees centigrade). Why the sight of a big object is usually attended by a large M, and feeling of heat by a large O, we understand no more than Thales could have if he had known the facts. With all our science we have learned nothing about the relations existing in the world of natural experience. We have discovered how to create a world between the elements of which rational relations do exist, and we exploit the empirical fact of its close parallelism with the natural world.

This is of the greatest importance in regard to the function of measurement in other sciences such as psychology and sociology. Here exactly the same considerations hold good, but whereas in physics the parallelism between the metrical concepts and ordinary experiences is the rule and its breakdown the exception, in the other sciences the reverse is more nearly true; at least any supposed measurement of a psychological attribute is much less uniformly related to actual experience than is normally the case in physics. To take but a single example, the primary importance of Intelligence Quotient is not that it measures "intelligence," whatever that may be, but that it stands in simple relations to other measurements (in particular, a relation approaching identity with further determinations of the same quantity with the same person). We may expect that in time a considerable system of relations between psychological measurements will be built up, but woe betide us if we imagine that its relation to the world of experience is other than purely empirical. A large IQ may go with a good performance in other specified operations, but its possessor may well be a gambling addict, and so one of the most "unintelligent" of persons.

It is in view of such facts as these that measurement must be defined in terms of its origin in the operations we perform, without reference to anything external. Having so defined it, we can begin its analysis. Each measurement includes a manual and a mental part; for example, in measuring length we lay an object along a specified scale (the manual part) and subtract the smaller from the larger of the end-readings (the mental part). We deliberately relax the precision of the specification in two respects. In the manual part we allow one element of the operation to be changed ad lib.; in the example of length we can make "the object" anything we like, and we call the result (merely as a name) the length of that object. In the mental part we allow ourselves to multiply the result of any fundamental measurement (that is, a measurement that does not include another measurement as a part of its prescription) by any number; we call

this (again merely as a name) "changing the unit of measurement."
The whole process is thus described without wandering outside into
a hypothetical "something to be measured."

---

## 1.2   On the Assessment of
## Academic Achievement
*Henry S. Dyer*

There are several purposes to which education and psychological
tests are customarily put. However, no matter what the tester hopes
to learn about the testee's behavior, it is almost invariably true that
it will be a developed or learned attainment which the test will
evoke. In other words, achievement.

Dr. Dyer has a very fresh, uncluttered way of talking and writing
about measurement and evaluation problems. This article is no
exception. In it you will find a careful, clear description of what the
field of measurement is about. You may be in for a surprise or two,
especially if you believe that tests can be expected to relieve the
professionals from the need to make judgments about the progress
students and counselees have made.

In these days of ferment in the curriculum, any large producer of
educational tests is likely to get strange and wonderful requests from
teachers suddenly smitten by the need to evaluate the new things
they are doing. The following letter, though purely imaginary, is
not untypical. It reflects a few of the mistaken ideas about testing
and the assessment of achievement which are prevalent:

*Dear Sir:*

*During this past academic year I have been giving a new course,
Marine Wild Life 106. I need some incontrovertible evidence to
prove to my suspicious colleagues that Marine Wild Life 106 is*

Reprinted with permission of the author and *Teachers College Record*,
**62,** 1960, 164–172.

*more comprehensive and effective than the course it has replaced, namely, Marine Wild Life 102.*

*Will you therefore please send me 92 copies of your standard-ized objective test in ichthyology? I am particularly interested in showing that my students have developed a true and deep appre-ciation of the love-life of our underwater friends.*

*Please rush the shipment, since I want to give the test as part of my final examination next Thursday.*

*Sincerely yours,*
*Professor Finn*

Although Professor Finn does not exist, he has many educational cousins who do, and who think, with him, that the purpose of educational evaluation is to demonstrate the truth of a foregone conclusion. It has never occurred to him that an investigation of Marine Wild Life 106 should be so planned as to permit negative findings to appear if, in fact, the course is not all he firmly believes it to be.

But what most bothers the professional tester about the many Professor Finns who are experimenting with new courses is the series of bland assumptions that lie behind the letters they write. The first such assumption is that one can prove something by giving a single test after the show is all over. The second is that a standard-ized objective test is standard and objective in some absolute sense, as though it had been made in heaven. The third is that testing agencies are like vending machines: All you have to do is put your nickel in the right slot, and out will come precisely the test you are looking for. All of which would be just dandy if true, but unfortu-nately none of these assumptions bears any noticeable relation to the facts of testing and the assessment of achievement.

## THE HUMAN SIDE OF TESTS

What Professor Finn does not appear to realize is that an educational test of any kind is primarily a human process, not a physical thing. It is a process that begins and ends in human judgment. It is a process that requires time, effort, and hard creative thinking, not only of the professional tester, but of the test user as well. It is a process that can take an infinite number of forms, depending on the purposes to be served and the conditions under which the testing is to be done. It is a process that can hardly be confined to the use of multiple choice questions and paper-and-pencil techniques if it is to provide the sort of rewarding illumination of the educational scene that some people hope for.

In what follows I shall discuss some of the essentials of the testing process as applied to the assessment of academic achievement and pay my respect to several of the knotty problems that bedevil the whole enterprise. The discussion will turn up more questions than answers, but if the questions are sufficiently disturbing, the outcome should be such as to nudge Professor Finn toward deeper wisdom in approaching his evaluation problem.

What do we mean by "academic achievement"? If it is something we are trying to assess, then it seems reasonable to ask first of all what it is. In current usage, it is a fuzzy term that may mean any one of a dozen unspecified things: the sum total of information a student has at his command when he finishes a course of instruction, the getting of a passing grade in a course regardless of what may lie behind the grade, the score on a test that has "achievement" in the title, and so on.

There are two ideas that can be used to pin down the notion of academic achievement a bit more precisely. The first idea is that academic achievement refers to the *identifiable operations* a student is expected to perform on the materials of a course, that is, on the facts, theories, problems, principles, and points of view which he encounters while taking the course. The second idea is that academic achievement refers to the *differences* between the number and the kinds of operations a student can and does perform at the beginning of a course and the number and kinds of operations he can and does perform at the end of a course.

The key terms in the definition of achievement are *identifiable operations* and *differences*. The emphasis on operations is supposed to suggest that it is what the student actually *does* that counts. We should think of achievement as something composed of transitive verbs with direct objects—verbs like *infer, generalize, recall, compare, analyze, evaluate, organize, criticize.* And we need to be sure that we can identify these operations by reference to specific tasks or questions that require them. ("What inferences can you draw from the following set of data?" "What general principle can you find that explains the behavior of the following political figures?" etc.)

The emphasis on the *differences* between what a student does at the beginning of a course and what he does at the end of a course call attention to the fact that academic achievement is a dynamic, not a static, concept; it is what has happened between then and now, not just what is happening now. Can the student now solve differential equations that he found impossible last October? Can he detect differences between Beethoven and Brahms that were not apparent to him earlier? Can he organize his thoughts in written form better than he did at the outset?

Clearly, under the definition, the assessment of academic achievement is a complicated business; it is not something that can be done merely by going out and buying a standardized test two weeks before the final examination. It requires that the teacher responsible for a course must himself be a major participant in the assessment job from start to finish. He may be able to get supplementary aid from published tests; he may find that the professionals in testing can give him useful ideas and point the way to sound strategy but the substance of the job of sizing up what he has done to his students rests with him.

How shall he proceed?

## CLARITY OF GOALS

Obviously, the first step is for him to get a clear idea of what he is trying to have his students achieve. What operations does he want them to perform in June that they could not perform last September? This may be an "obvious" first step, but a look around the classrooms of the country suggests that it is a step rarely taken. Almost invariably teachers are more concerned with what *they* are going to do in their courses than with what their *students* are going to do. Lessons and lectures are outlined, reading lists are laid out, visual aids are planned, but few teachers give much concentrated attention to what the fuss is really all about from the standpoint of the student. If a syllabus is prepared, it almost never gives any detailed description of what students are supposed to be able to do as a result of having been exposed to the instructor and the subject matter. There is usually a hope that students will be impressed, that they will remember something, and in a vague sort of way it is felt that the course experiences will do them good, that is, make better thinkers or better citizens of them. But there is very little disposition to get down to brass tacks and specify what kinds of student performance are deemed to reflect better thinking or better citizenship.

All of which is hardly surprising. Stating the goals of a course in a highly concrete manner takes more energy and imagination than most teachers have time for. One of the very practical problems in developing a sound assessment program is to find the time needed to carry out this essential first step.

Generally speaking the goals of achievement fall into three broad classes: informational goals, proficiency goals, and attitudinal goals. The informational goals refer to those items of information that students are expected to know and give forth on demand by the time they have completed a course. It would appear that these can be readily described simply by listing the topics, sub-topics, and sub-sub-topics the course is expected to cover. But this is only half the story. A fact in human knowledge is not just the name of something standing all by itself; it is a subject and a predicate. It is not just the name "sodium"; it is the sentence, "Sodium is a metal." Progress toward the informational goals of a course, therefore, is measured by the number and complexity of these subject-predicate relationships which the student can reproduce. In making the informational goals useful as a basis for assessing achievement, some explicit attention must be given to these relationships and to their degree of complexity. It is not sufficient to list topics and sub-topics and sub-sub-topics.

The large majority of teachers would disown the idea that the *only* kinds of goals they have in mind for their courses are informational goals. They would argue, and quite properly, that information is one of the goals, and a necessary one, but certainly not one of ultimate importance. This they argue, but their arguments are too often confounded by their own examinations, which demand facts and facts only. One of the hoariest criticisms brought against objective tests is that they test only for factual information, while essay tests get at the higher aspects of learning. This would be a cogent criticism except for two things: First, a well-made objective test need not be limited to the measurement of factual information; and second, essay tests are too frequently graded solely by counting the number of relevant facts that each student churns up.

Most of what we think of as "the higher aspects of learning" is contained in the proficiency goals of academic achievement, that is, proficiency in various kinds of skills, both manual and mental—manipulative skills, problem solving skills, evaluative skills, and organizational skills. Taken together, they add up to effective thinking and sound execution. But to be useful as guides in the assessment of achievement, they must *not* be taken together; they must be elaborated in detail and expressed in terms of the multitude of different kinds of specific tasks a student is expected to perform and in terms of the specific kinds of operations he must follow in performing them.

Unless the proficiency goals are elaborated in this fashion, they may be too easily overlooked or forgotten. Back in the 1930's a number of experiments in the teaching of science led to the conclusion that science courses without laboratory instruction were just as effective as science courses with laboratory instruction. The typical set-up was to divide science classes into two groups, one of which received laboratory work in addition to the regular course work and the other of which received no laboratory exercise. At the end of the course, the two groups would be compared by means of an achievement test in science. The differences in test scores between the two groups were generally negligible. Why? Because in setting up the tests, the proficiency goals peculiar to laboratory instruction had been overlooked. The only measures used had been measures related mainly to informational goals that have little or nothing to do with what goes on in a laboratory. Under these conditions, the finding of no difference in achievement between the two groups is essentially meaningless, since the relevant proficiency variables had not been taken into account. More recently Kruglak and his associates at Minnesota have taken a second look at this problem in science teaching, have devised tests aimed directly at the proficiency goals of laboratory instruction, and have come up with results of a more meaningful sort (7).

It is admittedly no easy matter to define all the proficiency goals in terms of student performance. One can flounder a long time over the types of performance that form the components of creative thinking, for instance, or skill in evaluative judgment. The result is that nobody has yet been able to produce a completely satisfactory and universally applicable method for assessing achievement in these areas. On the other hand, there have been some interesting attacks on the problem, and possibly in the course of time it may be solved (8, 10, 11). A giant step toward the solution will be made when teachers now uttering pious sentiments on the subject will get down to cases and try to define what they are really looking for when they speak of such things as "creative power" and "sensitivity to values."

Finally, there are the attitudinal goals—those educational objectives which are often blithely called the "intangibles." Everybody applauds them, but few teachers seem to know what to do about them. How does one define such goals as love of music or sense of social responsibility or enthusiasm for abstract ideas in such a way that they can be recognized when seen? What is it that a student does to demonstrate that he likes good literature? We have our dodges on matters of this sort: We count the books a student takes out of the library; we measure the amount of spare time he gives to good reading (provided, of course, we allow him any spare time at all); we engage him in conversation and try to judge from the fervor in his voice how far along the scale of appreciation his reading has brought him, or we ask him outright on some sort of rating schedule how well he likes Shakespeare and T. S. Eliot. But we suspect that these devices for uncovering attitudes are based on exceedingly tenuous inferences. Books may be taken out of the library not to be read, but to maintain an impressive looking book-shelf. The time spent in reading may really be spent only in an effort to avoid reality. Conversational fervor may be only good acting or the effect of one cocktail too many. And a rating schedule can almost always be faked if much depends upon it.

I dislike to be discouraging in this all-important matter of attitu-dinal goals, but thus far very few operations have been suggested which define them satisfactorily. There are some breaks in the clouds, though. At Pennsylvania State University a group of experi-menters has been trying to get a line on student attitudes toward television instruction. One device they have hit upon is to give the students generous samples of both TV instruction and conventional instruction, and then to permit them a genuine choice as to which type they would take for the remainder of the semester (3). This is a real operational definition of a specific attitude. It furnishes a fruitful clue for further development in defining attitudes in other areas, the general principle being that one defines attitudes in terms of live decisions that make an actual difference in what an individual will do or not do.

## MEASUREMENTS OF GOALS

Once the goals of instruction have been clearly set forth by describ-ing the operations students have to perform to attain them, the problem of devising tests and other techniques for assessing aca-demic achievement is at least seventy-five per cent solved. The reason is that an achievement test is in effect a sample of all the kinds of tasks that a given course of study is striving to get students to master. As such, the tests should in themselves constitute a definition of the goals to be attained. In putting together an appropriate sample of tasks and checking out their adequacy, there are technical matters in which the experienced tester may serve as a guide to the teacher. But, again, the questions of what to include or not to include, what is more important and what is less important, what constitutes a good response and what constitutes a poor response must in the last analysis be the teacher's decision if the test is to measure progress toward the goals *he* has in mind.

On the other hand, as mentioned above, teachers are busy people who are unlikely to find the time they need to do all that really should be done to work out the goals of their own instruction and to devise fully valid measures for assessing achievement. What are some of the practical compromises?

In the first place, although one is unlikely to find any published standardized test that in all respects fits the goals of a particular course or school, one may, by analyzing such tests question by question, possibly find one that comes reasonably close. Looking at a test question by question is important not only for determining a test's general suitability, but also for deciding what questions might properly be eliminated in assessing the performance of one's own students. Surprisingly, the notion of adapting a published test by dropping out irrelevant material seldom occurs to people, yet in many circumstances it is an obvious and justifiable procedure.

Standardized tests, when they can be found and adapted, have two important advantages for any program for assessing academic achievement. First, the makers of such tests have usually lavished a great deal of care on the preparation and try-out of each question to make sure that it is unambiguous, that it discriminates sharply between good and poor students, and that it is of the right level of difficulty for the group at which it is aimed. Second, two or more parallel forms of a standardized test are usually available, so that one has at his disposal the means for accomplishing a highly important part of the assessment job, that of measuring the student's perfor- mance twice—once at the beginning of the course and once again at the end.

## TESTING THINKING ABILITY

Until recently most standardized tests have concentrated rather heavily on the purely informational goals of instruction and have tended to neglect the proficiency goals. In the last few years, however, there has been a marked change in this respect. More and more tests are made up of questions that require the student to perform various mental operations well beyond the simple operation of re-calling learned facts. They are getting at problem solving and rea-soning processes of many kinds. Consider the following sets of questions drawn from a booklet describing the achievement tests of the College Entrance Examination Board (1). If the reader will take the trouble to wrestle with them, I think he will find that they challenge powers of thought well beyond simple memory, though they also require of the student a firm foundation of factual knowl-edge.

The first set of questions is intended to test the student's appre-ciation of those factors that must be controlled so that valid conclu-sions can be drawn from the results of a scientific experiment:

You are to conduct an experiment to determine whether the rate of photosynthesis in acquatic plants is affected by the addition of small amounts of carbon dioxide to the water in which the plants are growing. You have available all of the equipment and material generally found in a well-equipped science laboratory plus sev-eral well-rooted Elodea plants which are growing in a battery jar. It is evident that the plants are healthy because they are giving off bubbles of oxygen.

1. If the addition of carbon dioxide were to have an effect upon aquatic plants, almost immediately after bubbling the gas through the water you would expect to observe a noticeable change in the

    A) growth of the plants
    B) temperature of the water
    C) coloring of the plant leaves
    D) rate of bubble production by the plant
    E) amount of oxygen consumed by leaf respiration

2. If a carbon dioxide generator were not available for the experiment, an adequate supply of carbon dioxide might be pro-vided by

    A) placing a piece of carbon in the water in which the plants are growing
    B) burning a candle over the battery jar
    C) adding carbon tetrachloride to the water

D) pumping air into the water

E) blowing through a glass tube into the water

3. Which of the following materials would be *least* useful in identifying the escaping gas as oxygen?

A) A collection bottle

B) Glass tubing

C) A glass plate

D) Splints

E) Matches

4. Which of the following materials could be used to provide a source of carbon dioxide for this experiment?

A) Distilled water and carbon

B) Zinc and carbonic acid

C) Limestone and hydrochloric acid

D) Limewater and carbon

E) Sodium hydrozide and carbon

5. The addition of carbon dioxide could have no observable effect upon the rate of bubbling by the Elodea plants if you had

A) previously turned off the light

B) no means of regulating the carbon dioxide flow

C) no means of regulating the room temperature

D) a variable water temperature

E) no cover on the battery jar

6. Before you could conclude whether or not the rate of photosynthesis in aquatic plants in general is affected by the addition of small amounts of carbon dioxide to the surrounding water, you would have to repeat the experiment using

A) all the materials of the original experiment

B) an entirely different set of materials

C) other aquatic plants

D) other Elodea plants

E) some terrestrial plants

The following set of questions attempts to test the student's knowledge and understanding of United States foreign policy:

*Speaker I:* I don't think the United States has any business getting involved in the affairs of other nations, through foreign aid or anything else. We have prospered without aid from other countries. Why can't other nations do the same?

*Speaker II*: But we can't afford not to aid other nations. A foreign-aid program offers us a great opportunity to increase our prestige and we should take advantage of it. A nation which ignores other nations will not be regarded as important.

*Speaker III*: Maybe, but let's not forget the fact that foreign aid is also an investment in our own future. If we don't help other free nations, we can't expect to stay free ourselves.

*Speaker IV*: Let's be practical about this. If other nations are too weak to stand on their own two feet, we should help them, yes, but let's remember that when they become dependent on us we must also subordinate them to us. We can only justify foreign aid if we're going to protect our investment.

*Speaker V*: You're all so cold-blooded about this! It isn't a matter of practicality, but of moral obligation to aid other countries. If we could only renounce war, think of the money and material which would be available for constructive work.

1. A humanitarian point of view is best represented by Speaker
   (A) I    (B) II    (C) III    (D) IV    (E) V

2. Since the close of World War II, the United States has mainly justified its foreign-aid policy by arguments such as those advanced by Speaker
   (A) I    (B) II    (C) III    (D) IV    (E) V

3. Which speaker represents a point of view historically associated with the midwestern United States?
   (A) I    (B) II    (C) III    (D) IV    (E) V

4. Speaker IV would probably have approved of the
   1. Platt Amendment
   2. Roosevelt Corollary to the Monroe Doctrine
   3. Good Neighbor policy
      (A) 3 only
      (B) 1 and 2 only
      (C) 1 and 3 only
      (D) 2 and 3 only
      (E) 1, 2, and 3

Despite the progress that may have been made in developing standardized tests, one must always bear in mind that they can never do the whole job of assessing academic achievement in a particular situation. In the last analysis, if a teacher wants to measure those aspects of achievement peculiar to his own instruction he must resort to at least some tests of his own making. He can get some good ideas for approaching this enterprise from two books: *Taxonomy of Educational Objectives* (2) and *General Education: Explorations in Evaluation* (5). If one peruses these books looking for new testing ideas rather than faults, one may find much that is helpful in suggesting ways and means of measuring progress toward the goal of more effective thinking.

But the assessment of the student's growth in effective thinking is still not enough. Any teacher with a well-developed conscience is primarily concerned that his students shall acquire increasing maturity in their attitudes, that is, a more grown-up and informed approach to life and learning. The assessment of this aspect of achievement requires ingenuity and a willingness to experiment with tests that might be regarded as "off-beat."

## TESTING MATURITY

Two such instruments may be mentioned as examples. One, called *The Facts About Science* (9), looks on the surface like an ordinary factual test aimed at seeing how much the student knows about scientists and the sorts of things they do. Actually, however, the pay-off response to each of the scored questions represents a false stereotype of the scientist or his work, e.g., "A scientist has no sense of humor." The test has been used to see to what extent high school courses in science influence students away from these false stereotypes. The same approach could be taken to get at student attitudes toward many other social institutions and enterprises.

Another instrument carries the title *Sizing Up Your School Subjects* (6). It focuses on students' attitudes toward their current academic work and is especially designed for use in educational experiments where a given subject is being taught by two or more methods. Through an indirect approach, which almost certainly guarantees that the student will not fake his responses, it provides the means for comparing different courses or different methods of instruction in the same course with respect to the reactions of students to ten aspects of the material or the teaching. (E.g., What course is best at holding the student's attention? What course is regarded by the student as most valuable to him?) With a little imagination, the technique can be elaborated to cover the attitudes of students toward almost any feature of the academic work in which they are engaged.

## ALTERNATIVE DEVICES

One of the things that is holding back the development of new and better methods of assessing academic achievement, especially in the area of attitudes, is the tendency to think almost exclusively in terms of paper-and-pencil tests, particularly multiple choice tests. Multiple choice tests are useful up to a point. They can do more than most people realize in tapping a student's higher mental processes, and all the possibilities of multiple choice questions have not yet been fully explored. Nevertheless, the multiple choice test has, by its very nature, certain severe limitations. So do other forms of written tests, including essay tests.

To break out of this restricted mode of thinking we ought to consider how to exploit the possibilities in the so-called situational tests which psychologists have been working on in recent years. To what extent can such tests be adapted to the measurement of the "intangibles" of academic achievement? Situational tests are still highly experimental and full of technical problems, but they may well be the answer to the question of how to evaluate many of the subtle aspects of human behavior that can never be reached satisfactorily by paper-and-pencil devices.

One effort to apply a situational test in the classroom setting can be found in *The Russell Sage Social Relations Test* (4). On the surface, this is a test of the ability of a group of students to solve cooperatively a series of construction problems. It does in fact give a reasonably good measure of the group's effectiveness in this situation. If properly administered, however, it also yields information about other important aspects of group behavior: how well the students have learned to work together, how they respond to group control, how well they develop among themselves an efficient group organization, how they react on one another, and so on.

This sort of technique, and others like it, should eventually bring us closer to a truly adequate assessment of how students are attaining the attitudinal goals of instruction. Indeed, such techniques can do more. They can dramatize the importance of the goals by demonstrating how far we are falling short of achieving them. The development and application of good situational tests are expensive and time-consuming. Nevertheless, if we really wish to know what is happening to students in our classrooms, we are going to have to give up the notion that we can find out by relying on the "quick-and-dirty" tests that come cheap.

## ASSESSMENT IS CENTRAL

Education these days has become a major concern of national policy. It is in consequence the center of a good deal of bitter controversy, and the issues being debated (segregation, the source of school support, teachers' salaries, federal or local control, "standards") are so overriding that the question of how to assess student achievement seems by comparison to be of minor technical importance. Actually, it ought to be regarded as of central importance to the whole educational enterprise. Until we can reduce our vast ignorance of what is actually happening to the minds and hearts of students in the classrooms, until we can point up the goals of education in terms of what we want students to *do* physically, mentally, spiritually, and until we have better ways of knowing how well we are getting them to do these things, there is hardly much point to all the fuss about the so-called "larger issues." A comprehensive program to develop better methods for assessing achievement in all the classrooms of the country would go a long way toward taking the heat out of the controversies now plaguing us and would furnish the means for replacing the anarchy in education with new vitality and a sense of direction.

## REFERENCES

1. *A description of the College Board Achievement Tests*. Princeton, N. J.: College Entrance Examination Board, 1960.
2. BLOOM, B. S. (Ed.), *Taxonomy of Educational Objectives*. New York, N. Y.: Longmans, Green and Co., 1956.
3. CARPENTER, C. R., and GREENHILL, L. P., *An Investigation of Closed Circuit Television for Teaching University Courses*. University Park, Pa.: The Pennsylvania State University, 1958, p. 77.
4. DAMRIN, D. E., "The Russell Sage Social Relations Test: a technique for measuring group problem solving skills in elementary school children," *Journal of Experimental Education*, 1959, 28, 85–99.

5. DRESSEL, P. L., and MAYHEW, L. B., *General Education: Explorations in Evaluation.* Washington, D. C.: American Council on Education, 1954.

6. DYER, H. S., and FERRIS, A. H., *Sizing Up Your School Subjects.* Princeton, N. J.: Educational Testing Service, 1958.

7. KRUGLAK, H., and CARLSON, C. R., "Performance tests in physics at the University of Minnesota," *Science Education*, 1953, **37**:2, 108–121.

8. MacKINNON, D. W., "The highly effective individual," *Teachers College Record*, 1960, **61**, 367–378.

9. STICE, G., *The Facts About Science Test.* Princeton, N. J.: Educational Testing Service, 1958.

10. TAYLOR, C. W. (Ed.), *Research Conference on the Identification of Creative Scientific Talent.* Salt Lake City, Utah: University of Utah Press, 1956.

11. WILSON, R. C., "Improving criteria for complex mental processes," *Proceedings of the 1957 Invitation Conference on Testing Problems.* Princeton, N. J.: Educational Testing Service, 1957.

---

## 1.3    Educational Testing Service
### *Report of the President 1960–1961*
#### Henry Chauncey

Although the following passage is taken from a report concerning a particular yet outstanding testing and research organization, the general breadth of content and specific excellence of exposition which characterizes Dr. Chauncey's summary of how far the field has come in its short history is extremely important reading. Note his frank acknowledgment of the limitations of testing along with the advantages it has brought to many thousands of Americans.

You ought to be able to think of specific instances in which well-constructed tests are nearly irreplaceable for assessment and selec-

Reprinted with permission. Educational Testing Service, *Annual Report 1960–61*, Princeton, N. J.
From *Annual Report 1960–1961*. Reprinted with permission of Educational Testing Service, Princeton, N. J.

tion. In particular, this intelligent discussion should aid one to separate fact from diatribe in much of the public debate, which goes on nearly continually, about testing and its "supposed" effects on people.

Testing made significant progress during the 1960–61 year. But no one year tells the story of testing. Today's measurement techniques result from the work of many individuals and organizations over many years and represent a long evolution of development. Testing, to be understood at all, should be discussed in perspective and in context—in the perspective of its historical development and in the context of American education and a democratic society.

In this report, I want to review very generally the status of educational testing today, examine more specifically some recent developments in testing, and then summarize the highlights of the year's work at Educational Testing Service.

## TESTING IN PERSPECTIVE AND CONTEXT

Contemporary tests can be better understood, first of all, if one discards the notion that testing is something radically new. In one form or another, tests are as old as man himself. Testing, in its broadest sense, refers to any method of observing and measuring human behavior in order to evaluate and compare individuals. And man has been sizing up his fellow man since he first drew breath.

Testing, in short, has always been a fact of life. What is relatively new is the systematic improvement of tests and their wide application—a development that has occurred largely within the last 50 years.

Modern testing is both an art and a science. It is the art of fashioning and using many different kinds of devices and techniques for sizing up human beings and trying to foresee how they will make out as students, workers, and members of the community. Behind these techniques and devices is a new science, a growing body of theory drawn principally from psychology and mathematics and known as psychometrics. Both the art and the science are imperfectly developed and constantly changing, a characteristic of all arts and sciences. But the rate of development and improvement in testing is remarkable, considering the relatively short history of a systematic, scientific approach to the problem of determining individual differences.

## MAJOR KINDS OF TESTS

Today's tests may be divided into four major categories: aptitude tests, achievement tests, interest tests or inventories, and personality tests of various kinds. Aptitude tests seek to measure an individual's capacity to acquire the knowledge and skills that will enable him to perform a given kind of work. Achievement tests seek to measure the individual's mastery of certain knowledge and skills and his ability to apply what he has learned to the solution of new problems. Interest and personality tests, as their names imply, seek to determine what interests an individual has and what basic personality tendencies underlie his behavior.

None of these instruments is infallible, but some are good enough to provide valuable indications of individual abilities and achievement, which, *considered in relation to all other pertinent information*, can guide people in making important human decisions. In general, one could say that good modern tests can measure reasonably well what a person *knows*, less well what *interests* he has, and only poorly what he *is* and *may become*. In other words, good tests of academic and certain other specific aptitudes are reasonably reliable instruments, as are good tests of academic achievement. Interest tests and personality tests, often called inventories, are in a much more primitive stage of development at the present time.

Considerable work and research is going on in this difficult area of personality measurement. Some of it is promising and there may well be important breakthroughs within the next few years. Certainly a great deal of attention will be centered on efforts to devise reliable ways of determining motivation, creativity, interests, personality traits, and all the other intangibles that affect the way each individual approaches his life and his work.

## TESTS USED IN EDUCATION

Since our concern is educational testing, let me narrow the focus from testing in general to the kinds of tests used in education today. There is, of course, the teacher's own classroom test, which may be written or oral and may range from the ten-minute quiz to the full-fledged semester examination. And there are the standardized tests. These, in turn, may be designed for individual administration or for group administration; they may be "intelligence" tests, scholastic aptitude tests, achievement tests, interest tests, or personality tests.

Because of the many subtle differences among tests, it is important always to be specific about the kinds of tests under discussion. The kinds of tests to which the following remarks specifically refer are the multiple-choice tests of scholastic aptitude and achievement designed for group administration in systematic, large-scale testing programs.

The program may be one planned by and used within a school or school system. In this case, the school buys appropriate tests from a test publisher and uses them as long and often as it wishes. Or the program may be one administered on a nationwide scale under the sponsorship of some representative educational group or testing agency. In this case, the sponsoring group determines the policy and nature of the program, sees that tests are developed to serve the program's purpose, and arranges for administration of the tests on designated dates.

### CENTRAL PURPOSE OF TESTS

In either type of program, the central purpose of these tests is a dual one, a combination of aims. Their purpose is both to help the individual student understand and develop his academic abilities and to help educators make better judgments about individual students. The goal is to help students, not to coerce them, to highlight the vast range of individual differences, not to encourage conformity. The goal is also to help teachers, counselors, school principals, and college admissions officers do their difficult jobs better—to give them an additional kind of information that can be used in teaching, in evaluating instruction, in curriculum planning, in guidance, and in selection.

Consider the educational context in which these tests are used. It is a completely different situation from the one faced by educators a generation ago and no amount of nostalgia for the good old days will make either the teaching or testing methods of that period adequate for today's needs.

A generation ago, schools were uncrowded and students in any one school came from fairly homogeneous backgrounds. The American population was far less mobile. Going to college was something only a relatively small proportion of the youth of high school age contemplated. Today, some 45,000,000 students are enrolled in our elementary and secondary schools. They represent the widest possible diversity of backgrounds, abilities, and aspirations. Many of them transfer from school to school, as their families move for one reason or another. The current college and university enrollment is 4,399,000; by 1970, according to one projection, it may be as high as 7,000,000.

Within this context, how does the classroom teacher, at the start of the year, get some idea of the individual abilities of her 30 children so that she can plan her teaching and group her class? How can she arrive at an objective, impartial appraisal of the results of her instruction as the year draws to a close? How can the high school guidance counselor help several hundred students make sensible plans for college or work after graduation? How does the college admissions officer, faced with four or five applications for every opening, begin to evaluate the records of candidates who come from different kinds of schools all over the country?

In each of these situations—and many others—educators have found they can get some help by studying the results of appropriate scholastic aptitude and achievement tests taken by the students concerned. Teachers today have to teach, guide, place, and select students day in and day out—with or without tests. And, given the complexities of our educational system and the numbers of students being educated, most teachers feel they do a better job with objective tests than without them. This is why such tests are so widely used.

## TEACHERS AND TESTING

A favorite notion of the critics of multiple-choice tests of scholastic aptitude and achievement is that these tests are somehow isolated from education, that they are perpetrated by a self-seeking band of "test-makers" and imposed upon schools and colleges. This approach is factually incorrect. It underestimates the common sense of the educational profession by implying that teachers have been duped into accepting something that is unrelated to their teaching and administrative needs.

The truth is that testing is part of education and, like education itself, has passed through an evolution of trial and error. In their present form and prevalence, good objective tests of scholastic aptitude and achievement measure in a reasonably valid and reliable fashion certain abilities that educators want to measure and need to measure. They do it better than other testing techniques currently available and they do it without having a coercive or restrictive effect on the curriculum.

The fallacy of the notion that teachers are helpless victims of "test-makers" becomes clear when one examines the development of objective tests. Most of them are prepared by teachers. In some instances, a test publisher may commission an individual teacher to develop a test, with the help of measurement specialists and the critical review of other teachers in the field—just as book publishers commission teachers to write textbooks. In other instances, a test publisher may work with an advisory committee of several teachers in a particular field to develop new tests.

In the case of such large-scale testing programs as those of the College Entrance Examination Board, the control of testing policies and test content by teachers and scholars is explicit. The College Board itself is a voluntary membership association of schools and colleges. For every College Board test, there is a Committee of Examiners. Members are school and college teachers, representative of different kinds of educational institutions and outstanding scholars in the subject field to be tested.

These teachers work with the test development staff of Educational Testing Service, which administers the Board's testing programs, to plan the test content, write individual questions, review all proposed questions, decide which ones should go into the test, and review the final assembled form of the test.

The College Board also has a Committee on Examinations that assumes responsibility for reviewing all work of all Examiners. Thus, the development of College Board tests, and a continuing review of those tests, is in the hands of teachers and scholars. A similar situation exists for other testing programs administered by Educational Testing Service and for the tests published by our Cooperative Test Division. In an average year, some 500 teachers and scholars are involved in the design, preparation, or review of scholastic aptitude and achievement tests.

The tests are not exclusively the multiple-choice type. Some tests include essay questions and others the insertion of written answers. Over the years, test development committees have experimented with every known type of test question. They will continue to do so. But when they decide to use a complete multiple-choice test it is because evidence accumulated through careful research convinces them that this type of test is the fairest, most valid, reliable, and feasible way to accomplish the specific purposes of their program.

## ADVANTAGES OF MULTIPLE-CHOICE TESTS

The advantages of multiple-choice tests are frequently thought to be that they can be scored clerically or by machine and that they are relatively inexpensive. These are only minor virtues. The important qualities are three. The first is that a hundred questions, more or less, can be asked instead of six or twelve. This permits a much wider sampling of the subject matter and the student's abilities. It means that if a student for one reason or another does not do himself justice on one, two, or even half a dozen questions, he will not seriously affect his score.

Secondly, a test can be planned, and each question prepared, with the greatest possible care. The first step in developing an achievement test, for example, is to draw up a "blueprint" for the examination, specifying the abilities to be measured and the content to be covered. These specifications may be stated in a variety of ways, depending on the nature and complexity of the test. Sometimes a two-way grid is prepared, which enables each question to be classified in two dimensions—the ability to be measured and the subject matter covered. Such a grid for the Biology and General Science test in the National Teacher Examinations is reproduced on page 28.

Those responsible for the test then decide approximately how many questions should be written to cover each ability in each content area. When the questions are written and classified, the number of questions falling into each classification is recorded on the grid. A completed grid thus indicates at a glance the scope and balance of the test.

The third asset of multiple-choice tests is that they lend themselves readily to systematic study. Preliminary tests using newly-developed questions are tried out to determine whether, in fact, able students generally select as the best answer the response that the teachers who prepared the question considered the best answer. This is the point at which elements of ambiguity that may make it an ineffective question are spotted. If a question is found to be ambiguous, or if it does not generally elicit from good students the intellectual skills and reasoning powers it seeks to measure, the question is eliminated, or it is revised before it is used in an actual test.

ABILITIES

| NTE Biology and General Science Item Distribution — SUBJECT MATTER | Understanding of basic scientific concepts and principles | Ability to distinguish basic concepts from those which are irrelevant or inappropriate | Ability to anticipate and diagnose concepts likely to prove easy or difficult for students | Ability to select and devise appropriate demonstrations for effective teaching | Ability to recognize and utilize appropriate sources of information | Ability to give a lucid explanation of scientific concepts and principles | Ability to apply scientific concepts and principles to every-day experience | Ability to evaluate student learning | Ability to stimulate and guide the individual student | TOTAL |
|---|---|---|---|---|---|---|---|---|---|---|
| Chemistry | | | | | | | | | | |
| Physics | | | | | | | | | | |
| Astronomy | | | | | | | | | | |
| Geology | | | | | | | | | | |
| Meteorology | | | | | | | | | | |
| Histology | | | | | | | | | | |
| Botany | | | | | | | | | | |
| Zoology | | | | | | | | | | |
| Human anatomy and physiology | | | | | | | | | | |
| Biology and human welfare | | | | | | | | | | |
| Heredity and evol. | | | | | | | | | | |
| Total | | | | | | | | | | |

28

## ERRORS INHERENT IN MEASUREMENT

In any aptitude or achievement test, the objective is to get the best possible sample of a student's ability and knowledge. The larger the sample, the more representative the sample, and the better the individual questions, the better the test will be. But even the best test is subject to error—because all possible content is not sampled, because authorities may differ in their evaluation of responses, and because language itself is imprecise.

Those who prepare good multiple-choice tests recognize all three sources of error. They seek to reduce all three by the processes I have described: 1) they include many questions in the test, thus increasing the size of the sample; 2) they ask several outstanding teachers and scholars to come to a consensus in evaluating intended responses to any question; 3) they eliminate ambiguity of language as much as possible by trying out new questions and studying student responses before including the questions in an actual test. In addition to all this care in preparation of the test, they conduct extensive research after the test results are in, to determine the relationship of test scores to the subsequent performance of students.

## IMPORTANCE OF WISE AND SENSIBLE USERS

The best test is no good unless it is used properly, by individuals fully aware of the fact that tests are but *samples* of behavior, subject to sampling errors, and that therefore a test score is not an absolute, unchanging truth. It is but an *estimate* and predictions based on it are but estimates.

People who use test results wisely know this. They know that an individual's test scores can vary, even on the same test given at different times. They know, too, that no scholastic aptitude or achievement test measures a student's "innate ability" or his "intelligence" or his "creativity." They have found, however, that good tests can measure reasonably well a student's *developed* abilities to perform certain academic tasks. And they know that these abilities are the result of whatever mental capacities the student was born with *plus* whatever opportunities he has had (and taken) to develop those capacities.

With these facts in mind, it is obvious that a test score by itself means very little. It takes on meaning only in relation to all other information about an individual. The wise and sensible user, therefore, does not make decisions on the basis of test scores alone. On the other hand, the kind of information provided by good tests cannot be ignored by conscientious educators seeking all possible information about students before making important decisions.

Let me illustrate with two actual cases what can happen when good tests are used wisely and sensibly. The first is reported by an admissions officer at a distinguished Eastern university for men:

"We recently had to decide what student should receive a special scholarship, available to an undergraduate with 'unusual creative ability and stamina' in writing, art, or music. There were a number of candidates and the decision was close. The scholarship went to a senior with unusual talent as a painter and a good three-year record in his college courses.

"The interesting point about it is that this student would never have been admitted to this university three years ago on the basis of his high school grades alone. He came from a school in western Pennsylvania where he ranked 87 in a class of 146. Yet the school principal felt that the boy had great potential and fully endorsed him.

"Then the boy's College Board test scores came in. They were not startling as far as the Achievement Tests were concerned, but good enough. The Scholastic Aptitude Test scores, however, particularly the verbal score, were way up there. We accepted the young man on the strength of his test scores, which, in effect, supported the school principal's evaluation of the boy's promise."

The second case is reported by a guidance counselor in a large urban high school:

"Roger was a quiet boy—the kind who causes no trouble, therefore goes by unnoticed. That was the story of his life—just going along with the group.

"The picture changed when Roger took a series of standardized tests in grade 8. His teacher was amazed to find he scored high above grade level in achievement tests and that his IQ score was about 136. Roger has since been encouraged to be more outgoing and has responded favorably. Today, as a senior, he stands almost at the head of his class, is a class officer, has a five-piece dance band, and plans to enter a seminary in September.

"I believe Roger might have gone through unnoticed had not the test results jolted his teacher into realizing that she was dealing with a superior student who was in a shell and needed help to mature."

## THE QUALITY AND USE OF TESTS

Educators and testing experts agree that some tests are poor tests and that even good tests are sometimes used for the wrong purposes. They further agree that test results are too often over-emphasized, and that not all test users are wise and sensible. But this picture is changing. Although the rate of progress may be slower than one might desire, progress is being made.

To argue that multiple-choice tests should be abolished because all such tests are not perfect, or because they are not always used as they should be, is specious reasoning. It is the same as saying that all automobiles should be abolished because some are poorly built or driven by reckless drivers—or that all books should be banned because some are poorly written or influence readers in undesirable ways.

To argue that tests should be abolished because they are "unfair to the underprivileged child" is equally specious. It is not the test that is unfair to the underprivileged child—it is the hard facts of social and economic circumstance and inadequate education that are unfair. Test results inevitably reflect the opportunities a student has had for learning. If educational and cultural opportunities are unequal, the test results will also be unequal.

Recent experiments in junior high schools located in underprivileged areas of large cities have demonstrated that when a concerted effort is made to improve the teaching and guidance of children in these schools, and to expose them to cultural opportunities outside of school, such students subsequently work harder, get better grades—and do better on tests. This is a result to be expected. It underlines the fact that tests measure the academic abilities a student had developed up to the time he takes the tests, and that these abilities are influenced by the quality of his education and his environment.

Because good tests do reflect the extent to which a student has developed his academic abilities, they provide a basis for estimating the student's subsequent academic performance. Many studies have shown that tests perform this predictive role very well. From the measurement and prediction point of view, then, the tests themselves are fair. The "unfairness" lies elsewhere. If it is due to poor education and poor environment, only major efforts, starting early in the school years and continuing over a period of time, can produce a significant improvement in the student's ability to handle increasingly difficult academic work.

## THE DEMOCRACY OF MULTIPLE-CHOICE TESTS

If one looks at educational testing in perspective and context, a good case can be made for the view that objective tests promote certain democratic values to which most Americans subscribe. This country is a multitudinous, heterogeneous nation. We are dedicated to the principle of equal opportunity and we believe that justice should be done each individual according to his merit. We try to recognize and respect individual differences and we attempt to accommodate to local and regional differences. We believe in change and we strive for progress. Because our present civilization is in part founded on it, we have faith in science and the wise application of technology. These are some of the traditional values that, along with historical, social, and economic factors, have contributed to the present character of American education—and of educational testing.

In a vast nation where talent may be anywhere, and where we advocate its right to be discovered and developed, large-scale testing that is reliable and efficient, albeit somewhat impersonal, is a necessity. If it did not exist, it would have to be invented. Unlike the personal interview, the classroom, or the teacher's subjective evaluation, the objective test is a common touchstone. It gives all students who take it the same chance, asks them to run the same race—even though they have had different economic backgrounds, different educational, cultural, and social opportunities.

If these opportunities have been seriously inadequate, the student may do poorly on the test. But this very fact highlights the degree to which Americans have failed to provide equal educational opportunity for all children according to their abilities. It may even help more people to become aware of the fact that talent and ability are developed in direct proportion to the excellence of educational opportunity.

## RESPONSIBILITIES OF THE CRITIC

As tests become better and more widely used, it is both inevitable and desirable that they be talked about, written about, examined, and criticized. Those responsible for multiple-choice tests welcome this scrutiny. Tests, with all their limitations, are as good as they are today only because they have been constantly examined and criticized.

But the critic, too, has a responsibility: the responsibility to know what he is talking about, to avoid personal prejudice, and to approach the subject in perspective and context. In an earlier report,* I discussed in some detail certain specific criticisms of objective tests; there is no need to repeat that discussion here. It does seem important, however, to point out a few instances of what can only be called an irresponsible approach to the critical role.

1. First, there is occasionally the deliberate use of inflammatory, emotionally-tinged words such as the "tyranny" of testing, the reference to "mass-produced tests," the statement that "your child's future is controlled by electronic machines." These words may make good headlines, snare readers, and stir up controversy—but they have no real basis in fact. No evidence of tyranny exists; tests are not mass-produced, they are individually produced; electronic machines have no control over the child's future, but simply perform scoring, clerical, and computational operations faster than they can be performed any other way.

2. Second, there is the critic who condemns tests because they do not do what he wants them to do, regardless of the fact that they are not designed to do this. For example, no knowledgeable person would claim that a scholastic aptitude test can unerringly identify the "truly creative" student, or the "strongly motivated" student, or the "highly gifted" student. Yet the tests are attacked on the grounds that they do not accomplish these feats. What a good scholastic aptitude test does do is this: *it indicates in a reasonably reliable way the relative ability of students* and *it identifies the group of students with high academic ability in which the creative, gifted individual is most apt to be found.*

3. Third, there is the critic who extracts individual test questions out of context, decides they are ambiguous, and concludes that the "highly gifted" student will come to the same conclusion, select an answer that is not the intended correct response, and therefore be penalized.

There are several things to be said about this approach. In the first place, there is no evidence that highly gifted students react in

---

* Educational Testing Service, *Annual Report 1958–59*, pp. 43–57.

this fashion. All available evidence indicates that gifted students score in the upper ranges on multiple-choice tests. In the second place, language depends on context for meaning and can never be reduced to the precision of a mathematical formula. What we are trying to get at in testing is the student's ability to deal with language as it is and as he will have to deal with it all through life—complete with semantic difficulties.

For example, in one type of multiple-choice question the student is asked to read a paragraph or passage and then select the most nearly accurate statement, out of five possible statements, describing or interpreting what is said in the passage. He is asked, in short, to comprehend the passage. Yet the purpose of such questions some-how escapes the critic bent on finding ambiguity. One such individual once cited a specific test question as a prime example of ambiguity, criticizing the "muddy" language of the passage the student was asked to comprehend. The passage in question came from the *Federalist* papers; the objective of the question was to test the student's ability to comprehend and deal with the language in a type of source material he would frequently study in college.

4. Fourth, there is the editorial approach to the subject of testing that is narrow, even provincial, and based on inadequate research of existing facts. This approach is particularly evident in articles about college admissions testing. One national magazine, for instance, recently introduced an article on college entrance tests with an editorial note beginning this way: "This spring hundreds of thousands of high-school students will take the College Board tests which will largely determine their chances of getting a higher education—and this may affect their whole future."

As it stands, this sentence is inaccurate and misleading. The words ". . . which will largely determine their chances of getting a higher education . . ." simply are not true. They reflect a lack of knowledge of the extent to which other information about a student —school record, references, interview reports—is used in determining college admissions. They also reflect a lack of knowledge about the many "chances of getting a higher education" in this country.

There are roughly 1,800 to 2,000 institutions offering higher education in the United States; approximately 1,100 offer four-year undergraduate work and about 800 are junior colleges. Of these 1,900 institutions offering college-level work, about 600 currently require candidates for admission to take one or more College Board tests. Some of these (about 10) are state universities that require only out-of-state candidates to do so; others (60–70) require only certain candidates to take a College Board test for special reasons. Assuming a student could not get into any of these 600 colleges, he still has 1,300 more "chances of getting a higher education."

Moreover, among the colleges requiring College Board tests, there is such a wide diversity of purpose, curriculum, academic standards, enrollment pressures, and other pertinent factors affecting admissions that a student who may not have much chance at one type of college within the group would have a very good chance at other types of colleges in this group.

As a matter of fact, this is exactly what happens. With the help of their counselors—*and* with the help of good scholastic aptitude and achievement tests—increasing numbers of students are assessing their own academic potential, learning what their chances are for admission to different types of colleges, and applying for admission to two or three different types rather than to three of a kind.

The result, obvious to all who will look and see, is that the "chances of getting a higher education" in this country are better than they have ever been. Whether this situation will continue depends not on tests and test scores, but on the willingness of the American people to support—financially and in every other way— the urgent necessity to expand our facilities for higher education and to demand that all institutions meet standards of excellence consonant with their purpose and the needs of their students.

---

## 1.4    Measurement in Relation to the Educational Process
### Dorothy C. Adkins

Dorothy Adkins suggests six steps or stages in the "cycle of activity comprising the educational process" where measurement necessarily

Address in commemoration of the Fiftieth Anniversary of the College of Education, The Ohio State University, Columbus, Ohio, April, 1957; also presented at Ohio University, Athens, Ohio, under the auspices of the Department of Psychology. Reprinted with permission of the author and *Educational and Psychological Measurement*, 18, 2, 1958.

makes an appearance. She makes clear the utility and rationale of mental measurement in terms of the three scaling techniques appropriate to educational assessment: nominal, ordinal, and interval scaling. The result is a concise definition of a psychological test which parallels the parable about how long a term paper ought to be: like the wrapping of a box, long enough to cover completely but with no bulges or loose ends.

Do you agree, and why, with her statement that "diversity of behavior" is the principal concern in mental measurement? How might the concepts of expanding stimulus sensitivity and response repertoires be applied in a typical classroom? To what extent does this conception of education lend itself to a variety of psychological tests? What specific types of tests could be utilized in Adkin's scheme of assessing changes in behavior?

This fairly long article is presented in its entirety because Dr. Adkins has pulled together in one place one of the best statements of the argument revealing the inseparable relationship between psychology, education, and measurement.

A *meaningful* analysis of the relation of measurement to education requires some generalizations first about what constitutes this process and then as to the nature of psychological measurement.

As a beginning, we can scarcely improve upon the trite but true observation that education entails change—not just any variation, to be sure, but rather progressive alteration or improvement in some sense, in the direction of behavior on the part of the learner that will be to his future advantage or to that of society. More specifically, let us reflect upon the kinds of modification educators hope to produce.

Some of the developments in learning theory should aid in such an analysis. Since this is not the occasion for dwelling at length upon the vagaries of learning theorists, only one systematic position has been chosen to provide a framework within which to describe the several types of behavioral changes that comprise education—that of B. F. Skinner. This selection has not been entirely at random, since I find much in his point of view with which to concur. Introduction of Skinnerian concepts at this point also will provide orientation for later argument as to the essence and value of psychological measurement, in which I shall take issue with his treatment of this topic.

Further, it will be relevant to a conclusion that much of education should be to the mastery level, a point at which I again can applaud some of his recent innovations.

According to Skinner's treatment of learning, educators seek, first, an increase in the variety of stimulus dimensions to which the learner will be sensitive and responsive. Second, enlargement of the learner's response repertoire is attempted. To put the matter otherwise, the number of discriminable stimuli to which already acquired responses may be made is to be augmented. This first aim entails forcing the learner to make stimulus distinctions in a previously undistinguished environment. Thus the person who has been required to make fine color discriminations comes to see colors not seen previously. This aspect of teaching may also be described as bringing behavior under the control of single properties or special combinations of stimulus properties—a procedure that leads to what is sometimes referred to as abstraction or concept formation.

The second purpose is to add to the number of new responses that will be made in the presence of familiar, or already discriminated, stimulus components. Here the task is two-fold: (1) to alter response topography in a particular direction, as in the acquisition of motor skills, through a process of response differentiation; and (2) to shape up or develop entirely new topographies that earlier had very low probabilities of emission. This latter aspect is somewhat reminiscent of the sudden emergence of a solution in the insight situation—an event that also had a low original probability.

To complete the picture, a third purpose of education is to extend the number of new responses to be made in novel stimulus situations.

Thus the expectation is that the educational process will change the relative frequency of appropriate behavior in both old and new situations or in fresh combinations of familiar stimuli. The notion of appropriate responses here should include their suitable timing. As Skinner would say, then, education makes particular forms of behavior more probable under certain circumstances or increases the probability that a fitting response will be made at a proper time.

This analysis does not mean that knowledge—in a sense the total learned response repertoire—is merely a set of mechanical connections between stimuli and responses mediated solely through paired-associates verbal memory. But verbal behavior does play a significant role in much that is called learning, and the learner himself may facilitate the process by initiating and carrying out his own verbal instructions. He learns how to attack problems, how to collect and survey relevant facts and materials, how to change his set when faced with a seemingly insoluble problem, how to test various solutions vicariously, how to apply principles in new settings, how to formulate hypotheses, to abstract, to generalize. Education, then, must transcend the establishment of routinized stimulus-response connections to equip the learner for coping with novel situations.

If this were not possible, tax-supported educational institutions long since would have closed their doors. For educators can scarcely anticipate the specific problems that learners will encounter five, 10, 15 years hence. As long as formal education is retained—and I do not anticipate its early demise—the only recourse is to modify behavioral repertoires in such a way that solutions to new problems will ensue. Fortunately, although often our efforts are woefully inefficient and our tests ill designed to reflect the attainment of this objective, substantial evidence exists that such behavioral changes occur and can be expedited through teaching.

If education is to alter the relations of stimuli or classes of stimuli to responses or types of behavior, one step will entail defining stimulus situations and the responses for which the frequency of occurrence is to be modified. Behavioral goals thus must be made concrete in terms of curricular content. Then the learner's environment must be so arranged that certain types of responses will be occasioned with increasing probability. The structuring of the learning situation will encompass not only the particular content but also teaching techniques that will facilitate an increasing probability of occurrence of appropriate responses when particular stimuli are present. Moreover, an essential part of the process, as will be seen in more detail presently, must be the prediction of the extent to which particular goals can be attained by particular learners and later the appraisal of the extent to which they have been reached.

The measurement of change in the learner—all too often informal, subjective, and unreliable—is an inescapable aspect of various phases of the cycle of activity comprising the educational process. For purposes of clarification, it may be separated into the following steps:

1. Defining behavioral goals or objectives.

2. Planning stimuli (that is, curricular materials) and teaching methods.

3. Predicting the degree to which the objectives can be attained.

4. Applying the teaching methods to the selected curricular content or adjusting the goals or the content and methods.

5. Testing achievement.

6. Defining new behavioral objectives in the light of how well the old ones were met, and so on.

This succession has been called a cycle because it has no boundaries. Each new series must be adjusted upon the basis of the results of the preceding ones. Throughout the sequence, evaluation of either current status of the learner or of change in him must be more or less continuous, whether or not the appraisal is recognized as such or is conducted by means of formal tests.

Returning to the first step, the behavioral goals defined cannot be realistic unless they are based upon a knowledge of the abilities of the prospective learners to reach alternative ends that might be set. At once becomes apparent the necessity of measuring both various kinds of aptitude and previous achievement.

The second phase of the cycle, planning the curricular content and teaching methods, must be related to previously acquired knowledge or skills of the learners and to the readiness with which they can acquire the contemplated new abilities. Again, the decisions need to take into account the learners' present status. Likewise, teaching techniques should be modified in view of the capacities of the learners.

The prediction of whether or not the goals are realistic, listed as the third step, requires consideration of the aims themselves, the selected curricular content, and the proposed teaching techniques in relation to the previous attainments and aptitudes of the learners. Will a particular learner, presented with certain stimuli with specified amounts of reading, explanation, drill, recitation, dosage, and so on, demonstrate the desired behavioral change? Or will his time and that of the teacher largely be dissipated? If a prediction is to be made—as indeed it should be—appraisal of the learners' abilities again must be made.

The fourth phase, the application of particular teaching methods to selected curricular content, can be successful only if the teacher is vigilant in measuring progress toward the desired objectives. If retardation is evident, then teaching technique may be altered, content supplemented, or the goal adjusted. The teacher also should be responsive to more rapid accomplishment of the objective than was anticipated, else otherwise excellent learners will shy away from scholarship through sheer boredom. Here assessment of change in the learner as it is occurring must be prominent.

The fifth step calls for a test of the attainment of the objective of a unit of instruction. Such a test could be regarded as one of current status. Whether or not the achievement reflected in the test can be attributed to the unit of the educational process in question or to the particular teaching involved can not be resolved by a single administration of a test, however. Rather, test results must be interpretable in terms of how much change they reflect. Two comparable tests, given before and after some particular experience, such as exposure to a segment of content by means of certain methods, often will permit an inference as to the extent to which variation in behavior has taken place. Sometimes a conclusion is warranted that such change as is evident is associated with the intervening events, especially if a control group or some other appropriate experimental design has been employed.

The educational process should be dynamic. It should not concentrate fixedly upon an unchanging ultimate goal the attainment of which eventually may be tested. Rather, a series of proximate or intermediate aims should be established, with each subject to constant readjustment in the light of frequent appraisals of the attainment of previous ones. Viewed in this light, the setting of educational objectives cannot be divorced from the appraisal of progress toward them.

Let us now indicate more precisely what is meant by mental measurement. When the length of an object is measured with a yard-stick, at one extreme of which the designation of zero has some rational significance and on which it makes sense to regard the units as physically equal, the statement that the length of one object is twice that of another is meaningful. Moreover, the assertion that one increase in length is a certain multiple of another can be justified.

On the other hand, the thermometer, while also scaled in equal units, has an arbitrary zero point. In such a situation, relative gains can be compared quantitatively. Thus an increase from 90° to 100° on a Fahrenheit scale is twice the amount of the gain in going from 50° to 55°. But a temperature of 100° can not be said to be twice as hot as one of 50°.

A scale lacking equal units while having an absolute zero—not an arbitrarily set zero point—is also possible. Thus at birth a child has zero words in his vocabulary, whether recognition or spoken or written word usage is implied. Because words differ in difficulty of acquisition, however, a 12,000-word vocabulary is not twice a 6,000-word vocabulary in any meaningful quantitative sense. Here is a scale with an absolute zero but without equal units. If choice must be made between a scale characterized by equal units and one originating at a rational zero, the former is more useful.

Some purists have argued that no measurement can occur unless both conditions are fulfilled. This is a defeatist point of view for mental measurement, because almost never can these requirements be met. To conclude from this fact that psychological measurement is obviated, however, is indeed unnecessary. With equal units useful comparisons among persons can be made despite the arbitrariness of the origin of the scale. What is more, lacking both of the ideal conditions for measurement, results of thousands of tests provide ample evidence of their value. If the process is not to be called measurement, another term can be used. The fact remains that when persons can be placed in rank order along some continuum, with an arbitrary zero and without exact knowledge of the distance between successive persons, valid predictions of future behavior very frequently can be made. The foregoing argument is tantamount to a confession that while in my more psychometric moments I may share the devotion of the savants to these niceties, like the more learned I am able to relegate them to the textbooks when it comes to appraising students' knowledge of test theory or the typing skill of prospective secretaries.

What, then, is a psychological test? Broadly speaking, it is a means of drawing inferences about persons, based upon their responses to a sampling of a field of behavior. If a person in a particular test situation responds in one way, the prediction is that he will behave in a certain manner in other stimulus situations and, usually, that his behavior will differ from that of persons who respond in other ways in the test situation. More concretely, when a problem is presented verbally, persons may be required to choose one from among several answers. If one option is considered best, then the inference is made that persons who select it will behave differently from those who make the poor choices. The prediction is limited to other behavioral situations of which the one presented in the question is a sample or to which it is related. The inference, if it is correct, supports the claim of validity of the test question. An incorrect conclusion for a large percentage of subjects, on the other hand, means that it is not valid for the purpose at hand.

The inferences in which interest centers when a test is constructed usually have had to do with prospective variations among individuals in their behavior. Little if any scientific or practical significance, from this point of view, has accrued to single test questions or composites to which all members of some group would respond in identical ways. Rather, when a test is administered to an assemblage of persons, commonly homogeneous in one or more characteristics, such as age, school grade, race, and so on, the purpose has been to gain knowledge of their differences in some other respect—some trait or ability. The principal concern in mental measurement, then, usually has been with diversity of behavior.

To the extent that the predictions of individual differences made from test scores agree with those observable in later performance, the test is said to have *predictive* validity. This type of validity is usually expressed in terms of a correlation coefficient between test scores and some independent measure of the criterion or the performance that was being predicted. This index of relationship is called a validity coefficient.

When an investigator gives attention to *content* validity, his immediate purpose is to determine how an individual would perform at present in a universe of situations of which a test provides a sample. Educators are interested in appraising immediate returns of certain units of instruction, with specified curricular content and teaching methods. Therefore, they can not escape attempting to assess the content validity of achievement measures. Here they consider the types of responses made in the test situation, for their own sake, so to speak. In the case of empirical validity, on the other hand, the focus is on the criterion behavior to be predicted, and the specific types of behavior in the test situation become of secondary interest only.

*Construct* validity focuses upon the degree to which the individual is characterized by some trait presumably reflected in the test score. The term trait, as used here, refers to a more or less integrated constellation of response tendencies that can be said to typify the individual. Construct validity thus is associated with an explanatory concept or with some theory underlying responses to a set of test items.

A criterion of performance may not be available in the initial phases of investigating some behavioral phenomena. Here resort is made to indirect evidence of construct validity. Educational testers ordinarily should be more interested in content and predictive validity, even though the first steps may entail consideration of the constructs or traits that are to be measured.

When the principal aim of a test is to assess how an individual performs at present, to measure immediate skills or abilities or knowledges, it often is referred to as an achievement or proficiency test. The emphasis upon specific types of acquired behavior is greater than upon more general hereditary factors. On the other hand, a test designed to measure potentialities for increasing one's range of stimulus sensitivity or his response repertoire is likely to be referred to as an aptitude test. Here the interest lies not in specific types of learned behavior but rather in broader abilities more influenced by native endowment and less by particular environmental factors.

The pragmatic distinction often made between aptitude and achievement tests is by no means hard and fast. For one thing, the same test may be used upon one occasion primarily as an aptitude test and upon another as a test of achievement. Thus an arithmetic test may provide an appraisal of present knowledge and skill in arithmetic, or it may be used to predict which individuals will be best able to learn algebra. In the second place, to test any aptitude requires use of some previously acquired stimulus sensitivity and response repertoire; thus the aptitude measure is contaminated with learning. Thirdly, scores on an achievement test also may be affected by aptitude differentials, because those with higher native potentialities for learning will have acquired more in a uniform period of practice or study. Hence relative differences in achievement, real though they may be, depend in part upon aptitude variability.

In any event, the ultimate purpose of an achievement test, like that of an aptitude test, is to predict future behavior. Seen in proper perspective, an achievement test must serve this function if it is to go beyond the narrow limits of today's activities. Indeed, were educators completely unable to predict future performance from present achievement, the process of education would become chaotic. Any basis for selecting curricular content, mastery of which presumably would have positive transfer to later situations, would disappear. The inescapable fact, then, is that we are interested in present achievement primarily because it permits a prediction of future performance, however informal and often neglected that prognosis is.

Frank acknowledgment of this fundamental purpose of educational achievement tests should lead to revisions in the measuring devices themselves, in the curriculum, and in teaching methods. Recall with me a study reported by Sidney Pressey in *Psychology and the New Education* in 1933. Students' scores on end-of-course examinations in various high-school and college subjects were compared with their performance on the same examinations after one and two years. To quote, "These students showed a knowledge of about three-quarters of the material covered in the test at the end of the course, less than half after one year and about one-quarter after two years." One hesitates to project these loss of retention curves to even one more year! Pressey himself speculates as to whether solace may be found in the thought that students retain general understanding, principles, points of view, methods of attack, rather than minimally essential facts. Although too many educational achievement tests are limited largely to facts acquired by rote memorization, Pressey concludes by arguing persuasively that we are but little better off in the higher echelons of the thought processes. Finally, he suggests that the slight permanence of much school learning is chargeable to the curriculum, which evidently is not based upon content needed or used outside the classroom.

Yet, while the foregoing argument may hold for, say, algebra, which may appear to fade through disuse, it can scarcely apply to the basic skills of reading and writing, for example, which are practiced quite regularly and in which college students also reveal little permanence of learning.

A repetition of such an experiment in almost any field would yield equally sobering results. The basic difficulty may lie in the fact that materials learned to a level below mastery disappear from our repertoires for the very reason that they are not fully mastered, so that correct responses are not made often enough to get sufficient reinforcement in the normal course of events to perpetuate them.

Surprisingly enough, although the advantageous effects of strategic degrees of overlearning upon relearning and eventual permanent mastery have been common knowledge to educators since the 1885 publication of Ebbinghaus' work, teaching practice reflects meager appreciation of them.

The suggested solution will lie in teaching each learner to the mastery level those materials that he is capable of really mastering, by suitable teaching methods and with more or less continuous progress appraisals based upon tests of defined educational objectives. The remedy is not simply to multiply the use of tests. More drastic surgery is indicated. Tests need to be integrated into the entire educational process, as heretofore suggested. To reiterate briefly, we must assess the present abilities of the learners, prepare curricular materials appropriate to the ability levels, adapt teaching methods to the learners and the content to be learned, establish appropriate degrees of overlearning by empirical means, and constantly appraise the learning as it is taking place.

Let us turn again to some general features of mental measurement. In a provocative chapter entitled "Function Versus Aspect" in his book *Science and Human Behavior,* Skinner points out that common, unchanging properties of behavior do not lead to trait names. Psychologists become interested in traits in order to describe differences in behavior. They arise from differences in the independent variables to which individuals have been exposed, an environmental factor; differences in their hereditary endowment; and differences in age and developmental status. Traits provide a way of representing the behavioral repertoires of different persons. Tests that measure such traits are inventories which list responses falling in certain classes and estimate their relative frequency of occurrence. So far so good. Then Skinner goes on to say that a second kind of variation in behavior arises from a difference in the rate at which changes in behavior take place. He remarks that a high score on an achievement test may be traced either to exposure to certain variables or to the rate at which they have taken effect or both. Then, although previously he claimed that an achievement test represents an inventory of behavior, he argues that traits of the second sort cannot be measured by inventory, thus cannot be measured by tests! He attaches scant importance to the fact that from a test one can make a prediction of future behavior. Moreover, he seems to deny the feasibility of inferences of the *rate* at which behavior has changed, drawn from inventories of response repertoires taken at different times.

Although Skinner recognizes that dissimilarities in traits are partially attributable to hereditary factors, he is primarily interested in variations arising from alterations in the independent variables to which individuals are exposed. He prefers to concentrate upon changes in behavior that can be observed as they occur in relation to one or more independent variables, for these he has more hope of controlling. Admittedly, to attempt to control effectively the response repertoire of an individual with only glia-cells in his cortex would not be very rewarding! We may as well recognize, too, that the educator really has little leverage over independent variables to which the learner has been exposed previously. But this does not mean that tests designed to tap native aptitudes or affected in unknown or even unanalyzable ways by differences in learners' previous environments are not useful. Educators need such appraisals in planning their work effectively.

Skinner also finds himself uncomfortable because any sensible interpretation of an individual's score on a test depends upon knowledge of how other persons have performed on it. Since the tester is interested in present traits and in future behavior in which individual differences exist, this is no limitation whatever. To make prognoses of later differences in one trait from knowledge of how the individuals vary now is indeed the straightforward approach to mental measurement. Typically, then we do not want a measure to be independent of a sample of subjects. This point of view is in no sense inconsistent with interest in having all members of a particular group master all of a content unit, although to be sure the emphasis at the point of testing this group is not upon individual differences. Even so, the fact that one learner achieves 100% mastery, as revealed by a test, eventually can best be interpreted in the light of the performance on the same test of other learners, exposed to different teaching methods or curricular materials.

Skinner regards as the most conspicuous feature of an aspect description of behavior its failure to advance the control of behavior. As an argument for this conclusion, he notes that from the measurement of a set of traits the suitability of an individual to a given task can be judged. But then he concludes that the only practical step is to accept or reject him, based upon the faulty premise that the measurement of traits does not suggest ways of altering his suitability to the task. At this point, he claims that we need a measure appropriate to a functional process.

Measures of performance on the same psychomotor test made at eight different stages of practice have been included in a factor analysis study reported in *Psychometrika* in 1954 by Edwin Fleishman and Walter Hempel, Jr. They found considerable and systematic changes in the factor structure of the test as practice on it increased. Thus differences in abilities required by a test—or traits, if you will—can be studied as a function of variations in an independent variable, amount of practice. Such a study design seems close to meeting Skinner's demands for a functional analysis. Yet it is also a study of traits. Note, moreover, that here the practice or training material and the test material were identical.

Skinner's speculations about Robinson Crusoe's appraisals of his own abilities seem equally fallacious. Crusoe must have had a certain repertoire of behavior, certain frequencies of response, and he must have been able to discriminate stimuli of given complexities, must have been intelligent in being quick to solve problems, etc. All of this, according to Skinner, he could have observed and measured; but he could not have measured his I.Q. since he could not have devised a test on which his score would be divested of length, level of difficulty, and allotted time. This is delusive, however. What particular problems of daily life did he solve? How difficult were they? How many solutions did he produce in an allotted time? Here are the same arbitrary—and necessary—features to which Skinner was objecting when he referred to the inability of Crusoe to measure his I.Q. (Perhaps, also, we should remind Skinner that the I.Q. would have provided an inappropriate measure of adult intelligence in any case and that Crusoe's survival doubtless was contingent upon his possession of certain more specific abilities in requisite amounts rather than upon his having a high average score on a "hodgepodge of unknown factors combined at unknown weights," to borrow a phrase from L. L. Thurstone.)

The educational process is expensive, to the society that supplies the dollars and to the learner who contributes the time. As teachers' salaries rise and as the number of pupils increases, the total cost becomes larger. Despite the fact that I think teachers are grossly underpaid, I would at the same time point out that our educational system demands radical improvement. Consider, if you will, the hundreds of hours that are devoted to instruction in English by the time a person becomes a college senior. Then ponder his inability to write. Turn to arithmetic, the time devoted to fruitless drill, and later to algebra and geometry. Then reflect upon the ineptitude of a typical college student in solving the most elementary equation or even in adding a column of figures. Recall the idiosyncrasies in spelling that confront you in personal correspondence. Contemplate the current reading hubbub, by no means without foundation. Shudder at the prevalent superstitions and gullibility of the American public.

This does not mean that we should return to the "good old days," nor that as a people we are worse off than our immediate forbears as far as reading, writing, and arithmetic are concerned. More of us are about equally bad off, and the total effect is thus more devastating. A large part of what transpires under the name of education should be regarded candidly as serving primarily the function of custodial care of the callow. (It also, of course, provides an outlet for members of the teaching profession. And it slows down traffic on school days.) This safekeeping of the young is by no means a thankless endeavor, because it frees parents for several hours a day for other pursuits and hence presumably contributes to their tranquility. Thus the national trend toward starting children to school at earlier ages and keeping them there through early adulthood is not unrelated to the relief of parents from some of the responsibility for their care. As far as progress toward educational objectives is concerned, however, no one believes that schools operate at anywhere near 100 per cent efficiency.

This is not a criticism of individual teachers nor of the profession of teaching. It is an indictment of an educational system within which teachers operate and which is so firmly entrenched by long tradition that no single teacher or group of teachers or school can hope to resist it. Indeed, widespread and drastic educational change is warranted.

Consider a more or less typical fifth-grade group. With a mean age of around 10, it may contain some as young as 8 and others who have repeated a grade or more and who are thus as old as 13, or even older. Their general intelligence, in terms of the rather coarse I.Q. measure, will vary from perhaps 55 to as high as 170 or more. Their mental ages (equally crude, of course) might range from around 7 to 15 or so. If the school is large enough, some ability grouping doubtless would be used to reduce these ranges. Even so, they are typically pretty large. Children's differences in the several more or less native aptitudes that go to make up the common general intelligence measure are enhanced by the fact that they have acquired widely varying degrees of competence in the many skills and knowledges to which they have been exposed. So what happens? With notable exceptions, every child is given identical assignments, exposed to essentially the same teaching methods with the same amount of learning time, and tested occasionally by identical tests. Teachers are well aware that the amounts learned under such conditions will vary markedly, and achievement tests commonly reveal wide ranges of ability. So inured are we to these differences that their very presence provides a clue to the validity of the tests. When the majority of scores cluster about a particular point, we say that the test is not discriminating among individuals, leading to the conclusion that it is not a valid measuring device. If all learners do well on a test, we plan to replace it by one more difficult in order to reflect the different degrees of mastery of subject matter that our educational system insures will exist.

Under such a plan, the educationally poor become more impoverished, but the rich are not strengthened. By the nature of the system, the weaker student is forced to endure failure over and over again. Aside from the questionable desirability of such negative motivation, the blighting effects of constant frustration upon personality development should be a matter of grave concern. The abler student, on the other hand, often experiences success too readily, with no genuine effort. This painless achievement again may have harmful outcomes when the student later encounters situations that require exertion.

Along what lines lies a solution, short of providing a private tutor for every child? The first major need is for extensive curriculum revision, in the direction of a large number of learning units scaled according to difficulty within subject-matter areas. Each such area should be limited to a body of knowledges or set of related skills that require the same pattern of abilities, which include both the effects of native aptitudes and previously acquired knowledges or skills. An initial step in scaling learning units would be the testing of these abilities of prospective learners. Then tentative curricular units could be tried out with groups of varying ability patterns by different methods of presentation. Doubtless experienced teachers could effectively reduce the number of methods to be tried by excluding in advance the ones likely to be least effective. Comprehensive subject-matter tests based upon materials taught by whatever method is current in a particular school would provide a start. Then, by some combination of expert teacher judgment and empirical test data, the units of instruction could be placed in appropriate order. The next step would be to develop mastery tests for each unit. These would be entirely different from the tests commonly now administered at the end of a unit of instruction, in which the teacher is disappointed if he can not observe wide individual differences. Rather, the learner would be expected to persist at curricular units of a given difficulty level until he had achieved a standard degree of mastery, at which time he would be ready for the next higher level.

Note some of the features of such an educational plan. The learner is not frequently assigned content entirely beyond his current ability level. Nor is he ever wasting time upon materials absurdly easy for him. He rarely experiences failures. The questionable luxury of not exerting effort is disallowed. The learner competes always at his own ability level, not being exposed to content for which he lacks prerequisites. He becomes well acquainted with his limitations as well as with his strengths. His degree of mastery of what he is learning is continuously appraised, so that at all times both he and his teacher can know exactly how he is progressing.

Does this emphasis upon positive motivation and mastery of one learning unit before proceeding to the next mean that by some magic, at the end of several years of exposure to the educational process, we will have been able to eliminate the individual differences so conspicuous at its beginning? Not at all. If anything, the discrepancies will be more pronounced. Moreover, reporting upon such differences as will exist to prospective employers or to higher educational institutions could well be more detailed and far more precise than under the present system. In 1984, we may be able to say to an employer or to a university that John Doe has mastered mathematics unit 1728, English grammar 642, spelling 1021, physics 305, and so on. The personnel officers will by that time have conducted studies to enable them to predict from such data his relative chances of success as an outer-space radiological isotopist or as a student in a modern household engineering curriculum.

Are steps now being taken to reduce the formidable inefficiency and wastage of this mass baby-sitting movement that goes under the guise of the educational process? Undoubtedly isolated schools and rare teachers exist in contradiction to the perhaps shocking phraseology in which I have characterized modern education. But are there discernible trends, omens of significant departures from an educational system geared to presenting identical doses of pabulum to be partially digested within a uniform allotment of time? I am not to be satisfied—not should you be—by having each teacher know the I.Q. of her every pupil, by further applications of "ability grouping," by myriad "opportunity rooms," or by what need no longer be called "progressive education." What we must seek is a situation in which a sizeable share of curricular materials, graded according to the ability pattern and levels required, is presented to the learner in such a way that he can work at his own rate with a record of his progress constantly available to him and to his teacher. The measurement approach must be applied in the scaling of the curricular units as well as in the appraisals of progress. A dearth of such graded learning units exists. In fact, one is hard pressed to cite any aside from Ernest Horn's admirable early work in grading 3500 common words as to spelling difficulty and the contributions of Guy Buswell and others in elementary arithmetic.

A study aimed at the production of graded reading exercises, beginning with ones appropriate for elementary school grade 4 and continuing to the graduate school level, has recently been undertaken by Thelma G. Thurstone in the Psychometric Laboratory at the University of North Carolina. Currently the project involves 4500 items; and once they have been scaled, additional items can readily be added. This study should represent a major advance in the teaching and evaluation of reading skills.

The same B. F. Skinner with whom I have agreed and disagreed in turn is also developing scaled curricular materials as one phase of his work on teaching machines, about which many of you will have heard. Briefly, his plan calls first for the careful preparation of such materials appropriately ordered as to difficulty. Successive elements of each learning unit are presented to the learner in a window of a machine. He is alternately given information, required to practice or apply the information, and tested on each phase until he has mastered the unit. The machine can be set in several ingenious ways, so that, for example, the learner must finally proceed through a mastery test, say, three times in succession without error. Moreover, the robot can reject questions on which the learner has already demonstrated mastery so that he need not devote time to them. Skinner himself, as I interpret him, has misgivings about the reactions of both teachers and testers to his inventive approach to the educational process. He seems apprehensive lest they fear that they will soon be out of business, the teachers because the machine will be presenting materials in their stead and the testers because somehow appraisals of mastery will no longer be needed. To the contrary, teachers as both curriculum specialists and test construction experts will be needed in large numbers, even aside from their roles as discussion leaders, motivators, socializers, stimulators of creative thought, and so on. Skinner, in spite of his possibly ephemeral scorn of aspect testing, will come to recognize that such measurement is a very integral feature of his teaching machine. If his plans fully materialize, posterity may consign his pigeons to extinction and pay homage to him chiefly as the sponsor of the century's most massive measurement movement.

Pressey experimented with a similar idea in the late twenties or early thirties. He had a machine, like a miniature cash register, by which a student could indicate answers to objective test questions and immediately learn whether his answer was right or wrong. Basically the same idea was adopted by Angell and Troyer in their Self-Scorer. It also provides a means whereby a student taking a test continues to select answers until he obtains the right one, which is revealed by a red mark under the hole on the answer sheet that he has punched out. While we await the commercial feasibility of Skinner's latest venture, a relatively simple and inexpensive device such as this one may help to span the breach between instruction and testing. It is practicable for a small number of questions in daily discussion periods or for longer achievement tests.

On a less dramatic front, such college examiners as Paul L. Dressel at Michigan State College, working over the past several years with the instructional staff on evaluation of the objectives of college courses, has pursued an integrated approach to evaluation and teaching to the extent that they become indistinguishable from many points of view. To quote Dressel: "Evaluation does not differ from instruction in purposes, in methods, or in materials and can be differentiated from instruction only when the primary purpose is that of passing judgment on the achievement of a student at the close of a period of instruction."

The general outlines of an educational system that I have presented and the significant role that I have visualized for measurement in relation to the educational process may seem a far cry from such an institution of higher learning as, for example, Sarah Lawrence College. There, according to the jacket of *Essays in Teaching*, edited by its president, Harold Taylor, exists "a freedom of intellectual inquiry unencumbered by the apparatus of assignment and tests." This is so overwhelming that I perforce discredit it. Simply because assignments are not organized or just because they are adjusted to the individual students does not mean that no assignments are made. As for tests, from what I have heard and read about the evaluation of students' abilities, needs, and interests at Sarah Lawrence, far more examining is done there than at the average college. The disuse of end-of-course marks or of any kind of grades that resemble the familiar A, B, C's or the 70-to-100 scale does not indicate lack of measurement. The fact that much of the evaluation depends upon subjective impressions gleaned from essays and individual conferences rather than upon objective examinations does not signify that no measurement is taking place. Conceivably, such testing, based upon close personal contact between student and teacher, may be both less reliable and more valid than many of the objective tests currently extant. As I am sure will be clear by now, however, for a country-wide educational program I would rather place my chips on a more orderly curriculum and a more highly organized plan for measurement, closely geared together at every stage of the educational process.

# 2 *Essentials of a Useful Test*

## 2.1 Reliability and Confidence
### *Alexander G. Wesman*

Do you agree with the author that the reliability of the test itself is far more crucial than scorer reliability? What implications does the concept of reliability have for assessing the consistency of measurement of essay exams?

The chief purpose of testing is to permit us to arrive at judgments concerning the people being tested. If those judgments are to have any real merit, they must be based on dependable scores—which, in turn, must be earned on dependable tests. If our measuring instrument is unreliable, any judgments based on it are necessarily of doubtful worth. No one would consider relying on a thermometer which gave readings varying from 96° to 104° for persons known to have normal temperatures. Nor would any of us place confidence in measurements of length based on an elastic ruler. While few tests are capable of yielding scores which are as dependable as careful measurements of length obtained by use of a well-marked (and rigid!) ruler, we seek in tests some satisfactory amount of dependability— of "rely-ability."

It is a statistical and logical fact that no test can be valid unless it is reliable; knowing the reliability of a test in a particular situation, we know the limits beyond which validity in that situation cannot rise. Knowing reliability, we know also how large a band of error surrounds a test score—how precisely or loosely that score can be interpreted. In view of the importance of the concept of reliability, it is unfortunate that so many inadequacies in the reporting and use of reliability coefficients are to be found in the literature. This

From *Test Service Bulletin No.* 44, May 1952. Reprinted with permission of The Psychological Corporation, N. Y.

article is intended to clarify some aspects of this very fundamental characteristic of tests.

Reliability coefficients are designed to provide estimates of the consistency or precision of measurements. When used with psychological tests, the coefficients may serve one or both of two purposes: (1) to estimate the precision of the test itself as a measuring instrument, or (2) to estimate the consistency of the examinees' performances on the test. The second kind of reliability obviously embraces the first. We can have unreliable behaviour by the examinee on a relatively reliable test, but we cannot have reliable performance on an unreliable instrument. A student or applicant suffering a severe headache may give an uncharacteristic performance on a well-built test; the test may be reliable, but the subject's performance is not typical of him. If, however, the test items are ambiguous, the directions are unclear, or the pictures are so poorly reproduced as to be unintelligible—if, in short, the test materials are themselves inadequate—the subject is prevented from performing reliably, however propitious his mental and physical condition.

This two-fold purpose of reliability coefficients is reflected in the several methods which have been developed for estimating reliability. Methods which provide estimates based on a single sitting offer evidence as to the precision of the test itself; these include internal consistency estimates, such as those obtained by use of the split-half and Kuder-Richardson techniques when the test is given only once, as well as estimates based on immediate retesting, whether with the same form or an equivalent one. When a time interval of one or more days is introduced, so that day-to-day variability in the person taking the test is allowed to have an effect, we have evidence concerning the stability of the trait and of the examinee as well as of the test. It is important to recognize whether a reliability coefficient describes only the test, or whether it describes the stability of the examinees' performances as well.

## HOW HIGH SHOULD A RELIABILITY COEFFICIENT BE?

We should naturally like to have as much consistency in our measuring instruments as the physicist and the chemist achieve. However, the complexities of human personality and other practical considerations often place limits on the accuracy with which we measure and we accept reliability coefficients of different sizes depending on various purposes and situations. Perhaps the most important of these considerations is the gravity of the decision to be made on the basis of the test score. The psychologist who has to recommend whether or not a person is to be committed to an insitution is obligated to seek the most reliable instruments he can obtain. The counselor inquiring as to whether a student is likely to do better in one curriculum or another may settle for a slightly less reliable instrument, but his demands should still be high. A survey of parents' attitudes towards school practices needs only moderate reliability, since only the *average* or group figures need to be highly dependable and not the specific responses of individual parents. Test constructors experimenting with ideas for tests may accept rather low reliability in the early stages of experimentation—those tests which show promise can then be built up into more reliable instruments before publication.

It is much like the question of how confident we wish to be about decisions in other areas of living. The industrial organization about to hire a top executive (whose decisions may seriously affect the entire business) will usually spend large sums of time and money to obtain reliable evidence concerning a candidate's qualifications for the job. The same firm will devote far less time or money to the hiring of a clerk or office boy, whose errors are of lesser consequence. In buying a house, we want to have as much confidence in our decision as we can reasonably get. In buying a package of razor blades, slim evidence is sufficient since we lose little if we have to throw away the entire package or replace it sooner than expected. The principle is simply stated: the more important the decision to be reached, the greater is our need for confidence in the precision of the test and the higher is the required reliability coefficient.

## TWO FACTORS AFFECTING THE INTERPRETATION OF RELIABILITY COEFFICIENTS

Actually, there is no such thing as *the* reliability coefficient for a test. Like validity, reliability is specific to the group on which it is estimated. The reliability coefficient will be higher in one situation than in another according to circumstances which may or may not reflect real differences in the precision of measurement. Among these factors are the range of ability in the group and the interval of time between testings.

### Range of Talent

If a reliability estimate is based on a group which has a small spread in the ability measured by the test, the coefficient will be relatively low. If the group is one which has a wide range in that particular talent, the coefficient will be higher. That is, the reliability coefficient will vary with the range of talent in the group, even though the accuracy of measurement is unchanged. The following example may illustrate how this comes about. For simplicity, we have used small numbers of cases; ordinarily, far larger groups would be required to ensure a coefficient in which we could have confidence.

In Table 1 are shown the raw scores and rankings of twenty students on two forms of an arithmetic test. Looking at the two sets of rankings, we see that changes in rank from one form to the other are minor; the ranks shift a little, but not importantly. A coefficient computed from these data would be fairly high.

Now, however, let us examine only the rankings of the five top students. Though for these five students the shifts in rank are the same as before, the importance of the shifts is greatly emphasized.

TABLE I.    RAW SCORES AND RANKS OF STUDENTS ON TWO FORMS OF AN ARITHMETIC TEST

| Student | Form X | | Form Y | |
|---|---|---|---|---|
| | Score | Rank | Score | Rank |
| A | 90 | 1 | 88 | 2 |
| B | 87 | 2 | 89 | 1 |
| C | 83 | 3 | 76 | 5 |
| D | 78 | 4 | 77 | 4 |
| E | 72 | 5 | 80 | 3 |
| F | 70 | 6 | 65 | 7 |
| G | 68 | 7 | 64 | 8 |
| H | 65 | 8 | 67 | 6 |
| I | 60 | 9 | 53 | 10 |
| J | 54 | 10 | 57 | 9 |
| K | 51 | 11 | 49 | 11 |
| L | 47 | 12 | 45 | 14 |
| M | 46 | 13 | 48 | 12 |
| N | 43 | 14 | 47 | 13 |
| O | 39 | 15 | 44 | 15 |
| P | 38 | 16 | 42 | 16 |
| Q | 32 | 17 | 39 | 17 |
| R | 30 | 18 | 34 | 20 |
| S | 29 | 19 | 37 | 18 |
| T | 25 | 20 | 36 | 19 |

Whereas in the larger group student C's change in rank from third to fifth represented only a ten per cent shift (two places out of twenty), his shift of two places in rank in the smaller top group is a forty per cent change (two places out of five). When the entire twenty represent the group on which we estimate the reliability of the arithmetic test, going from third on form X to fifth on form Y still leaves the student as one of the best in this population. If, on the other hand, reliability is being estimated only on the group consisting of the top five students, going from third to fifth means dropping from the middle to the bottom of this population—a radical change. A coefficient, if computed for just these five cases, would be quite low.

Note that it is not the smaller number of cases which brings about the lower coefficient. It is the narrower range of talent which is responsible. A coefficient based on five cases as widespread as the twenty (e.g., pupils A, E, J, O, and T, who rank first, fifth, tenth, fifteenth, and twentieth respectively on form X), would be at least as large as the coefficient based on all twenty students.

This example shows why the reliability coefficient may vary even though the test questions and the stability of the students' performances are unchanged. A test may discriminate with satisfactory precision among students with wide ranges of talent but not discriminate equally well in a narrow range of talent. A yardstick is unsatisfactory if we must differentiate objects varying in length from 35.994 to 36.008 inches. Reliability coefficients reflect this fact, which holds regardless of the kind of reliability coefficient computed. It should be obvious, then, that *no reliability coefficient can be properly interpreted without information as to the spread of ability in the group on which it is based.* A reliability coefficient of .65 based on a narrow range of talent is fully as good as a coefficient of .90 based on a group with twice that spread of scores. Reliability coefficients are very much a function of the range of talent in the group.

### Interval Between Testings

When two forms of a test are taken at a single sitting, the reliability coefficient computed by correlating the two forms is likely to overestimate somewhat the real accuracy of the test. This is so because factors such as mental set, physical condition of examinees, conditions of test administration, etc.—factors which are irrelevant to the test itself—are likely to operate equally on both forms, thus making each person's pair of scores more similar than they otherwise would be. The same type of overestimate may be expected when reliability is computed by split-half or other internal consistency techniques, which are based on a single test administration. Coefficients such as these describe the accuracy of the test, but exaggerate the practical accuracy of the results by the extent to which the examinees and the testing situation may normally be expected to fluctuate. As indicated above, coefficients based on a single sitting do not describe the stability of the subjects' performances.

When we set out to investigate how stable the test results are likely to be from day to day or week to week, we are likely to underestimate the test's accuracy, though we may succeed in obtaining a realistic estimate of stability of the examinees' performances on the test. The underestimation of the test's accuracy depends on the extent to which changes in the examinees have taken place between testings. The same influences mentioned above—mental set, physical condition of examinees, and the like—which *increase* coefficients based on a single sitting are likely to *decrease* coefficients when testing is done on different days. It is unlikely for example, that the same persons who had headaches the first day will also have headaches on the day of the second testing.

Changes in the persons tested may also be of a kind directly related to the content of the particular test. If a month has elapsed between two administrations of an arithmetic test, different pupils may have learned different amounts of arithmetic during the interval. The second testing should then show greater score increases for those who learned more than for those who learned less. The correlation coefficient under these conditions will reflect the test's accuracy *minus* the effect of differential learning; it will not really be a reliability coefficient.

For most educational and industrial purposes, the reliability coefficient which reflects *stability of performance* over a relatively short time is the more important. Usually, we wish to know whether the student or job applicant would have achieved a similar score if he had been tested on some other day, or whether he might have shown up quite differently. It would be unfortunate and unfair to make important decisions on the basis of test results which might have been quite different had the person been tested the day before or a day later. We want an estimate of reliability which takes into account accidental changes in day-to-day ability of the individual, but which has not been affected by real learning between testings. Such a reliability coefficient would be based on two sittings, separated by one or more days so that day-to-day changes are reflected in the scores, but not separated by so much time that permanent changes, or learning, have occurred.* Two forms of a test, administered a day to a week apart, would usually satisfy these conditions. If the same form of a test is used in both sittings, the intervening time should be long enough to minimize the role of memory from the first to the second administrations.

Ideally, then, our reliability coefficient would ordinarily be based on two different but equivalent forms of the test, administered to a group on two separate occasions. However, it is often not feasible to meet these conditions: there may be only one form of the test available, or the group may be available for only one day, or the test may be one which is itself a learning experience. We are then forced to rely on coefficients based on a single administration. Fortunately, when such coefficients are properly used they usually provide close approximations to the estimates which would have been obtained with alternate forms administered at different times.

## SOME COMMON MISCONCEPTIONS

### Reliability of Speed Tests

Although estimates of reliability based on one administration of the test are often satisfactory, there are some circumstances in which *only* retest methods are proper. Most notable is the case in which we are dealing with an easy test given under speed conditions. If the test is composed of items which almost anyone can answer correctly given enough time but which most people tested cannot finish in the time allowed, the test is largely a measure of speed. Many clerical and simple arithmetic tests used with adults are examples of speed tests. Internal consistency methods, whether they are of the Kuder-

---

*A coefficient which is based on two testings between which opportunity for learning has occurred is a useful statistic. It may provide evidence of how much individual variation in learning has taken place, or of the stability of the knowledge, skills or aptitudes being measured. It is similar to a reliability coefficient, and is in part a function of the reliability of the two measurements; but such a coefficient should not be interpreted as simply estimating reliability—it requires a more complex interpretation.

Richardson or of the split-half type, provide false and often grossly exaggerated estimates of the reliability of such tests. To demonstrate this problem, two forms of a simple but speed-laden clerical test were given to a group. For *each* form the odd-even (split-half) reliability coefficient was found to be over .99. However, when scores on Form A were correlated with scores on Form B, the coefficient was .88. This latter value is a more accurate estimate of the reliability of the test.* Many equally dramatic illustrations of how spurious an inappropriate coefficient can be may be found readily, even in manuals for professionally made tests.

If a test is somewhat dependent on speed, but the items range in difficulty from easy to hard, internal consistency estimates will not be as seriously misleading as when the test items are simple and the test is highly speeded. As the importance of speed diminishes, these estimates will be less different from the coefficients which would be obtained by retest methods. It is difficult to guess how far wrong an inappropriate coefficient for a speeded test is. *Whenever there is evidence that speed is important in test performance, the safest course is to insist on an estimate of reliability based on test-and-retest,* if necessary with the same but preferably with an alternate form of the test.

### Part vs. Total Reliability

Some of the tests we use are composed of several parts which are individually scored and the part scores are then added to yield a total score. Often, reliability is reported only for the total score, with no information given as to the reliability of the scores on the individual parts. This may lead to seriously mistaken assumptions regarding the reliability of the part scores—and, thus, of the confidence we may place in judgments based on the part scores. The longer a test is, other things being equal, the more reliable it is; the shorter the test, the lower is its reliability likely to be. A part score based on only a portion of the items in a test can hardly be expected to be as reliable as the total score; if we treat the part score as though it has the reliability of the total score, we misplace our confidence—sometimes quite seriously.

As an example, we may look at the Wechsler Intelligence Scale

---

* *Manual for the Differential Aptitude Tests,* Revised Edition, p. 65. The Psychological Corporation, 1952.

for Children, one of the most important instruments of its kind. Five subtests are combined to yield a total verbal Score for this test. The reliability coefficient for the Verbal Score, based on 200 representative ten-year-olds, is .96—high enough to warrant considerable confidence in the accuracy of measurement for these youngsters. For the same population, however, a single subtest (General Comprehension) yields a reliability coefficient of only .73—a far less impressive figure. If we allow ourselves to act as though the total test reliability coefficient of .96 represents the consistency of measurement we can expect from the Comprehension Subtest, we are likely to encounter unpleasant surprises on future retests. More importantly, any clinical judgments which ignore the relatively poor reliability of the part score are dangerous. Test users should consider it a basic rule that *if evidence of adequate reliability for part scores is missing, the part scores should not be used.*

### Reliability for What Group?

This question may be considered as a special case under the principles discussed above with respect to range of talent. It is worth special consideration because it is so often ignored. Even the best documented of test manuals present only limited numbers of reliability coefficients; in too many manuals a single coefficient is all that is made available. On what group should a reliability coefficient be based?

When we interpret an individual's test score, the most meaningful reliability coefficient is one based on the group with which the individual is competing. Stated otherwise, the most appropriate group is that in which the counselor, clinician or employment manager is trying to make decisions as to the relative ability of the individuals on the trait being measured. Any one person is, of course, a member of many groups. An applicant for a job may also be classified as a high school or college graduate, an experienced or inexperienced salesman or bookkeeper, a local or out-of-state person, a member of one political party or another, below or above age thirty, etc. A high school student is a boy or girl; a member of an academic, trade or commercial school group; a member of an English class, a geometry class, or a woodworking or cooking class; a freshman or a junior; a future engineer or nurse or garage mechanic. Obviously, it would be impossible for a test manual to offer reliability for *all* the groups of which any one individual is a member.

The appropriate group is represented by the individual's present competition. If we are testing applicants for clerical work, the most meaningful reliability coefficient is one based on applicants for clerical work. Coefficients based on employed clerical workers are somewhat less useful, those based on high school graduates are still less useful; as we go on to *more general* groups—e.g., all high school students or all adults—the coefficients become less and less meaningful. Similarly, as we go to *less relevant* groups (even though they may be quite specific) the reliability coefficients are also less relevant and less meaningful. The reliability of a test calculated on the basis of mechanical apprentices, college sophomores, or junior executives reveals little of importance when we are concerned with clerical applicants. What we need to know is how well the test discriminates among applicants for clerical work. If we can define the population with even greater specificity and relevance—e.g., female applicants for filing jobs—so much the better. *The closer the resemblance between the group on which the reliability coefficient is based and the group of individuals about whose relative ability we need to decide, the more meaningful is that coefficient of reliability.*

**Test Reliability vs. Scorer Reliability**

Some tests are not entirely objective as to scoring method; the scorer is required to make a judgment as to the correctness or quality of the response. This is frequently true in individually-administered tests (Wechsler or Binet for example), projective techniques in personality measurement (Rorschach, Sentence Completion, etc.) and many other tests in which the subject is asked to supply the answer, rather than to select one of several stated choices. For tests such as these, it is important to know the extent of agreement between the persons who score them. Test manuals usually report the amount of agreement by means of a coefficient of correlation between scores assigned to a set of test papers by two or more independent scorers.

Such a correlation coefficient yields important information—it tells us how objectively the test can be scored. It even contributes some evidence of reliability, since objectivity of scoring is a factor which makes for test reliability. Such a coefficient should not, however, be considered a reliability coefficient for the test; it is only an estimate of *scoring* reliability—a statement of how much confidence we may have that two scorers will arrive at similar scores for a given test paper. Moreover, it is possible for a test to be quite unreliable as a measuring instrument, yet have high scoring objectivity. We should remember that many objective tests—those in which the person selects one of several stated options—are not very reliable, yet the scoring is by definition objective. A short personality inventory may have a retest reliability coefficient of .20; but if it is the usual paper-and-pencil set of questions with a clear scoring key, two scorers should agree perfectly, except for clerical errors, in assigning scores to the test. The coefficient of correlation between their sets of scores might well be 1.00.

In short, information as to scorer agreement is important but not sufficient. The crucial question—How precisely is the test measuring the individual?—is not answered by scorer agreement; a real reliability coefficient is required.

## A PRACTICAL CHECK-LIST

When reading a test manual, the test user would do well to apply a mental check-list to the reliability section, raising at least the following questions for each reliability coefficient:

1. What does the coefficient measure?
   a. Precision of the test—coefficient based on single sitting?
   b. Stability of examinees' test performances—coefficient based on test-and-retest with a few days intervening?

2. Is it more than a reliability coefficient? . . . does it also measure constancy of the trait? . . . is the coefficient based on test-and-retest with enough intervening time for learning or similar changes to have occurred?

3. Do scores on the test depend largely on how rapidly the examinees can answer the questions? If so, is the reliability coefficient based on a test-and-retest study?

4. Are there part scores intended for consideration separately? If so, is each part score reliable enough to warrant my confidence?

5. Is the group on which this coefficient is based appropriate to my purpose? Does it consist of people similar to those with whom I shall be using the test?

6. Since a reliability coefficient, like any other statistic, requires a reasonable number of cases to be itself dependable, how large is the group on which the coefficient is based?

If, and *only* if, the coefficients can be accepted as meeting the above standards, one may ask:

7. In view of the importance of the judgments I shall make, is the correlation coefficient large enough to warrant my use of the test?

A reliability coefficient is a statistic—simply a number which summarizes a relationship. Before it takes on meaning, its reader must understand the logic of the study from which the coefficient was derived, the nature of the coefficient and the forces which affect it. Statistics may reveal or conceal—what they do depends to a very large extent on the logical ability and awareness the reader brings to them. Figures do lie, to those who don't or won't understand them.

---

## 2.2   Test Validity over a Seventeen-Year Period

*E. B. Knauft*

This study illustrates the relative success that tests can have in predicting criterion behavior, even over extended periods of time. Note that even a relatively short test can, for certain purposes be a quite satisfactory measure.

A 15-minute general mental ability test, known as LOMA-1, has been administered to applicants in the home office of the Aetna Life Affiliated Companies since 1937. The most recent validity study of this test, although generally confirming previous studies, was felt to be of interest because it covers a period of 17 years.

The principal finding concerns the relationship between test score and job level the employee has attained over a period of years. The analysis was based on 692 persons hired between 1937 and 1949 and still employed by the company on March 1, 1954. These persons

Reprinted with permission of the author and *Journal of Applied Psychology*, **39**, 5, 1955.

were tested at the time they were employed. A product-moment correlation of +.60 was obtained between LOMA test score and present job classification of the 692 employees. The classification system for these jobs includes seven grades or classes ranging from simple clerical jobs such as file clerk to complicated decision-making jobs such as senior underwriter and senior claim examiner. The great majority of these employees started in one of the bottom three classes. The company adheres to a policy of promotion from within, and it is very unusual for anyone to be initially employed on a job above the third class from the bottom. The correlation of +.60 thus indicates that the LOMA test score is a fairly good predictor of the extent to which an employee will be promoted over a period of years.

TABLE 1    RELATIONSHIP BETWEEN JOB CLASS AND LOMA SCORE

LOMA Score

| Job Class | 0–99 N | 0–99 % | 100–119 N | 100–119 % | 120 and Over N | 120 and Over % | Mean Score |
|---|---|---|---|---|---|---|---|
| Decision-making 3 | 0 | 0 | 1 | 1 | 6 | 3 | 148.6 |
| Decision-making 2 | 4 | 1 | 8 | 5 | 58 | 25 | 133.7 |
| Decision-making 1 | 10 | 4 | 23 | 13 | 60 | 26 | 123.9 |
| Complicated clerical 2 | 61 | 21 | 59 | 34 | 57 | 24 | 105.7 |
| Complicated clerical 1 | 87 | 31 | 56 | 32 | 38 | 16 | 94.8 |
| Simple clerical 2 | 100 | 35 | 23 | 13 | 11 | 5 | 79.2 |
| Simple clerical 1 | 24 | 8 | 3 | 2 | 3 | 1 | 70.0 |
| Total | 286 | 100 | 173 | 100 | 233 | 100 | |

Table 1 summarizes the relationship between job class attained and LOMA score. The number and percentage of persons falling in each job class are given for each of three score categories.

A second criterion for evaluating the effectiveness of the LOMA test is the individual's present job performance. In several departments production records were available for simple and complicated clerical jobs which are on a wage incentive plan. The criterion used was the mean of 14-weeks bonus efficiencies of employees who had been on the job long enough to be producing at a relatively constant rate. The bonus efficiency represents net production with allow-

TABLE 2    RELATIONSHIP BETWEEN LOMA SCORE AND PRODUCTION

| Department | No. Cases | Criterion Reliability | Validity Coefficient |
|---|---|---|---|
| A | 36 | .92 | .40* |
| B | 23 | .91 | .48* |
| C | 14 | .94 | .29 |
| D | 19 | .87 | .32 |

*Significant at 5% level of confidence.

ances for time on "non-bonus" activities. Results obtained from four departments used in this study are summarized in Table 2. Criterion reliabilities are based on a correlation between odd and even weeks for 16 weeks. Validity coefficients are product-moment correlations between the production criterion and LOMA score.

Although the LOMA test appears to be most effective as an aid to prediction of job class eventually attained, indications from four small samples suggest that at least in some instances it is also effective as a partial predictor of performance on various kinds of clerical jobs.

## 2.3   Measurement and the Teacher

*Robert L. Ebel*

The unqualified question, "How good is this test?" directed at one who is knowledgeable in measurement inevitably leads to an arched eyebrow and the counterquestion, "What do you plan to use the test for?"

From *Educational Leadership*, **20**, Oct. 1962, 20–24. Reprinted with permission of the author and the Association for Supervision and Curriculum Development.

The following article, written by an outstanding authority in the field, enunciates and explains clearly ten selected principles which, if well understood, should give the reader useful knowledge to aid in both the selection and construction of tests. Furthermore, Dr. Ebel leaves one with a new appreciation for the viewpoint that measurement and instruction are inseparable aspects of an integrated process. One can hardly take place without the other. And only to the degree that the teacher or psychological worker skillfully considers both aspects in his professional planning will he attain the goals he has set for his instructional or therapeutic efforts.

## TEN USEFUL PRINCIPLES

The principles of measurement of educational achievement presented in this article are based on the experience and research of a great many people who have been working to improve classroom testing. The particular principles discussed here were selected on the basis of their relevance to the questions and problems which arise most often when tests of educational achievement are being considered, prepared and used. While some of the principles may seem open to question, we believe a case can be made in support of each one.

1. *The measurement of educational achievement is essential to effective education.*

Learning is a natural, inevitable result of human living. Some learning would occur even if no special provision were made for it in schools, or no special effort were taken to facilitate it. Yet efficient learning of complex achievements, such as reading, understanding of science, or literary appreciation, requires special motivation, guidance and assistance. Efforts must be directed towards the attainment of specific goals. Students, teachers and others involved in the process of education must know to what degree the goals have been achieved. The measurement of educational achievement can contribute to these activities.

It is occasionally suggested that schools could get along without tests, or indeed that they might even do a better job if testing were prohibited. It is seldom if ever suggested, though, that education can be carried on effectively by teachers and students who have no particular goals in view, or who do not care what or how much is being learned. If tests are outlawed, some other means of assessing educational achievement would have to be used in their place.

2. *An educational test is no more or less than a device for facilitating, extending and refining a teacher's observations of student achievement.*

In spite of the Biblical injunction, most of us find ourselves quite often passing judgments on our fellow men. Is candidate A more deserving of our vote than candidate B? Is C a better physician than D? Is employee E entitled to a raise or a promotion on his merits? Should student F be given a failing mark? Should student L be selected in preference to student M for the leading role in the class play?

Those charged with making such judgments often feel they must do so on the basis of quite inadequate evidence. The characteristics on which the decision should be based may not have been clearly defined. The performances of the various candidates may not have been observed extensively, or under comparable conditions. Instead of recorded data, the judge may have to trust his fallible memory, supplemented with hearsay evidence.

Somewhat similar problems are faced by teachers, as they attempt to assess the achievements of their students. In an effort to solve these problems, tests have been developed. Oral examinations and objective examinations are means for making it easier for the teacher to observe a more extensive sample of student behavior under more carefully controlled conditions.

The price that must be paid for a test's advantages of efficiency and control in the observation of student achievements is some loss in the naturalness of the behavior involved. In tests which attempt to measure the student's typical behavior, especially those aspects of behavior which depend heavily on his interests, attitudes, values or emotional reactions, the artificiality of the test situation may seriously distort the measurements obtained. But this problem is much less serious in tests intended to measure how much the student knows, and what he can do with his knowledge. What is gained in efficiency and precision of measurement usually far outweighs what may be lost due to artificiality of the situation in which the student's behavior is observed.

3. *Every important outcome of education can be measured.*

In order for an outcome of education to be important, it must make a difference. The behavior of a person who has more of a particular outcome must be observably different from that of a person who has less. Perhaps one can imagine some result of education which is so deeply personal that it does not ever affect in any way what he says or does, or how he spends his time. But it is difficult to find any grounds for arguing that such a well concealed achievement is important.

If the achievement does make a difference in what a person can do or does do, then it is measurable. For the most elementary type of measurement requires nothing more than the possibility of making a verifiable observation that person or object X has more of some defined characteristic than person or object Y.

To say that any important educational outcome is measurable is not to say that satisfactory methods of measurement now exist. Certainly it is not to say that every important educational outcome can be measured by means of a paper and pencil test. But it is to reject the claim that some important educational outcomes are too complex or too intangible to be measured. Importance and measurability are logically inseparable.

4. *The most important educational achievement is command of useful knowledge.*

If the importance of an educational outcome may be judged on the basis of what teachers and students spend most of their time doing, it is obvious that acquisition of a command of useful knowledge is a highly important outcome. Or if one asks how the other objectives are to be attained—objectives of self-realization, of human relationship, of economic efficiency, of civic responsibility—it is obvious again that command of useful knowledge is the principal means.

How effectively a person can think about a problem depends largely on how effectively he can command the knowledge that is relevant to the problem. Command of knowledge does not guarantee success, or happiness, or righteousness, but it is difficult to think of anything else a school can attempt to develop which is half as likely to lead to these objectives.

If we give students command of knowledge, if we develop their ability to think, we make them intellectually free and independent.

This does not assure us that they will work hard to maintain the status quo, that they will adopt all of our beliefs and accept all of our values. Yet it can make them free men and women in the area in which freedom is most important. We should be wary of an educational program which seeks to change or control student behavior on any other basis than rational self-determination, the basis that command of knowledge provides.

*5. Written tests are well suited to measure the student's command of useful knowledge.*

All knowledge can be expressed in propositions. Propositions are statements that can be judged to be true or false. Scholars, scientists, research workers—all those concerned with adding to our store of knowledge, spend most of their time formulating and verifying propositions.

Implicit in every true-false or multiple-choice test item is a proposition, or several propositions. Essay tests also require a student to demonstrate his command of knowledge.

Some elements of novelty are essential in any question intended to test a student's command of knowledge. He should not be allowed to respond successfully simply on the basis of rote learning or verbal association. He should not be asked a stereotyped question to which a pat answer probably has been committed to memory.

*6. The classroom teacher should prepare most of the tests used to measure educational achievement in the classroom.*

Many published tests are available for classroom use in measuring educational aptitude or achievement in broad areas of knowledge. But there are very few which are specifically appropriate for measuring the achievement of the objectives of a particular unit of work or of a particular period of instruction. Publishers of textbooks sometimes supply booklets of test questions to accompany their texts. These can be useful, although all too often the test questions supplied are of inferior quality—hastily written, unreviewed, untested, and subject to correct response on the basis of rote learning as well as on the basis of understanding.

Even if good ready-made tests were generally available, a case could still be made for teacher-prepared tests; the chief reason being that the process of test development can help the teacher define his objectives. This process can result in tests that are more highly relevant than any external tests are likely to be. It can make the process of measuring educational achievement an integral part of the whole process of instruction, as it should be.

7. *To measure achievement effectively the classroom teacher must be (a) a master of the knowledge or skill to be tested, and (b) a master of the practical arts of testing.*

No courses in educational measurement, no books or articles on the improvement of classroom tests, are likely to enable a poor teacher to make good tests. A teacher's command of the knowledge he is trying to teach, his understanding of common misconceptions regarding this content, his ability to invent novel questions and problems, and his ability to express these clearly and concisely; all these are crucial to his success in test construction. It is unfortunately true that some people who have certificates to teach lack one or more of these prerequisites to good teaching and good testing.

However, there are also some tricks of the trade of test construction. A course in educational measurement, or a book or article on classroom testing can teach these things. Such a course may also serve to shake a teacher's faith—constructively and wholesomely— in some of the popular misconceptions about the processes of testing educational achievement. Among these misconceptions are the belief that only essay tests are useful for measuring the development of a student's higher mental processes; that a test score should indicate what proportion a student does know of what he ought to know; that mistakes in scoring are the main source of error in test scores.

8. *The quality of a classroom test depends on the relevance of the tasks included in it, on the representativeness of its sampling of all aspects of instruction, and on the reliability of the scores it yields.*

If a test question presents a problem like those the student may expect to encounter in his later life outside the classroom, and if the course in which his achievement is being tested did in fact try to teach him how to deal with such problems, then the question is relevant. If the test questions involve, in proportion to their importance, all aspects of achievement the course undertakes to develop, it samples representatively. If the scores students receive on a test agree closely with those they would receive on an independent, equivalent test, then the test yields reliable scores.

Relevance, representativeness and reliability are all matters of degree. Procedures and formulas for calculating estimates of test reliability are well developed, and are described in most books on educational measurement. Estimates of representativeness and relevance are more subjective, less quantitative. Yet this does not mean that relevance and representativeness are any less important than reliability. The more a test has of each the better. While it is possible to have an irrelevant and unrepresentative but highly reliable test, it is seldom necessary and never desirable, to sacrifice any one of the three for the others.

Either essay or objective test forms can be used to present relevant tasks to the examinees. Ordinarily, the greater the novelty of a test question, that is, the smaller the probability that the student has encountered the same question before, or been taught a pat answer to it, the greater its relevance. Because of the greater number of questions involved, it is sometimes easier to include a representative sample of tasks in an objective than in an essay test. For the same reason, and also because of greater uniformity in scoring, objective tests are likely to yield somewhat more reliable scores than are essay tests.

9. *The more variable the scores from a test designed to have a certain maximum possible score, the higher the expected reliability of those scores.*

Reliability is sometimes defined as the proportion of the total variability among the test scores which is not attributable to errors of measurement. The size of the errors of measurement depends on the nature of the test—the kind and the number of items in it. Hence for a particular test, any increase in the total variability of the scores is likely to increase the proportion which is not due to errors of measurement, and hence to increase the reliability of the test.

Figure 1 shows some hypothetical score distributions for three tests. The essay test consists of 10 questions worth 10 points each, scored by a teacher who regards 75 as a passing score on such a test. The true-false test consists of 100 items, each of which is worth one point if correctly answered, with no subtraction for wrong answers. The multiple-choice test also includes 100 items, each of which offers four alternative answer options. It, too, is scored only for the number of correct answers given, with no "correction for guessing."

Note, in the data at the bottom of Figure 1, the differences among the tests in average score (mean), in variability (standard deviation), in effective range and in estimated reliability. While these are hypothetical data, derived from calculations based on certain assumptions, they are probably reasonably representative of the results most teachers achieve in using tests of these types.

It is possible to obtain scores whose reliability is above .90 using 100 multiple-choice items, but it is not easy to do, and classroom teachers seldom do it in the tests they construct. It is also possible to handle 100-point essay tests and 100-item true-false tests so that their reliability will equal that of a 100-item multiple-choice test. But again, it is not easy to do and classroom teachers seldom succeed in doing it.

Hypothetical Score Distributions for Three Tests.

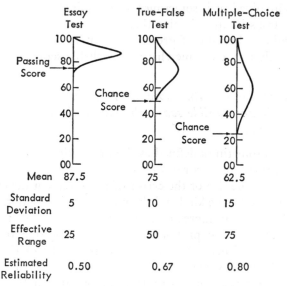

| | Essay Test | True-False Test | Multiple-Choice Test |
|---|---|---|---|
| Mean | 87.5 | 75 | 62.5 |
| Standard Deviation | 5 | 10 | 15 |
| Effective Range | 25 | 50 | 75 |
| Estimated Reliability | 0.50 | 0.67 | 0.80 |

FIG. 1

10. *The reliability of a test can be increased by increasing the number of questions (or independent points to be scored) and by sharpening the power of individual questions to discriminate between students of high and low achievement.*

Figure 2 illustrates the increases of test reliability which can be expected as a result of increasing the number of items (or independent points to be scored) in a test. Doubling the length of a 10-item test whose reliability coefficient is .33 increases the reliability to .50.

Relation of Test Reliability to Test Length

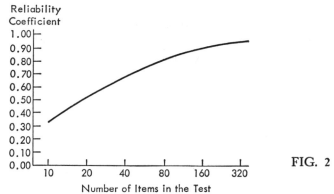

Reliability
Coefficient

FIG. 2

Number of Items in the Test

Doubling again brings it up to .67, and so on. These estimates are based on the Spearman-Brown formula for predicting the reliability of a lengthened test. While the formula requires assumptions which may not be justified in all cases, its predictions are usually quite accurate.

Figure 3 shows how the maximum discriminating power of an item is related to its level of difficulty. These discrimination indices are simply differences between the proportions of correct response from good and poor students. Good students are those whose total test scores fall among the top 27 percent of the students tested. Poor

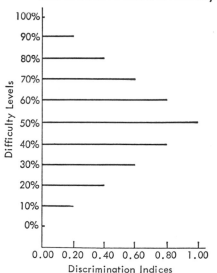

Maximum Discrimination Attainable With
Items at Different Levels of Difficulty

Difficulty Levels

FIG. 3

Discrimination Indices

students are those whose scores make up the bottom 27 percent. An item of 50 percent difficulty does not necessarily have (and usually will not have) an index of discrimination of 1.00. Its discriminating power may be zero, or even negative. But items of middle difficulty have higher ceilings on their discriminating power. What is more important, they not only can have, but usually do have, greater discriminating power than very easy or very difficult items. An item that no one answers correctly, or that everyone answers correctly, cannot discriminate at all. Such an item adds nothing to the reliability of a test.

In summary, the 10 principles stated and discussed in this article represent only a sample of the important things classroom teachers need to know about educational measurement. These principles, and the brief discussion of each presented here, may serve to call into question some common practices in classroom testing, or to suggest some ways in which classroom tests might be improved. They are not likely, and are not intended, to say all that needs to be said or do all that needs to be done to improve educational measurement in the classroom. It is our sincere belief, however, that a teacher whose classroom testing reflects an understanding of these principles will do a better than average job of measuring student achievement.

# 3 *Reliability and Validity*

## 3.1 The Correction for Guessing
### *Jerome E. Doppelt*

Validity can be described as the freedom from errors of measurement which a test enjoys. The following article discusses in a comprehensive way the problems revolving around purging from tests the contamination attributable to guessing.

The author sums up by an appeal or recommendation for semantic clarity. He suggests that the correction for guessing would be better named "a penalty for answering wrong." Try to decide, if you can, under what circumstances a test could be made more valid through the technique discussed in this article.

When Pat and Mike laid down their picks and shovels and decided to apply for the job of mechanic's helper, they realized they would be competing with each other. Only one job was available. They consequently were not surprised when the personnel director asked them to take a test of mechanical comprehension to help the company decide which man would be selected.

Pat, a cautious man, carefully read the directions for the test, learned he was to choose the best answer to every question from the three choices that were given, and proceeded to take the test. He found he was quite sure of his answers to 36 of the 60 questions; for the remaining questions he could sometimes rule out one of the choices but he just could not select one answer with complete confidence. Pat felt it would be best not to try.

Mike, on the other hand, was generally more willing than Pat to take a chance. After he answered the 23 questions with which he had no difficulty, he decided to answer the remaining questions as

From *Test Service Bulletin No.* 46, Jan. 1954. Reprinted with permission of The Psychological Corporation, N. Y.

best he could. As luck and partial information would have it, Mike managed to answer correctly 13 of the 37 items about which he had had doubt.

The results of the scoring of the test papers were 36 rights and no wrongs for Pat; 36 rights and 24 wrongs for Mike.

The test-maker had realized that people will react differently when faced with multiple-choice test questions which they cannot answer with confidence. Some will not respond to such questions; others will risk answering them. Consequently the test score was defined as the number of correct answers minus one-half the number of wrong responses. Thus Pat's score was 36 and Mike's score was 24.

In this instance, the correction for guessing resulted in a higher score for Pat than for Mike. Since we know how the two men took the test, it seems entirely fair for Pat to receive the higher rating. But how often do we know what has gone on in the minds of the examinees?

All people who have scored or used multiple-choice tests know that there exist several "formulas" for obtaining scores. We find among objective and semi-objective tests such different scoring formulas as the number of right answers, the number of right answers minus the number of wrong responses, Rights minus ½ Wrongs, Rights minus ⅓ Wrongs, Rights minus ¼ Wrongs, and the like. Psychometricians can usually tell, after a quick glance at the test content, what the scoring formula will be. If the test is of the completion type, the formula is the number of right answers; if the test is of the multiple-choice type, the number of right answers is often reduced by an amount equal to the number of wrong responses divided by one less than the number of options per item.

The scoring formula for a particular test is determined by applying the laws of chance in an attempt to correct for the effect of guessing on the part of the examinee. In a test made up of five-choice items, for example, the examinee may be expected to guess correctly the answer to one out of every five items he doesn't know or can't solve. The total number of right answers therefore includes the number of items answered correctly on the basis of information plus the number of correct guesses. But how does one know how many answers are guesses? To determine the number of correct guesses we make use of the number of wrong responses. Thus, for every four wrong responses it is assumed the examinee made one correct guess. Consequently, the number of correct guesses is estimated for a five-choice test by dividing the number of wrong responses by four. This is the correction for guessing and it is subtracted from the number of right answers. Note that the basic assumption is that all wrong responses plus some of the right ones are classified as chance responses or guesses.

Usually a "guess" is interpreted as a positive statement or action based on chance. An omission or the withholding of a response is ordinarily not considered a guess. It is interesting, therefore, to find that in any given group, how much difference the so-called correction for guessing makes depends on the number of omissions rather than on the number of actual guesses (which we never know). If everyone in a group taking a test answers *all* the items, the uncorrected scores (the number of right answers) will be perfectly correlated with corrected scores which take into account the number of wrong responses. The numerical values of the corrected and uncorrected scores will of course be different but the relative positions or ranks of individuals in the group will be exactly the same. This can be demonstrated mathematically and will be true *regardless of whether the wrong answers are due to chance responses, misinformation or partially correct information.* The same situation exists if all students have the same number of omitted items, even though the specific omitted items differ from student to student. It is only when the number of omissions ranges from very few to very many that a correction factor assumes significance.

What does the "corrected" score mean? Is it an indication of the number of items to which the examinee definitely knows the answers because the number of correct guesses has been subtracted? After some consideration, one can see that the corrected score does not actually mean this. For the correction formula to be strictly applicable, the examinee must have made pure chance responses to all the items which he marked incorrectly and to some of the items which he marked correctly. For that to occur, all of the options for an item to which the examinee responds by chance must seem to him equally likely to be right. Ordinarily, if the examinee is even half awake when he is taking the test, all the options will not be equally attractive. He can probably rule out some of the options quite readily. It is also obvious that influences other than chance enter into the picture. It is entirely possible that an examinee answers an item incorrectly because he has definite misinformation on the topic or because he has partial information which misleads him. In such cases, he did not really guess at the answer, in a chance sense. Since the examinee rarely chooses purely by chance among the possible answers presented to him, the basic assumption underlying the correction for guessing is violated. In some instances the correction for guessing may overcorrect and in other instances, it may undercorrect. In general, the correction for guessing probably yields a reasonable approximation of the true situation not because of the inherent soundness of its assumptions but rather because it tends to be a compromise between too much correction and not enough correction.

If the correction for guessing is based on conditions which are practically never met, some terms and concepts regarding the meaning of test scores should be altered. For example, it is not uncommon to hear that a particular student or applicant got no more than a "chance score" on a test if he answered twenty items correctly out of a total of 100 five-choice items. It is felt that such a score is not more than the effect of chance, and the correction for guessing if he tried every item will reduce this score to zero. It is no more accurate to say that this student got a "chance score" than it is to say that a pair of loaded dice respond to the laws of chance. There is probably no such thing as a chance score on a test appropriate to the person and the situation unless the examinee is blindfolded when he takes the test. Zero scores and negative scores, which sometimes result from a correction for guessing, are not indications of no knowledge whatsoever regarding the materials in the test. Such scores are probably obtained through the interaction of (a) positive correct information on some items, (b) guessing and partial information and positive misinformation on other items, and (c) overcorrection for guessing.

The correction for guessing is widely used in scoring power tests and there are some situations in which its use is advisable. Some students are bold, and answer questions when they are not sure of the answers while their more timid colleagues would rather omit those questions. If the test score is simply the number of correct responses, there will be a premium for boldness. In such instances, it seems reasonable to correct the scores by subtracting a proportion of the number of wrong responses. It would, however, be more logical to call the correction factor a penalty for wrong responses than to call it a correction for guessing.

When an item is omitted in an untimed test we can generally assume that the examinee had the opportunity to read the question but, for one reason or another, refused to respond. Speed tests present a somewhat different problem. True speed tests are made up of questions which are extremely easy and the examinee will almost always answer correctly if he has the opportunity to read the item. Most of the omissions in a pure speed test are due to the fact that the examinee never got a chance to answer the items because the time was up before he could reach them. In tests of this type we usually find very few or no omissions and relatively few wrong answers between the first item and the last item attempted. Consequently there is no need for using a correction scheme. The number of right answers is entirely adequate as a score.

Many tests may best be described as a mixture of power and speed. In such tests speed is an important factor, but the items vary in difficulty and are generally arranged in order of difficulty. Between the first and the last items attempted the examinee is very likely to encounter questions which he cannot answer with certainty and he must then decide whether or not he will risk a guess. There may be considerable variation in the number of omissions up to the last item attempted and in the number of wrong responses. If this is found to be the case, the situation is similar to that found in power tests. A corrected score may then be advisable. There are, however, great differences among tests of the mixed power and speed type in the extent to which items are omitted or answered incorrectly. The actual effectiveness of a correction applied to the number of right answers must be evaluated for each test separately.

Before leaving the topic of speeded tests we should note a situation which occasionally arises. Many speeded tests are scored by merely recording the number of right answers. A test-wise examinee who knows how the test is scored may answer the questions to the best of his ability until shortly before the time is up. He may then hastily record 'an answer to each of the remaining items without even stopping to read the questions. He is thus almost bound to pick up some points of score without any danger of incurring a penalty. If this kind of test-taking occurs with any frequency, it would be advisable to apply a correction to the scores.

It is the fond hope of those who construct power tests that the examinees will answer all the items. If this were to happen, there would be no need for correcting scores. We know, however, that there are differences among examinees in their willingness to leave items unanswered. It is likely that more people might be induced to answer more items if the directions for the test stated that omissions would be counted as wrong responses or if all were encouraged to guess whenever they did not know the answers. Such directions would doubtless disturb those educators who feel that encouraging students to guess makes for loose thinking and disrespectful attitudes toward learning. This view may have validity if tests are being used for moralistic or character-building purposes alone, but this is rare. Usually a test's essential function is that of a measuring instrument and as such it should be kept as uncontaminated as possible. One source of contamination is the matter of boldness vs. caution in taking the test. The imposition of a penalty for wrong answers is an attempt to control this type of contamination. More effective control would be achieved if all students were encouraged to be equally bold, so to speak, by answering every item.

What can be said, in summary, about the correction for guessing? In the first place, "correction for guessing" is essentially a misnomer; the correction could more properly be called a penalty for answering wrong. Some of these wrong answers may have been given in accordance with the laws of chance but more of them probably are based on misinformation or partial information.

Second, the basic assumption underlying the correction for guessing is the concept of the "chance score." Thus one expects a proportion of the number of items to be answered correctly on the basis of chance. This concept is misleading and may make it appear that the examinee knows the answers to fewer questions than he really does know.

Third, the correction for guessing makes a difference in the relative positions of individuals in a group if there is considerable variation in the number of omitted items. To eliminate a premium for willingness to answer items, it seems advisable to use corrected scores. It should be remembered, however, that such corrected scores are an attempt to rule out the effects of differential boldness in taking the test rather than a method for getting a true picture of the examinee's knowledge.

Fourth, when a comparison of the corrected and uncorrected scores on a power test shows considerable discrepancies in relative standing of the examinees, the question is not which type of score should be used. The question is whether or not the test is really a power test and whether it is appropriate for use with the group.

The fundamental purpose in giving a test is to obtain samples of behavior which will permit comparisons with respect to some reasonably well defined attribute among individuals in the group tested. Effective discrimination among the examinees must be demonstrated for each test in specific situations. There is no reason to believe that any scoring formula contributes materially to a test's discriminating power.

Many published tests require use of a correction formula to obtain the score. The user of such tests must necessarily abide by the scoring instructions since otherwise he cannot compare his scores with the norms. In making his own objective tests, the teacher or personnel man need not feel that a correction for guessing is essential to the construction of a good test. Reliability and validity may still be obtained with either corrected or uncorrected scores.

---

## 3.2   The Present Status of the Culture-Fair Testing Movement

*Nadine M. Lambert*

The idea of culture-fair tests presents an interesting dilemma. Some psychologists feel that cultural group differences in ability do exist, and that present standardized tests penalize most minority groups. On the other hand, there are some who believe that this situation is irrelevant. They contend, since available tests accurately predict academic success, that if schools are established to reach specific learning objectives, and if tests are available to identify those children whose chances for success are small, then these tests are fulfilling a major role.

Which position is most tenable for you? What are some *advantages* to be derived from developing a truly culture-fair test? Can such a test ever be developed?

The historical development of tests of mental ability has not ignored the fact that environment influences performance. What the development of the intelligence test movement has shown us, however, is

---

Reprinted with permission of the author and *Psychology in the Schools*, 1, 3, 1964.

that the degree to which psychologists have wished to deal with environment and the totality of cultural influences as they affect measured intellectual performance as vacillated.

The problem of culture bias in tests has not been ignored in the literature. Notable among those who have argued for a clear-headed look at how much tests handicap such children and in turn perpetuate a particular system of educational emphasis is Davis (1948). In the Midcentury White House Conference on Children and Youth (1951) he pointed out that unless America finds and trains effectively more children from the vast lower socio-economic groups with undeveloped educational potential, this country will be seriously threatened by the competitive developments of European and Asian countries. He contended that the discovery of such children has been restricted by the fact that "standard" intelligence tests have been culturally biased in favor of the higher socio-economic groups. A great amount of evidence is available to demonstrate that children from higher socio-economic families do consistently better as a group on traditional intelligence tests than those from lower economic levels (Eells, 1951; Lucas, 1953; McNemar, 1942). Davis further hypothesized that when cultural factors are controlled, average, real intellectual ability is at the same level for all economic groups. Eells (1951) suggested that finding real intellectual ability where it was not previously noticed was the central responsibility for intelligence testing. His emphasis was on the fact that if good tests of basic problem solving ability could be developed and these tests could measure ability to solve real life problems of the kind that are important, school authorities could use such tests as a basis for curriculum planning and as a basis for educational evaluation.

The Davis Eells Games were published in 1953. They were developed to measure basic intellectual potential which was free of socio-economic cultural bias. These tests have gone through some revealing studies since they were published, and they have been demonstrated to be not free from the bias which the authors had hoped to avoid.

The late Irving Lorge (1952) in an incisive critique of the movement for cultural free tests points out that the efforts for development of such tests are motivated by the desire to show that there are no real differences between groups. He cites evidence from ability tests which shows over and over again that men and boys do less well than women and girls on certain types of test items. Since group means of male and female subjects are hypothesized to be equal, test authors have included enough items favoring men as well as women so that the resulting test has added bias and taken away bias to accomplish the original motive-equal means. Lorge feels that to deny differences between groups is to build a house on a shifting foundation in measurement. To make unbiased tests of ability is to try to reduce group differences, which may be, and probably are real, to zero. If tests can be developed which show no difference between groups, they are not biased—no difference, no bias. Culture-fair tests therefore often are tests measuring single types of ability. With tests measuring several types of ability, culture-fair tests must achieve this by subtracting out of the tests the items which differentiate between cultural groups. The result is development of culture-fair tests that reduce the uncommon characteristics of two groups by eliminating them; thus we often have tests with no verbal items, no verbal instructions, and which are abstract but concerned with figural abstractions rather than verbal ones. Lorge raises the issue that if such tests can be developed, what do we have when finished. The problem of establishing their validity still remains and as long as we have performance on learning tasks and teacher judgment through grades (which necessarily involve culture) what good are tests which predict these criteria less well than traditional tests of mental ability?

Lorge would have psychologists measure difference with as great a variety of tasks as possible. When differences can be reduced by changes in opportunity, credit should be given to the tests which showed an initial difference. He would reinforce the movement in differential psychology and attempt to appraise the interaction of endowment and opportunity. The task for the development of culture-fair tests is not only to reduce differences resulting from socio-economic status. In many parts of the United States and in other English-speaking countries, culture-fair tests would offer a great advantage in evaluating persons from other cultural and racial groups. Testing of Indian children in the Southwest United States as well as the problems in testing children of Mexican background has occupied a few psychologists for some time. Testing African natives is the particular concern of the South African whites who wish to use the natives in industry. The Canadian provinces and the United States are interested in evaluating the abilities of Eskimo and Indian children for educational programs. The great influx of migrants in the last few years to Australia has increased need for the use of tests which will evaluate basic intellectual endowment and contribute to the knowledge or prediction of the success of people from different cultural backgrounds in educational and industrial endeavors.

## EXAMPLES OF CULTURE-FAIR TESTS

### Davis Eells Games (1953), World Book Company

This test was developed to measure ability of children of differing socio-economic levels. It is composed of a number of items which require no reading nor attention to instructions written on the test forms. Several studies (Cooper, 1958; Richie, 1954; Rosenblum, 1955) have questioned the cultural bias of the test and some of the initial claims for socio-economic fairness are no longer made. The test may have value for use with poor readers (Justman, 1955), but Smith (1956) has indicated that auding ability (ability to understand spoken language) is a major source of bias in the test.

### IPAT—A Culture-Free Intelligence Test. Cattell, R. B., Psychological Corporation

This is a test containing figure analogies and figure reasoning items (Cattell, 1940). There are three levels; I, 4–8 years, II, 8–12 years and III, adults. Marquardt (1955) demonstrated that with children from low, middle and high socio-economic groups IPAT Level I was as influenced by socio-economic status as the Stanford Binet but this was not true of Levels II and III. Marquardt ignores the fact in her conclusion that the items on the lower end of the Stanford Binet Scale are not heavily weighted with school learning and achievement and this may have accounted for the similar variability on the IPAT and the Binet. As the items on the Stanford Binet become more difficult, they are more heavily weighted with achievement and one would expect greater discrepancy between this and the IPAT.

Anastasi (1953) tested Puerto Rican children from bi-lingual homes with the IPAT and found that the over-all performance of this group was considerably lower than that reported on the norming sample by Cattell. An analysis of variance of the results showed that there was significant variance attributed to the subjects as well as to the test session. She concluded that there was marked improvement of performance from first to second testing regardless of whether the test was given in English or Spanish. The discrepancy between the bi-lingual performance and the performance of the norming sample was attributed to low socio-economic status, bilingualism, lack of test sophistication and poor emotional adjustment to school.

The IPAT was used by Keehn (1955) with Lebanese children in order to determine how well the results agreed with teachers' judgments of intelligence. The Progressive Matrices, a French Dominoes Test and Number series were also administered. Correlation of test score with estimates of intelligence as seen by teachers ranged from −.20 to .52. A factor analysis showed that all tests had saturation on a single factor presumed to be by the authors. Although the tests were heavily-loaded on a single factor, they were only slightly correlated with either academic marks or teacher judgments. These results remind one of the arguments offered by Lorge for continuing the bias in tests or determining what so-called culture-fair tests are really measuring. It may be that what is involved in the IPAT as well as the other tests which were used has little relationship to performance in Lebanese schools.

*Raven's Progressive Matrices. Raven, J. C. H. K. Lewis & Co., London and Psychological Corporation, New York*

The progressive matrices were developed to be a test of "g." They contain three sets of colored matrices which require increasingly difficult figure reasoning abilities. Factorially they measure complex spatial ability and reasoning by analogy. The test has its rationale in Spearman's cognitive principles and the manual reports a "g" saturation of .82. Martin (1954) administered the Progressive Matrices and the Wechsler Intelligence Test for Children (WISC) to 100 Indiana school children between 9 and 10 years. The IQs ranged from 74 to 141 on the WISC with a mean of 107. The correlations between the WISC IQs and the Progressive Matrices were from .83 for the Performance Scale, .84 for the Verbal Scale and .91 for the Full Scale. These correlations are close to the estimated reliability for the WISC and indicate that the tests may be measuring some common ability. These results do not tell us much about the use of the test with various socio-economic groups or with other cultural groups.

Barratt (1956) administered the Progressive Matrices and the WISC to the same children but he reports correlations from .70 to .75 between the two tests. These correlations are considerably lower than those reported by Martin.

Ninety Navajo children attending the U. S. Indian school in Albuquerque were given the Progressive Matrices and the Goodenough Draw a Man (Norman, 1955). The results of this study showed that performance on the Progressive Matrices was consistently inferior to that on the Draw a Man. Other native populations are reputed to have equally poor scores on the Progressive Matrices. Raven in correspondence with Norman, the author of this study, states that African children in French-African colonies seem to "think" differently from Europeans. When they acquire the European's ways of thinking, they begin to perform the matrices test in a more equivalent fashion.

### A Semantic Test of Intelligence. Rulon, P. J., Harvard University

At the 1952 Invitational Conference on Testing Problems, Philip Rulon (1952) introduced basic test item types for a test of intelligence which reduced common verbal symbols to a minimum and attempted by the test items to imitate semantic relationships of symbols and concepts. The test requires no understanding of any language and is administered in pantomine. Little research is available on the use of this instrument with various socio-economic groups of children of other cultures. It is included in the list of culture-fair tests because it represents another approach to the problem of developing test items free from bias.

### Goodenough Draw a Man. Goodenough, F. (1926)

While the Draw a Man test is not commonly used as a measure of intelligence in school children, some research has been completed to determine whether what is required to complete this test (drawing the human figure) is affected by culture. Britton (1954) studied social class influences on the test and found that while IQ scores for the DAM were considerably lower than those for verbal tests commonly used in schools, the correlation with socio-economic status was .11. The DAM was administered to children in Lebanon and the scores show that the IQs decline with age from 5 to 10 years except in the school where education was the most similar to that of Western children. The results also showed differences between high and low status Armenian children.

*Gestalt Continuation Test. Hector, H. (1960)*

This test is in a developmental phase in South Africa and attempts to provide a task for illiterate testees who have had no previous experience with paper and pencil. It also assumes that the ability to trace sequences of angular patterns and continue them reflects an individual's degree of intelligence in the sense of general adaptability. Correlations for 152 illiterates between the Gestalt Continuation Test and Biesheuvel Adaptability Battery were from .38 to .48. The reliability is estimated at .74 to .76. The task requires the continuation of a geometric pattern of straight lines. It is scored either by counting the number of gestalts completed correctly or by counting the number of lines in the longest correct sequence (Tekane, 1960).

*7 Squares Test. Hector, H. (Bradley, 1960)*

Bradley used the 7 Squares Test devised by Hector to determine whether education of natives affected ability to make meaningful arrangements of 7 black squares. The author found that education had little effect, but suggests the use of this test is still in an experimental stage.

### SUMMARY OF THE ATTEMPTS TO PRODUCE CULTURE-FAIR TESTS

From the list of available culture-fair tests we see that there has been an attempt to translate verbal material into pictures which should have equal difficulty for high and low socio-economic groups and attempts to use figural reasoning and figure analogies to be measures of ability. The use of drawings of the human figure has also been explored as well as some new tests to continue gestalt patterns and to produce meaningful representations from abstract materials. Thus far the research on all of these instruments has shown that the results are affected not only by socio-economic status, but by ethnic and cultural origins. What, if anything, can be said about the possibilities of measurement without cultural bias? It would have to be re-stated that these results support Lorge's contentions mentioned earlier and certainly they support Dyer's comments on measurement of human ability (1960). Dyer contends that since any ability test is made up of a series of pieces of the environment to which the pupil is expected to react in one way or another, it is impossible to sample a common denominator of all cultures. Dyer suggests that while it theoretically is possible to find test items which might be pretty comparable to all the subcultures of a cultural group, they might

when completed predict very little in the way of meaningful validity criteria. He suggests that those psychologists who are interested
in improving the lot of the culturally underprivileged should direct
their attentions not to changing the tests, but to improving the
quality of educational opportunity. The work of the New York
City Schools in replacing cultural experiences where they were
missing for Puerto Rican and Negro pupils and finding that the test
scores improved as the students began to achieve more in school is a
good example of what is implied in Dyer's point of view.

## TESTING ACTIVITIES IN VARIOUS PARTS OF THE ENGLISH-SPEAKING WORLD WHICH HAVE IMPLICATIONS FOR THE CULTURE-FAIR TESTING MOVEMENT

### South Africa

Two tests, the Gestalt Continuation Test and the 7 Squares Test
have already been mentioned as examples of the type of material
which is being produced in South Africa for testing illiterates. Dr.
Simon Biesheuvel who is director of personnel research of the South
African Council for Scientific and Industrial research has been
working in this special testing field for a number of years. His work
has been directed toward evaluating the hundreds of thousands of
black workers who show up regularly for work in the mines. His
responsibility is not only to make some prediction about how well
they will perform on the job, but also to select those men who show
some aptitude for supervisory activities.

The workers are assigned to training courses and the personnel
research group administers tests designed to classify the workers
into non-mechanical duties, mechanical duties and supervisory duties. These tests are administered by means of silent pictures. Dr.
Biesheuvel found that the men were confused by still-life pictures,
but that silent motion pictures were most useful in communicating
the task demanded by the test. As he takes the test, the worker gets
the idea of starting and stopping with instructions, the idea of speed
and accuracy, and some understanding of the task involved. By
doing so, he demonstrates his degree of adaptability by transferring
his experience in the testing situation to other tasks. The men who
perform best on the adaptability tests are given leadership tests
which involve putting small groups of men through physical tasks in
which they have to work as a team and in which it is possible for a

man to show whether he has the capacity to direct the work of others.

Biesheuvel has not tried to compare the performance of these workers with performance of workers from other cultures. He feels strongly that there are no culture-free tests and that even concepts like straight lines have cultural implications and values. Their work has been to construct tests which solve the task at hand—to locate the best workers for the mines and find those with supervisory ability. They have been quite successful, but they do not generalize the usefulness of their instruments beyond these results.

## United States

Aside from the limitations or even deterioration of measured ability in our culture, certain special ethnic groups in the United States demonstrate dramatically special testing problems. A year ago last summer I had an opportunity to discuss some problems in Indian education with Dr. A. A. Wellck, Director of the University of New Mexico Counseling Center, and Mr. Herbert Blatchford, Consultant to the New Mexican Department of Education, who is stationed in Gallup, New Mexico, the Indian Capitol of the U. S. Mr. Blatchford is a Navajo and it is partly for this reason that he is assigned to working with Navajo children. The Navajos present special problems to education in New Mexico. The Navajos have stubbornly maintained their special culture for centuries. The Pueblo Indians, Hopis and Zunis have accommodated to the teaching of the mission fathers, and participate more fully in what amounts to Spanish-American general culture. On the other hand, the Navajos who refer to themselves as the "Denay," which means the chosen people, have resisted erosion of their old ways.

One of their particular problems in school is their slow work pace. Navajo children who seem perfectly happy and well adjusted in school tend to meet any scholastic assignment as if there were all the time in the world. If they are given any speeded test, even with exhortations to work as fast as they can, they proceed dutifully, but at a more leisurely pace. For example, their scores on a California Test of Mental Ability (CTMM) or Otis (Higher Form) are always markedly depressed because they do not finish. They do better on a test such as the School and College Ability Test (SCAT) which is relatively unspeeded, but it is apparent that no existing test is satisfactory. Even the WISC presents a picture which seems to be markedly out of proportion to what observers feel is their true potential. The Navajo children earn few time bonus points on WISC performance scores even though they may completely understand what they are supposed to do and proceed skillfully. Their familiarity with objects presented is usually as great as that of the Pueblos or Hopis, but their work pace results in lower scores. In this case, deliberateness and inability to accept speed make the existent measurement devices more unsuitable for them than for other Southwest Indians.

Mr. Blatchford uses the School and College Ability Tests, and feels that they predict pretty well the degree to which the Navajos will succeed in school. These tests are not only heavily culture bound, but they involve speed and previous achievement. However, as Mr. Blatchford puts it, "We are interested in what makes these Indians unique, but when it comes to determining how they will do in school, we need measures of scholastic potential, not culture-fair tests."

Dr. A. A. Wellck, Director of Counseling and Testing, from the University of New Mexico is responsible for the state testing program and for the compilation of measurement data throughout New Mexico. He concurs with Mr. Blatchford in his views on the limitations of so-called culture-fair tests and also states that no culture-fair tests are used in the state testing program in New Mexico even though there is a very high percentage of Spanish-American and Indian children attending schools in the state. The experience of specialists in New Mexico is that the culture-fair tests have little value and that scholastic predictors are the most usable sources of information for educational application.

Dr. H. T. Manuel of the University of Texas is presently revising and standardizing the successors to the Cooperative Inter-American Tests published by Educational Testing Service in 1950. This work is financed largely by the U. S. Office of Education. The tests in preparation are scholastic ability tests and reading tests for use from the primary grades to the first year of college. While these tests are not designed to be culture-fair in the sense that is usually meant by the term, they offer another approach to the problem of measuring people from different ethnic and cultural backgrounds. This approach is to translate material into the native tongue and then pretest, conduct item studies, formulate final editions and standardize the tests.

Dr. Pablo Roca who was formerly Technical Director of the Department of Education in Haito Rey, Puerto Rico, presently with the U. S. Office of Education, has just published under the auspices of the Psychological Corporation, a Spanish edition of the Wechsler Intelligence Test for Children. This approach is essentially the same as that undertaken by Manuel, and represents a translation of existing English language test material and the subsequent standardization of the items on a different cultural population.

Another attempt at evaluating learning ability of children from different cultural groups which is at the same time a departure from the approaches described thus far is the unpublished work of Arthur R. Jensen at the University of California in Berkeley. He located four groups of children—high and low IQ Mexican-Americans, and high and low IQ Anglo-Americans by means of the California Test of Mental Maturity. The children comprised an unselected population from fourth and fifth grades in eastern Contra Costa County in California. Learning tasks were administered to the four groups of children. The tasks were composed of recall of familiar objects, serial learning, and paired associates learning. The child responded in either English or Spanish. He found a significant nationality x IQ interaction with the low IQ Mexican-American children performing better than the low IQ Anglo-Americans, while there was little difference at the high IQ levels. The same tasks were administered two weeks later and the results showed that the reliabilities of the tests were substantial. He concludes that the development of a complete battery of direct learning tests should have promise for improving the assessment of learning ability and the diagnosis of educational disabilities, especially in ethnic and cultural groups.

Jensen's procedure is comparable to an approach suggested by Sorenson (1963) where the time spent in learning and the number of errors recorded in a programmed learning task could replace traditional IQ tests as measures of intelligence.

## Canada

In the Province of British Columbia,[1] regular testing in the schools includes children who are Chinese, Japanese, Indian and Eskimo as

[1] The author is indebted to Dr. Clifford Conway, Director, Division of Tests Standards and Research, Province of British Columbia, for this information.

well as "white." The performance of these ethnic groups of children must be interpreted in terms of selective immigration and does not offer much in the way of information about the fairness of existing tests for these groups. Recently in this province the recording of racial origin of children has been frowned upon as an aspect of segregation. As a result there is no indication on school records as to the cultural or ethnic background of the child. This makes it relatively impossible to gather any data about how well particular children perform in intelligence tests or school tasks. Children from different cultural groups are incorporated into regular classes and teachers are instructed not to segregate the pupils into special classes or to treat them differently in any way. Indian and Eskimo children attend public schools, private and residential schools. The efforts of those charged with the responsibility of Indian Education (Renaud, 1958) are directed toward acculturation of these youngsters. The success of the acculturation program can be measured by the degree to which the gap between the "whites" and the ethnic groups closes as they proceed through the school grades. Snider (1961) studied acculturated Indian high school students in northern Idaho. His findings demonstrate that the performance of the acculturated group was comparable to the performance of other children with whom they went to school, and in some learning areas there were no significant differences between the two groups.

These data offer little in the way of enlightenment about the use of culture-fair measurements to evaluate Indian and Eskimo learning potential in Canada. While non-verbal tests are frequently used, they are selected because they minimize reading handicap rather than because they offer common cultural denominators which would make them fair measures for these pupils.

The efforts of educators in Canada have been to look at the Indian and Eskimo as he compares to others in his own tribe or ethnic group as well as to compare him with children not of his ethnic group but of the same age. Here again the need is enunciated for as wide a variety of measures resulting in as broad a description of the pupil as possible. No one test is believed to do the job of measuring native potential and these educators are aware of the limitations of the tests which they use. They deal with cultural handicaps not by trying to perpetuate their effect on education, but to reduce them so pupils thus handicapped can profit more from instruction.

## Australia

Even though there are a great variety of racial, ethnic and cultural groups in Australia, little work has been done at a national level with tests designed to be culture-free. Mr. S. S. Dunn, who is the Assistant Director of the Australian Council for Educational research and in charge of the Test Division, writes that there has been little work on the topic. A few small studies have been conducted in which such tests as the Progressive Matrices have been used with New Australians and Australian aborigines, but the results are inconclusive. Mr. Dunn writes that "to prepare a culture-free test, one must assume that you can find a content that is equally familiar in all cultures, an impossibility, or that one can divorce the quality of thought processes in problem solving from familiarity with content." He goes on to say that "In my opinion quality of thinking cannot be divorced from familiarity with the content area in which the thinking takes place. Thus, a non-verbal test which uses such non-verbal symbols as triangles, squares, etc., is not culturally free when used to test, say, two races, one of which is far more familiar with the symbols than the other." Empirically, researchers have found that Asian students do less well on Progressive Matrices than one would expect from their scholastic results. Even though the test is completely abstract in content, it is not a "fair" test for the Asian students.

## Overview of Work in Progress

These comments certainly confirm the fact that measurement specialists in different parts of the world are in essential agreement about the value and use of culture-fair tests. From these major sources of professional opinion and action in measurement, one must conclude that culture-fair tests as they are now described may have value in assessing certain aspects of the cognitive abilities of those tested, but they lose meaning when scores from one cultural group are compared with scores from another. The approach of those responsible for evaluating abilities of people from a complex culture is to design tests with specific predictive potential in mind and then to test their validity against the criterion. This is the approach in South Africa. Translation of English language tests into other languages and then standardizing them is another approach. Omitting the goal of fairness in testing and evaluating students on how well they will succeed in specific scholastic tasks is still another approach. Finally it has also been noted that measuring the ability to learn new tasks has potential in evaluating the degree to which students may succeed in subsequent learning situations.

## SUMMARY AND CONCLUSION

There is a paradox in the theory and practice of educators who would, on the one hand speak up for the need to understand individual differences, and on the other hand continue to support educational programs which sublimate such differences to single standard evaluations of accomplishment. John H. Niemeyer, writing in the September 12, 1959, issue of *The Saturday Review*, estimates that perhaps one-half of the pupil population of the nation is culturally deprived. "It is these young people," states Mr. Niemeyer, "whom our schools, staffed generally with teachers whose eyes are focused on an Anglo-Saxon middle class way of life and who utilize educational procedures geared to that way of life, are leaving almost entirely untapped." In the current emphasis in education on academic excellence, one must remember that large numbers of youth come from backgrounds where cultural deprivations exist; cultural deprivations which have a decided negative effect upon effective intellectual learning. The New York City program, Higher Horizons, has shown that by removing some of the cultural deficiencies, children who otherwise would have dropped out of high school or not succeeded beyond graduation have a much greater chance of developing into educated citizens. Such new programs in education show that there is promise in programs of acculturation with the resultant improvement in the youngster's ability to profit from education. Such programs do not provide, however, much information as to how to locate those students who have ability to profit from such educational and cultural opportunity when their test scores are far below average because of cultural interaction with the test material.

The tests now used to measure scholastic potential can predict traditional school success quite adequately. Many of them have been continually improved over the years so correlations between scholastic ability and achievement are quite high. What has happened has been that as education has become more and more standardized, ability tests have become more and more refined to predict this common standard. There is a single criterion for educational success in most courses taught in school. To the extent that these criteria have factors in common with ability tests, the prediction is good and the validity of the ability test is established.

Such comments lead next to the question of what happens when the common standard for achievement is changed. The National Science Foundation, interested in improving instruction in the physical and biological sciences, contracted with Educational Testing Service to develop achievement tests to measure performance in the new science curricula. One interesting finding (Ferris, 1961) was that scores on the School and College Ability Tests (SCAT) do not predict scores on the new physical science achievement tests as well as they predict scores on other achievement tests. This finding is especially interesting since the achievement tests were designed to measure anticipation and thinking in science problems. Ferris reports that many students below the 75 percentile on SCAT were able to achieve as well as, or better than, students above this cut-off point. Ferris believes that a type of ability is measured by the achievement tests which is not being measured by the traditional scholastic aptitude tests. *Further efforts of this type which change educational curricula and subsequently or concomitantly investigate the degree to which these new learnings can be predicted by existing or newly-developed ability tests are extremely important.* Such efforts involve proposed changes in curricula which can be described and implemented into the school setting. *They provide some encouragement for a wider variety of achievement and success for some students who might get passed over by the more traditional educational programs.* [This is a very important point. The author is suggesting in this paragraph how educators can put ability tests to a rather unorthodox use. Not for assessing developed abilities in pupils but rather for verifying the possibility that a curricular innovation can be introduced and its effects reliably measured. Note in particular the portions we have italicized. Eds.]

The problem in developing culture-fair tests lies, just as in test development problems of any type, in deciding on what types of items and cognitive abilities such tests should include. After the test development process has been concluded the tests must be validated against acceptable criteria. If there are educational criteria which can be established, which are different from the traditional ones, as in the case of the Physical Science Study Committee work by Ferris, it may be possible to validate revised ability tests against new educational criteria. If such criteria do not exist, the problem of obtaining meaningful validity information still remains. There is nothing wrong with developing ability tests which are reliable and which can be shown to measure important individual differences. Such a task is descriptive of the work of Raven, Cattell, Davis and Eells reported previously. These tests seem to have fair reliability and validity for measuring individual differences of the particular behavioral tasks involved, but research has shown that the predictive validity in estimating school achievement is fairly weak. Some new way of classifying or evaluating the usability of such tests as the Progressive Matrices or the IPAT and the others which have been mentioned is necessary, and new criteria against which to validate the tests may also be necessary.

Haggard (1952) summarizes the test development problems for culture-fair tests and lists four areas which need research consideration: (1) existing tests have measured only a very narrow range of mental abilities, namely those related to verbal or academic success, and have ignored many other abilities and problem-solving skills, which are perhaps more important for adjustment and success— even in a middle class society; (2) existing tests have failed to provide measures of the wide variety of qualitative differences in the modes or processes of solving mental problems; (3) even culture-fair tests have ignored the differences in cultural training and socialization on the repertoire of experience of not only different cultural groups, but on the sub-groups of culture as well; (4) mental functioning has been considered in isolation and must be related to culturally determined personality and values of the individual.

A review of the item types of culture-fair tests would certainly support Haggard's contention that only a narrow range of abilities has been provided for. Test developers have substituted abstract figural reasoning for abstract verbal reasoning items. Often spatial abilities predominate and determine the degree to which a student is able to perform well on these tests. In other cases, items which favor a lower cultural group have been included in order to make the test less biased. Items measuring social intelligence—an often factored mental ability (Thorndike, 1926)—are added to the Davis Eells Tests in order to make them more fair for lower socio-economic groups. Anastasi (1961), however, suggests that all cultural groups on which test information is obtained should be tested by as wide a variety of tests as possible. It is an obvious fact that groups do not occupy the same relative position when compared in different intellectual traits. She goes on to suggest that some meaningful classification of tests by the factors which the tests are measuring would be most useful.

If one refers to Guilford's Structure of Intellect (1956; 1958), the variety of test item types used on the many culture-fair tests take on new meaning. First of all it becomes possible to suggest a position for each of the tests in terms of Guilford's three classifications of intellectual activities—operations, products, and contents. Thus the more traditional ability tests—those not designed to be culture-fair—can be (if the factor structure of the test is known) arranged in this matrix according to the abilities which are being measured. The culture-fair tests, if their factor structure is known, could also be arranged in this matrix. What would result would be some overlapping of intellectual factors measured by some of the culture-biased and culture-fair tests. In most cases there would be little overlap since it is hypothesized that culture-fair tests as they are now designed are measuring different intellectual abilities from the abilities measured by conventional ability tests.

If the existing culture-fair tests could be administered in batteries with tests of reference factors (French, 1951), information could be given about the types of intellectual abilities that they are measuring. This would add greatly to our knowledge of the uniqueness or commonness of the culture-fair materials.

An extension of this approach would also be useful and contribute to our knowledge of cultural differences as they vary with performance on intellectual tasks. Such a study would be patterned after the work of Swineford (1948) who studied general, verbal and spatial factors as they differ in performance of boys and girls, change with increase in mental maturity, vary with bright and dull pupils, and predict success in school performance.

Tests with items having symbols and semantics which are common to a variety of cultures, measuring a number of the established factors, could be placed with tests of reference factors in a battery. This battery could be then administered across sub-cultural groups within a given culture, and across distinct cultural or ethnic groups. The results would add greatly to our enlightenment of how these groups differ. Prediction of success in a variety of educational tasks and life situations for that particular cultural or ethnic group from a combination of tests would then increase our knowledge of how valid such batteries are as predictors of useful, practical criteria for that culture.

**REFERENCES**

ANASTASI, ANNE, and CRUZ, D., "Language development and non-verbal IQ of Puerto Rican children in New York City," *J. abnorm. soc. Psychol.*, 1953, **54**, 357–366.

ANASTASI, ANNE, and CORDOVA, F. A., "Some effects of bilingualism upon the intelligence test performance of Puerto Rican children in New York City," *J. educ. Psychol.*, 1953, **44**, 1–19.

ANASTASI, ANNE, *Differential psychology*. New York: Macmillan, 1958.

ANASTASI, ANNE, "Psychological tests: uses and abuses," *Teachers Coll. Rec.*, 1961, **62**, 389–393.

BARRATT, E. S., "The relationship of the Progressive Matrices and the Columbia Mental Maturity Scale to the WISC," *J. consult. Psychol.*, 1956, **20**, 294–296.

BRADLEY, D. J., "The ability of black groups to produce recognizable patterns on the 7-Squares Test," *J. nat. Inst. Personnel Res.*, 1960, **8**, 142–144.

BRITTON, J. H., "Influence of social class upon performance on the 'Draw a Man' Test," *J. educ. Psychol.*, 1954, **45**, 44–51.

BURKE, H. R., "Raven's Progressive Matrices—A review and critical examination, *J. genet. Psychol.*, 1958, **93**, 199–228.

CATTELL, R. B., "A culture-free intelligence test," *J. educ. Psychol.*, 1940, **31**, 161–179.

COLEMAN, W., and WARD, ANNIE W., "A comparison of the Davis Eells and Kuhlman Finch scores of children from high and low s-e status," *J. educ. Psychol.*, 1955, **46**, 465–469.

COOPER, J. G., "Predicting school achievement for bi-lingual pupils," *J. educ. Psychol.*, 1958, **49**, 34–36.

DAVIS, A., *Social class influences upon learning* (The Inglis Lecture, 1948). Cambridge, Mass.: Harvard Univer. Press, 1948.

DAVIS, A., and EELLS, K., *Manual for the Davis Eells test of general intelligence.* Yonkers on Hudson, New York: World Book Co., 1953.

DAVIS, A., "Socio economic influences upon children's learning," *Proceedings of midcentury White House conference on children and youth.* Report of conference sessions, Washington, D. C., December 3–7, 1950. Raleigh, North Carolina: Health Publications Institute, Inc. 1951.

DENNIS, W., "Performance of Near Eastern children on the Draw a Man Test," *Child Develpm.*, 1957, **28**, 427–30.

Dyer, H., "A psychometrician views human ability," *Teachers Coll. Rec.*, 1960, **61**, 394–403.

Eells, K., *Intelligence and cultural differences*. Chicago: Univer. of Chicago Press, 1951.

Ferris, F. L., "Some new science curricula and their measurement," *Proceedings of the western regional conference on testing problems*. Los Angeles: Educational Testing Service, 1961.

French, J. W., "The description of aptitude and achievement tests in terms of rotated factors," *Psychometr. Monogr.*, 1951, 5.

Geist, H., "Evaluation of culture-free intelligence," *Calif. J. educ. Res.*, 1954, **5**, 209–214.

Goodenough, Florence, *The measurement of intelligence by drawings*. Yonkers, New York: World Book Co., 1926.

Guilford, J. P., "The structure of intellect," *Psychol. Bull.*, 1956, **53**, 267–293.

Guilford, J. P., "New frontiers of testing in the discovery and development of human talent," *Proceedings of the seventh annual western regional conference on testing problems*. Los Angeles: Educational Testing Service, 1958.

Haggard, E. A., "Techniques for the development of unbiased tests," *Proceedings invitational conference on testing problems*. Princeton, New Jersey: Educational Testing Service, 1952.

Hector, H., "Results from a simple Gestalt Continuation Test applied to illiterate black mineworkers," *J. nat. Inst. Personnel Res.*, 1960, **8**, 145–147.

Indian and Eskimo Welfare Commission, *Residential education for Indian acculturation*. Ottowa, Ontario: Oblate Fathers in Canada, 1958.

Justman, J., and Aronow, Miriam, The Davis Eells Games as a measure of the intelligence of poor readers," *J. educ. Psychol.*, 1955, **46**, 418–22.

Keehn, J. D., and Prothro, E., "Non-verbal tests as predictors of academic success in Lebanon," *Educ. psychol. Measmt.*, 1955, **15**, 495–498.

Knief, Lotus, and Stroud, J. B., "Intercorrelations among various intelligence, achievement, and social class scores," *J. educ. Psychol.*, 1959, **50**, 117–120.

Lorge, I., "Difference of bias in tests of intelligence," *Proceedings invitational conference on testing problems*. Princeton, New Jersey: Educational Testing Service, 1952.

LUCAS, C. M., *Survey of the literature relating to the effects of cultural background on aptitude test scores*. Research Bulletin. Princeton, New Jersey: Educational Testing Service, 1953.

McNEMAR, Q., *The revisions of the Stanford Binet scale*. Boston: Houghton-Mifflin, 1942.

MARQUARDT, DOROTHY I., and BAILEY, LOIS L., "An evaluation of the culture-free test of intelligence," *J. genet. Psychol.*, 1955, 87, 353–358.

MARTIN, A. W., and WEICHERS, J. E., "Raven's Colored Progressive Matrices and the Wechsler Intelligence Scale for Children," *J. consult. Psychol.*, 1954, 18, 143–4.

NORMAN, R. D., and MIDKIFF, KATHERINE L., "Navajo children on Raven Progressive Matrices and Draw a Man Test," *Southwest J. Anthrop.*, 1955, 10, 129–136.

RAVEN, J. C., *Guide to using Progressive Matrices*. London: H. K. Lewis, 1951.

RENAUD, A., "Indian education today," *Anthropologica*, 1958, 6, 15–22.

RICHIE, ALICE, "A comparison of the Kuhlman Anderson with the Davis Eells Intelligence Tests in a fifth grade," *Calif. J. educ. Res.*, 1954, 5, 186.

ROCA, P., *Escala De Intelligencia Wechsler Para Ninos*. New York: Psychological Corp., 1961.

ROSENBLUM, S., KELLER, J. E., and PAPNIA, N., "Davis-Eells Test performance of lower class retarded children," *J. consult. Psychol.*, 1955, 19, 51–4.

RULON, P. J., "A semantic test of intelligence," *Proceedings invitational conference on testing problems*. Princeton, New Jersey: Educational Testing Service, 1952.

SAWREY, J. M., "The predictive effectiveness of two non-verbal tests of intelligence in first grade," *Calif. J. educ. Res.*, 1955, 5, 133.

SMITH, T. W., *Auding and reading skills as sources of cultural bias in the Davis Eells Games and California Test of Mental Maturity*. Unpublished doctoral dissertation, Univer. of Southern California, 1956.

SNIDER, J. G., "Achievement test performance of acculturated Indian children," *Alberta J. educ. Res.*, 1961, 7, 39–41.

SORENSON, A. G., "The use of teaching machines in developing an alternative to the concept of intelligence," *Educ. psychol. Measmt.*, 1963, 23, 323–30.

SWINEFORD, FRANCES, "A study in factor analysis: The nature of the general, verbal and spatial bifactors," *Supplementary Educational Monographs*, Univ. of Chicago Press, 1948, 67.

TEKANE, I., "A new and objective scoring method for the Gestalt Continuation Test," *J. nat. Inst. Personnel Res.*, 1960, 8, 148–150.

THORNDIKE, E. L., *The measurement of intelligence.* New York: Teachers Coll., Columbia Univer., 1926.

WOODS, W. A., and TOAL, R., "Subtest disparity of Negro and white groups matched for IQ's on the Revised Beta Test," *J. consult. Psychol.*, 1957, **21**, 136–8.

---

## 3.3   The Stability of Achievement Test Results from Grade to Grade

*Roger T. Lennon*

This article deals with the reliability of achievement test results projected from one grade to another. Its significance seems to lie in the fact that it is an empirical attempt to objectively predict achievement at one grade based upon achievement test results at a lower grade level. The results indicate that as one attempts to predict criterion behavior which is relatively far removed from the predictor test, the errors of predictability tend to increase. Can you explain this result in terms of principles of measurement? What do the results of this study suggest to you in terms of using achievement test results at various grade levels to predict achievement in later years?

This paper is concerned with a study of three related problems in the interpretation of achievement test results for a community: (1) How stable or consistent are the results of achievement tests from grade to grade in a community? (2) To what extent is terminal achievement consistent with achievement at various earlier grades?

Reprinted with permission of the author and *Educational and Psychological Measurement*, **11**, 1951, 121–127.

(3) To what extent are results at any given grade level representative of performance as a whole?

The data reported were obtained in connection with the standardization of the present (1946) edition of the *Metropolitan Achievement Tests*. They are based on the results for 81 of 250 communities which participated in the standardization program; these 81 communities in which all public-school pupils in grades 2 through 8 were tested, exclusive of a few very small communities whose results are based on such few cases as to be of limited dependability. The communities are, for the most part, small ones; about two-thirds are of less than 10,000 population. They are drawn from 36 states.

All tests were administered within two months of the opening of schools in the fall of 1946, the appropriate battery of the Metropolitan series being used at each grade. The figures reported are based on an analysis of a random sample of approximately 25 per cent of the total number of cases in each community. For this random sample the mean standard score in each subtest of the *Metropolitan Achievement Tests* for each grade in each community was computed; these standard scores constitute, for each subtest, a continuous scale of approximately equal units, so that direct comparison of scores is possible regardless of the battery used. It is the relationships among these community means for various grades and subjects with which this paper is concerned.

## STABILITY OF ACHIEVEMENT FROM GRADE TO GRADE

The first problem with which this paper deals is that of the consistency of results for successive grades—knowing the achievement level in a given grade, how well can the achievement of pupils in, let us say, the next higher or next lower grade be estimated?

Table 1 summarizes the correlations between community mean scores on the various subtests in adjacent grades. Means and standard deviations of the various distributions are given in Table 2. These correlations are measures of the extent to which communities tend to maintain the same relative standing as judged by test results for successive grades. In this respect they shed some light on the matter of how dependable a picture of school achievement is yielded by test results for single grades or for selected grades in the system.

The correlations in Table 1 range from a value of .331, between the Arithmetic Problems scores in the second and third grades, to

.694 between the Reading scores in the third and fourth grades. The majority of the correlations are between .50 and .65; the median value is .57.

Although the correlations are all positive and, in general, of sizable magnitude, it can readily be seen that there would be a large error involved in attempting to estimate relative achievement status in any grade from the status even in an adjacent grade; and, as will be shown below, an even larger error involved in estimating it from the performance in grades further removed. This is a fact which has not always been appreciated by test users who follow the practice of "spot-testing" in certain grades, and who attempt to make inferences with respect to a general level of achievement on the basis of results in one or two grades.

TABLE 1    CORRELATIONS BETWEEN MEAN STANDARD SCORES FOR ADJACENT GRADES ON SUBTESTS OF METROPOLITAN ACHIEVEMENT TESTS, FOR A GROUP OF 81 COMMUNITIES

| Subtest | Grades | | | | | |
|---|---|---|---|---|---|---|
| | 2–3 | 3–4 | 4–5 | 5–6 | 6–7 | 7–8 |
| Reading | .646 | .694 | .577 | .640 | .582 | .519 |
| Vocabulary | .569 | .637 | .647 | .668 | .571 | .514 |
| Arith. Fund. | .533 | .669 | .691 | .598 | .605 | .548 |
| Arith. Prob. | .331 | .551 | .470 | .546 | .456 | .560 |
| English | | | .557 | .579 | .570 | .441 |
| Spelling | | .417 | .499 | .503 | .506 | .450 |
| Literature | | | | | .593 | .469 |
| History | | | | | .535 | .400 |
| Geography | | | | | .544 | .604 |
| Science | | | | | .683 | .575 |

It is noteworthy that the correlations between the means for adjacent grades are no higher at the upper-grade levels than at the lower. One might have assumed that more stable relative rankings would have been achieved at later grade levels, but this does not prove to be the case. Although the differences among subjects are not great with respect to stability from grade to grade, the Reading, Vocabulary, Arithmetic Fundamentals and Science tests appear to yield slightly more consistent rankings in successive grades than do the other tests.

TABLE 2   MEANS AND STANDARD DEVIATIONS OF SUBTEST STANDARD SCORES, METROPOLITAN ACHIEVEMENT TESTS, BY GRADE, FOR A GROUP OF 81 COMMUNITIES

| Subtest | Grade | | | | | | | | | | | | |
|---|---|---|---|---|---|---|---|---|---|---|---|---|---|
| | 2 | | 3 | | 4 | | 5 | | 6 | | 7 | | 8 | |
| | M | SD | M | SD | M | SD | M | SD | M | SD | M | SD | M | SD |
| Reading | 114.1 | 6.0 | 141.6 | 6.1 | 165.1 | 7.3 | 180.5 | 8.0 | 195.5 | 7.2 | 204.0 | 7.5 | 215.0 | 7.7 |
| Vocabulary | 121.1 | 6.6 | 143.0 | 6.5 | 165.8 | 7.0 | 178.5 | 7.3 | 197.1 | 8.1 | 205.0 | 7.6 | 216.3 | 7.4 |
| Arith. Fund. | 137.4 | 3.3 | 137.8 | 2.4 | 154.6 | 5.1 | 171.2 | 6.0 | 196.7 | 10.3 | 221.1 | 9.7 | 244.6 | 12.6 |
| Arith. Prob. | 137.4 | 3.3 | 149.6 | 2.5 | 164.9 | 4.0 | 178.2 | 5.1 | 198.9 | 6.9 | 211.5 | 7.0 | 224.0 | 10.0 |
| English | | | | | 164.6 | 7.0 | 178.3 | 6.8 | 197.5 | 8.5 | 206.6 | 7.8 | 218.2 | 7.0 |
| Spelling | | | 142.3 | 6.7 | 163.9 | 7.7 | 179.4 | 6.1 | 197.3 | 6.0 | 209.9 | 7.4 | 228.7 | 8.9 |
| Literature | | | | | | | | | 197.1 | 7.6 | 206.4 | 8.9 | 217.1 | 8.8 |
| History | | | | | | | | | 199.2 | 7.3 | 207.6 | 7.5 | 217.2 | 8.7 |
| Geography | | | | | | | | | 199.0 | 8.7 | 209.4 | 8.6 | 216.8 | 9.7 |
| Science | | | | | | | | | 200.8 | 8.8 | 209.3 | 8.5 | 225.6 | 11.2 |

Recognizing that the relative status of communities does not remain altogether the same from grade to grade, it is still reasonable to inquire how great or how important *are* the differences in relative standing which may be expected from one grade to the next? If the fourth grade in a system, for example, is three months below the norm in reading, how likely is it that the fifth grade will be at or above the norm? It is clear that to answer such questions we must have information on the variability of increments in mean scores between successive grades.

TABLE 3        STANDARD DEVIATIONS OF DIFFERENCES BE-
TWEEN MEAN SCORES IN SUCCESSIVE GRADES, BY SUBTEST

|              | Grades |       |       |       |       |        |
|--------------|--------|-------|-------|-------|-------|--------|
| Subtest      | 2–3    | 3–4   | 4–5   | 5–6   | 6–7   | 7–8    |
| Reading      | 5.1 2* | 5.4 4 | 7.1 4 | 6.5 5 | 6.7 6 | 7.4 9  |
| Vocabulary   | 6.1 3  | 5.8 3 | 6.0 4 | 8.3 5 | 7.4 9 | 9.4 10 |
| Arith. Fund. | 2.9 3  | 3.9 2 | 4.4 2 | 8.2 4 | 8.9 3 | 10.9 5 |
| Arith. Prob. | 3.5 3  | 3.3 2 | 4.8 2 | 5.9 3 | 7.3 6 | 8.4 7  |
| English      |        |       | 6.5 4 | 7.1 6 | 7.6 6 | 7.9 7  |
| Spelling     |        | 7.8 5 | 7.1 4 | 6.0 4 | 6.4 4 | 8.6 6  |
| Literature   |        |       |       |       | 7.6 9 | 9.2 10 |
| History      |        |       |       |       | 7.2 9 | 8.9 11 |
| Geography    |        |       |       |       | 8.3 9 | 8.3 12 |
| Science      |        |       |       |       | 6.9 5 | 9.4 7  |

* The second entry in each column expresses the difference in terms of months of grade equivalent.

In a group of typical communities, such as these are as far as can be told, the average increment from grade to grade, in terms of grade equivalent is, of course, one year. Now we may ask, what is the variability of these increments? By what amount do the increments for communities tend to depart from the expected year? Table 3 presents the standard deviations of the differences, by subject, between the means for adjacent grades, both in terms of standard scores and in months of grade equivalent. It will be observed that at the lower grades, communities tend to be quite similar with respect to the amount of increment between successive grades, in terms of grade equivalent. In the upper grades, on the other hand, the variation among communities in the amount of increment from grade to grade is much larger. This is, of course, partly a function of the fact that the variability both of individual pupils' scores and of community means tends to increase as one goes up through the grades.

On the basis of the data in Table 3, we may determine the probability of an increment of any given magnitude between mean scores for successive grades. The data thus provide an additional basis for the interpretation, by a community or school system, of the average gain its pupils make in a subject from grade to grade. The data indicate, for example, that it is far more serious, in the sense of far more uncommon, for a system to show a gain of only six months of grade equivalent in spelling between the third and fourth grades, than to show a similar gain of six months in literature between the sixth and seventh grades.

## PREDICTION OF TERMINAL ACHIEVEMENT

There is a certain logic in establishing as one criterion for evaluating the achievement of schools, their relative standing based on tests given as their pupils near the close of their school career. This study permits us to determine what the relationship is between achievement in certain selected earlier grades and "terminal" achievement, defined for present purposes as achievement at the eighth-grade level.

Table 4 presents the correlations between mean scores by sub-tests at selected earlier grade levels, on the one hand, and eighth-grade status, on the other. The values in the last column repeat those in the last column of Table 1. The correlations range from .11 for Arithmetic Problems, between second-grade level and terminal status, to .625 for Science results between the sixth-grade level and terminal achievement. In general, for the skill subjects—Arithmetic, English, and Spelling—there is but slight relationship between results at earlier grades and eighth-grade achievement, most of the $r$'s being under .35. The agreement between Reading Vocabulary measures at earlier grades and at the eighth-grade level is somewhat higher but still far from sufficient to permit very accurate estimation of the eighth-grade status of a school or community from its performance in the lower grades.

Table 4 reveals that for the skills tests, other than reading, the results in the later grades seem to agree a little more closely with final achievement than second- or third-grade results.

TABLE 4    CORRELATIONS BETWEEN MEAN SCORES AT SELECTED GRADE LEVELS AND "TERMINAL" ACHIEVEMENT (8TH GRADE MEAN SCORE) BY SUBTEST

| Subtest | Grade 2 | Grade 3 | Grade 5 | Grade 6 | Grade 7 |
|---|---|---|---|---|---|
| | | | Grade 8 and | | |
| Reading | .507 | .464 | .540 | | .519 |
| Vocabulary | .430 | .334 | .458 | | .514 |
| Arith. Fund. | .131 | .245 | .398 | | .548 |
| Arith. Prob. | .113 | .178 | .314 | | .560 |
| English | | | .423 | | .441 |
| Spelling | | .268 | .332 | | .450 |
| Literature | | | | .457 | .469 |
| History | | | | .485 | .400 |
| Geography | | | | .573 | .604 |
| Science | | | | .625 | .575 |

It must be recognized, of course, in interpreting these correlations that we are dealing with the relationship between performance in a lower grade and performance of a different group in the same system at the eighth grade, and that these relationships cannot be assumed to be identical with those which would obtain between the performance of a group now in an early grade in a community and the performance of that same group when it reaches the end of its elementary schooling. These latter relationships are, strictly speaking, the ones with which it would be more accurate to deal when we speak of the prediction of terminal achievement from earlier status, but it is the author's belief that the picture thus revealed would be very similar to the one presented by these data.

## REPRESENTATIVENESS OF RESULTS IN ANY GRADE

How representative of a community's general, or average, achievement in a subject are the results in that subject for any given grade? The data in Table 5 bear on this question. In this table are shown the correlations between the mean scores by subject in selected grades

TABLE 5   CORRELATIONS BETWEEN MEAN SCORES AT
SELECTED GRADE LEVELS AND "AVERAGE" ACHIEVEMENT
BY SUBTEST

| Subtest | Average and | | | |
|---|---|---|---|---|
| | Grade 2 | Grade 5 | Grade 6 | Grade 8 |
| Reading | .744 | .846 | | .720 |
| Vocabulary | .694 | .791 | | .703 |
| Arith. Fund. | .451 | .752 | | .766 |
| Arith. Prob. | .435 | .673 | | .731 |
| English | | .794 | | .685 |
| Spelling | .623 | .723 | | .698 |
| Literature | | | .812 | .817 |
| History | | | .807 | .797 |
| Geography | | | .810 | .860 |
| Science | | | .853 | .879 |

and a measure of "average" achievement in each subject, found by
averaging (actually by totaling) mean scores in all grades in the
given subject. These correlations are, to be sure, spurious to a
certain extent because the average includes the measure for the
grade in question; this is more serious for the correlations dealing
with the content subjects (Literature, History, Geography, and
Science) inasmuch as the averages in these fields are based on results
for three grades only. With the exception of the arithmetic results at
the second grade the results for any subject in any grade yield
relatively high correlations with the average performance in the
subject. The median value of these correlations is about .75.

**SUMMARY**

Analyses of the correlations between mean achievement test scores
of a community for a given grade, and mean scores for other grade
levels, indicate that there are marked variations in the relative standing of a community as measured at various levels. Therefore, generalizations from test results in any given grade as to performance in
other grades, final status, or average status, are to be made with
caution.

# 3.4    Validity and Reliability Defined

*Joint Committee on Standards for Educational and Psychological Tests and Manuals*

Below are reprinted two sections taken from the latest officially endorsed statement of suggested standards for measurement instruments and procedures, *Standards for Educational and Psychological Tests and Manuals.* The complete 40-page report, which can be purchased from the American Psychological Association, is the product of five years of effort by a joint committee comprised of representatives from the three professional groups most intimately concerned with testing and is considered a revision of the 1954 *Technical Recommendations for Psychological Tests and Diagnostic Techniques* and the *Technical Recommendations for Achievement Tests.*

You will find here clear, precise descriptions of the three most useful validity concepts and of the general concept of reliability. Note particularly the care with which the authors avoid misleading the reader in the latter discussion. Reliability is to be no longer given a convenient label such as "consistency," or "test-retest," but rather it is recommended to attach a brief descriptive statement denoting the source of error variance which was permitted to contribute to the total variance when the test was tried out on a norming sample.

**VALIDITY**

Validity information indicates the degree to which the test is capable of achieving certain aims. Tests are used for several types of judgment, and for each type of judgment, a different type of investigation is required to establish validity. For purposes of describing the uses for three kinds of validity coefficients, we may distinguish

---

Reprinted with permission of a Joint Committee of the American Psychological Association, American Educational Research Association, and the National Council on Measurement in Education, and of the publisher, the American Psychological Association, Inc., copyright 1966.

three of the rather numerous aims of testing:

1. *The test user wishes to determine how an individual performs at present in a universe of situations that the test situation is claimed to represent.* For example, most achievement tests used in schools measure the student's performance on a sample of questions intended to represent a certain phase of educational achievement or certain educational objectives.

2. *The test user wishes to forecast an individual's future standing or to estimate an individual's present standing on some variable of particular significance that is different from the test.* For example, an academic aptitude test may forecast grades, or a brief adjustment inventory may estimate what the outcome would be of a careful psychological examination.

3. *The test user wishes to infer the degree to which the individual possesses some hypothetical trait or quality (construct) presumed to be reflected in the test performance.* For example, he wants to know whether the individual stands high on some proposed abstract trait such as "intelligence" or "creativity" that cannot be observed directly. This may be done to learn something about the individual, or it may be done to study the test itself, to study its relationship to other tests, or to develop psychological theory.

Different types of tests are often used for each of the different aims, but this is not always the case. There is much overlap in types of tests and in the purposes for which they are used. Thus, a vocabulary test might be used (a) simply as a measure of present vocabulary, the universe being all the words in the language, (b) as a screening device to discriminate present or potential schizophrenics from organics, or (c) as a means of making inferences about "intellectual capacity."

To determine how suitable a test is for each of these uses, it is necessary to gather the appropriate sort of validity information. The kind of information to be gathered depends on the aim or aims of testing rather than on the type of test. The three aspects of validity corresponding to the three aims of testing may be named content validity, criterion-related validity, and construct validity.

*Content validity* is demonstrated by showing how well the content of the test samples the class situations or subject matter about which conclusions are to be drawn. Content validity is especially important for achievement and proficiency measures and for measures of adjustment or social behavior based on observation in selected situations. The manual should justify the claim that the test content represents the assumed universe of tasks, conditions, or processes. A useful way of looking at this universe of tasks or items is to consider it to comprise a *definition* of the achievement to be measured by the test. In the case of an educational achievement test, the content of the test may be regarded as a definition of (or a sampling from a population of) one or more educational objectives. The aptitudes, skills, and knowledges required of the student for successful test performance must be precisely the types of aptitudes, skills, and knowledges that the school wishes to develop in the students and to evaluate in terms of test scores. Thus evaluating the content validity of a test for a particular purpose is the same as subjectively recognizing the adequacy of a definition. This process is actually quite similar to the subjective evaluation of the criterion itself. Unless, however, the aim of an achievement test is specifically to forecast or substitute for some criterion, its correlation with a criterion is *not* a useful evaluation of the test.

*Criterion-related validity* is demonstrated by comparing the test scores with one or more external variables considered to provide a direct measure of the characteristic or behavior in question. This comparison may take the form of an expectancy table or, most commonly, a correlation relating the test score to a criterion measure. Predictive uses of tests include long-range forecasts of one or more measures of academic achievement, prediction of vocational success, and prediction of reaction to therapy. For such predictive uses the criterion data are collected concurrently with the test; for example, when one wishes to know whether a testing procedure can take the place of more elaborate procedures for diagnosing personality disorders. A test that is related to one or more concurrent criteria will not necessarily predict status on the same criterion at some later date. Whether the criterion data should be collected concurrently with the testing or at a later time depends on whether the test is recommended for prediction or for assessment of present status.

*Construct validity* is evaluated by investigating what qualities a test measures, that is, by determining the degree to which certain explanatory concepts or constructs account for performance on the test. To examine construct validity requires a combination of logical and empirical attack. Essentially, studies of construct validity check on the theory underlying the test. The procedure involves three steps. First, the investigator inquires: From this theory, what hypotheses may we make regarding the behavior of persons with high and low scores? Second, he gathers data to test these hypotheses. Third, in light of the evidence, he makes an inference as to whether the theory is adequate to explain the data collected. If the theory fails to account for the data, he should revise the test interpretation, reformulate the theory, or reject the theory altogether. Fresh evidence would be required to demonstrate construct validity for the revised interpretation.

A simple procedure for investigating what a test measures is to correlate it with other tests. We would expect a valid test of numerical reasoning, for example, to correlate more highly with other numerical tests than with clerical perception tests. Another procedure is experimental. If it is hypothesized, for example, that form perception on a certain projective test indicates probable ability to function well under emotional stress, this inference may be checked by placing individuals in an experimental situation producing emotional stress and observing whether their behavior corresponds to the hypothesis.

Construct validity is ordinarily studied when the tester wishes to increase his understanding of the psychological qualities being measured by the test. A validity coefficient relating test to criterion, unless it is established in the context of some theory, yields no information about *why* the correlation is high or low, or about how one might improve the measurement. Construct validity is relevant when the tester accepts no existing measure as a definitive criterion of the quality with which he is concerned (e.g., in measuring a postulated drive such as need for achievement), or when a test will be used in so many diverse decisions that no single criterion applies (e.g., in identifying the ability of Peace Corps trainees to adapt to new cultures). Here the traits or qualities underlying test performance are of central importance. It must be remembered, however, that, without a study of criterion-related validity, a test developed for diagnosis or prediction can be regarded only as experimental.

These three aspects of validity are only conceptually independent, and only rarely is just one of them important in a particular situation. A complete study of a test would normally involve information about all types of validity. A first step in the preparation of a predictive (*criterion-related*) instrument may be to consider what constructs are likely to provide a basis for selecting or devising an effective test. Sampling from a *content* universe may also be an early step in producing a test whose use for *prediction* is the ultimate concern. Even after satisfactory *prediction* has been established, information regarding *construct* validity may make the test more useful; it may, for example, provide a basis for identifying situations other than the validating situation where the test is appropriate as a predictor. To analyze *construct* validity, all the knowledge regarding validity would be brought to bear.

The three concepts of validity are pertinent to all kinds of tests. It is the intended use of the test rather than its nature that determines what kind of evidence is required.

Intelligence or scholastic aptitude tests most often use criterion-related validity to show how well they are able to predict academic success in school or college, but the nature of the aptitudes measured is often judged from the content of the items, and the place of the aptitude within the array of human abilities is deduced from correlations with other tests.

For achievement tests, content validity is usually of first importance. For example, a testing agency has a group of subject-matter specialists devise and select test items that they judge to cover the topics and mental processes relevant to the field represented by the test. Similarly, a teacher judges whether the final test in his course covers the kinds of situations about which he has been trying to teach his students certain principles or understandings. The teacher also judges content when he uses a published test, but he can appropriately investigate criterion-related validity by correlating this test with tests he has prepared or with other direct measures of his chief instructional objectives. When the same published achievement test is used for admissions testing, it may reasonably be checked against a later criterion of performance. In any theoretical discussion of what is being measured by the achievement test, a consideration of construct validity is required. Whether the score on a science achievement test, for example, reflects reading ability to a significant degree, and whether it measures understanding of scientific method rather than mere recall of facts are both questions about construct validity.

Development of a personality inventory will usually start with the assembly of items covering content the developer considers meaningful. Such inventories are then likely to be interpreted with the aid of theory; any such interpretation calls for evidence of construct validity. In addition, a personality inventory must have criterion-related validity, if, for example, it is to be used in screening military recruits who may be maladjusted.

Interest measures are usually intended to predict vocational or educational criteria, but many of them are also characterized by logical content and constructs. This makes it more likely that they can provide at least a rough prediction for the very many occupations and activities that exist and for which specific evidence of criterion-related validity has not been obtained.

For projective techniques, construct validity is the most important, although criterion-related validity using criteria collected either concurrently with the testing or afterwards may be pertinent if the instruments are to be used in making diagnostic classifications.

## RELIABILITY

Reliability refers to the accuracy (consistency and stability) of measurement by a test. Any direct measurement of such consistency obviously calls for a comparison between at least two measurements. (Whereas "accuracy" is a general expression, the terms "consistency" and "stability" are needed to describe, respectively, form-associated and time-associated reliability.) The two measurements may be obtained by *retesting* an individual with the identical test. Aside from practical limitations, retesting is not a theoretically desirable method of determining a reliability coefficient if, as usual, the items that constitute the test are only one of many sets (actual or hypothetical) that might equally well have been used to measure the particular ability or trait. Thus, there is ordinarily no reason to suppose that *one* set of (say) 50 vocabulary items is especially superior (or inferior) to another comparable (equivalent) set of 50. In this case it appears desirable to determine not only the degree of response variation by the subject from one occasion to the next (as is accomplished by the retest method), but also the extent of sampling fluctuation involved in selecting a given set of 50 items. These two objectives are accomplished most commonly by correlating scores on the original set of 50 items with scores by the same subjects on an independent but similar set of 50 items—an "alternate form" of the original 50. If the effect of content-sampling *alone* is sought (without the effects of response variability by the subject), or if it is not practical to undertake testing on two different occasions, a test of 100 items may be administered. Then the test may be divided into two sets of 50 odd-numbered items and 50 even-numbered items; the correlation between scores on the odd and the even sets is a "split-half" or "odd-even" correlation, from which a reliability (consistency) coefficient for the entire test of 100 items may be estimated by the Spearman-Brown formula (involving certain generally reasonable assumptions). Essentially the same type of estimated reliability coefficient may be obtained from item-analysis data through use of the Kuder-Richardson formulas (which involve various assumptions, some more reasonable and exact than others). It should be noted that despite the possible heterogeneity of content, the odd-even correlation between the sets of items may be quite high if the items are easy and if the test is administered with a short time limit. Such odd-even correlations are in a sense spurious, since they merely reflect the expected correlation between two sets of scores each of which is a measure of rate of work.

From the preceding discussion, it is clear that *different methods of determining the reliability coefficient take account of different sources of error.* Thus, from one testing to the other, the retest method is affected not only by response variability of the subjects but also by differences in administration (most likely if different persons administer the test on the two occasions). Reliability coefficients based on the single administration of a test ignore response variability and the particular administrative conditions: their effects on scores simply do not appear as errors of measurement. Hence, "reliability coefficient" is a generic term referring to various types of evidence; each type of evidence suggests a different meaning. It is essential that *the method used to derive any reliability coefficient should be clearly described.*

As a generic term reliability refers to many types of evidence, each of which describes the agreement or consistency to be expected among similar observations. Each type of evidence takes into account certain kinds of errors or inconsistencies and not others. The operation of measurement may be viewed as a sample of behavior; in a typical aptitude or achievement test the person is observed on a particular date as he responds to a particular set of questions or stimuli, and his responses are recorded and scored by a particular tester or system. The occasion is a sample from the period of time within which the same general inquiry would be pertinent; some sampling error is involved in selecting any one date of observation. The items that constitute the test are only one of many sets (actual or hypothetical) that might have been used to measure the same ability or trait. The choices of a particular test apparatus, test administrator, observer, or scorer, are also sampling operations. Each such act of sampling has some influence on the test score. It is valuable for the test user to know how much a particular score would be likely to change if any one of these conditions of measurement were altered.

There are various components that may contribute to inconsistency among observations: (a) response variation by the subject (due to changes in physiological efficiency, or in such psychological factors as motivation, effort, or mood): these may be especially important in inventories of personality; (b) variations in test content or the test situation (in "situational tests" which include interacting persons as part of the situation, this source of variation can be relatively large); (c) variations in administration (either through variations in physical factors, such as temperature, noise, or apparatus functioning, or in psychological factors, such as variation in the technique or skill of different test administrators or raters); and (d) variations in the process of observation. In addition to these errors of observation, scoring-error variance in test scores reflects variation in the process of scoring responses as well as mistakes in recording, transferring, or reading of scores.

*The estimation of clearly labeled components of error variance is the most informative outcome of a reliability study*, both for the test developer wishing to improve the reliability of his instrument and for the user desiring to interpret test scores with maximum understanding. The analysis of error variance calls for the use of an appropriate *experimental* design. There are many different multivariate designs that can be used in reliability studies; the choice of design for studying the particular test is to be determined by its intended interpretation and by the practical limitations upon experimentation. In general, where more information can be obtained at little increase in cost, the test developer should obtain and report that information.

Although estimation of clearly labeled components of error variance is the most informative outcome of a reliability study, this approach is not yet prominent in reports on tests. In the more familiar reliability study the investigator obtains two measures and correlates them, or derives a correlation coefficient by applying one of several formulas to part or item scores within a test. Such a correlation is often interpreted as a ratio of "true variance" to "true variance plus error variance." Many different coefficients, each involving its own definition of "true" and "error" variance, may be derived from a multivariate reliability experiment with the presence of controls for such factors as those of content, time, and mode of administration. Hence, any single correlation is subject to considerable misinterpretation unless the investigator makes clear just what sampling errors are considered to be error in the particular coefficient he reports. The correlation between two test forms presented on different days has a different significance from an internal-consistency coefficient, for example, because the latter allocates day-to-day fluctuations in a person's efficiency to the true rather than to the error portion of the score variance.

In the present set of *Standards*, the terminology by which the 1954 *Technical Recommendations* classified coefficients into several types (e.g., coefficient of equivalence) has been discarded. Such a terminological system breaks down as more adequate statistical analyses are applied and methods are more adequately described. Hence it is recommended that test authors work out suitable phrases to convey the meaning of whatever coefficients they report; as an example, the expression, "the stability of measurements by different test forms as determined over a 7-day interval," although lengthy, will be reasonably free from ambiguity.

# 4   Test Score Interpretations

## 4.1   The Concept of Validity in the Interpretation of Test Scores

### Anne Anastasi

Test scores are generally useful as predictors of future performance or as estimates of current level of capacity or attainment. The author of this article makes an important point: psychological tests provide the same *kind* of information that other observational techniques would yield.

Labels attached to tests, such as "intelligence" and "aptitude," often lead to misperceptions by testers. They infer, incorrectly, some mysterious, elusive property which can be elicited from testees *only* by certain tests. A little reflection will reveal that the concept "intelligence" existed long before modern testing began.

Anastasi's use of the term "extenuating circumstances" serves to illustrate that *any* test can be valid for *some* purpose. What specific implications does this notion have for, say, classroom uses and interpretations of psychological tests?

If asked to define "validity," most psychologists would probably agree that validity is the closeness of agreement of a test with some independently observed criterion of the behavior under consideration. It is only as a measure of a specifically defined criterion that a test can be objectively validated at all. For example, unless we define "intelligence" as that combination of aptitudes required for successful school achievement, or for survival on a certain type of job, or in terms of some other observable criterion, we can never either prove or disprove that a particular test is a valid measure of "intelligence." The criterion may be expressed in very broad and general terms,

Reprinted with permission of the author and *Educational and Psychological Measurement*, **10**, 1, 1950, 67–78.

such as "those behavior characteristics in which older children in our culture differ from younger children reared in the same culture," but, however expressed, it defines the functions measured by the particular test. To claim that a test measures anything over and above its criterion is pure speculation of the type that is not amenable to verification and hence falls outside the realm of experimental science.

To the question, "What does this test measure?", the only defensible answer can thus be that it measures a sample of behavior which in turn may be diagnostic of the criterion or criteria against which the particular test was validated. Nor is there any circularity implicit in such a definition of validity, since a psychological test is a device for determining within a relatively short period of time what could otherwise be discovered only by means of a prolonged follow-up. For example, with a psychological test we may be able to predict within a certain margin of error which applicants will succeed on a given job or which students will be able to complete a medical course satisfactorily. Logically, the same information could have been obtained, even more precisely, by hiring all job applicants or admitting to medical school all students wishing to enroll, and observing the subsequent performance of each subject. The latter procedure is obviously so time-consuming and wasteful, however, as to be completely impracticable. Hence the tests make a real contribution in permitting predictions in advance of lengthy observations. Another advantage of standardized psychological tests is that they make possible a comparison of the individual's performance with that of other persons who have been observed in the same sample situation represented by each test. In other words, the tests provide norms for evaluating individual performance.

Prediction and comparison with norms represent valuable contributions which psychological tests can render to our knowledge of individual behavior, the practical benefits of these contributions having been widely demonstrated. It is of fundamental importance, however, to bear in mind that psychological tests do not provide a different *kind* of information from that obtained by any other observation of behavior. The use of such labels as "intelligence," "aptitude," "capacity," and "potentiality" has probably done much to make test users lose sight of the empirical validation of tests. A number of current disagreements regarding the interpretation of test results and the susceptibility of tested abilities to training may be

traceable to a failure to take due cognizance of validation procedures. Many test users apparently give only preliminary and possibly perfunctory attention to validation data, in order to reassure
themselves at the outset that the test is "satisfactory." Their interpretation of the scores obtained with such a test, however, often
takes no account of the validation data and is expressed in terms
which bear little or no relation to the criterion.

Perhaps one of the most common examples of such an inconsistent treatment of test validity is proved by what we may call the
argument of "extenuating circumstances." Let us suppose that a
child obtains an IQ of 58 on a verbal intelligence test, and that the
examiner subsequently finds evidence of a fairly severe language
handicap in this child owing to foreign parentage. It is a common
practice to conclude in such a case that the obtained IQ is not
"valid," on the grounds that the verbal content of the test rendered
it unsuitable for testing such an individual. At this point we may
inquire, however, "On the basis of *what criterion* is this IQ invalid?" Certainly the obtained IQ may be a valid measure of the
behavior defined by the criterion against which the particular test
was validated. It is very likely that the same language handicap
which interfered with performance on this test will interfere with
the child's behavior in other linguistic situations of which this test
is an adequate index. The correspondence with the criterion may
thus be just as close for this child as for children without a language
handicap. In school, for example, the language handicap would
probably interfere with the child's acquisition of important skills
and information. The resulting academic backwardness, together
with the original language handicap itself, would, in turn, affect
certain aspects of job performance and other areas of adult activities. Conversely, any remedial efforts designed to eliminate the
language handicap would produce an improvement, not only in
the tested IQ, but also in the broader area of behavior of which
this test is a predictor.

It should be added parenthetically that language handicap has
been chosen as an example only for purposes of discussion. A number of other "extenuating circumstances," such as visual or auditory
defects, emotional and motivational factors, inadequate schooling,
and the like, could have served equally well to illustrate the point.
Similarly, the discussion has been limited to intelligence tests, since it

is chiefly in connection with these tests that many confusions regarding validity have arisen. The entire discussion applies equally well, however, to all types of psychological tests.

Specifically, how does the case cited in our illustration, as well as others of its type, differ from those in which no question is raised regarding the "validity" of the test or its applicability to the particular individual? First, in the present case the examiner has direct and certain knowledge regarding at least one of the factors which *determine* the subject's subnormal performance, viz., language handicap. In other cases, the principal determining factor might be inferior schooling facilities, parental illiteracy, cerebral birth injuries, a defective thyroid, or any of a large number of psychological or biological conditions. Yet it is doubtful whether the IQ would be considered "invalid" in all of these cases simply because it proved possible to point to a specific condition as the determining factor in the poor test performance. To be sure, in many cases of low IQ, the examiner has little or no knowledge about the circumstances or conditions which lead to the intellectual backwardness. But such ignorance is obviously no more conducive to "valid" testing. Quite apart from the question of validity, the examiner should, of course, make every effort to understand why the individual performs as he does on a test. The fullest possible knowledge of the individual's pre- and post-natal environment, structural deficiencies, and any other relevant conditions in his reactional biography is desirable for the most effective use of the test data. But to explain *why* an individual scores poorly on a test does not "explain away" the score. There are always reasons to account for an individual's performance on a test. Language handicap is just as real as any other reason.

A second distinguishing feature of our example is that such a language handicap is usually *remediable*. The individual need not be permanently backward in intellectual performance, but with special training he may in large measure compensate for past losses in intellectual progress. Susceptibility to treatment is, however, a matter of degree. Many of the conditions determining intellectual performance, whether structural or functional, are amenable to change under special treatment. Moreover, conditions for which no effective therapy is now known may yield to newly developed treatments in the future. The distinction in terms of remediability is thus rather tenuous. Nor does such a distinction have any direct bearing upon the validity of a measuring instrument. A thermometer may be a valid index of fever, despite the fact that the administration of medicine will cure the fever.

Thirdly, some may point out that language handicap is not *hereditary* and may maintain that for this reason its influence upon test performance ought to be "ruled out." Such an objection contains a tacit assumption that psychological tests are primarily concerned with those individual differences in behavior which can be attributed to heredity. Since the number of hereditary conditions which have been clearly related to behavior differences are extremely few, such a policy, if followed consistently, would mean the virtual cessation of psychological testing. Moreover, the connection between hereditary mechanisms and behavior is so remote and indirect as to render the distinction between hereditary and environmental factors in behavior largely an academic one (cf., e.g., 2). Above all, it should be noted that no *criterion* against which any psychological test has been validated is itself traceable to purely hereditary factors. Hence no such test has been proved to be a valid measure of individual differences in hereditary characteristics.

A fourth point to be considered is that of *comparability*. It may be objected that the individual who is handicapped by language difficulties, sensory deficiencies, or similar "extenuating circumstances" is not comparable to the validation group on which the test norms were established. The requirement of comparability in the application of psychological tests needs further clarification. If individuals are entirely similar in all of the conditions (psychological, physiological, etc.) which influence the behavior measured by a particular test, individual differences will disappear, all subjects receiving the same score. Obviously no test is designed to measure behavior independently of the conditions which determine such behavior—that would be a logical absurdity as well as an empirical impossibility. *When the conditions in which the individual differs from the standardization group affect the test and the criterion in an approximately equal manner and degree, the validity of the test for that individual will not be appreciably influenced by the lack of comparability of the individual to the standardization group.* [Italics added. Eds.]

This question of "comparability" pertains not so much to the measurement of behavior as to the analysis of the etiology of behavior differences. It is only when attributing the observed individual differences in test scores to a particular factor or class of factors that the investigator must make certain that other contributing factors have been reasonably constant. For example, if a few individuals in a group have a language handicap while the rest do not, we could not ascribe individual differences in performance within this group to structural differences in the nervous system, or to any other factor whose contribution to behavior we may be investigating. The same limitation would apply, however, if educational opportunities, family traditions, incentives for intellectual activities, or any other factor were not held constant. The fact that the influence of language handicap, sensory deficiencies, and a few other conditions is more readily apparent does not place such conditions in a different category. The question of comparability applies equally to all conditions other than the one under investigation.

A fifth consideration pertains to the use of test scores in *prediction*. Could an IQ obtained by a child with a language handicap serve as a basis for predicting the subsequent behavior of the individual? As long as the language handicap remains, the test score can provide an accurate prognosis of the child's behavior in situations demanding the type of verbal responses sampled by the test. It is only in this sense that *any* psychological test makes predictions possible. Within a certain margin of error, behavior can be predicted *under existing conditions*. But if, for example, any detrimental conditions such as poor schooling, sensory deficiencies, or the like are corrected, then performance on *both* test and criterion will show improvement. In discussions of test *reliability*, various writers during the past twenty-five years have pointed out that a psychological test should be expected to reflect changes in behavior at different times and under different conditions.[1] For test scores to remain constant when conditions affecting the subject's behavior have altered would indicate a crude and relatively insensitive measuring instrument, rather than a highly "reliable" one. The same logic applies to validity. If the subjects' test scores remain unchanged despite the modification of conditions which affect criterion performance, the test cannot have high validity.

Closely related to the problem of prediction is the *scope or breadth of influence* of any given condition upon the individual's behavior. For example, the presence of a loud, irregular noise during

---

[1] Cf., e.g., 1, 4, 5, 6, 9, 10, 11, 12, 15, 18, 19.

the testing would probably affect the score on that test, without influencing the individual's behavior in other situations. A toothache or a severe cold on the day of the testing would be further illustrations of narrowly limited conditions. In the case of these conditions, the prognostic value of the test for the individual would indeed be reduced, in much the same manner that holding an ice cube in the mouth would invalidate an oral thermometer reading of bodily temperature. Conditions such as language handicap, however, affect the individual's behavior in a much broader area than that of the immediate test situation. They may thus influence both criterion and test score in a similar manner.

The import of the above analysis is that validity should be consistently interpreted with reference to the *specific criteria* against which the given test was validated. It also follows that validity is not a function of the test but of the use to which the test is put. A test may have high validity for one criterion and low or negligible validity for another. The attitude that a good test has "high validity" and a poor test has "low validity" is still too prevalent among test users. Tests cannot be validated in the abstract, nor is the usual concept of validity itself universally applicable to psychological testing. It is only when tests are employed for predictive or diagnostic purposes that the correlation with an external criterion is relevant at all. In many investigations concerned with fundamental behavior research, tests are employed merely as behavior samples obtained under standardized (i.e., uniform) conditions, without reference to the correlations of these samples with other, "every-day-life" behavior samples (i.e., practical criterion measures). When the maze-learning behavior of white rats is tested, for example, the maze is not first "validated" against the rats' success in finding food in a grocery basement, or their ability to avoid contact with prowling cats, or any other criteria of achievement in the rats' extra-laboratory or workaday world. The investigator may quite reasonably argue that for the study of the particular principles of behavior which he is investigating, maze-learning is as "good" a sample of behavior as cat-avoiding, and that he has no more reason for validating the former against the latter than vice versa.

Fundamentally, any validation procedure proves a measure of the relationship between two behavior samples. As Guilford has recently expressed it, "In a very general sense, a test is valid for anything with which it correlates" (7, p. 429). The process can be regarded as irreversible only when one of the behavior samples has greater importance than the other for a specific purpose.[2] In such a case, the more important behavior sample is designated the "criterion." No basic difference exists between "criteria" on the one hand and "tests" on the other. They are merely different samples of behavior whose interrelationships permit predictions from one to the other. We *could* predict intelligence test scores from school achievement, although the process would be needlessly time-consuming. In such a case, the intelligence test scores would constitute the criterion.

The criterion is not *intrinsically* superior in any sense. It is well known, for example, that many commonly used criteria, such as school grades or job advancement, may be influenced by many factors "extraneous" to the quality of the individual's performance. Yet, if it is our object to predict such criteria, with all their irrelevancies and shortcomings, then the correlation of a given test with such criteria *is* the validity of the test in that situation. To be sure, the immediate criterion against which a test is validated may itself have been chosen as a convenient index or predictor of a broader and less readily observable area of behavior. For example, a pilot aptitude test may be validated against performance in basic flight training, the latter being in turn regarded as an approximate index of achievement in more advanced training and even possibly of ultimate combat performance. Such "successive validation" would be quite consistent with the relativity of predictors and criteria. It might be noted parenthetically that it is only when criterion measures are themselves used as predictors of further behavior that one may legimately speak of the reliability and validity of the criterion itself (cf. e.g., 8).

Validation against a "practical" criterion is essential for many uses to which tests are put. It should not be assumed, however, that only tests which have been validated against some criterion considered important within a particular cultural setting can be used in

---

[2] To be sure, when the relationship between the two variables is curvilinear, prediction will not be equally accurate in both directions, since $\eta_{xy} \neq \eta_{yx}$. In such cases, however, there is no a priori reason to expect that the correlation will be any higher when predicting the "criterion" from the "test" than when predicting the "test" from the "criterion."

behavior research. In order to be able to generalize from any obtained test score, we need only to know the relationships between
the tested behavior in question and other behavior samples, none of
these behavior samples necessarily occupying the preeminent position of a criterion. Thus, if the investigator is interested in the
possible use of maze-learning performance as a basis for predicting
the rats' behavior in other learning situations, he will have to correlate the subjects' maze-learning scores with their scores in a variety
of other learning tasks. If a common factor is identified through
these different learning scores, the "factorial validity" (7) of any
one of the tests in predicting that which is common to all of them
can be determined. On the other hand, if no single learning factor is
demonstrated, then the area within which predictions can be made
must be accordingly narrowed to fit the confines of whatever common factor does become evident. Investigations conducted to date
on human subjects, for example, have failed to indicate the presence
of a common "learning factor" (20, 21), and animal studies have
revealed even greater specificity (cf., e.g., 14, 16, 17). But such
specificity, if further corroborated, is an empirically observed fact
whose discovery is useful in its own right in advancing our knowledge of behavior; it should not be construed as a weakness of the
tests.

Whether we are dealing with common factors and "factorial
validity" or with "practical validity" in the prediction of every-day-
life criteria, the question of validity concerns essentially the interrelationships of behavior samples. In the latter case, one sample is
represented by the test and another, probably much more extensive
sample, by the criterion. In the former case, the different tests which
are correlated constitute the behavior samples. Nor should the terminology of factor analysis mislead us into the belief that anything
external to the tested behavior has been identified. The discovery of
a "factor" means simply that certain relationships exist between
tested behavior samples.

The common misconception that the criterion is in some mysterious fashion more basic than the test probably results, in part, from
the belief that tests measure hypothetical "underlying capacities"
which are distinguishable from observed behavior. Discussions of
psychological tests often become hopelessly entangled because of
the implicit supposition that tests can be validated against such

underlying capacities as criteria. Any operational analysis of actual validation procedures reveals the futility and absurdity of such an expectation.

In this connection we may consider a monograph by Thomas (13), which sounds a note of acute pessimism regarding the use of mental tests as "instruments of science." Through a careful and systematic logical analysis, the author demonstrates the fallacies inherent in any attempts to interpret psychological tests as measures of "innate abilities," hypostatized "fundamental human capacities," and the like. He clearly recognizes that "the methodology of mental testing provides no way of operationally defining an ability and a performance as distinct . . . entities" (13, p. 75). But, in his final conclusions, the author seems to exhibit the same confusions which he had previously sought to eliminate.[3] For example, in the attempt to evaluate the scientific usefulness of psychological tests, he raises such questions as the following: "Do two identical scores mean that the same kind and amount of psychological processes were employed? Do they mean similar sociological backgrounds of experience? Do they mean a qualitatively similar adaptation to the immediate test environment? Do they mean that comparable amounts of psychic tension were built up or that similar amounts of nervous energy were expended?" (13, p. 77). By way of reply he adds: "The achievement of such scientific meanings as these from the current methodology of mental testing is probably too much to expect, for test results at present are notoriously ambiguous in what they signify about the sociopsychological ingredients of the recorded performances" (13, p. 77).

Two weaknesses are apparent in such an argument. First, the testing of behavior is being confused with an analysis of the factors which determine behavior. Secondly, despite his earlier advocacy of an operational definition of "ability," the author now appears to be chasing the will-o'-the-wisp of "psychological processes" which are distinct from performance. He seems thus to be demanding that in

---

[3] These confusions in the fundamental argument do not detract from the value of certain more specific points discussed in this monograph, such as the limitations of ordinal scales, and the concepts of difficulty value and homogeneity in test construction. But these problems have also been analyzed by other writers, in a somewhat more constructive manner (cf., e.g., 3, 10).

order to be proper instruments of science, psychological tests should measure functions which by definition fall outside the domain of scientific inquiry!

In summary, it is urged that test scores be operationally defined in terms of empirically demonstrated behavior relationships. If a test has been validated against a practical criterion such as school performance, the scores on such a test should be consistently defined and treated as predictors of school performance rather than as measures of hypostatized and unverifiable "abilities." It is further pointed out that conditions which affect test scores may also affect the criterion, since both test scores and criteria are essentially behavior samples. The extent or breadth of such influences is a matter for empirical determination, rather than for a priori assumption. Moreover, the validity of a psychological test should not be confused with an analysis of the factors which determine the behavior under consideration. Finally, it should be noted that the distinction between test and criterion is itself merely one of practical convenience. The scientific use of tests is not predicated upon the assumption that criteria are a separate class of phenomena against which all tests must first be validated. Essentially, generalization and prediction in psychology require knowledge of the interrelationships of behavior, regardless of the situation in which such behavior was observed.

**REFERENCES**

1. ANASTASI, A., "The Influence of Practice upon Test Reliability," *Journal of Educational Psychology*, **XXV** (1934), 321–335.

2. ANASTASI, A. and FOLEY, J. P., JR., "A Proposed Reorientation in the Heredity-Environment Controversy," *Psychological Review*, **LV** (1948), 239–249.

3. COOMBS, C. H., "Some Hypotheses for the Analysis of Qualitative Variables," *Psychological Review*, **LV** (1948), 167–174.

4. CRONBACH, L. J., "Test 'Reliablity': Its Meaning and Determination," *Psychometrika*, **XII** (1947), 1–16.

5. DUNLAP, J. W., "Comparable Tests and Reliability," *Journal of Educational Psychology*, **XXIV** (1933), 442–453.

6. GOODENOUGH, F. L., "A Critical Note on the Use of the Term 'Reliability' in Mental Measurement," *Journal of Educational Psychology*, **XXVII** (1936), 173–178.

7. GUILFORD, J. P., "New Standards for Test Evaluation," *Educational and Psychological Measurement*, **VI** (1946), 427–438.

8. Jenkins, J. G., "Validity for What?" *Journal of Consulting Psychology*, X (1946), 93–98.

9. Kuhlmann, F., *Tests of Mental Development*. Minneapolis: Educational Test Bureau, 1939.

10. Loevinger, J., "A Systematic Approach to the Construction and Evaluation of Tests of Ability," *Psychological Monographs*, LXI (1947), 4.

11. Paulsen, C. B., "A Coefficient of Trait Variability," *Psychological Bulletin*, XXVIII (1931), 218–219.

12. Skaggs, E. B., "Some Critical Comments on Certain Prevailing Concepts Used in Mental Testing," *Journal of Applied Psychology*, XI (1927), 503–508.

13. Thomas, L. G., "Mental Tests as Instruments of Science," *Psychological Monographs*, LIV (1942), 3.

14. Thorndike, R. L., "Organization of Behavior in the Albino Rat," *Genetic Psychology Monograph*, XVII (1935), 1.

15. Thouless, R. H., "Test Unreliability and Functional Fluctuation," *British Journal of Psychology*, XXVI (1935–1936), 325–343.

16. Van Steenberg, N. J. F., "Factors in the Learning Behavior of the Albino Rat," *Psychometrika*, IV (1939), 179–200.

17. Vaughn, C. L., "Factors in Rat Learning: An Analysis of the Intercorrelations Between 34 Variables," *Psychological Monographs*, XIV (1937), 69.

18. Wherry, R. J., and Gaylord, R. H., "The Concept of Test and Item Reliability in Relation to Factor Pattern," *Psychometrika*, VIII (1943), 247–264.

19. Woodrow, H., "Quotidian Variability," *Psychological Review*, XXXIX (1932), 245–256.

20. Woodrow, H., "The Relation Between Abilities and Improvement with Practice," *Journal of Educational Psychology*, XXIX (1938), 215–230.

21. Woodrow, H., "Factors in Improvement with Practice," *Journal of Psychology*, VII (1939), 55–70.

## 4.2   Critics of Psychological Tests: Basic Assumptions: How Good?

*Marvin D. Dunnette*

In the past few years, many articles have appeared in popular form, expressing a disdain for psychological and educational testing. Dunnette attempts to isolate some of the more popular objections to testing, and then analyze them in terms of known measurement techniques. Do you think he handles the objections satisfactorily? Can you state further evidence to refute the objections raised in the article?

First, let us consider some of the major assumptions made by Hoffman (1962) in his book, *The Tyranny of Testing*, and consider the relative validity of each. Later, we will comment on some of the broader charges made by other critics and the relative validity of these.

Conveniently, Hoffman spells out his assumptions on page 150 of his book. The first is as follows:

"The tests deny the creative person a significant opportunity to demonstrate his creativity and favor the shrewd and facile candidate over the one who has something to say."

I personally know of no evidence to suggest that tests stifle the creative person. The major problem with making such a charge or assumption is that little satisfactory research has been done to define the so-called trait of creativeness. The usual procedure has been simply to call people "creative" who happen to score high on so-called "creativity" tests. Recently, Robert Thorndike (1963) has

Paper presented as part of a symposium, "Professional Views of Some Recent Protests Against Psychological Testing," at the Midwestern Psychological Association meetings in Chicago, May 1963. Reprinted with permission of the author and *Psychology in the Schools*, 1, 4, 1964.

analyzed the relative factorial purity of the content of the standard IQ tests and of the so-called creativity or divergent thinking tests. He finds that tests of creativity actually correlate more highly with convergent thinking tests than they do with themselves. Evidence such as this is hardly sufficient to sustain an argument that the so-called trait or behavior which we label "creative" has been successfully measured by tests now available. Unfortunately, the usual approach is to label persons as creative who score high on these factorially poorly defined "creativity" tests rather than on the basis of any behaviorally defined reference outside the tests themselves.

Hoffmann cites the study by Getzels and Jackson (1962) described in their book, *Creativity and Intelligence.* Unfortunately the Getzels and Jackson study is a particularly poor example of what I have just discussed. In their study Getzels and Jackson define creativity on the basis of scores on a variety of measures of fluency and divergent thinking. In one part of their study they contrast two groups selected on the basis of high scores on IQ tests and creativity tests, respectively. The average IQ of the students selected on the basis of IQ tests was 150 whereas the average IQ of students selected on the basis of the "creativity" tests was only 127. Getzels and Jackson report that these two groups who differ by 23 points in IQ *did not differ on standard multiple choice achievement examinations.* Yet Hoffmann says on page 146 of his book,

> "In view of the above how much faith can we have in the IQ as an unbiased predictor of scholastic achievement even when the scholastic achievement is measured by multiple choice methods. Think of the number of gifted students who were penalized in our schools because they lack the IQ knack."

It is difficult for me to understand how Hoffmann can use the data of the Getzels and Jackson study to make such a comment. Just the opposite is, in fact, true: the "low ability" (IQ = 127) students were not penalized on achievement examinations; they scored the same as the "high ability" (IQ = 150) students.

Even so, there seems to be a widely held misconception that teachers somehow like the highly "creative" children less well than the highly intelligent children. As a matter of fact Getzels and Jackson are often cited as evidence and they do state that "the high IQ students are preferred over the average students by their teachers, the creativity students are not." The actual facts as shown by the Getzels and Jackson data are that teachers' preferences were in the same direction for *both* groups and of very nearly the same magnitude. The difference, however, was not statistically significant for the "creative" children. Thus the reader and the public is left by this cavalier treatment of data with the unjustified impression that the teachers prefer the "high IQ's" to the "high creatives." In my opinion, this is irresponsible reporting of research data—reporting that is nicely designed to lead people with an axe to grind (such as Mr. Hoffmann) astray.

Let us consider a second assumption made by Hoffmann. He says:

> "They penalize the candidate who perceives subtle points unnoticed by less able people including the test makers. They are apt to be superficial and intellectually dishonest with questions made artifically difficult by means of ambiguity because genuinely searching questions did not readily fit into the multiple choice format."

A comment such as this of course ignores the massive amount of careful research which actually goes into the construction and final validation of a test item. For example, it is well known that distractors are purposely written to "fool" the less able person. We know that information about responses made by persons of different levels of knowledge shows without question that the degree of ambiguity perceived by the examinee is inversely related to his knowledge of the subject matter. In other words in a good test item the less one knows the more ambiguous does the question appear. In spite of this, Hoffmann states on page 67 "and the more one knows about the subject the more glaring the ambiguities become." Hoffmann, of course, has no evidence to support this assumption.

A further assumption made by Hoffmann may be stated as follows:

> "they take account of only the choice of answer and not of quality of thought that lead to the choice," and "They neglect skill and disciplined expression."

Hoffmann apparently feels very strongly that objective examinations fail to assess a mysterious entity which he calls "quality of thought" or that they give little opportunity for "disciplined expression." Naturally, he offers no definitions for these mysterious attributes and he certainly suggests no reliable nor valid way of measuring them. In fact Hoffmann seems diligently to resist all references to the concepts of reliability and validity.

In addition to the fact that Hoffmann fails to define quality of thought or disciplined expression, it is noteworthy that he gives in Chapter 3 a series of very convincing arguments for *not* using essay examinations to measure so-called quality of thought or disciplined expression. For example, Hoffmann states that it is difficult in writing an essay question to choose a topic which will be fair to all examinees. He further states that even if a topic finally is chosen it is extremely difficult to determine whether the essay is actually relevant to the question, further that it is difficult to overcome the problem of negative halo due to poor handwriting, poor spelling, or poor punctuation. He brings up the problem of different graders of essay examinations using different standards and he even cites the difficulty of the grader changing his standards as he moves through the examinations which he must grade. Hoffmann concludes that essay exams may be unfair, indeed that they are unfair for the testing of the students.

Thus Hoffmann works himself into a corner by criticizing objectives exams because they fail to assess quality of thought or disciplined expression; yet he leaves no alternative for assessing these non-defined entities by any other means (such as by essay exams).

In his discussion of this problem he cites a study by the Educational Testing Service showing that a 90 minute essay test was less good than an objective exam, the English Composition Test, for predicting faculty ratings in English Composition. Faced with this evidence that an essay exam is less worthy, Hoffmann simply argues that these results are silly and that they could not possibly have been obtained. He appears to be using logical analysis in order to overcome or to reject empirical results. Essentially, of course, Hoffmann is simply confusing content with predictive or concurrent validity.

Finally, perhaps the potentially most damaging assumption and the one which would be the most difficult for Hoffmann to sustain has to do with the effect of tests in the identification of individual merit. He states,

"They have a pernicious effect on education and the recognition of merit."

Furthermore, he seems to be concerned about the idea that multiple choice testing might somehow be "efficient" and he feels that efficiency is bad in and of itself. For example, on page 90 he states,

> "Let us not sacrifice too much for the sake of efficiency. In some respects the dictatorship is more efficient than a democracy and the lie detector more efficient and scientific than the jury. The efficient Nazis made medical experiments directly on men and women."

After reading this I find myself very curious about Mr. Hoffmann's stand on fluoridation of water which certainly must be regarded as one very efficient way of decreasing the incidence of dental caries. However, lest I be charged with arguing in the same manner as I am accusing Mr. Hoffmann of doing, let me hasten to offer something in a more positive vein.

Actually, standardized testing is one of the great success stories of our time. Perhaps this has been no better pointed out than in the book, *Excellence*, by John Gardner (1961). Psychological testing for the first time enables us to look at the many facets of an individual instead of making judgments based on the so-called "lump of dough" doctrine. Now we can truly measure and assess the individuality of each person in society and through careful guidance help individuals realize the potentialities indicated by psychological testing instruments. Gardner illustrates the lump of dough doctrine and the lack of any recognition of individuality by citing the experience of a friend who visited a small provincial school in France. Gardner states,

> "The teacher seemed to find it impossible to separate his judgment of a pupil's intelligence from his judgment of the pupil's cleanliness, good manners, neatness of dress and precision of speech. Needless to say his students from the upper and upper-middle social class excelled in these qualities."

Today, through objective tests we can identify the many abilities of children and for the first time do a good job of mapping the true individuality of each and every child. In other words, tests provide us with the best means available for assessing individuality and discovering and rewarding individual merit. In my opinion this function is undoubtedly the greatest strength of testing and it is an entirely fallacious and unfounded assumption on the part of Hoffmann that tests are instead working against the recognition of individual merit and the wise and humane utilization of human resources. The creative genius of men such as Terman, Thurstone, Guilford and Strong cannot be nullified by a few Hoffmanns, Packards, Grosses, or Whytes.

Now I would like to turn briefly to points made by Hoffmann which I believe are essentially worthwhile and with which I am in essential agreement.

First, Hoffmann is unhappy with the terms "underachiever" and "overachiever." So am I. As a matter of fact, tests have never shown predictive or concurrent validities which exceed .60 or .70. It would seem under these conditions to be wiser to use the terms "overscorer" and "underscorer" rather than to assume and to label persons in terms of their achievement as is done by the widely used terms, under and overachiever.

Secondly, Hoffmann argues that statistics should not take precedence over rational analysis of an item's content. I would tend to agree with this statement. Even if empirical validity did show that an item was valid, if a wrong answer were keyed, I would not then proceed to use this wrongly keyed answer. Thus, I would say that empirical validity should not necessarily carry the day over content validity and in so saying I am in essential agreement with Hoffmann. Unfortunately, Hoffmann completely ignores the fact that statistical validation of test items is most often an effective means of discovering poor and ambiguous items. Nowhere in his book does Hoffmann mention that item analysis is primarily a means of identifying poorly keyed and ambiguous items.

Finally, Hoffmann may not be aware of it but he does call attention to the possibility of heteroscedastic and non-linear relationships. It would certainly be well for more psychologists to recognize the possibility of such relationships more generally. One of the approaches to item analysis which is suggested then by this complaint of Hoffmann's is a more thorough analysis of the item characteristic curve for each of the items in the pool being submitted to analysis. This is a wise and a needed procedure as has already been pointed out by Dr. Astin.

Now, I should like to consider more generally some of the assumptions made by other writers who have complained about psychological testing, including such persons as Vance Packard,

Jacques Barzun, Martin Gross, William Whyte, Allan Harrington and others.

One of the major assumptions running throughout these writings is that "mind" can't be measured. It would appear that most of these gentlemen feel that "mind" somehow is such a warm and mysterious human quality that they resist the idea of being able to learn or to predict anything about it. It is as if they seek to retain this particular "mystery system" as being outside the realm of scientific study. We know, of course, that if "mind" is defined as behavior, it can indeed be measured. As a matter of fact, as has already been stated, perhaps the greatest accomplishment of psychology thus far has been the measurement of the individuality of man. We know that we can, through various psychological techniques assess the individuality of persons and make rather good predictions about their future behavior. Perhaps the greatest recent success attesting to this is the selection of the Peace Corps candidates who are now serving overseas. I do not know what the current "hit rate" is for the Peace Corps selection project but I do know that of the first 600 persons who went overseas only 6 had to be returned and that 2 of these returned because of a death in the family. I would say that the assumptions that "mind" or behavior cannot be measured is entirely negated by the evidence we have at hand.

Secondly, the writers against psychological testing seem to make an assumption which is the exact opposite from that just discussed. They assume that testing will lead to conformity by picking persons who are all of the same mold or all of the same type. This, of course, assumes that "mind" can be measured only too well and is a sharp contradiction from the assumption that mind can't be measured. Of course we know that our psychological measures aren't *that* good but even if they were we have widespread evidence showing that the compensatory model seems to be of major significance for predicting behavior. Thus even though we have a series of tests which combine into a multiple prediction which is highly valid, we know that any given person would show a great deal of intra-individual trait variability. This was pointed up nicely by a recent study involving the early identification of management potential conducted by the Standard Oil Company of New Jersey. In their study it was possible to develop a battery with a cross-validated multiple correlation of .70 for identifying more effective and less effective managers. However, the managers did not fit a common mold when the various individual tests of the battery were examined. Some managers were high on one kind of test (such as verbal fluency); other managers, though low on this test, seemed to "make-up for it" by having a pattern of education and work experience in their backgrounds which compensated in a sense for their lower measured ability. Thus, again, one of the great principles of psychological testing which is ignored by these critics is the fact of intra-individual trait variability. The fact that people do differ within themselves has long been recognized and submitted to careful study by psychologists.

A third common complaint about psychological testing is that it is an invasion of privacy. It is possible that this criticism may have some merit. This is the point, of course, at which it is incumbent upon the users of psychological tests to demonstrate the validity of any items which might otherwise be regarded as an invasion of privacy. A major point usually ignored by critics of psychological testing when they discuss the invasion of privacy is the distinction between institutional and individual decisions. If a firm is using a test to assess candidates and an individual desires employment with that firm, the use of the test is for the purpose of helping the institution to make a hiring decision; the purpose is not to give guidance or to protect the privacy of the individuals being tested. It is true, but perhaps beside the point, that an increase in the accuracy of institutional decisions will, over the long run, be accompanied by an increasing proportion of accurate or "correct" individual decisions.

Finally, it should be noted that the critics very rarely suggest any alternatives to psychological testing. Gardner in his book, *Excellence*, says the following:

> "Anyone attacking the usefulness of the tests must suggest workable alternatives. It has been proven over and over again that the alternative methods of evaluating ability are subject to gross errors and capable of producing grave injustices."

Thus it would appear that the alternatives are to return to the Industrial Dark Ages when personnel decisions were made on the basis of hair color or shape of head or perhaps more realistically on the basis of family background or family status. Although most critics carefully avoid suggesting alternatives, Allen Harrington in his book, *Life in the Crystal Palace*, does suggest some interesting ones, on p. 60 he says,

"Once long ago it seems hiring was done in a rough and ready way. It still is by the firms that are too small to maintain an employee relations staff or by companies that expect a certain amount of turnover."

And on p. 61 he states further:

"Employer and applicant made an intuitive connection. By intuition, I mean perception through unconscious logic. We tried to see into each other beyond the things we said, behind the polite formalities. We sought to discover what the other was really like. Sometimes one was the victim of whimsical judgment. A businessman I know always scrutinized a visitor's shoes in order to determine his character. He could he said, "Read" an applicant by studying his footwear, the shine, the repair of the heels, and so on. Another employer after World War II despised anyone who had been in the Air Force. He was a former infantryman and had once been bombed and wounded by our own planes."

Thus it is apparent that the alternatives, when they are suggested, are clearly ridiculous. Let us consider, for example, how Harrington would have reacted to a personality test inventory which had the following three items in it:

1. My heels are often run down          True or False.

2. I love to have my shoes shined          True or False.

3. I worry a good deal about the appearance of          True or False. my feet.

Certainly items such as this would be received by great anguish and gnashing of teeth. However, they are simply objective statements of the examination of the visitor's shoes which seems in Harrington's rather inconsistent manner of thinking to be a preferred selection technique.

### CONCLUSION

I believe that our careful examination of the assumptions made by the various critics of psychological testing can lead to only one conclusion: The basic assumptions are erroneous and fallacious; they are based for the most part on lack of information, as apparently is the case for Hoffmann, or more seriously on a refusal to accept the strong evidence showing that individuality *can* be assessed with *accuracy* and in such a way as to give better recognition to real merit than has ever before been the case in either our educational or industrial institutions.

---

## 4.3   When Are Test Scores Different?

*James L. Lister*

A crucial area of educational and psychological assessment involves making behavioral inferences from test information. Lister suggests an important first step in judging the significance of differences in test scores. Serious interpretive errors can result when observed test score *differences* reflect chance or random errors. The suggestions in this article will aid interpretation through the use of a simple statistic to distinguish between real and chance differences.

A trend in educational and psychological testing has been the development of tests which yield several scores. Multi-score tests now provide the counselor with scores that purport to measure independently several components of intelligence as well as achievement in a half-dozen subject areas. While the decisions for which test information is sought should usually be based on several kinds of information, the use of multi-score tests presents counselors with one difficult problem: how large a difference between two subtest scores should a counselor demand before he is willing to conclude that the *true scores* are really different?

An individual's *true score* refers to the average of all the scores he might obtain by taking an unlimited number of equivalent forms of the same test. It is assumed that the characteristic being measured remains unchanged, and the variation among obtained scores is a result of random errors of measurement. Since any one test score is subject to random variation, *differences* between test scores are also somewhat unstable. This paper is an attempt to aid counselors in taking account of the instability of score differences.

Reprinted with permission of the author and *The School Counselor*, Dec. 1964.

For example, what should the counselor conclude about the following discrepancy between a student's scores?

Reading comprehension—42nd percentile rank.

Arithmetic computation—68th percentile rank.

The difference of 26 percentile ranks certainly *appears* large enough to constitute a real difference. There are, as will be explained later, more than five chances [1] in one hundred (assuming the average reliability of the subtests is .90) that the observed difference results from random errors rather than a true difference in abilities.

This paper provides a method for reliably determining the significance of such profile [2] differences.

Apparent differences between scores often serve as the basis for such interpretative statements as these:

"Your mechanical aptitude is not as high as your verbal fluency."

"Your reading comprehension is low in relation to your reading speed."

"Considering the difference between your verbal and quantitative scores, your chances for success are probably greater in journalism than in engineering."

"You're surprised to find your Persuasive score higher than your Artistic score?" [3]

---

[1] This refers to a significance level of 5%. The writer recommends this level for interpreting scores to students. When providing information to students, few counselors would be willing to risk more than five chances in one hundred of interpreting a random difference as a real one.

[2] "Profile" refers to a graphic or tabular presentation of a student's results on *one test* which yields two or more separate scores. The principles of profile interpretation also apply to comparisons of one student's scores on different tests. When this is done, however, two conditions must be met: (a) scores on the different tests must be reported in the same score form, and (b) all tests must be based on the same or equivalent normative groups. Some test publishers (Educational Testing Service and California Test Bureau, for example) have used the same standardization groups for two related tests, usually academic aptitude and achievement. When the different tests are not standardized on the same group, it is difficult to determine whether the norm groups can be considered equivalent.

[3] Interpretation of score differences on forced-choice inventories such as the *Kuder Preference Record* present difficulties beyond those considered in this paper. For discussion of such problems, see Robert H. Bauernfiend. "The Matter of Ipsative Scores." *Personnel and Guidance Journal*, 1962, **41**, 210–217.

Each of the preceding statements is based upon the assumption that the observed difference between two scores is sufficient evidence of a corresponding difference between the two traits, abilities, or dimensions represented by the scores. Too often such assumptions are invalid.

When a difference is observed between a pair of subtest scores on a test profile, a counselor must follow one of two courses of action:

1. *He may conclude that the observed difference is negligible and that the scores indicate essentially the same standing on both tests.* In other words, the counselor assumes that differences as large as those observed would frequently result from random errors of measurement, even when the student's true score on subtests A and B are equal.

2. *He may conclude that the observed difference is large enough to indicate that the student differs in terms of his standing on the two tests.* In this case, the counselor assumes that if the student's true scores, on subtests A and B are equal, random errors of measurement would rarely produce a difference of this size.

Without stable guidelines, counselors are likely to differ in their interpretations of marginal score differences. Some differences are often large or small enough to present no problems of interpretation. Borderline differences, however, do not clearly warrant either interpretative decision. When in doubt, Counselor X may ignore observed differences between scores, (Alternative 1) whereas Counselor Y may emphasize such differences as real and meaningful, (Alternative 2). Such preference may represent constant, stable biases: the bias of Counselor X tends to *withhold* reliable information from students; the bias of Counselor Y tends to provide them with *erroneous information.* It is, therefore, essential that the counselor make unbiased decisions regarding score differences. While most counselors would agree that the student should be responsible for final decisions, counselors have an ethical responsibility for clearly and accurately reporting test results. A counselor should not overlook any technique that reduces the probability of providing students with invalid information about themselves.

## A RECOMMENDED PROCEDURE

To enable counselors to avoid the dangers outlined above, the following suggestions are given. These suggestions permit counselors

to interpret profile differences with a minimum of error and computation. This approach allows counselors to determine differences
with a 5 per cent margin of error. By following this procedure,
therefore, a counselor would be in error approximately five times
for every 100 differences he interprets to students.

This procedure is based upon a statistical measure called the
*standard error of a difference*. Such a measure is used to describe the
range of differences between scores on two subtests. Thus, if the
standard error of a difference between two scores is 5 points, one
would expect to find a difference greater than 5 points in favor of
either subtest about 32 times in 100. A difference of 10 points or
more in favor of either subtest (twice the standard error of the
difference) should occur only about five times in 100.

Although the *standard error of measurement* has sometimes been
recommended as a way of interpreting profile differences, it is
actually an inappropriate technique, since it provides only an estimate of the variability of a person's score on *one separate* subtest.
The standard error of the difference, however, provides an estimate
of the fluctuation or instability of the *differences* between a person's
scores on *two separate subtests*. Use of the standard error of measurement requires a larger difference between two scores than is
actually necessary. Reliance upon it would, therefore, lead counselors to ignore profile differences which reflect real differences in the
characteristics measured.

The standard error of a difference is not included in many test
manuals. Notable exceptions include the *Cooperative General
Achievement Tests*, the *1963 California Tests of Mental Maturity*,
and the *Differential Aptitude Tests*. When not reported in the test
manual, the standard error of a difference can be computed from the
formula:

$$
\begin{matrix} \text{the standard error} \\ \text{of a difference} \end{matrix} = \sqrt{\left(\begin{matrix}\text{standard error of}\\ \text{measurement of}\\ \text{Subtest 1}\end{matrix}\right)^2 + \left(\begin{matrix}\text{standard error of}\\ \text{measurement of}\\ \text{Subtest 2}\end{matrix}\right)^2}.
$$

Multiplying the standard error of a difference by 1.96 gives the size
of the difference large enough to give a counselor a 5 percent
margin of error in interpreting differences. The value 1.96 is used
because 1.96 standard deviations on both sides of the mean include
95 percent of the area under a normal curve.

TABLE 1    T-SCORE EQUIVALENTS OF PERCENTILE RANKS

| Percentile Rank | T-Score | Percentile Rank | T-Score | Percentile Rank | T-Score |
|---|---|---|---|---|---|
| 99 | 73 | 71–74 | 56 | 18–19 | 41 |
| 98 | 71 | 68–70 | 55 | 15–17 | 40 |
| 97 | 69 | 64–67 | 54 | 13–14 | 39 |
| 96 | 68 | 60–63 | 53 | 11–12 | 38 |
| 95 | 67 | 56–59 | 52 | 9–10 | 37 |
| 94 | 66 | 51–55 | 51 | 8 | 36 |
| 93 | 65 | 50– | 50 | 7 | 35 |
| 92 | 64 | 45–49 | 49 | 6 | 34 |
| 90–91 | 63 | 41–44 | 48 | 5 | 33 |
| 88–89 | 62 | 37–40 | 47 | 4 | 32 |
| 86–87 | 61 | 33–36 | 46 | 3 | 31 |
| 83–85 | 60 | 30–32 | 45 | 2 | 29 |
| 81–82 | 59 | 26–29 | 44 | 1 | 27 |
| 78–80 | 58 | 23–25 | 43 | | |
| 75–77 | 57 | 20–22 | 42 | | |

Example: Suppose that a ninth-grade student earned scaled scores of 12 and 15, respectively, on the vocabulary and mathematics subtests of an achievement test. Should the counselor emphasize the difference or ignore it? To answer the question, we find that in grade nine the standard error of measurement was:

vocabulary      3 scaled score points
mathematics    4 scaled score points

The standard error of the difference between these two tests is equal to:

$$\sqrt{(3)^2 + (4)^2} = \sqrt{25} = 5.$$

And, $1.96 \times 5 = 9.80$. Since the observed difference of 3 scaled score points is much less than the obtained value, the counselor should assume that the student has the same relative standing in these two areas.

When standard errors of measurement are not reported in the same type of unit employed in profile interpretation, the procedure described below should be followed. This requires finding percentile rank equivalents of profile scores.

TABLE 2    INTER-TEST DIFFERENCES REQUIRED FOR INTER-
PRETATION

| Average Reliability of Two Tests | Differences in T-Score Units Required for Interpretation |
|:---:|:---:|
| .95 | 6.2 |
| .90 | 8.8 |
| .85 | 10.7 |
| .80 | 12.4 |
| .75 | 13.9 |
| .70 | 15.2 |
| .65 | 16.4 |
| .60 | 17.5 |
| .55 | 18.6 |
| .50 | 19.6 |

*Source:* After Cronbach, L. J., *Essentials of Psychological Testing.* New York: Harper
and Brothers, Inc., 1960, p. 287.

Several multi-score tests report scores as percentile rank equivalents. In such instances, counselors can reliably determine whether differences between pairs of scores should be considered true by the following steps:

1. Using Table 1, convert the percentile ranks to T-scores.

2. Find the difference between the two T-scores.

3. Find the average reliability of the two subtests.

4. Compare the obtained T-score difference with the corresponding value in Table 2.

If the obtained difference is equal to or greater than the value in Table 2, the difference could be interpreted as significant. Otherwise, it should be disregarded.[4]

*Example:* Suppose that on an interest inventory, a student's percentile ranks were 35 and 76 respectively, on the commercial and mechanical subtests. Obviously a difference of 31 percentile ranks *appears* quite meaningful. The procedure outlined above gives a more definite answer, however. By reference to Table 1, we find

---

[4] It must be remembered that there is a variable relationship between percentile ranks and T-scores. Thus, a difference of five percentile ranks near the middle of the distribution (35 and 40, for example) would be equivalent to only one T-score unit, but near the extremes of the distribution (90 and 95, for example), the same difference would be equivalent to four T-score units.

that the T-score equivalents of these percentile ranks are 46 and 57. The difference between them is 11. The average reliability of the two subtests is .85; therefore, the difference just exceeds the required difference of 10.7 T-score units. One would be justified in concluding that this student's true score on the mechanical subtest exceeds his true score on the clerical subtest.

Counselors who interpret Scholastic Aptitude Test scores to students should note that the T-score values in Table 2 can be converted to College Board scores by multiplying them by 10 (T-scores have a mean and standard deviation of 50 and 10, while comparable values for College Board scores are 500 and 100). Since the average reliability of the Verbal and Mathematics sections of the Scholastic Aptitude Test is around .90, observed differences must equal 88 points before they can be considered significant.

Most of the steps described above are clerical in nature. With some supervision, a secretary could determine the size of differences required for all tests used in the school testing program. A few hours of clerical time seems a modest expenditure for increased reliability in the interpretation of test results.

---

## 4.4   Norms Must Be Relevant
*Harold G. Seashore and James H. Ricks, Jr.*

One of the first procedures teachers can use in the selection of appropriate tests is an analysis of the norm group for standardized tests. In this article the authors suggest some crucial considerations in the interpretation of tests based upon the concept of a norm. It is important to know that a standardized test could be valid and reliable, but totally inappropriate for certain populations of pupils.

The usual purpose of testing is to understand someone better— whether it be a child in school, a patient in a clinic, a youth planning his career, an applicant for a job, an employee being considered for

From *Test Service Bulletin No.* 39. Reprinted with permission of The Psychological Corporation, N. Y.

promotion, a soldier being classified for special training, or an older person seeking help in adjusting to retirement. Usually, we wish to make predictions of future behavior. Two things are essential if testing is to contribute to understanding the individual: the test chosen must be *appropriate for the person and the purpose of the testing*, and we must know something about *how others have performed on the test*. Norms provide this second essential. Even if a test is appropriate, reliable, and valid, a score obtained from it is meaningless until it is compared with other scores.

Here we encounter another essential: not only must we have other scores for purposes of comparison, but these other scores—the norms—must be *relevant*. They will be meaningless or even misleading if they are not based on groups of people with whom it is sensible to compare the individuals we are counseling or considering for employment. Seems obvious, doesn't it? But, perhaps because it does seem so obvious, the relevance of norms often receives less attention than the number of cases or the way the norms are expressed.

This is going to be a discussion of relevance—a consideration of whether, and when, norms mean anything. We will assume throughout the rest of this argument that the number of cases in the normative group is large enough to assure stability, and that all the proper statistical requirements have been met. We will not worry about whether the norms are expressed as standard scores, percentiles, ratios, age or grade equivalents, or cut-off scores. The question is what kind of norms (provided they are appropriately computed and expressed and are stable) do we need in order to make intelligent use of somebody's test score.

*Norms should yield meaning in terms of the particular purpose for which the testing is done.* Because tests are given for a variety of reasons, a variety of kinds of norms is needed. Many of the persons we test should have their scores evaluated by comparison with several reference groups.

Suppose Sue has a score of 152 points on the *General Clerical Test*. She is a senior in a commercial high school finishing the secretarial course. Her advisor, fortunately, not only has available the norms tables in the 1950 edition of the manual for this test but also has accumulated (a) norms in her own school on the past three successive classes of girls finishing in the commercial department, (b) the same information for the secretarial course, and (c) the norms tables or cut-off scores for three local companies which recruit girls from this school. Let us look at Sue's "status" which she, her counselor, and a local employment manager desire to understand better.

1. In comparison with commercial high school senior girls in general, Sue's percentile rank is

    a) from the manual ................................. 85

    b) on local senior norms ........................... 75

2. In comparison with commercial high school senior girls finishing secretarial training, Sue's rank is

    a) from the manual ................................ 75

    b) on local norms .................................. 60

3. Sue's percentile rank can also be determined

    a) on firm X's *all-clerical-applicant* norms .............. 60

    b) on firm X's *secretarial applicant* norms ............... 32

4. Firm Y sets a critical score of 130 for all office workers and 150 for stenographic applicants.

5. Firm Z has set 175 points as its minimum score for considering a beginning stenographer.*

We shall not go into detail about how the counselor and employment officer would use these data, since the reader can readily appreciate the richness of interpretation which is made possible by having more than one set of norms. It is clear that a person's score may have many meanings.

Frequently test publishers encounter a desire for *norms based on the "general population."* It is an understandable desire. Testing without a clearly understood purpose in mind may or may not be forgivable; but in fact test users have been known to start with little more than a vague intention to help somebody toward success or to help themselves choose better workers. Having given the *Minnesota Clerical Test* to Bill, who is male, eighteen years old, a recent graduate from high school, and interested in becoming an accountant, they may be confused when faced with the necessity of deciding whether to use norms that compare him with others of his age,

---

*It should scarcely need stressing that besides *General Clerical Test* scores other factors (such as her stenographic proficiency) will enter into considering Sue's employability. Maybe Firm Z has to consider that she is a daughter of an important customer!

or those comparing him with his educational equals, or those representing employed accountants. So, down in the records goes Bill's percentile rank based on the general (or at least the male adult) population—probably the least useful of all the possible ratings that could have been assigned to him.

Historically, the concepts of mental age and intelligence quotient (and the related educational age and educational quotient) were based on an assumption of complete generality of the norms. World War I yielded Alpha and Beta norms on young-enlisted-men-in-general; in later use, the words "young soldier" were frequently read as simply "adult." When we find that Ned has an IQ of 110, we would like to read into that value a comparison of Ned with all children—at least with those of his age in our broad American culture. Nowadays, of course, sophisticated test users generally realize that even the best sampling available has failed to represent some groups—regional, racial, socio-economic, or the like—in their proper proportions.

There are a few situations—primarily clinical ones—in which we really desire to compare Ned and Bill and Sue with children-in-general and Miss Zembro and Mr. Arnold with adults-in-general. The measurement of a person's abilities—particularly over-all general intelligence—in terms of national norms is sometimes desired. For instance, a broad and representative basis for comparison is needed for evaluating children suspected of a mental defect or for estimating reading readiness among kindergarten children. In surveys, national norms may be used to discover the status of a group (say eighth graders in a city) or to judge the educational success of the community in training their youngsters.

However, there is a serious limitation of the use of such national norms in counseling and personnel work. It helps little to know that Sue's score on a clerical test places her at the 63rd percentile on some people-in-general norms. We are not counseling her in general or employing her in general. We need at least the specificity of norms which will permit us to interpret her score in terms of high school graduates and in terms of women only, because the labor market she is entering consists mainly of high school graduates and because we know that she will be competing for a job with women (who, as a group, excel men in most clerical tasks).

*Legitimate and illegitimate general norms abound in current test manuals.* People-in-general norms are legitimate only if they are based upon careful field studies with appropriate controls of regional, socio-economic, educational, and other factors—and even then only if the sampling is carefully described so that the test user may be fully aware of its inevitable limitations and deficiencies. The millions entering the armed forces during World War II provided the basis for some fairly good norms on young adult men, though mainly on tests not available to the public. The standardization of the *Wechsler Intelligence Scale for Children* is a recent attempt to secure a representative smaller sample of children aged 5–15 for setting up tables of intelligence quotients which may be considered generalized norms for children. The earlier work of Terman's group to set up good national norms on a small, well-chosen sample is well known. In the standardizing of some educational achievement tests, nationwide samplings of children of each appropriate grade or age and from different types of schools in all parts of the country are sought in an effort to produce norms that are truly general for a given span of grades or ages.

Unfortunately, many alleged general norms reported in test manuals are not backed even by an honest effort to secure representative samples of people-in-general. Even tens or hundreds of thousands of cases can fall woefully short of defining people-in-general. Inspection of test manuals will show (or would show if information about the norms were given completely) that many such massed norms are merely collections of all the scores that opportunity has permitted the author or publisher to gather easily. Lumping together all the samples secured more by chance than by plan makes for impressively large numbers; but while seeming to simplify interpretation, the norms may dim or actually distort the counseling, employment, or diagnostic significance of a score.

With or without a plan, everyone of course obtains data where and how he can. Since the standardization of a test is always dependent on the cooperation of educators, psychologists and personnel men, the foregoing comments are not a plea for the rejection of available samples but for their correct labeling. If a manual shows "general" norms for a vocabulary test based on a sample two-thirds of which consists of women office workers, one can properly raise his testwise eyebrows. There is no reason to accept such norms as a good generalization of adult—or even of employed-adult-vocabulary. It is better to set up norms on the occupationally homogeneous two-thirds of the group and frankly call them norms on female office workers. Adding a few more miscellaneous cases does not make the sample a truly general one.

As a rule, then, in reading a test manual we should reject as treacherous any alleged national or general norms whose generality is not supported by a clear, complete report on the sample of people they represent, or norms which are obviously opportunistic accumulations of samples weighted by their size according to chance rather than logic. *Look for the evidence!*

* * *

The dilemma of the test publisher is acute. It is difficult to provide genuinely general norms when these are desirable, and it is impossible to supply all the detailed norms that would be useful.

If the author and the publisher decide that general or national norms are appropriate, they must accept the responsibility of obtaining scores from representative groups and of combining the groups in accordance with a plan that makes sense when compared with census data. No less a responsibility is the reporting in detail of the sources of the data and the rationale of any adjustments that may have been made. If they cannot do this, or choose not to, the limitations of the norms must be properly described. Attempts to hodge-podge handy data into one mass normative table merit severe criticism.

But suppose the publisher and author agree that they have no truly national norms and furthermore do not believe them useful for the test in question. What choices do they then have? The *number* and the *variety* of less-than-general groups are crushing. In theory, norms should be collected for every meaningful subgroup of the population against which any individual's test scores might be compared. Ideally, the *General Clerical Test* (for example) should have tables of norms for many educational levels, experience levels, age levels, fields of clerical work, and for various combinations of these. Furthermore, there should be regional norms, state norms perhaps, local community norms, and finally, specific norms for each firm and school using the test. No one would need all of these but someone would find use for each of them! Eventually it may be hoped that we will even have norms for test scores earned in adolescence by persons grouped according to the job in which they succeeded as adults.

The test user probably never will have at hand all the varieties of norms he really wants and needs. Even the most excellent test manuals do not present enough tables of norms, although those included in the better manuals are well-documented and very useful. What then is the solution of the test author's and publisher's dilemma? How can the test user help himself? By way of summary let us try to formulate a few principles which can serve as practical guides.

1. *Avoid unjustified "general" norms.* Undocumented, people-in-general norms should not be presented because there is no cogent reason for collecting, publishing or using them.

2. *Define national norms.* So-called national norms on tests should be carefully expressed as generalizations for important and sense-making subgroups, such as the grade groups on the *Metropolitan Achievement* or the *Differential Aptitude Tests*, or the age groups on the *Wechsler Intelligence Scale for Children.* In the case of national or regional norms especially is it essential that the sampling procedure be described in sufficient detail for understanding and evaluation by others.

3. *Combine populations with care, and only when the resulting group has definite meaning.* Lumping several groups is as logical, in some instances, as presenting them separately. For example, in the 1950 revision of the *General Clerical Test* Manual all of the samples of *female applicants for office work* were lumped (after being presented separately). The publisher sought data wherever they might be found rather than by plan, but the grouping seemed sensible in order to provide a starting basis for users who have not yet established local norms. As in the case of national norms, it is absolutely essential that the original groups entering such a composite norms table be described and that the reasons which justify combining them be stated plainly. At all times, the distortion that results from merging incongruous data into improperly weighted larger groupings (usually done only in order to make the number of cases look more impressive) should be avoided.

4. *Report all the genuinely useful data available.* Lacking data on the enormous variety of educational, occupational, or clinical groups which would be needed to provide *all* the possible sets of norms, authors and publishers must of course present what data they have available. It would have been unfortunate if failure to cover *all* trades and professions had prevented E. K. Strong, Jr., from providing us with the scoring scales that he was able to develop for his

*Vocational Interest Blank.* There is a healthy trend in manuals such as those for the *Bennett Mechanical Comprehension Test Form AA*, the *Wesman Personnel Classification Test*, the *Kuder Preference Record*, and others, to present percentile equivalents or other norms for a dozen or more described groups. Small and ill-defined groups should be omitted from the standardization tables and reported only if they are of very special interest for some reason.

5. *Accumulate and use local and special-group norms.* Local norms should be constructed by the user for appropriate groupings of cases. This is of great importance, both for personnel selection tests used by a firm and for tests used in educational and vocational counseling. It may be necessary to begin by using reasonably appropriate norms published in the test manual, but local norms should be prepared as soon as a hundred or more cases have been accumulated and should be revised from time to time as the testing program continues and additional data become available. While published percentile or standard score norms may provide a temporary starting point, cut-off scores for hiring purposes should be established *only* on the basis of specific local experience and not merely taken from published reports.

6. *Feed local and special norms back to help build the body of knowledge available to test users.* Better norms can be made available in test manuals only if psychologists, educators, counselors, and personnel men accept a responsibility almost as demanding as the responsibility of the author and publisher. Tests are useful to us because of the work that others have already invested in them; we can repay this debt by contributing our own experience to the common treasury of normative and other data. This may be accomplished by articles in professional journals, or simply by sending the data to the publisher for inclusion in revisions of test manuals. If anyone is uncertain as to the appropriate methods of collecting data so that they will be useful to others as well as in his own daily work, The Psychological Corporation on request will gladly suggest recording and reporting methods.

No meaningful information can emerge from testing Sue, Bill, Ned, Miss Zembro or Mr. Arnold unless we can evaluate their raw scores by means of norms which are relevant to our reasons for testing these individuals in the first place. Our better understanding of an individual through tests depends, then, largely upon our having diverse and well-defined sets of norms. Such accumulation of norms is a duty of authors and publishers. And the thousands of test administrators hold a key position in developing these more useful and interpretable bases for comparing test performances.

# 5 *Measuring Cognitive Variables*

## 5.1 Misconceptions About Intelligence Testing

*Warren R. Good*

Warren R. Good, in this article, reaches the conclusion that misinterpretation of psychological test data is a common fault of those using tests. Do you agree? He objects to the concept of a nonverbal IQ. Is his reasoning a justification for abolishing the use of nonverbal instruments? Many test users see nonverbal tests as extremely advantageous. What specific benefits can be derived from the use of nonverbal tests? Try to formulate the reasons why in choosing an intelligence test, the tester must examine the test, item by item, to be reasonably certain it is appropriate for his purposes.

There seems to be a lot of confusion nowadays about intelligence tests and the meaning of intelligence quotients. For example, many teachers now in service have been taught that 60 percent of the children have IQ's 90–109, 14 percent 110–119 and again 80–89, 6 percent 120–129 and 70–79, 1 percent above 130, and 1 percent below 70; and that those with IQ's below 70 are feebleminded. None of this is "true" today. Many teachers have been easily converted to an ill-founded confidence in verbal and nonverbal IQ's, primary abilities, and culture-free tests. Whatever the merits of these "newer" developments may be, teachers should choose and interpret on the basis of understanding rather than acceptance of propaganda. These and other blunders apparently result from poor knowledge of fundamental intelligence-test theory.

When we try to measure intelligence we seek an indication of *capacity* for learning and adaptation. This indication must be obtained by inference, because the potentiality for development is

Reprinted with permission of the author and *University of Michigan School of Education Bulletin*, May 1954.

constantly in the process of being realized. Hence we must resort to the assumption that mental ability—what the individual knows and can do on intellectual tasks—will vary with capacity if opportunities for development and motivation have been equal. And we infer "intelligence" from mental ability. But we cannot measure ability directly, either; what we measure is performance. And so, it goes like this: we measure performance, from which we infer ability, from which we infer capacity.

The basic conditions for validity of our inferences—equality of opportunity and motivation—demand what might reasonably be called "normal" environment, comparable, so far as test effects are concerned, with that of the children on whom the test was standardized. And opportunities to have learned the kinds of things involved in the specific test items must be equalized. Our chances of getting such equalization are certainly best at zero (no opportunity at all) and infinity, or to be practical, at *plenty*—far more opportunity than would be needed to learn the thing if the individual were mature enough. For example, children have abundant opportunities to learn what arms, legs, nose, ears, and hair are, and to learn the names and uses of familiar household objects. Intelligence tests are often at fault because a good many items relate to special interests or opportunities, but even the best tests will be unsatisfactory for some children in almost any group, because of differences in background.

Once this principle of equal opportunity is understood, teachers can judge for themselves whether test items are suitable for measuring intelligence, and will soon learn to choose good tests for the purpose. In the last analysis the validity of intelligence test items always depends on judgment.

The pathetic arguments favoring "nonverbal IQ's" for duller children are at best questionable. In general, language is a highly sensitive indicator of intelligence and, barring specific handicap, there is no evidence that those who cannot understand or use their native language with facility are likely to be endowed with some special kind of "general mental ability" that cannot be adequately measured by verbal tests. The issue here, as always in intelligence testing, is equality of opportunity to have learned the kind of thing demanded. One technique for evening out the accidental differences in opportunity is to sample broadly from the many types of items and activities that are judged to show "relative facility in learning." But, to avoid language in an intelligence test is to reject the most versatile and most important means of communicating thought. In case of specific handicap—defect of speech or hearing, or difference of languages—we resort to non-language tests through necessity, not because they are "just as good." Even for young children, our best intelligence tests make considerable use of language, although that does not necessarily mean having the pupil read—which is not a suitable means of setting the task unless he can read well enough for the purpose.

I have just been examining the test booklets filled out by 133 high school students on a test which purports to yield a verbal and a nonverbal IQ. The correlation between the two is only .36 for this group, and the helter-skelter differences are highly questionable in consideration of (1) the very unsatisfactory statistical characteristics of the subtests, (2) the dubious validity of many specific items, and (3) internal evidence on the quality of responses.

As for verbal and nonverbal IQ's, there has never been any justification for such terminology. What we have is verbal and nonverbal test items or tests, all designed to measure general intelligence; and if IQ's obtained with verbal and nonverbal tests differ greatly there is reason for grave doubt of the validity of either or both.

The broad sampling needed for good intelligence tests may have to be restricted for special purposes, such as obtaining comparable measurements where languages differ or cultural patterns are conspicuously dissimilar. Such an attempt was illustrated by the "culture-free" tests which have been so severely criticized. Here too, the major criterion is equality of opportunity to have learned the kind of thing demanded, and American schools do not require the exclusion of the common culture to achieve cultural fairness in intelligence tests. To exclude it is to throw out our most useful indicators of mental ability.

The search for "primary mental abilities" is concerned with finding the major components of the groups of abilities which may be judged to reflect intelligence. But so far, competent analysts are not agreed on the identification of such abilities or on the validity of tests which purport to measure them as separate abilities.

A common characteristic of intelligence tests is that they yield IQ's. The original Binet tests measured directly in mental age credits, but nearly all tests nowadays are point scales, the IQ's being determined statistically from the distribution of point scores. If these determinations were valid in relation to the definition of an IQ, the distributions of IQ's obtained from the various tests on the market would be alike—they would have the same standard deviation—and the IQ's would be comparable, in this respect, at least. But these standard deviations vary from about 10 to about 26; so a very bright youngster might have, taking extremes, an IQ of 130 on one test and an IQ of 178 on another. Or, a child might have an IQ of 80 on one test and be judged a bit subnormal, and have an IQ of 48 on another and be classified as an imbecile.

The standard deviation of IQ's on the first Stanford-Binet scale was about 13. The distribution of IQ's given in the first paragraph of this article was based on that scale, which has been obsolete since 1937, when it was superseded by the present revision. The newer standard deviation is reported as 16.4, and makers of many other intelligence tests now try to get about the same dispersion—with considerably varying degrees of success.

An IQ, then, is likely to be a pretty shifty measure of mental ability unless it is interpreted in terms of how commonly such an IQ occurs in the general population; that is, in terms of the statistical characteristics of the test used. The IQ's yielded by different tests cannot be assumed to be comparable. At least some teachers in each school, therefore, should know enough about elementary statistics to make the necessary analysis.

Many teachers are disturbed by the increasing numbers of "feeble-minded" children in school, as indicated by IQ's below 70. As Tredgold pointed out many years ago, the sound definition of feeble-mindedness refers to the lowest $x$ percent of the population. Without an agreement on $x$, we formerly had estimates running all the way from one feeble-minded person in 2500 to one in 16. The American consensus on what $x$ should be was expressed for the old Stanford-Binet as the portion having IQ's below 70. That was 1 percent. On the present Stanford-Binet it's nearly 4 percent. To identify the feeble-minded as the lowest 1 percent nowadays we should take those with IQ's below 60 on the Stanford-Binet and other tests with similar IQ dispersion.

The term IQ has been so grossly abused and it is so inappropriate to the shifting values yielded by various tests the writer thinks that we probably should abandon it altogether. The test scores would be far easier to interpret if the school made its own conversion of the raw point scores into standard scores of some sort (Z-scores, for example, which have a mean of 50 and a standard deviation of 10), and made comparisons with national norms if requisite data were available.

In any case, I should say that we do too much intelligence testing and then misinterpret—or ignore—the results. Once in three or four years should be often enough to measure a student's mental ability, and the tests then used should not attempt the speculative or the impossible. In considering tests for selection, fancy claims and high costs should be automatically suspect, and tests under favorable consideration should be carefully studied (and actually taken by the teachers who made the selection) to make judgments of local validity, ease of administration and scoring, adequacy of manuals, and so on. Finally, the results of the intelligence testing should be interpreted in light of the characteristics of the test used, and especially —until we can do better—of the IQ distribution for that test.

---

## 5.2 American Attitudes toward Intelligence Tests
### Orville G. Brim, Jr.

Testing always occurs in a social context. This article recommends that a more professional use of intelligence tests will serve to allay some of the many misgivings people have about the use of tests. Do you agree? What specific suggestions do you have to help meet the common objectives of psychological tests? Do the objectives cited suggest a dilemma or do you feel some concrete attempts can be developed to solve this recurring controversy?

"Given tests as they are now, do you think it is fair (that is, just) to use intelligence tests to help make the following decisions?"

To decide who can go to certain colleges
To put children into special classes in school

Reprinted with permission of the author and *American Psychologists*, Feb. 1965.

To decide who should be hired for a job
To decide who should be promoted

If one asks a representative group of Americans over 18 these questions, he finds that many of them are against the use of intelligence tests. Forty-one percent are opposed to using tests to help decide on admission of students to colleges; 37% are against using tests in job selection, and 50% against their use to help decide on job promotions; about one-fourth are opposed to using intelligence tests to help establish special classes in school.

One might expect that a younger group of respondents, having had more experiences with tests, would be more favorable in their attitudes. This is not true. High school students in the United States are even more strongly opposed to the use of intelligence tests. Fifty-three percent are against using tests in job hiring; 62% against their use in deciding on promotion; and 54% think it unfair to use tests to help select students for colleges. Almost half are even opposed to using intelligence tests to help in establishing special classes in schools.

How are we to account for this opposition to the use of standardized ability tests by such a substantial number of Americans? Psychologists have the primary responsibility in this country for the development and use of tests in the national interest. Only by facing the existence of a strong antitesting sentiment in the population, by making a professional appraisal of its causes, and by taking effective action will their responsibility be discharged.

Two years ago Russell Sage Foundation began a program of research on the social consequences of standardized ability tests. The data just reported come from two opinion surveys which are part of the program. In the first study a national sample of 1,500 adults was interviewed. In the second study a questionnaire was administered to 10,000 students in a national sample of 60 secondary schools; these included 40 public, 10 private, and 10 parochial schools. The data reported here are from the 40 public high schools, with over 5,000 respondents.

Results of the two surveys are only partially analyzed at this point, but they do provide some insights and hypotheses about antitesting sentiment. This report is divided into two parts. The first deals with five criticisms of tests. The second goes on to examine the basic sources of these criticisms as they arise from human nature and society.

## CRITICISMS OF TESTS

When we examine antitesting sentiment as expressed by both lay and professional groups today we find one or more of the following issues to be involved:

Inaccessibility of test data
Invasion of privacy
Rigidity in use of test scores
Types of talent selected by tests
Fairness of tests to minority groups

Consider the first, the inaccessibility of records. It is natural for a person to have an interest in any facts about himself. If someone else knows something about him that he, himself, does not know, then, of course, he will try to find it out, especially if it is something of such importance as his intelligence test score.

Most secondary school students believe that they should be told the actual scores they get on ability tests; but they are not getting this information now. Although almost all of them wish they had received specific, precise information about their test performance, 38% got no feedback at all, and another 24% got only a general idea. Adults, of course, are interested in their children's intelligence, yet 34% of those in our national sample reporting that their children took at least one test never got any information about their children's test performances.

I know the reasons we do not, routinely, give information to people about their test scores. One is that those who do poorly may find the information disturbing. Another is the possible misinterpretation of test scores, and their too rigid use by the inexperienced (a child may be labeled both in his own mind and his parents' as a result of his early test performance).

Even so, it seems to me to be callous on our part to go on ignoring the natural interest of the respondent in his performance, and denying him reasonable information. The American Psychological Association's Committee on Psychological Assessment has recommended that research be undertaken on the effects of communicating psychological information, including experimentation with different methods of feedback. But we cannot wait for research to be completed to start work on a coherent and sensible policy: Steps must be taken to establish a collaborative relationship between tester and respondent in which both gain information of value to them.

A second major criticism of testing is that it constitutes an invasion of privacy. This is a growing concern to many persons because test data are a key part of the new concept of the career record or dossier, which will accompany a person throughout his life. But, who is to keep the record and who is to have access to it? This criticism, to be sure, is directed more to tests of motives, beliefs, and attitudes than to tests of intelligence; but it is pertinent to our general theme, because if legislation is ever passed eliminating personality tests, intelligence tests could well be destroyed along with them.

Psychologists have defended the use of personality inventories by claiming that the data would be confidential, its access limited to competent research persons. The fact is that confidentiality cannot be protected. Psychologists are misinformed in thinking that test responses have the character of a privileged communication. Test results are subject to subpoena by any group with proper legal authority and easily can become a matter of public record.

Therefore, many are concerned about the legal rights of the individual to refuse to give out information about himself. The concern is legitimate and we must listen. The issue is: Under what conditions can the state invade an individual's right to privacy? Where national security is at stake, the state can invade; for instance, conscription, and the psychological testing associated with it, is legitimate. Also justified is the use of intelligence and achievement tests in the nation's public education system, for it is a valuable diagnostic device helping the school system do a better job of educating the students.

But, even though testing by psychologists often is justified on the ground that it benefits the respondents, there are many occasions when the use of tests by psychologists invades privacy without justification. Indeed, one could question the legitimacy of asking the questions reported on subsequently in this paper—questions which were asked of a "captive audience" of public high school students. Perhaps one justifies it because of its eventual contribution to knowledge, on the assumption that the growth of social science knowledge is a public good. But is this really sufficient? A serious matter is involved here, and psychologists must work through their moral philosophy on this point and chart a new section in our code of ethics.

A third objection to tests is their use early in the life of an individual to determine his life chances. Rigid use of tests makes no allowance for possible changes in either the person or his future environments. This is all the more a point for criticism because the public believes that intelligence increases throughout life, viewing it more as knowledge and wisdom than as a quality with a large genetic component.

The public attitude toward intelligence is shown by our survey data in a number of ways. Half of our high school respondents say intelligence tests measure mostly (or only) learned knowledge, while only 13% view tests as measuring mostly inborn talent. The high school students (three quarters of them) say that intelligence increases throughout life, that their older siblings are more intelligent than they, and that while they are not as smart as their fathers right now, they will be considerably smarter than their fathers 10 years from now.

No wonder, then that with this concept of intelligence there is antagonism to the use of intelligence tests. Two actions are indicated: The public is not, of course, wholly right in its confusion of wisdom with intelligence; some education about the nature of intelligence tests and their value would be in order. But, on the other hand, there can be no doubt that actual use of test results in many schools (and other settings) is much too rigid, being at variance not only with these public views but with what we ourselves know about test reliability and predictive validity. What we need is provision for continuous appraisal of an individual's performance after he has been allocated to one or another environment; a special class in school, a certain college, a particular job. Psychometric theory permits one to appraise the probabilities of subsequent success, but we must not fail to safeguard ourselves from treating the probabilities as certainties. There are some test users—in schools, the Civil Service, the military establishment—who must be converted from their belief that once they have assigned an individual to a given path in life their work has ended. They must realize instead that they have a continuing responsibility to find out if their decisions prove to be right.

A fourth source of antagonism toward intelligence tests is that they deny opportunity to persons with different and possibly highly valuable talents. Since the opportunity structure in American education, and to some extent in occupations, is organized around intelligence tests, there will be resentment from those who do not think intelligence is very important.

Those who hold such a view maintain that intelligence tests are restricted in the talent they measure, and that the valued qualities of man are diverse and multiple in nature—creativity, ambition, honesty, concern for the general welfare of man. More studies on the independence of intelligence from commonly valued characteristics such as creativity, or altruism, or achievement would be of help in defining the degree to which the issue is a real one.

The fifth criticism of tests of ability is that they screen out from opportunities for advancement those individuals from a background of cultural deprivation, who because of the deprivation give an inferior performance on the tests. Fortunately Joshua Fishman and his colleagues (Deutsch, Fishman, Kogan, North, & Whiteman, 1964) have completed their analysis of this problem. Their action recommendations command the attention of all psychologists.

I would like just to add this observation. Those of culturally deprived backgrounds are frequently members of minority groups against which society discriminates. Minority groups, as such, should be favorably inclined to the use of ability tests, since tests constitute a universal standard of competence and potential. When tests are substituted for discriminatory methods of educational placement and discriminatory methods of job selection and promotion, they increase the opportunities of minority group members because they measure ability rather than social status. Tests therefore should be viewed with favor by this segment of the culturally deprived.

Our data seem to show this. A comparison of Negro and white adult respondents, controlled for social class, shows that at the lower social class levels Negroes have the more favorable attitude toward the use of tests in job selection and promotion (although no differences exist for higher social class levels).

Now, to conclude this part: Some criticisms can be met, I believe, by giving heed to familiar recommendations to psychologists. The criticisms involving too rigid usage and inappropriate interpretation of test results of deprived children can be dealt with directly by increased education, training, and supervision of those responsible for the use of tests. Since individuals themselves sometimes misinterpret the meaning of their test scores, an accompanying public education program would be desirable.

Other criticisms cannot be met this easily. I refer to the questions regarding the invasion of privacy, the inaccessibility of records, and the kinds of talent that psychologists want to nurture. These are not matters of educating others, or of technical improvements in tests, but of a carefully reasoned legal, moral, and scientific position which the American psychologist chooses to take.

If these five criticisms can be met by effective action then many critics will be quieted. There are many men of good will toward tests who favor their use, subject to improvements along the lines indicated.

## BASIC SOURCES OF CRITICISMS

I now want to go on to consider a sharply different group of issues: not the criticisms raised about tests, but the personal and social characteristics of some of the critics themselves. For a significant number of these critics, the familiar objections that I have just reviewed are often merely superficial expressions of their more fundamental opposition. The attempt to classify these deeper sources of antitest sentiment leads to noting at least four types of opposition.

First, there is opposition arising from one's general personality characteristics. Second, there is opposition arising from one's general system of values. Third, opposition develops as a consequence of the individual's experience with intelligence tests; antagonism is bred in the loss of self-esteem a person may have suffered as a result of poor performance. Last, opposition arises from the restrictions on one's life opportunities, which also result from poor performance on tests.

Although we do not as yet have data on all four of these I want to touch on each to give a full picture.

Those who object to psychological testing may do so by virtue of their personality characteristics. It is likely, for example, that strong opposition exists among those people who are distinctly hostile to any self-examination, introspection, or self-understanding. These are the people who are also authoritarian in interpersonal relations, intolerant of diversity in ideology or beliefs, and strongly opposed to most forms of social change. The association of this personality type with extremist groups in our country, especially the extreme right-wing political groups, is commonly recognized, and it is understandable that such groups are pushing for legislation banning the use of tests.

The personality syndrome of these persons might well be examined more carefully in our own studies. Although I have no data to report at this time, we did include several scales measuring defensiveness and anti-introspection in our study of the high school students. We are presently analyzing the relationship of these scales to attitudes toward psychological tests. It should be understood, moreover, that little is known about how "authoritarian" personality characteristics relate to the type of objection directed against psychological tests. Will the authoritarian person emphasize invasion of privacy or some other objection? The determining factors undoubtedly involve situational influences as well as personality characteristics. The important point to recognize, however is that given the personality structure, one or more of the five objections mentioned above is sure to be raised.

The second source of opposition to ability tests is one's general belief about how a society should be organized. One's attitudes, favorable or unfavorable, are rooted in the basic and conflicting themes of American democracy—whether men really are equal, and if they are, what one is to do about the obvious differences between them. In his book entitled *Excellence*, John Gardner (1961) distinguishes between the three ways in which societies can be organized: according to an equalitarian philosophy, or with an inherited aristocracy, or as a result of open competition. Which type of organization a person believes is best should strongly influence his attitudes toward the use of ability tests in his society.

From the equalitarian viewpoint men are equal, and differences in ability should be equalized by differential treatment. Ability tests are incompatible with this view because the rationale of ability tests is that there are individual differences of an important kind, and that tests are able to detect such differences.

In an aristocratic society one is given money, power, and prestige according to his parents' social position, and the aristocracy is maintained through ingroup marriage. The doctrine of opening avenues of achievement in a society according to biological inheritance, rather than to social inheritance, is a direct challenge to the established aristocratic social order, and the use of ability tests would not be condoned.

In contrast with these two value systems is the belief that open competition between different types and levels of ability is a social good. In each generation a talented elite should rise to the top, to be replaced next generation by others bearing no necessary blood relationship to them. Each individual has the right to contribute to society as much as he is able, according to his talents. Since tests identify the talented and make it possible to provide them with opportunities for full development of their capacities, a favorable view of intelligence tests should follow.

According to our two surveys, how do Americans feel about these questions? The data show that US students have a less aristocratic outlook than adults. The high school group more often says that parents should not be allowed to pass on their wealth and prestige and that people of wealth and position should not marry their own kind. For the high school students it is the equalitarian position rather than the belief in open competition, which they take as their own. More high school students than adults say that everyone should go to college; more believe there is no difference in intelligence between social groups; and to back up this belief, more of them disagree with the view that the more intelligent should get better schooling and have the most opportunities. It should follow that the high school students are more opposed to the use of ability tests than are the adults: you will recall that this is the case.

There is other evidence of the linkage of these beliefs to test attitudes: Within the adult population our intragroup analyses show those adults who hold equalitarian views to be the ones who say most frequently that intelligence tests are unfair. (We have not yet completed our within-group analysis for the high school students, but I am certain that this result will hold up.)

If the difference in social philosophy between the generations reflects a historical change, then antitest sentiment is growing. If it is an age difference only, then expect to find most of the antitest sentiment in the younger population. In either event we see that there is a link between opposition to tests and one's general scheme of values.

A third important source of opposition to ability tests is the wounded self-esteem of those who may have done poorly on such tests. We are not ready with any full analysis, but have some suggestive data from the high school group. We note that there are several necessary conditions for test scores to have an impact on self-esteem.

First, one must believe intelligence itself is important. Among a long list of desirable characteristics, intelligence is rated as extremely important by the largest number of respondents with the exception of good health. Also, in another question, more than a third viewed intelligence as more important than any other thing for success in life.

Second, if test scores are to have an impact, one must view them as accurate. Again, the high school respondents included two-thirds who said tests are accurate, even highly accurate, with 18% holding the view that they are inaccurate.

Third, the respondents must have received information about their intelligence as a result of taking standardized ability tests. About 40% said they had received no such information from ability tests; the other three-fifths did.

Fourth, the test information received must present a picture of the respondent less desirable than the one he holds. In the normal course of things half the population would get test scores below normal. However, the self-descriptions of our high school respondents find 43% saying they are above average, another 33% saying they are average, and only 8% rating themselves below average, at all. Thus, many of these must have been disappointed in the test information they received. We see, then, that all four conditions are met.

Now comes a curious fact. What is actually reported about the effects of receiving information is that 24% raised their intelligence estimate as a result of the test, 16% made no change, and 7% lowered it. Another one-third said it had no effect or could not remember. How is one to account for this preponderance of raised estimates? This suggests first that the test scores are misinterpreted. We know that the students report receiving only vague and general scores, subject to loose interpretation. Or, it may be a simple misunderstanding such as that a score of 90 is viewed as a high score when one starts with a base of 0, as they are used to in a school grading system.

But other data show that increasing self-estimates of intelligence are a general phenomenon not linked solely to receiving test data. Whatever the source of influence on intelligence, the influence is upward. When one asks whether the school marks they have received caused them to change their mind about how intelligent they are, the same thing occurs, 28% changing upward, and 10% changing downward. Moreover, changes resulting from any experience other than test scores or marks show 70% raising their estimate, 28%

lowering it. This suggests a selective use of information designed to protect one's self-esteem, in which those who receive data which upgrades their ability estimates remember it and use it, and those who receive the contrary data forget it or explain it away. The disagreeable experience in the receipt of an unexpectedly low test score may be defended against by forgetting, but the residue of displeasure may well remain and be directed in general ways into resentment against tests. This would be particularly the case in the high school group because of their more frequent and near universal test experience.

The fourth major source of resentment against tests is any punishing effects they may have had on the individual's life chances. We asked both groups of respondents for their perceptions of the influence of tests on such things as educational, occupational, military, and other kinds of opportunities. Very few effects were reported by either group, and those that were mentioned were almost wholly positive. It may simply be that for the adults there has been little impact of tests, while the high school students have not yet entered into military or career choices; indeed, the tenth graders have not yet faced college entrance. Our high school group 10 years from now might report more negative experiences, but for now it appears that it is the impact of test scores on personal feelings rather than life opportunities which is a main matter of concern.

Our review of these four fundamental sources of opposition to tests leads to the conclusion that psychologists must be concerned about the society in which tests are used. Testing does not occur in isolation; there is always a social context. Test scores have a social meaning. They have impact on man's self-esteem; they influence his life chances; they engage his deepest political and social attitudes. These forces must be understood as part of the social setting in which intelligence testing is carried on.

**REFERENCES**

DEUTSCH, M., FISHMAN, J. A., KOGAN, L., NORTH, R., and WHITMAN, M., "Guidelines for testing minority group children, *Journal of Social Issues*, 1964, **22** (2, Suppl.), 127–145.

GARDNER, J. W., *Excellence*. New York: Harper, 1961.

GOSLIN, D. A., *The search for ability: Standardized testing in social perspective*. New York: Russell Sage Foundation, 1963.

## 5.3 Alternatives to Intelligence Testing

*Joseph O. Loretan*

Many people still hold the belief that intelligence is inherited and essentially unchangeable. Reprinted below is a talk given by Dr. Loretan at the 1965 Invitational Conference on Testing Problems, sponsored by Educational Testing Service. The reader will discover, in reading this presentation, that at least in the City of New York the "immutable" IQ is not only regarded as a myth but also as a decoy which tends to deflect educators from more effective teaching. Current best developmental psychological theory suggests that a very small proportion of the differences in mental ability noted between children can be attributed to genetic factors. Therefore, the logical direction for educational evaluation planning to go is toward some such blending of curricular and measurement materials as suggested here.

Isn't it an interesting and strange commentary on the inertia which has plagued education to find that it was Binet in the early 1900's, who first gave the rationale for the approach to the measurement and *improvement* of intelligence which 60 years later is finally beginning to be implemented on a moderately large scale?

When I was invited to speak on the topic, "Alternatives to Intelligence Testing," Bob Ebel was kind enough to ask me if I preferred some other wording of the topic. My response was that I would use the suggested title. My reason for this was that I wanted an opportunity to clarify the position that we have taken in our school system, and the particular title was to the point.

When New York City dropped the administration of group intelligence tests, the newspapers sprouted such headlines as "New York City Bans Intelligence Testing," "IQ Scores Dropped in Major City in the Nation." In fact, one publication stated, "Intelligence

From *Proceedings: 1965 Invitational Conference on Testing Problems,* 19–30. Reprinted with permission of the author and Educational Testing Service, Princeton, N. J.

*Out* in New York City." One mother wrote, "Are you sleeping nights now that you have taken away the IQ's of our children?"

Shortly after the "first shock wave," came the second. Now that we had eliminated the administration of group IQ tests, the public assumed that we must have been prepared to *substitute* another test. When it was learned that ETS was working on a cooperative project with New York City, it was taken for granted that they were coming up with another type of IQ test. Therefore, at this time, let me start by saying, unequivocally, we are not developing a substitute for the group intelligence test. It has never been our objective to *substitute* or interchange another type of group IQ test for the present group intelligence test. It *has* been our purpose, however, to develop an *alternative* to the IQ tests—in the form of a series of tasks that very early, almost immediately, in the young child's school experience, will involve him in activities that will help him to grow intellectually. I therefore appreciate the title Dr. Ebel assigned because we are interested in *alternatives*, not alternates. I am equally grateful for the *opportunity* of a forum not only to set forth some of the reasons for seeking alternatives, but also to discuss briefly *one* of the alternatives.

I should like first to discuss why the group intelligence tests have been discontinued in New York City, and why, instead of using tests to *measure* intelligence, we are substituting teaching and learning tasks to *develop* intelligence, using measurement or assessment simply as a by-product.

## THE NATURE AND PURPOSE OF GROUP IQ TESTS

The group IQ test was an offspring of the individual test developed by Binet in the early 1900's. At that time, before Binet had turned most of his attention to psychometrics, he concerned himself with the educability of intelligence, taking five or six aspects of intelligence that he thought could be trained. He organized classes to prove that "mental orthopedics" could be used to improve the ability to memorize, reason, and perceive. Working among the poor in Paris, he suggested that learning and environment interacted and that with a richer environment one's mental abilities could be improved. To quote him:

> A child's mind is like a field for which an expert farmer has advised a change in the method of cultivation, with the result

that in place of desert land we now have a harvest. It is in this particular sense, the one which is significant, that we say that the intelligence of children may be increased. One increases that which constitutes the intelligence of a school child, namely, the capacity to learn to improve *with instruction* (1).

Yet in years to come, Binet's hypothesis was largely neglected. Training of mental abilities was not considered possible. Some of the experimental work of Thorndike and others was used as proof that attempts to "improve the mind" in a general way through a study of a specific discipline was useless.

The presumption that genetic factors weighed very heavily in intelligence also discouraged attempts at intellectual training. Now these concepts have been modified and exemplified in the research of Bruner, Piaget, Guilford, and others. IQ is no longer considered "constant," nor is it deemed to measure all aspects of intelligence.

Our present group IQ test was conceived with the purpose of testing children more economically, since individual testing, then and now, is prohibitive in terms of time, trained personnel, and expense. However, the early group IQ test was constructed with a conscience. It tried to retain aspects of the individually administered test. It took four hours to administer and included many of the elements of the individual test. But even the most enthusiastic proponents of this group IQ test knew that something had to give, as four hours of testing was far too much for any youngster in a classroom situation. So it was whittled away until it was reduced to a 45-minute test—its present form.

In 45 minutes a youngster is tested on verbal meanings, space, reasoning, number concepts, and word fluency. This capsulized version of the test is given to a class or large group of youngsters at a time of day, week, or month that is administratively convenient for the school system. It is usually administered by a teacher whose only qualification for administering the test is the ability to read the "Directions to Teachers" on the first page of a test manual.

As a result of this 45-minute exposure to a test, a student is sent on a road marked "slow," "average," or "bright"—in many cases, with this single stroke his destiny is ordained.

Furthermore, the vocabulary and concepts in most of the group IQ tests are foreign to many children in our large and varied country (and certainly to many children in New York City). We have not been able to "extract" cultural biases from our tests and yet we use these tests with children who are culturally different. The assumption inherent in general intelligence tests that children have had very similar background experience has not been valid in the past, nor is it in 1965.

Now, let us look at our youngster—identified, labeled, and classified. He is placed more often than not in a class with youngsters of "equal ability." As one teacher said, "Once you know a child's IQ, you tend to see him through it. You adjust your teaching to his ability or level of intelligence." Thus the IQ becomes a self-fulfilling prophesy to the child as well as the teacher. An IQ means that there is something innate, a part of your body, a part of your soul that tells you what you are worth. What is worse, the general public thinks IQ means brain power you either were born with or not. You can't do anything about it.

Yet we know that an IQ test tells only *how the pupil performs on a limited number of tasks at the time he takes the test.* As stated by Chauncey and Dobbin (3) in *Testing: Its Place in Education Today:* "No intelligence test opens the window in the student's skull through which psychologists and scientists can ascertain the amount of latent brightness or intelligence he has. Nor can any test trick a person psychologically or otherwise into revealing how much brilliance or stupidity he possesses."

A 45-minute test, which yields a minimum of valid information, may assure a child with a "high IQ" the interest of his teacher in furthering his education, for he has "potential." It may, in turn, make him smug and content and lead him to live off his inborn talent —something like an annuity. This can end in disaster, since only effort and interest can help him succeed.

What about the youngster with the "low IQ"? He thinks little of himself; teachers feel they can do little with him or for him, and because of an unreliable instrument (certainly one of limited objectives), he may be excluded from the opportunity to discover and develop his intelligence. An average score may be the most harmful of all, for it may be a placebo that relegates the youngster to being like all the rest—accepting mediocrity with initiative stifled—and all this as a result of a 45-minute test given at the most three times in a student's career.

Yet, study after study proves that IQ's can be elevated with good teaching and by increased motivation on the part of students. Some children's IQ's may vary as much as 40 points from one period of their lives to another. New York City's Demonstration Guidance Project yielded perhaps the most dramatic results. Students in a selected junior high school were given remedial reading, mathematics, speech, group and individual guidance with stress on college and career planning, and cultural enrichment. The project also tried to improve the self-images of the participating students and to develop pride in their cultural background. In the current report issued in 1963, students who were in the project from 1956 to 1959 gained an average of 8 points in IQ. Those in the project from 1957 to 1960 gained an average of 15 points in IQ. The range was from a gain of 5 points to 40 points. If, as the research indicates, an educational program can "reverse deprivation effects," should we not address our curricula and our energies to discovering what *type* of educational program can do this?

Piaget hypothesizes that almost all human beings are born with approximately the same set of biologically inherited reflexes. Except for the unfortunate few who are biologically deficient (have reflexes missing) or who suffer injury in the processes of gestation and birth, *everybody starts life with about the same set of reflexes.* Piaget hypothesizes that intellect is not inherited but *generated.* (A theoretical discussion of whether it can be generated wholly out of human experience would be interesting, but it would not fulfill the purpose of this paper.)

## AN ALTERNATIVE TO IQ TESTING

Accepting the rationale of the educability of intelligence through human experience, I offer a report of experimental work being carried on in a cooperative venture of New York City public schools and Educational Testing Service. This alternative to IQ testing we call "Let's Look at First Graders." The rationale is based on several assumptions: 1) Intelligence is essentially a set of developed skills rather than an inherited characteristic. 2) Intellectual skills develop as a result of the child's continuous interaction with his environment. 3) Children are inherently motivated to explore and master their environment. 4) Intellect develops through a sequence of related stages that produce *qualitative change* in the way children think and are able to deal with the world.

John Dewey said ". . . the primary root of all educational activity is in the *instinctive, impulsive attitudes and activities of the child"* (5). He denied or certainly under-emphasized the importance of *"the presentation and application of external material."* "Let's Look at First Graders," however, is based on the theory of *intervention,* of presenting and applying external material, with education the intervening factor between the child and his environment. "Let's Look at First Graders" has three elements—observational, developmental and appraisal. Element I is an observation guide. It asks the teacher to become an *observer,* to look at the child as he proceeds through a series of learning experiences. This guide is divided into six broad areas. The major areas and the behavioral concepts discussed are:

| MAJOR AREA | CONCEPT |
|---|---|
| 1. Basic Language Skills | Auditory Discrimination and Attention<br>Listening Comprehension<br>Learning to Communicate<br>Language for Thinking |
| 2. Concepts of Space and Time | Learning Shapes and Forms<br>Spatial Perspective<br>The Notion of Time |
| 3. Beginning Logical Concepts | Logical Classification<br>Concepts of Relationship |
| 4. Beginning Mathematical Concepts | The Conservation of Quantity<br>One-to-One Correspondence<br>Number Relations |
| 5. The Growth of Reasoning Skills | Understanding Cause and Effect<br>Reasoning by Association<br>Reasoning by Inference |
| 6. General Signs of Development | Growing Awareness and Responsiveness<br>Directed Activity<br>General Knowledge<br>Developing Imagination |

In order to help teachers observe the behavior of children in these different areas, many examples are provided *in the guide:* Can the children identify or supply words that rhyme with another word? Can they tell about sounds they hear? Can they get the meaning of words from the tone of voice or gestures of a classmate? For each of the major areas I've just mentioned many behavioral clues are furnished in the guide. By noting and recording how the student reacts to these tasks or experiences, as observed in the course of the teaching and learning activities, teachers form a picture of the child's developing abilities and instruction. This can be used to help him develop further.

Now these tasks or skills that I refer to were not developed solely in the cloistered halls of Princeton. The content of this observation guide is a blend of information from two sources. The staff members of Educational Testing Service spent a whole year in the classrooms of New York City. By combining the research and theory of behavioral psychology with the actual tasks that teachers *can* observe in the classroom, it has been possible to list the behavioral signs of intellectual development of children which both researchers and teachers think are important. However,

> . . . it was apparent from the beginning of the project that there are children for whom the classroom circumstances are so strange or so threatening that they simply withdraw and reveal *little behavior of any kind*. These are the "hard-to-see" children who rarely engage in any classroom activities in which their developed intellectual skills *can be* observed. So the project was planned to consist of a *second* phase or element—Developmental. Concentration in this phase has been upon the development of various materials and tasks for *eliciting intellectual behavior*. If, for any one of several reasons, the teacher is unable to see important signs of intellect in the spontaneous behavior of children in the usual activities, lessons, games, she may use these tasks and materials to make sure they have an opportunity to demonstrate certain skills and understandings (4).

Some of the tasks or puzzles are amenable to full classroom demonstrations, while others seem more appropriate to present to small groups or individuals within a class. The teacher may be presenting a puzzle or task primarily for observational purposes, but the activity is one in which the child can see for himself whether he is right or wrong, even if it means children manipulate the toy or puzzle frequently on their own. The balance beam is such a toy. This is a stick balanced on a fulcrum. Each side of the stick is numbered from 1 to 10. Weights can be placed at the numbered locations on each side of the stick. One child, or a team of two, can experiment by balancing the stick and develop the insight that there are regularities in number relations.

A teacher who decides to use a developmental task for instructional purposes must consider varying the theme since a single exposure to the task in most instances will not achieve mastery. While the tasks used for a particular instructional purpose must obviously focus on the same concept (requiring the same understanding or application of a principle), the problems should be somewhat varied in content. In one or two instances, the guide suggests a developmental task in the form of a game that may be repeated without loss of instructional value. But for the most part, the tasks suitable for class demonstrations or instruction cannot be presented to the children over and over again without losing their effectiveness. What is called for in this situation is teacher *ingenuity* in devising variations of the task while retaining its *essential* principles.

You notice, of course, the emphasis on *teacher ingenuity*. Over the past 50 years, certain processes of specialization have been developing in education which overlap the function of the classroom teacher. In one of these specializations—that of estimating the intellectual capacities of children—the role of the teacher has been diminished almost to the vanishing point. It is now accepted, almost without question, that, with a sufficiently comprehensive system of testing, school authorities can *tell the teacher* what the learning characteristics of each child are and will be.

The shortcomings of such an attitude are so obvious to an experienced teacher that they need not be recounted here. It is enough to say that this project is an effort to restore to the domain of the classroom teacher the process of estimating and fostering the intellectual development of children who are just entering school. Its logic is based on the fact that the classroom teacher sees his pupils every day and gets to know them better than anyone else in the school system. Its method grows out of the fact that intellect—"intelligence"—cannot be seen directly as an abstract thing but can only be observed as it is *put to work by the child* on problems that are meaningful to him. This logic and method together represent an attempt to bring into a single, useful focus all that research has shown us about the intellect of young children in general and all that teachers can observe about their pupils in particular. In other words, we do not sit back and just wait for things to happen, since very often important learnings have little chance of happening in the ordinary course of events in a first grade classroom, or in other classrooms for that matter.

Here is one of the differences between this project and a testing situation. Whereas tests ask the question and expect the student to respond, drawing from his own experiences, this guide does not make the assumption that all children have had these experiences. For those children who in a testing situation would get an answer incorrect because of lack of experience, this guide provides developmental activities that bring them step-by-step to the point where they *can* answer the question.

Let me give you an example of the differences between a testing requirement and this project. One of the widely used group tests includes a question that requires the student to *Mark the one that does not belong*. (Incidentally, this is a test administered in Grade 2.) The youngster then has 24 opportunities to prove that he knows the classification of objects. However, if he does not know how to classify, he has 24 opportunities to be wrong. In "Let's Look at First Graders," instead of asking this question through "24 varieties," specific tasks are presented to the learner. First he is asked to match one of a pair of mittens or rubbers or any other article of clothing with its mate. He is then given practice in identifying pictures using sets of cards and finding the pictures that match. He is *then* asked to match or sort objects on the basis of identical perceptual qualities. For example: objects of the same color, size, or shapes go together, bells of the same pitch go together. The developmental tasks continue to include experience upon experience that allow the child to match, sort, or relate things on the basis of their functional properties, on the basis of their use or function, on the basis of various subclasses, on the basis of modifying the concept in the light of a new experience or new information (e.g.—*some* farm animals can be pets), and to relate a single object to two or more classes—an orange is like a ball (round) and a cake (food).

If you review many of the group IQ tests, you will see that questions on classification are on a most primary and superficial level. They are almost solely absolute in nature. They are not asking the student to think beyond the obvious. In "Let's Look at First Graders," as children receive new information and have a variety of experiences, they gradually develop more abstract concepts for classifying things. They see, for example, that certain things may go together because they have *similar qualities*, though not identical ones: these things have color and those don't, these things are all hard objects and those are all soft.

Up to this point, I have described about two elements of "Let's Look at First Graders": an observation guide that includes behavioral tasks through which teachers can observe the levels of development of their students; and developmental activities or lessons which help to develop these abilities of the students. (*In other words, many of the tasks have instructional value*. And it is at this point that what is often called "assessment" or "measurement" blends wholly into what is really teaching.) Now I wish to discuss the third aspect or element of this project—the written exercises. Perhaps this final element is the most "testlike" of any. However, while the written exercises are similar in some ways to any test in existence, they do contain at least two important features that make them quite distinct.

In the first place, *the exercises are related to the various theoretical concepts in the guide*. They are refinements of the developmental aspects of the project, designed to tap the child's understanding and developed ability in the areas of:

| | |
|---|---|
| Shapes and Forms | Mathematics |
| Spatial Relations | Communication Skills |
| Time Concepts | Logical Reasoning |

Secondly, *they are designed to give the child extensive practice* before any "measure-for-the-record" is made. In each area mentioned above there are actually five exercises, one to be given on each day of the week for a selected number of weeks. The first three lessons are for practice and instructional purposes. For example, in the material in logical reasoning, the class discusses ways of grouping objects. While the logical concept for which understanding is sought is the same each day, the material used each day is different. Only the results of the last two exercises will be recorded by the teacher as a measure of the child's developed skill in that area. By this procedure we hope not only to give the child an opportunity to become familiar with the mechanics of "test-taking" but also to instruct him in those concepts which we consider important enough to test for. In effect, we are attempting to make instructional materials and "test" materials one and the same thing. We are not predicting, we are diagnosing, teaching, evaluating. As Bruner would say, how much can a child make of the best hints we might give him, the best trots, the best tools, the maximum theoretical props? We are not assuming the child has had an experience; we create the lesson in which an experience takes place.

In their final form, the written exercises will be designed to give the teacher information on a number of aspects of the child's developed intellectual skills throughout the school year. Tentatively at least, it is planned that this information will include both a learning rate score (an index of the child's improvement with instruction) and an achievement score (the result of his performance on the last two exercises).

## UNDERSTANDING THROUGH INSTRUCTION

At the Invitational Conference in October 1963, I asked Henry Chauncey how we could help New York City teachers better understand and assess the intellectual development of every entering school child so that every child could be taught more effectively. The answer evolved over this period of time, is that we can understand and assess the intellectual development of entering school children by presenting them with activities that *develop* their concepts, and on the basis of *these concepts* we can then assess where they are and in which direction they must move. Children are observed, or assessed, or understood, or whatever word you wish to use, in the course of *teaching activities*. This is the most important part of this project. As you obtain a picture of the child's developing abilities, you then plan your instruction to help him develop further.

I think at this point, if I were asked to rename this guide, I would prefer to call it "Let's Look at First Graders—A Guide to a Curriculum For Young Children." If each of these tasks were expanded and others included, I could think of no better curriculum for first graders.

At the Invitational Conference in 1964, I asked another question: Why are we starting so late in a child's school career to observe and to help him in developing his intellect?

Until the mid 1950's, the theory persisted that children should not have their infancy spoiled by going to school "too early." The theories of Washburn and his contemporaries persisted: the very young child was just not ready for school. In the face of later research, however, a new attitude began to prevail. Bloom (2), in describing general intelligence and using the absolute scales of intellectual development formulated by Thorndike, Thurstone, and Heines, suggests that 50 percent of development takes place between conception and age 4; 30 percent between ages 4 and 8; and 20 percent between 8 and 17 (2, p. 109). He does not subscribe to the thesis that intelligence is a physical or neurological growth function analogous to height growth and that it must have a definite terminal growth point. However, Bloom does propose that intelligence as presently measured does reach a plateau in the period of ages 10 to 17 and that further development is likely only if powerful forces in the environment encourage further growth and development (2, p. 81).

If we accept the view that as much development takes place in the first 4 years of life as in the next 13, any years lost in a poor environment are almost irretrievable. This also suggests the great importance of the first few years of elementary school, as well as the preschool period, in the development of learning patterns and general achievement. Failure to develop learning patterns in these years may lead to failure throughout the student's school career. Bloom, in another study, further breaks down the figures and estimates that 17 percent of growth takes place between the ages of 4 and 6. From this one might well infer that schooling during these years can have far-reaching effects on a child's learning patterns.

In closing, I should like now to return to the title of this paper, "Alternatives to Intelligence Testing." I propose that an alternative to intelligence testing is *teaching;* that we assess progress only of what we teach, after we teach it, and that this progress is not the result of something innate, but of "external materials," of intervention through teaching.

**REFERENCES**

1. BINET, ALFRED, *Les Idées Modernes sur les Enfants,* Paris: Ernest Flammarien, 1909, 54–55.
2. BLOOM, BENJAMIN S., *Stability and Change in Human Characteristics,* New York: John Wiley & Sons., Inc. 1964, 68.
3. CHAUNCEY, HENRY and DOBBIN, JOHN E., *Testing: Its Place in Education Today,* New York: Harper & Row, 1963.
4. EDUCATIONAL TESTING SERVICE, *From Theory to the Classroom,* New York: Board of Education, City of New York, 1965.
5. THE "DEWEY" SCHOOL, from *The Elementary School Record,* Chicago: The University of Chicago, 1900.

# 6 *Measuring Noncognitive Variables*

## 6.1 How and Why to Classify Affective Educational Objectives
### *David R. Krathwohl, Benjamin S. Bloom, Bertram B. Masia*

The following selection sets forth some important reasons why schools must appraise noncognitive psychological changes in students and describes the rationale certain experts chose to enable them to select what they hoped would be a highly useful classificatory system for affective behaviors.

Teachers and applied psychologists want as much to measure emotional status and growth as they do changes and levels of ability. In order to do so, appropriate tools must be developed. Satisfactory instruments have been far too slow in appearing. These authors give some cogent explanations for this snail-paced progress and offer the currently best schematization for hastening needed production of objective measurement tools in the area of human emotional learning.

### LIMITED EVALUATION OF AFFECTIVE OBJECTIVES

One of the reasons the cognitive domain presented us with a more easily solvable problem than the affective domain was the tremendous wealth of evaluation material we found being used for grading and certifying student achievement. Faculty, examiners, administrators, and even students accept the need for and value of such material.

When we looked for evaluation material in the affective domain we found it usually in relation to some national educational research

From *Taxonomy of Educational Objectives, Handbook II, The Affective Domain*, 1964. Reprinted with permission of David McKay Co., Inc.

project or a sponsored local research project (for which a report had to be written). Only rarely did we find an affective evaluation technique used because a group of local teachers wanted to know whether students were developing in a particular way. It was evident that evaluation work for affective objectives was marginal and was done only when a very pressing question was raised by the faculty or when someone wished to do "educational" research.

It is not entirely fair to imply that evaluation of the attainment of affective objectives is completely absent from the regular activities of schools and teachers. Undoubtedly almost every teacher is on the alert for evidence of desirable interests, attitudes, and character development. However, most of this is the noting of unusual characteristics or dramatic developments when they are almost forced on the teacher's attention. What is missing is a systematic effort to collect evidence of growth in affective objectives which is in any way parallel to the very great and systematic efforts to evaluate cognitive achievement.

## EROSION OF AFFECTIVE OBJECTIVES

We studied the history of several major courses at the general education level of college. Typically, we found that in the original statement of objectives there was frequently as much emphasis given to affective objectives as to cognitive objectives. Sometimes in the early years of the course some small attempt was made to secure evidence on the extent to which students were developing in the affective behaviors.

However, as we followed some of these courses over a period of ten to twenty years, we found a rather rapid dropping of the affective objectives from the statements about the course and an almost complete disappearance of efforts at appraisal of student growth in this domain.

It was evident to us that there is a characteristic type of *erosion* in which the original intent of a course or educational program becomes worn down to that which can be explicitly evaluated for grading purposes and that which can be taught easily through verbal methods (lectures, discussions, reading materials, etc.). There is a real shift in intent that comes with time. It may be true that it is easier to teach and evaluate cognitive objectives. But we really doubt that this is the sole determining influence and believe that a number of forces are responsible for the erosion of intentions.

## SCHOOL GRADING AND AFFECTIVE OBJECTIVES

The failure to grade students' achievement on affective objectives accounts for a large portion of the erosion. Cognitive achievement is regarded as fair game for grading purposes. Examinations may include a great range of types of cognitive objectives, and teachers and examiners have little hesitation in giving a student a grade of A or F on the basis of his performance on these cognitive achievement examinations. In contrast, teachers and examiners do not regard it as appropriate to grade students with respect to their interests, attitude, or character development. To be sure, a student who is at one extreme on these affective objectives may be disciplined by the school authorities, while a student at the other extreme may be regarded so favorably by teachers that he receives whatever rewards and honors are available for the purpose (e.g., the teacher's attention, appointment to prestige classroom positions, etc.).

A considerable part of the hesitation in the use of affective measures for grading purposes stems from the inadequacy of the appraisal techniques and the ease with which a student may exploit his ability to detect the responses which will be rewarded and the responses which will be penalized. In contrast, it is assumed that a student who responds in the desirable way on a cognitive measure does indeed possess the competence which is being sampled. For instance, if we wish to determine whether a humanities course has resulted in "an interest in seeking and enjoying a wide variety of musical experiences," we may attempt to appraise the variety of musical experiences the student has voluntarily participated in prior to, during, and subsequent to the humanities course. We hesitate to trust the professed evidence that a student has developed such an interest, because we have difficulty in determining the difference between a natural or honest response and one that is made solely to please the teacher, and we may even have some question about the accuracy of the student's recall of such experiences. On the other hand, if our objective is "the development of the ability to become sensitive to and perceptive of different aspects of a musical work," we may present him with a series of musical selections which are likely to be unfamiliar to him. Then, by careful questioning, determine which elements he has perceived and which he has not. We would not hesitate to assign him a grade on the second objective, but we would have considerable hesitation about failing the student or giving him a high grade on the basis of our evidence on the first objective. However, though this difficulty with affective measures presents a series of technical problems, they could probably be solved with very substantial effort.

A much more serious reason for the hesitation in the use of affective measures for grading purposes comes from somewhat deeper philosophical and cultural values. Achievement, competence, productivity, etc., are regarded as public matters. Honors are awarded for high achievement, honor lists may be published by the Dean, and lists of National Merit Scholarship winners may be printed in newspapers. In contrast, one's beliefs, attitudes, values, and personality characteristics are more likely to be regarded as private matters, except in the most extreme instances already noted. My attitudes toward God, home, and family are private concerns, and this privacy is generally respected. My political attitudes are private; I may reveal them if I wish, but no one can force me to do so. In fact, my voting behavior is usually protected from public view. Each man's home is his castle, and his interests, values, beliefs, and personality may not be scrutinized unless he voluntarily gives permission to have them revealed. This public-private status of cognitive vs. affective behaviors is deeply rooted in the Judaeo-Christian religion and is a value highly cherished in the democratic traditions of the Western world.

Closely linked to this private aspect of affective behavior is the distinction frequently made between education and indoctrination in a democratic society. Education opens up possibilities for free choice and individual decision. Education helps the individual to explore many aspects of the world and even his own feelings and emotion, but choice and decision are matters for the individual. Indoctrination, on the other hand, is viewed as reducing the possibilities of free choice and decision. It is regarded as an attempt to persuade and coerce the individual to accept a particular viewpoint or belief, to act in a particular manner, and to profess a particular value and way of life. Gradually education has come to mean an almost solely cognitive examination of issues. Indoctrination has come to mean the teaching of affective as well as cognitive behavior. Perhaps a reopening of the entire question would help us to see more clearly the boundaries between education and indoctrination, and the simple dichotomy expressed above between cognitive and affective behavior would no longer seem as real as the rather glib separation of the two suggests.

## SLOW ATTAINMENT OF AFFECTIVE OBJECTIVES

Another cause of the erosion in affective objectives has to do with the immediacy of results. A particular item of information or a very specific skill is quickly learned and shows immediate results on cognitive examinations. Even more complex abilities may be learned in a one-semester or one-year course, and the evidences of the learning may be seen in the examination given at the end of the course. In contrast, interests, attitudes, and personality characteristics are assumed to develop relatively slowly and to be visible in appraisal techniques only over long periods of time, perhaps even years. Whether these assumptions are sound can only be revealed by much more evidence than is now available.

It is even possible that just the opposite may be true; namely, that affective behaviors undergo far more sudden transformations than do cognitive behaviors. What is even more probable is that certain objectives in the cognitive and affective domain may be quickly learned or developed, whereas other objectives in both domains may be developed only over a long period of time. Implicit in the *Taxonomy* is the assumption that objectives which fall into the first categories (e.g., *Knowledge, Receiving*) are likely to be learned more rapidly and more easily than objectives which fall into the later and "higher" categories (e.g., *Synthesis, Generalized set*). In any case, a useful classification of affective and cognitive objectives and behaviors would help to expose these assumptions about change (as well as the conditions required for change) in the different types of objectives, whether they be cognitive or affective.

## TEACHING FOR AFFECTIVE LEARNING IN RELATION TO COGNITIVE LEARNING

Before closing this discussion of causes of the erosion of affective objectives, we should point up the distinction between objectives as goals to be worked for directly and objectives which are assumed to be the by-products of other objectives (Sawin and Loree, 1959). For a long time it was assumed that if a student learned the information objectives of a course he would, as a direct consequence of this information learning, develop the problem-solving objectives in that course. Thus the teacher's responsibility was reduced to that of providing learning experiences to develop the information in students, and the examination was designed to appraise the students' progress toward the information objectives. As a result of the research and writings of Tyler (1934, 1951), Furst (1958), Dressel (1958), and others this belief in the "automatic" development of the higher mental processes is no longer widely held. However, there still persists an implicit belief that if cognitive objectives are developed, there will be a corresponding development of appropriate affective behaviors. Research summarized by Jacob (1957) raises serious questions about the tenability of this assumption. The evidence suggests that affective behaviors develop when appropriate learning experiences are provided for students much the same as cognitive behaviors develop from appropriate learning experiences.

The authors of this work hold the view that under some conditions the development of cognitive behaviors may actually destroy certain desired affective behaviors and that, instead of a positive relation between growth in cognitive and affective behavior, it is conceivable that there may be an inverse relation between growth in the two domains. For example, it is quite possible that many literature courses at the high-school and college levels instill knowledge of the history of literature and knowledge of the details of particular works of literature, while at the same time producing an aversion to, or at least a lower level of interest in, literary works. Clearly there is need for conclusive experimentation and research on the relations between the two domains. Here, again, the specificity which a taxonomy can introduce into both domains is likely to reveal conditions under which one conclusion is sound as well as point to situations where the opposite conclusion is tenable.

Perhaps one of the most dramatic events highlighting the need for progress in the affective domain was the publication of Jacob's *Changing Values in College* (1957). He summarizes a great deal of educational research at the college level and finds almost no evidence that college experiences produce a significant change in students' values, beliefs, or personality. Although he has been criticized for his methods, definitions, and assumptions, his critics have not responded by pointing up changes in the affective domain which he had overlooked. Jacob's work has stimulated a considerable amount of soul searching at the college level and is undoubtedly responsible for an increase in interest and research in this area. We must pay our respects to Jacob for increasing our own determination to complete this Handbook.

## CLARIFICATION OF COGNITIVE AND AFFECTIVE OBJECTIVES

More than two decades of work on cognitive objectives have produced specific and meaningful results. Few serious workers now use such terms as "critical thinking," "problem solving," or "higher mental processes" as statements of objectives. These terms may be used to describe large goals and aims of education, but in describing the objectives of a course with specific sequences of learning experiences, curriculum makers have more recently made use of terms like "application of principles," "interpretation of data," "skill in recognizing assumptions," etc. These terms are further defined behaviorally, enabling teachers to analyze an examination or evaluation technique to determine whether it does or does not appraise the kinds of educational outcomes they have specified. This greater precision in specifications has, of course, evolved from a considerable amount of interaction between teachers and evaluators. General statements of objectives have been gradually refined and restated until the operational consequences for evaluation instruments became explicit. Furthermore, the consequences of these objectives for the development of learning experiences have become more and more clear as the result of the operational definitions provided by statements of behavior and evaluation instruments. The effectiveness of learning experiences in helping students attain selected objectives has also become clearer through the use of appropriate evaluation instruments in educational research. Such research has stimulated efforts to develop learning theory and learning principles which deal more directly with these highly specific educational objectives. All this is not an attempt to describe a Utopian situation in which cognitive objectives, learning experiences, and evaluation techniques have been developed so well that little further work is now needed. Far from this, we have barely scratched the surface of the tremendous potential for clarification and development of cognition.

However, the situation with respect to affective objectives is so primitive that little in the way of meaning is at present conveyed by statements of objectives. For example, here are six objectives selected from the literature, which purport to state outcomes in the affective domain:

1. The student should develop an attitude of faith in the power of reason and in the methods of experiment and discussion.

2. The student should develop attitudes of intelligent self-criticism in matters of effective expression and correct form of writing.

3. The student should develop an appreciation for the rights and feelings of others.

4. The student should have deep wells of feeling that manifest themselves not only in a passionate hatred of injustice, a "divine discontent," and an unwillingness to be a passive bystander in the presence of violently pressing social issues, but also in active and joyous identification of his own happiness with the larger social good.

5. The student should become interested in good books.

6. The student should develop an appreciation of classical music.

It will be noted that each of these states a general term like "interest," "attitude," or "appreciation" followed by an object such as books, music, people, etc. What is meant by "interest" may range from simply knowing that the object exists to a passionate devotion to this type of object or activity. For example, some possible interpretations of objective 5 may be the following:

The student should be able to distinguish between good books and not-so-good books.

The student should want to know more about what makes a book good.

The student should read an increasing number of books which experts classify as good.

The student should express a desire to read more good books.

The student should purchase good books for his personal library.

An evaluator attempting to develop an evaluation instrument to appraise growth toward objective 5 could infer almost anything he desired and construct the instrument accordingly. However, in that case the specification of the objectives of instruction would pass from the teachers to the examiners. This would represent a shift in control of instruction and outcomes from the teachers responsible for the learning experiences to the evaluators who devise the instruments for appraising the results of instruction. We regard this as an undesirable shift, since it places educational direction (and control) in the hands of a small number of instrument makers. Furthermore, it is likely that those teachers who, through vague statements of objectives, have yielded control over objectives to the examiners will not make major contributions to the development of learning experiences which will enable students to grow in the ways specified by the objectives.

## THE CONTRIBUTIONS OF A TAXONOMY OF AFFECTIVE OBJECTIVES

If affective objectives and goals are to be realized, they must be defined clearly; learning experiences to help the student develop in the desired direction must be provided; and there must be some systematic method for appraising the extent to which students grow in the desired ways.

It is our hope that the *Taxonomy* will be of service in defining more clearly the objectives in this domain. If it does nothing more, it will serve to indicate that many of the present objectives in this domain are so general as to be meaningless.

It is our hope also that the *Taxonomy* will help teachers become aware of the techniques which are available for appraising growth of students toward various categories of objectives and for assessing other affective changes, whether intended or not. Perhaps this will further stimulate the development of better methods of evaluation in this domain.

Finally, it is our hope that the *Taxonomy* will provide a bridge for further communication among teachers and between teachers and evaluators, curriculum research workers, psychologists, and other behavioral scientists. As this communication process develops, it is likely that the "folklore" which we have presented in the beginning of this chapter can be replaced by a somewhat more precise understanding of how affective behaviors develop, how and when they can be modified, and what the school can and cannot do to develop them in particular forms.

## THE SEARCH FOR AN AFFECTIVE CONTINUUM

Perhaps the most difficult part of the task of building the affective domain of the *Taxonomy* was the search for a continuum that would provide a means of ordering and relating the different kinds of affective behavior. It was presumed that the affective domain, like the cognitive, would be structured in a hierarchical order such that each category of behavior would assume achievement of the behaviors categorized below it. But it did not appear likely that the principles of "simple to complex" and "concrete to abstract" would provide as appropriate a basis for structuring the affective domain as they had provided for the cognitive domain. Some additional construct had to be found.

An analysis of affective objectives was undertaken to determine their unique characteristics. It was hoped that among these we would find what was needed to structure an affective continuum. Combined with the structuring principles from the cognitive domain, we might then expect the affective structure to begin with simple, concrete, less pervasive behaviors having a little of some characteristic as yet unspecified. These levels would be the building blocks for the more complex, abstract, and pervasive behaviors having much more of this unspecified characteristic. The problem was to define the then unspecified characteristic and the principle by which it would structure the continuum.

As has already been indicated in previous chapters, the materials from which this continuum was to be educed were the objectives dealing with interests, attitudes, values, appreciation, and adjustment. These terms were all found to have too wide a variety of meanings to serve, themselves, as the focal points through which to construct a continuum. But an analysis of the range of meanings used for each of these terms did lead to an understanding of the characteristics of the affective domain which would have to be both encompassed and ordered. It also led to the formulation of the principle needed to establish a continuum.

This analysis found, for instance, that objectives dealing with interests describe behavior ranging all the way from the student's merely *being aware* that a given phenomenon exists (so that he will at least give it his attention when it is present) through behavior where he is increasingly willing to attend and respond to a phenomenon, to behavior where he is expected to *avidly seek* out the phenomenon in question and to be totally absorbed in it. Throughout the range, it is expected that the student will *feel positively* toward the phenomenon, but at the "high interest" end he is expected to be fairly enamored of it.

The term "attitude" was also found to include objectives with a wide range of behaviors. On the one hand, it is used to describe the involvement of the student who is willing to grant that he has a *positive feeling about something* when he is asked about it. At the other extreme, it is expected that his commitment is such that *he goes out of his way* to express it and even seeks instances in which he can communicate it to others. Objectives dealing with attitudes frequently require the individual to have a *clear conception* of his attitude which he can verbalize.

When we speak of an individual as holding a value, the same range of behavior described for attitudes comes into play. Further, both the terms "attitude" and "value" may refer to behavior which has either rather specific referents as its object, e.g., one's next-door neighbors, or much more general and pervasive referents, e.g., all minority groups. In the latter instances, although the terms "attitude" and "value" are still usually employed, the behavior is often better described as a bundle of attitudes *organized* into an attitude cluster or a value complex.

The term "appreciation," like "interest," may refer to such a simple behavior as a person's being aware of a phenomenon and *being able to perceive it.* It may require that the individual be able to verbalize it (in which instance it may become almost a cognitive rather than an affective objective). It may require only that the individual *experience a pleasant feeling* when he perceives the phenomenon.

Of the terms analyzed, the widest range of meanings is probably accorded the term "adjustment." Central to any definition of adjustment is an *interrelation of one aspect* of the person *with another* in such a way that within this organization some kind of balancing may take place. The term may refer to such behaviors as appear in the social interaction between two persons, or it may *refer to one's whole outlook on life.* It may refer to the internal balancing of self-concept and self-ideal or to the balancing of overt behavior with some role concept.

If the discussion so far does not completely describe the range of behavior in the objectives of the affective domain, it does at least outline its major components. What guideposts for an affective continuum can be gleaned from them? In the paragraphs above, material has been italicized which seemed to indicate the behavioral components which must be provided for in the affective-domain structure. From these it is clear that we must first provide a level at which the stimulus is attended to so it can enter the organism's life and be perceived. This would cover the less complex aspects of interest and appreciation objectives.

Similarly, we must provide a range of levels describing the extent to which the individual interacts with the phenomenon and the basis on which he does it: does he do it only when the situation presses on him so that some behavior is evoked, or does he go out of his way to display this interaction? This would provide for some of the behaviors implied in the objectives calling for development of interests and appreciation and the less complex attitudes.

Provision must be made at some point in the continuum for the first appearance of the emotional quality which is an important distinguishing feature of the appreciation, attitude, value, and adjustment objectives in the affective domain. Further, we need to provide the range of emotion from neutrality through mild to strong emotion, probably of a positive, but possibly also of a negative, kind.

From the description of attitudes, values, and adjustment, it is clear that the continuum must provide for the organization and interrelation of values and attitudes and for whatever steps accompany or are prerequisite to such organization.

Finally, the range of behaviors to be encompassed and the way these are organized into value systems and philosophies of life suggest that the continuum should provide for various levels of organization to be delineated.

At one stage in our work in this domain it was hoped that by appropriately delimited definitions of such terms as interest, attitude, value, etc., we could build the components into a string of guideposts tied to the common terms in the field. But such definitions were difficult to devise, and their meanings tended to drift into the connotations and denotations which these terms encompassed in common parlance.[1] When we abandoned this, we tried to fit the

---

[1] Readers interested in gaining a perspective on the matter of definitions as they relate to this effort should examine Chapter 1, "Definitions in Education," in Scheffler (1960). In Scheffler's terms we initially tried to obtain descriptive definitions of common terms which would permit their use to structure a continuum. We found we could do this only if we gave these terms noninventive stipulative definitions, and we feared the stipulations attached to these definitions would be lost when the terms were used outside the context of the *Taxonomy* structure. An examination of the category headings will show that we finally sought less commonly used terms, where, though we were still using noninventive stipulative definitions, the definitions given these terms and their desciptive definitions were more congruent.

components into the various theories of learning and theories of personality which were extant in the field. While we were able to find the components in almost all the formal theories, we did not find any one theory which structured the components into a single continuum and which sufficiently clarified the meanings of a representative range of objectives chosen from the literature.

The more we carefully studied the components, however, the clearer it became that a continuum might be derived by appropriately ordering them. Thus the continuum progressed from a level at which the individual is merely *aware* of a phenomenon, being *able to perceive it*. At a next level he is *willing to attend* to phenomena. At a next level he *responds* to the phenomena with a *positive feeling*. Eventually he may feel strongly enough to *go out of his way* to respond. At some point in the process he conceptualizes his behavior and feelings and *organizes* these conceptualizations into a structure. This structure grows in complexity as *it becomes his life outlook*.

This ordering of the components seemed to describe a process by which a given phenomenon or value passed from a level of bare awareness to a position of some power to guide or control the behavior of a person. If it passed through all the stages in which it played an increasingly important role in a person's life, it would come to dominate and control certain aspects of that life as it was absorbed more and more into the internal controlling structure. This process or continuum seemed best described by a term which was heard at various times in our discussions and which has been used similarly in the literature: "internalization." This word seemed an apt description of the process by which the phenomenon or value successively and pervasively becomes a part of the individual.

When we tried this concept as an organizing principle, we found we were able to construct a meaningful continuum. When we tried it with objectives, we found it helpful in delimiting and describing them and in classifying them into this structure. Our method of choice of an organizing structure was a combination of analytic and pragmatic criteria. The process termed "internalization" was chosen because it encompassed and combined the components which were present when we analyzed the behaviors implied by objectives belonging in the domain. It gave an ordering to these components which appeared to be reasonably parallel to some of our theories about how learning takes place with affective objectives. It helped to define operationally the kinds of tasks a teacher faces in this domain. It appeared to provide a means for cutting through the tangle of conflicting and inadequate learning theories without tying the structure to any one of them. It was consistent with the behavioral point of view of education which places the focus of learning within the individual, and it constructed a continuum of his behavior. It helped to simplify and clarify the meaning of both terse and lengthy complex affective objectives if we analyzed them from this point of view.

Once we decided to adopt it, our problems became (1) to define more completely what was meant by the word "internalization," in relation both to some of its previous uses and to similar terms used by psychologists and educators; (2) to describe the way it appears in the structuring of an affective continuum and the way that continuum can be arbitrarily but meaningfully divided into stages or levels; (3) to relate the affective continuum to commonly used affective terms; (4) to test the structure against some research evidence.

## INTERNALIZATION: ITS NATURE

The description of the process of internalization is not a product of any one theory or point of view. As we see it, it is not a new concept but a useful combination of old ones. English and English define it as "incorporating something within the mind or body; adopting as one's own the ideas, practices, standards, or values of another person or of society."

English and English's definition of internalization as "incorporating . . . within [oneself]" or "adopting as one's own" epitomizes the major aspect of internalization. As viewed in the *Taxonomy,* however, internalization may occur in varying degrees, depending on the extent to which there is an adoption of others' values. Thus in the *Taxonomy* internalization is viewed as a process through which there is at first an incomplete and tentative adoption of only the overt manifestations of the desired behavior and later a more complete adoption.

English and English note that the term is a close relative of the term "socialization," which, though it is "often used as a synonym . . . [properly means] . . . conformity in outward behavior without necessarily accepting the values." They define socialization as "the process whereby a person . . . acquires sensitivity to social stimuli . . . and learns to get along with, and to behave like, others in his group or culture." They also note that it is a major part of the acquisition or personality.

English and English's concept of socialization helps to define a portion of the content of the affective domain—that which is internalized—as well as the first part of the process itself. But even as a description of the content of the affective domain this definition must be interpreted broadly, since "sensitivity to social stimuli" must include the arts as well as others' behavior.

This definition suggests that the culture is perceived as the controlling force in the individual's actions. It is true that the internalization of the prevailing values of the culture describes the bulk of contemporary objectives. But it is equally true that our schools, in their roles as developers of individualism and as change agents in the culture, are not solely concerned with conformity. Internalization as defined in the *Taxonomy* provides equally for the development of both conformity and nonconformity, as either role pervades individual behavior. The term "internalization," by referring to the process through which values, attitudes, etc., in general are acquired, is thus broader than socialization, which refers only to the acceptance of the contemporary value pattern of the society.[2]

An old educational axiom states that "growth occurs from within." The term "internalization" refers to this inner growth which takes place as there is "acceptance by the individual of the attitudes, codes, principles, or sanctions that become a part of him-

---

[2] Internalization of socially disapproved as well as socially approved behavior is possible and does occur. But except as such behavior is used as an educational goal or objective, there is no attempt to encompass it in this framework. Thus, in general, fear, regression, and the various forms of social maladjustment, though of concern to many psychological theorists, lie outside the scope of educational objectives and therefore are not encompassed by the *Taxonomy*. On rare occasions, however, some "negative" emotion such as disgust or indignation (e.g., when racial equality is not observed) or fear (e.g., of bodily injury when safety rules are violated) may appear in an educational objective. It may be restated in its more usual form to stress the positive side (e.g., commitment to the observation of racial equality, conformance to safety rules). By such restatement, the present structure could be used for either positively or "negatively" oriented objectives.

self in forming value judgments or in determining his conduct." This growth takes place in different ways. One of these ways is the increased emotional impact of the experience. At the lowest levels of the internalization continuum there is little emotion in the behavior. At this end the individual is mainly just perceiving the phenomenon. At the middle levels, emotional response is a recognized and critical part of the behavior as the individual actively responds. As the behavior becomes completely internalized and routine, this emotion decreases and is not a regular part of most responses.

Another aspect of the growth is the extent to which external control by the environment yields to inner control as one ascends the continuum. Thus at the lowest end of the continuum, inner control serves only to direct attention. At higher levels, inner control produces appropriate responses, but only at the bidding of an external authority. At still higher levels, inner control produces the appropriate responses even in the absence of an external authority. Indeed at still higher levels, these responses are produced consistently despite obstacles and barriers.

These different aspects of growth suggest that it is probable that the internalization continuum is multidimensional. Certainly it has a simple-to-complex aspect as well as a concrete-to-abstract one. There is the external-to-internal control transition. There is an emotional component that increases up to a point on the continuum. Finally there are the conscious-to-unconscious aspects and cognitive aspects of organization of attitudinal components. (The latter are considered in more detail in the next chapter.)

Any continuum can be more easily and precisely defined if it is unidimensional. But it seems unlikely that we can account for affective phenomena with a unidimensional continuum at this state of our knowledge. We have found the term "intelligence" an extremely useful concept, even though it may be argued that it is multidimensional. It is hoped that internalization will prove a similarly useful basis for this structure, even though it, too, is probably multidimensional . . .

## INTERNALIZATION AS IT APPEARS IN THE TAXONOMY STRUCTURE

The process of internalization can be described by summarizing the continuum at successive levels as they appear in the *Affective Domain Taxonomy*. The process begins when the attention of the student is captured by some phenomenon, characteristic, or value.

As he pays attention to the phenomenon, characteristic, or value, he differentiates it from the others present in the perceptual field. With differentiation comes a seeking out of the phenomenon as he gradually attaches emotional significance to it and comes to value it. As the process unfolds he relates this phenomenon to other phenomena to which he responds that also have value. This responding is sufficiently frequent so that he comes to react regularly, almost automatically, to it and to other things like it. Finally the values are interrelated in a structure or view of the world, which he brings as a "set" to new problems.

Even from this abstract description it can be seen that the internalization process represents a continuous modification of behavior from the individual's being aware of a phenomenon to a pervasive outlook on life that influences all his actions.

While this description of the process seemed reasonably satisfactory, if a hierarchical structure was to be provided and more adequate description of the process developed, it was clear that the continuum needed to be divided into steps or stages. In so far as possible, when this was done, the breaking points between steps were located where there appeared to be some kind of transition, such as the addition of a new component or kind of activity. Since the boundaries of the categories are completely arbitrary and can be defended only on pragmatic grounds, it is possible that later work may suggest that other breaking points would be more satisfactory. The divisions between major categories have proved quite useful in the analysis of objectives. We feel more sure of the major divisions than of the subcategories, some of which appear to be easier to delineate than others . . .

We begin with the individuals being aware of the stimuli which initiate the affective behavior and which form the context in which the affective behavior occurs. Thus, the lowest category is 1.0 *Receiving*. It is subdivided into three categories. At the 1.1 *Awareness* level, the individual merely has his attention attracted to the stimuli (e.g., he develops some consciousness of the use of shading to portray depth and lighting in a picture).[4] The second subcategory,

---

[4] This same objective is successively modified to carry it through many of the levels of the continuum. Readers who would like a fuller description of the reasoning behind the classification of this objective at any level should turn to pages 65–68 in Chapter 5, where the same example is used and its development through the hierarchy is explained in detail.

1.2 *Willingness to receive*, describes the state in which he has differentiated the stimuli from others and is willing to give it his attention (e.g., he develops a tolerance for bizarre uses of shading in modern art). At 1.3 *Controlled or selected attention* the student looks for the stimuli (e.g., he is on the alert for instances where shading has been used both to create a sense of three-dimensional depth and to indicate the lighting of the picture; or he looks for picturesque words in reading).

At the next level, 2.0 *Responding*, the individual is perceived as responding regularly to the affective stimuli. At the lowest level of responding, 2.1 *Acquiescence in responding*, he is merely complying with expectations (e.g., at the request of his teacher, he hangs reproductions of famous paintings in his dormitory room; he is obedient to traffic rules). At the next higher level, 2.2 *Willingness to respond*, he responds increasingly to an inner compulsion (e.g., voluntarily looks for instances of good art where shading, perspective, color, and design have been well used, or has an interest in social problems broader than those of the local community). At 2.3 *Satisfaction in response* he responds emotionally as well (e.g., works with clay, especially in making pottery for personal pleasure). Up to this point he has differentiated the affective stimuli; he has begun to seek them out and to attach emotional significance and value to them.

As the process unfolds, the next levels of 3.0 *Valuing* describe increasing internalization, as the person's behavior is sufficiently consistent that he comes to hold a value: 3.1 *Acceptance of a value* (e.g., continuing desire to develop the ability to write effectively and hold it more strongly), 3.2 *Preference for a value* (e.g., seeks out examples of good art for enjoyment of them to the level where he behaves so as to further this impression actively), and 3.3 *Commitment* (e.g., faith in the power of reason and the method of experimentation).

As the learner successively internalizes values he encounters situations for which more than one value is relevant. This necessitates organizing the values into a system, 4.0 *Organization*. And since a prerequisite to interrelating values is their conceptualization in a form which permits organization, this level is divided in two: 4.1 *Conceptualization of a value* (e.g., desires to evaluate works of art which are appreciated, or to find out and crystallize the basic assumptions which underlie codes of ethics) and 4.2 *Organization of a value system* (e.g., acceptance of the place of art in one's life as one of dominant value, or weighs alternative social policies and practices against the standards of public welfare).

Finally, the internalization and the organization processes reach a point where the individual responds very consistently to value-laden situations with an interrelated set of values, a structure, a view of the world. The *Taxonomy* category that describes this behavior is 5.0 *Characterization by a value or value complex,* and it includes the categories 5.1 *Generalized set* (e.g., views all problems in terms of their aesthetic aspects, or readiness to revise judgments and to change behavior in the light of evidence) and 5.2 *Characterization* (e.g., develops a consistent philosophy of life).

Stripped of their definitions, the category and subcategory titles appear in sequence as follows (see also Appendix A):

1.0 Receiving (attending)
   1.1 Awareness
   1.2 Willingness to receive
   1.3 Controlled or selected attention

2.0 Responding
   2.1 Acquiescence in responding
   2.2 Willingness to respond
   2.3 Satisfaction in response

3.0 Valuing
   3.1 Acceptance of a value
   3.2 Preference for a value
   3.3 Commitment (conviction)

4.0 Organization
   4.1 Conceptualization of a value
   4.2 Organization of a value system

5.0 Characterization by a value or value complex
   5.1 Generalized set
   5.2 Characterization

## 6.2    Psychiatric Evaluation of Candidates for Space Flight

### George E. Ruff, Edwin Z. Levy

The following article is from a paper by George E. Ruff, Captain, USAF (MC) and Edwin Z. Levy, Captain USAF (MC), Stress and Fatigue Section, Biophysics Branch, Aero Medical Laboratory, Wright Air Development Center, Wright-Patterson Air Force Base, Ohio, presented well before the first astronauts in America's space program were launched. It describes in moderate detail the great care which characterized both the selection and evaluation of candidates for space crew duty. Note how the authors demonstrate clearly the ability to utilize extensive background from a discipline oriented to personality pathology for finding and assessing outstanding strengths.

That the amalgamation of what to some seem incompatible approaches to personality study can indeed succeed brilliantly is supported by the almost fantastic performances chalked up by the men who rode America's first space vehicles into history during the early 1960's.

The high levels of stress expected in space flight require careful screening of potential pilots by psychological and physiological techniques. Since emotional demands may be severe, special emphasis must be placed on psychiatric evaluation of each candidate for a space mission.

The selection process begins with a detailed analysis of both the pilot's duties and the conditions under which he will carry them out. As long as we have had no direct experience with space flight, some

Prepared for presentation to 115th annual meeting, the American Psychiatric Association, Philadelphia, Pa., Apr. 29, 1959.
Reprinted with permission of the author and *American Journal of Psychiatry*, **116**, 1959, 385–391. (Although originally presented as a paper under joint authorship, the article was published in *American Journal of Psychiatry* under the name of George E. Ruff only.)

aspects of this analysis will necessarily be speculative. We must thus rely heavily on knowledge of behavior during stress situations in the past. As a result, data from military operations, survival experiences, and laboratory experiments have guided the choice of men for space missions now being planned.

Although striking exceptions are seen, the individuals who have done best under difficult circumstances in the past have been mature and emotionally stable. They have usually been able to harmonize internal needs with external reality in an effective manner. When subjected to stress, anxiety has not reached high enough levels to paralyze their activity.

After the requirements of the mission and the qualifications of the individual best suited to accomplish it have been decided, it is necessary to select measures for determining who has the most of each desirable characteristic and the least of each undesirable characteristic. This can be done by using interviews and projective tests to give an intensive picture of each individual. Objective tests supplement the personality evaluation and measure intellectual functions, aptitudes, and achievements. After examination of the background data, interview material, and tests results, clinical judgment is used to decide which men are psychologically best qualified for the assignment.

As firsthand knowledge of space flight increases, these procedures must be reexamined. When enough data have accumulated, predictions can be checked against performance criteria. Methods which predicted accurately will be retained and improved. Those with little value will be discarded. New measures can be added on the basis of increasing experience. Once correlation between psychological variables and the quality of performance have been determined, the accuracy of future selection programs should be raised.

A clinical approach of this type was used in selecting pilots for the first U. S. manned satellite experiment—NASA's Project Mercury. The objective was to choose men for a 2-year training program, followed by a series of ballistic and orbital flights. The pilot's duties will consist largely of reading instruments and recording observations. However, he will retain certain decision-making functions, and will be required to adapt to changing conditions as circumstances may demand.

By combining data on the nature of this mission with information on behavior during other stressful operations, the following general requirements were established:

1) Candidates should have a high level of general intelligence, with abilities to interpret instruments, perceive mathematical relationships, and maintain spatial orientation.

2) There should be sufficient evidence of drive and creativity to insure positive contributions to the development of the vehicle and other aspects of the project as a whole.

3) Relative freedom from conflict and anxiety is desirable. Exaggerated and stereotyped defenses should be avoided.

4) Candidates should not be overly dependent on others for the satisfaction of their needs. At the same time, they must be able to accept dependence on others when required for the success of the mission. They must be able to tolerate either close associations or extreme isolation.

5) The pilot should be able to function when out of familiar surroundings and when usual patterns of behavior are impossible.

6) Candidates must show evidence of ability to respond predictably to foreseeable situations, without losing the capacity to adapt flexibly to circumstances which cannot be foreseen.

7) Motivation should depend primarily on interest in the mission rather than on exaggerated needs for personal accomplishment. Self-destructive wishes and attempts to compensate for identity problems or feelings of inadequacy are undesirable.

8) There should be no evidence of impulsivity. The pilot must act when action is appropriate, but refrain from action when inactivity is appropriate. He must be able to tolerate stress situations positively, without requiring motor activity to dissipate anxiety.

The chances of finding men to meet these requirements were increased by the preselection process. Eligibility for the mission was restricted to test pilots who had repeatedly demonstrated their ability to perform functions essential for the Mercury project. Records of men in this category were reviewed to find those best suited for the specific demands of the mission. A group of 69 were then invited to volunteer. The 55 who accepted were given a series of interviews and psychological tests. On the basis of these data, 32 were chosen for the final phase of the selection program. This phase was designed to evaluate each candidate's medical and psychological status, as well as to determine his capacity for tolerating stress conditions expected in space flight.

The psychological evaluation included 30 hours of psychiatric interviews, psychological tests, and observations of stress experiments. The information obtained was used to rate candidates on a 10-point scale for each of 17 categories. Ratings were made on the basis of specific features of behavior—both as indicated by the past history and as observed during the interviews. Even though the general population was used as a reference group, the scales are normative only in an arbitrary sense. The 10 levels represent subjective decisions on which characteristics are ideal, which are average and which are undesirable. Although the reliability among raters is excellent, validation studies have not yet been done.

The categories are:

1) Drive: An estimate of the total quantity of instinctual energy.

2) Freedom from conflict and anxiety: A clinical evaluation of the number and severity of unresolved problem areas and of the extent to which they interfere with the candidate's functioning.

3) Effectiveness of defenses: How efficient are the ego defenses? Are they flexible and adaptive or rigid and inappropriate? Will the mission deprive the candidate of elements necessary for the integrity of his defensive system?

4) Free energy: What is the quantity of neutral energy? Are defenses so expensive to maintain that nothing is left for creative activity? How large is the "conflict-free sphere of the ego"?

5) Identity: How well has the candidate established a concept of himself and his relationship to the rest of the world?

6) Object relationships: Does he have the capacity to form genuine object relationships? Can he withdraw object cathexes when necessary? To what extent is he involved in his relationships with others?

7) Reality testing: Does the subject have a relatively undistorted view of his environment? Have his life experiences been broad enough to allow a sophisticated appraisal of the world? Does his view of the mission represent fantasy or reality?

8) Dependency: How much must the candidate rely on others? How well does he accept dependency needs? Is separation anxiety likely to interfere with his conduct of the mission?

9) Adaptability: How well does he adapt to changing circumstances? What is the range of conditions under which he can function? What are the adjustments he can make? Can he compromise flexibly?

10) Freedom from impulsivity: How well can the candidate delay gratification of his needs? Has his behavior in the past been consistent and predictable?

11) Need for activity: What is the minimum degree of motor activity required? Can he tolerate enforced passivity?

12) Somatization: Can the candidate be expected to develop physical symptoms while under stress? How aware is he of his own body?

13) Quantity of motivation: How strongly does he want to participate in the mission? Are there conflicts between motives—whether conscious or unconscious? Will his motivation remain at a high level?

14) Quality of motivation: Is the subject motivated by a desire for narcissistic gratification? Does he show evidence of self-destructive wishes? Is he attempting to test adolescent fantasies of invulnerability?

15) Frustration tolerance: What will be the result of failure to reach established goals? What behavior can be expected in the face of annoyances, delays, or disappointments?

16) Social relationships: How well does the subject work with a group? Does he have significant authority problems? Will he contribute to the success of missions for which he is not chosen as pilot? How well do other candidates like him?

17) Overall rating: An estimate of the subject's suitability for the mission. This is based upon interviews, test results, and other information considered relevant.

It can be seen that categories 1, 2, 4, and 10 are largely economic constructs; 3, 5, 6, and 7 are ego functions: while the rest are specific characteristics considered important for space flight. The categories represent many different levels of abstraction and are not independent dimensions. In the final analysis, they are less a means of quantifying data than of organizing their interpretation. Not only do they provide a method to compare one subject with another, but also tend to focus attention on the material most closely related to the mission requirements.

An initial evaluation of each man was made by two psychiatrists, through separate interviews during the preliminary screening period. One interview was devoted primarily to a review of the history and current life adjustment, while the other was relatively unstructured. Finally, ratings were compared, information pooled, and a combined rating made. Areas of doubt and disagreement were recorded for subsequent investigation.

The men accepted for the final screening procedure were seen again several weeks later, after an intensive evaluation of their physical status had been completed. Each candidate was reinterviewed and the following psychological tests were administered:

## MEASURES OF MOTIVATION AND PERSONALITY

1) Rorschach.

2) Thematic apperception test.

3) Draw-a-person.

4) Sentence completion test.

5) Minnesota multiphasic personality inventory.

6) Who am I?: The subject is asked to write 20 answers to the question, "Who am I?" This is interpreted projectively to give information on identity and perception of social roles.

7) Gordon personal profile: An objective personality test yielding scores for "ascendency," "responsibility," "emotional stability," and "sociability."

8) Edwards personal preference schedule: A force-choice questionnaire measuring the strengths of Murray's needs.

9) Shipley personal inventory: Choices are made from 20 pairs of self-descriptive statements concerning psychosomatic problems.

10) Outer-inner preferences: A measure of interest in and dependence on social groups.

11) Pensacola Z-scale: A test of the strength of "authoritarian" attitudes.

12) Officer effectiveness inventory: A measure of personality characteristics found in successful Air Force officers.

13) Peer ratings: Each candidate was asked to indicate which of the other members of the group who accompanied him through the program he liked best, which one he would like to accompany him on a two-man mission, and which one he would assign to the mission if he could not go himself.

## MEASURES OF INTELLECTUAL FUNCTIONS AND SPECIAL APTITUDES

1) Wechsler adult intelligence scale.

2) Miller analogies test.

3) Raven progressive matrices: A test of nonverbal concept formation.

4) Doppelt mathematical reasoning test: A test of mathematical aptitudes.

5) Engineering analogies: A measure of engineering achievement and aptitudes.

6) Mechanical comprehension: A measure of mechanical aptitudes and ability to apply mechanical principles.

7) Air Force officer qualification test: The portions used are measures of verbal and quantitative aptitudes.

8) Aviation qualification test (USN): A measure of academic achievement.

9) Space memory test: A test of memory for location of objects in space.

10) Spatial orientation: A measure of spatial visualization and orientation.

11) Gottschaldt hidden figures: A measure of ability to locate a specified form imbedded in a mass of irrelevant details.

12) Guilford-Zimmerman spatial visualization test: A test of ability to visualize movement in space.

In addition to the interviews and tests, important information was obtained from the reactions of each candidate to a series of stress experiments simulating conditions expected during the mission. Neither the design of these tests nor the physiological variables measured will be discussed. Psychological data were derived from direct observation of behavior, post-experimental interviews, and administration before and after each run of alternate forms of six tests of perceptual and psychomotor functions. These procedures were:

1) Pressure suit test: After dressing in a tightly fitting garment designed to apply pressure to the body during high altitude flight, each candidate entered a chamber from which air was evacuated to simulate an altitude of 65,000 feet. This produces severe physical discomfort and confinement.

2) Isolation: Each man was confined to a dark, soundproof room for 3 hours. While this brief period is not stressful for most people, data are obtained on the style of adaptation to isolation. This proce-

dure aids in identifying subjects who cannot tolerate enforced inactivity, enclosure in small spaces or absence of external stimuli.

3) Complex behavior simulator: The candidate was required to make different responses to each of 14 signals which appeared in random order at increasing rates of speed. Since the test produces a maximum of confusion and frustration, it measures ability to organize behavior and to maintain emotional equilibrium under stress.

4) Acceleration: The candidates were placed on the human centrifuge in various positions and subjected to different G loads. This procedure leads to anxiety, disorientation, and blackout in susceptible subjects.

5) Noise and vibration: Candidates were vibrated at varying frequencies and amplitudes and subjected to high energy sound. Efficiency is often impaired under these conditions.

6) Heat: Each candidate spent 2 hours in a chamber maintained at 130°. Once again, this is an uncomfortable experience during which efficiency may be impaired.

After all tests were completed, an evaluation of each man was made by a conference of those who had gathered the psychological data. Final ratings were made in each category described previously, special aptitudes were considered, and a ranking within the group was derived. By combining the psychiatric evaluations, results of the physical examinations and physiological data from the stress test procedures, the group was subdivided under the headings "Outstanding," "Recommended," and "Not Recommended." Finally, seven men were chosen from the list according to the specific needs of the Mercury project.

## IMPRESSIONS OF CANDIDATES FOR SPACE FLIGHT

Although the results of the selection program can't be assessed for several years, impressions derived from psychiatric evaluations of these candidates are of interest. In answer to the question, "What kind of people volunteer to be fired into orbit?" one might expect strong intimations of psychopathology. The high incidence of emotional disorders in volunteers for laboratory experiments had much to do with the decision to consider only candidates with records of effective performance under difficult circumstances in the past. It was hoped that avoiding an open call for volunteers would reduce the number of unstable candidates.

In spite of the preselection process, we were surprised by the low incidence of such disorders in the 55 candidates who were interviewed. For the 31 candidates who survived the initial screening and physical examination, repeat interviews and psychological tests confirmed the original impressions. There was no evidence for a diagnosis of psychosis, clinically significant neurosis, or personality disorder in any member of this group.

Certain general comments can be made concerning the 31 men who received the complete series of selection procedures. The mean age was 33, with a range from 27 to 38. All but one were married. Twenty were from the Midwest, Far West, or Southwest. Only two had lived in large cities before entering college. Twenty-seven were from intact families. Twenty were only or eldest children. (In this connection, it is perhaps worth noting that four of the seven men chosen are named "junior.") Pronounced identifications with one parent were about equally divided between fathers and mothers, although mothers with whom such identifications were present were strong, not infrequently masculine figures.

Impressions from the interviews were that these were comfortable, mature, well-integrated individuals. Ratings in all categories of the system used consistently fell in the top third of the scale. Reality testing, adaptability, and drive were particularly high. Little evidence was found of unresolved conflict sufficiently serious to interfere with functioning. Suggestions of overt anxiety were rare. Defenses were effective, tending to be obsessive-compulsive, but not to an exaggerated degree. Most were direct, action-oriented individuals, who spend little time introspecting.

Although dependency needs were not overly strong, most showed the capacity to relate effectively to others. Interpersonal activities were characterized by knowledge of techniques for dealing with many kinds of people. They do not become overly involved with others, although relationships with their families are warm and stable.

Because of the possibility that extreme interest in high performance aircraft might be related to feelings of inadequacy in sexual or other areas, particular emphasis was placed on a review of each candidate's adolescence. Little information could be uncovered to justify the conclusion that unconscious problems of this kind were either more or less common than in other occupational groups.

A high proportion of these men apparently passed through adolescence in comfortable fashion. Most made excellent school and social adjustments. Many had been class presidents or showed other evidence of leadership.

Most candidates entered military life during World War II. Some demonstrated an unusual interest in flying from an early age, but most had about the same attitudes toward airplanes as other American boys. Many volunteered for flight training because it provided career advantages or appeared to be an interesting assignment.

Candidates described their feelings about flying in a variety of terms: "something out of the ordinary," "a challenge," "a chance to get above the hubbub," "a sense of freedom," "an opportunity to take responsibility." A few look upon flying as a means of proving themselves or to build confidence. Others consider it a "way for good men to show what they can do."

Although half the candidates volunteered for training as test pilots, the others were selected because of achievements in other assignments. Most view test flying as a chance to participate in the development of new aircraft. It enables them to combine their experience as pilots and engineers. Their profession is aviation and they want to be in the forefront of its progress. Danger is admitted, but deemphasized—most feel nothing will happen to them. But this seems to be less a wishful fantasy than a conviction that accidents can be avoided by knowledge and caution. They believe that risks are minimized by thorough planning and conservatism. Very few fit the popular concept of the daredevil test pilot.

Although attempts have been made to formulate the dynamics underlying the pursuit of this unusual occupation, generalizations are difficult to make. Motives vary widely. While it is clear that conscious reasons may be unrelated to unconscious determinants, the variation in conscious attitudes illustrates the impossibility of a single explanation for a career which has different meanings for different individuals. One man, for example, stated that he enjoys flight testing because it allows him to do things which are new and different. He enjoys flying the newest aircraft available—vehicles that most pilots will not see for several years. Another is an aeronautical engineer who is primarily interested in aircraft design. He looks upon a flight test much as the researcher views a laboratory experiment.

Reasons for volunteering in project Mercury show a mixture of professionalism and love of adventure. Candidates are uniformly eager to be part of an undertaking of vast importance. On one hand, space flight is viewed as the next logical step in the progress of aviation; on the other, it represents a challenge. One man expressed the sentiments of the group by saying, "There aren't many new frontiers. This is a chance to be in one of them." Other expressions included: "a new dimension of flight," "a further stage in the flight envelope of the manned vehicle," "a chance to get your teeth into something big," "the sequel to the aviation age," "a contribution to human knowledge," "an opportunity for accomplishment," "the program of the future," "an interesting, exciting field," "a chance to be on the ground floor of the biggest thing man has ever done."

At the same time, most candidates were practical. They recognized that this project will benefit their careers. To some it is a chance to insure an interesting assignment. Most recognize the trend away from conventional manned aircraft and look upon the Mercury project as a means for getting into the midst of future developments. One said: "We're the last of the horse cavalry. There aren't going to be many more new fighters. This is the next big step in aviation. I want to be part of it." Most are aware of the potential personal publicity and feel this would be pleasant, but "not an important reason for volunteering."

Although all candidates are eager to make the flight, it is not their only concern. Most want to participate in development of the vehicle and have an opportunity to advance their technical training. The orbital ride is partly looked upon as a chance to test an item of hardware they have helped develop. Risks are appreciated, but accepted. Most insist they will go only when the odds favor their return. No one is going up to die. They are attracted by the constructive rather than the destructive aspects of the mission.

Psychological tests of these 31 men indicate a high level of intellectual functioning. For example, the mean full-scale scores for the seven who have been selected range from 130 to 141, with a mean of 135. The pattern is balanced, with consistently high scores on both verbal and performance subtests.

Projective measures suggest the same healthy adaptations seen in the interviews. Responses to the Rorschach, for example, were well organized. Although not overly rigid, they did not suggest much imagination and creativity. Aggressive impulses tended to be expressed in action rather than fantasy.

Behavior during the isolation and complex behavior simulator tests—which might be considered input-underload and input-over-load situations—showed evidence of great adaptability. No candidate terminated isolation prematurely and none viewed it as a difficult experience. As might be expected for this brief exposure, no perceptual changes were reported. Fifteen subjects "programed" their thinking in isolation. In five of these men, the attempt to organize thoughts was considered evidence of an overly strong need for structuring. Sixteen permitted random thought, relaxed and enjoyed the experience. Most slept at least part of the time.

When placed under opposite conditions—with too much to do instead of too little—the candidates were usually able to keep from falling hopelessly behind the machine. Only a few were troubled by the impossibility of making all responses promptly. The majority became content to do as well as possible, showing a gradually increasing level of skin resistance, even though working at a frantic pace.

Reactions to physiological stressors correlated positively with the psychiatric evaluations. Candidates who had been ranked highest on psychological variables tended to do best in acceleration, noise and vibration, heat, and pressure chamber runs. Their stress tolerance levels were among the highest of the hundreds of men subjected to these procedures in the past. Uncomplaining acceptance of the discomforts and inconveniences of this phase of the program appeared to reflect not only their strong motivation, but also their general maturity and capacity to withstand frustration.

In summary, it is suggested that the most reasonable approach to selecting men for doing something no one has done before is to choose those who have been successful in demanding missions in the past. To decrease the probability of error, a broad sample of behavior must be observed. Every effort should be made to make these observations as relevant to the expected demands of this mission as possible.

By selecting only those candidates who were able to adapt to whatever conditions confronted them, we hope we have found those who are best qualified for space flight. Our confidence is further strengthened by the attitudes of the men who were chosen. Most reflected the opinion of the candidate who, when asked why he had volunteered, explained: "In the first 50 years since the Wright brothers, we learned to fly faster than sound and higher than 50,000 feet. In another 5 years we doubled that. Now we're ready to go out 100 miles. How could anyone turn down a chance to be part of something like this?"

---

## 6.3    The Unique Functions of Assessment Procedures

*Lee J. Cronbach*

In this important excerpt from a very popular testing text, Professor Cronbach argues cogently in defense of the so-called impressionistic or, better-called, assessment procedures for gaining understanding about an individual personality.

Earlier in the chapter from which this portion is taken, the author demonstrated that failure almost inevitably follows attempts to make precise predictions about a person's particular likes, interests, and general adjustment from personality assessment procedures such as observational records and projective devices and techniques. The author has suggested, as one explanation, that such complex behaviors are best conceived as *divergent* phenomena, that is, multiple-determined and uniquely different for every person. He points out that "William James warned, psychology can establish general expectations but cannot hope to give biographies in advance."

Note carefully, however, that used appropriately, impressionistic technique is invaluable for gaining insights into a subject and for diagnostic hypothesis generation.

In the writer's opinion, assessment techniques have been asked to do a job for which they are ill suited. It has been necessary to emphasize the extensive and discouraging negative results on the use of clinical techniques as predictors, but there is another, more positive evaluation to be made.

Assessment techniques have three related features which set them apart from conventional psychometric methods. Stated simply, these are as follows:

They provide information both on typical response patterns and on stimulus meanings.

They cover a very large number of questions about the individual.

They provide information about different questions for different individuals.

## COVERAGE OF STIMULUS MEANINGS

The psychometric approach is to confront the individual with a carefully selected task or set of tasks which represent a criterion situation in some way. This description applies to proficiency tests, to aptitude tests, to questionnaires on typical performance, and to worksample performance tests such as the LGD.[1] We saw that even impressionistic interpretation of such samples of behavior gave valid predictions for civil service and OCS [2] selection. The essential assumption in this type of testing is that we can generalize from a sample of behavior to performance in *one class* of situations.

A person's behavior changes from situation to situation, however, and when one must understand the person as a whole, or must select situations to fit him, a simple prediction by sampling within one class is impossible. One must begin to learn what situations mean for him. Much of the content of an interview deals with situational meanings: attitudes toward parents, former employers, school subjects, etc. The thematic projective tests elicit similar information, though in a more disguised and perhaps less censored form.

The Semantic Differential is the only psychometric technique designed to study meanings the person gives to significant others. Even this procedure, though structured and quantifiable, is interpreted impressionistically when a single individual is under study. Hence there is no psychometric technique for obtaining information about the subject's reactions to various persons and situations—unless one wishes to prepare dozens of questionnaires or Q sorts, each dealing with one person or situation. While research along the lines recently opened by Osgood and G. A. Kelly may lead to well-

---

[1] Leaderless Group Discussion
[2] Officers' Candidate School

controlled psychometric techniques, at this time there is no alternative to some type of clinical assessment if we want attitudinal information covering a wide range of objects. It is unfortunate that there have been no controlled validation studies to show just how well such procedures as TAT[3] and Semantic Differential identify significant attitudes. Virtually all systematic validation of impressionistic methods has examined their adequacy as measures of traits (i.e., of response information).

## BANDWIDTH

Shannon's "information theory" (1949), developed for the study of electronic communication systems, provides a model for considering the second important feature of assessment methods. He distinguishes two attributes of any communication system: bandwidth and fidelity.

Home record players have made "high fidelity" familiar to everyone. The complementary concept of bandwidth refers to the amount of complexity of information one tries to obtain in a given space or time. The fidelity of recording depends upon the width of the groove; if grooves are crowded together to put more music on a record, fidelity suffers. Fidelity could be improved over present standards by designing record and playback systems which would carry less information (e.g., a 33-rpm record lasting only ten minutes instead of thirty). With other things held constant, any shift in the direction of greater fidelity reduces bandwidth; and increase in bandwidth may be purchased at the price of fidelity. In any particular communication system there is an ideal compromise between bandwidth and fidelity. The record industry settled on the 33-rpm "long-play" record; the FCC allows the FM station a bandwidth of 22 kilocycles.

The classical psychometric ideal is the instrument with high fidelity and low bandwidth (Cronbach and Gleser, 1957; Hewer, 1955, pp. 3–19). A college aptitude test tries to answer just one question with great accuracy. It concentrates its content in a very narrow range, using correlated items to increase reliability. Because its parts are highly correlated, part scores give little information for choosing majors or diagnosing weaknesses. Most other excellent

---

[3] Thematic Apperception Test—a projective technique in which the subject tells a story elicited by a picture.

predictors such as the LGD participation score and the peer rating have similar limitation to one central variable.

At the opposite extreme, the interview and the projective technique have almost unlimited bandwidth. Whereas the aptitude test may devote three hours to obtaining just one score, the interviewer may cover twenty topics in a half-hour, and note an even larger number of traits. In some TAT studies ratings were made on more than forty variables, all on the basis of about an hour's testing. The individual description adds a dozen or more statements about individual traits or attitudes not commonly encountered.

There are tests with intermediate bandwidths, and a particular technique like the Binet or MMPI [4] may be used as a narrowband method by some testers and as a wideband method by others. All the validity studies we have reviewed substantiate Shannon's principle: increases in complexity of information are obtained only by sacrificing fidelity. The Wechsler Verbal IQ is highly valid. Patterns of subtest scores are of some but quite limited value. And interpretations of response to single items, or judgments about observed processes are distinctly untrustworthy. The most successful combinations of large bandwidth with relatively high fidelity are the GATB [5] and the SVIB,[6] both of which are designed for counseling where many alternatives must be considered and useful prediction can be made from about a dozen scores.

Extremely large bandwidth is disadvantageous because the information becomes too unreliable for use. Extremely small bandwidth, on the other hand, is appropriate only where there is one specific, all-important question to be answered, to which all testing effort should be devoted. While no rule can be given specifying the ideal bandwidth for testing, we can point to conditions favoring wider or narrower bandwidth:

The first is the number and relative importance of decisions to be made. If an institution is concerned with a simple decision and only one outcome, it should concentrate on the information most relevant to that decision. (Example: a college wishing to admit students who will make good academic records, without regard to values, social or emotional adjustment, or probable post-college career.) If many outcomes or alternatives are to be considered, more types of infor-

[4] Minnesota Multiphasic Inventory (personality)
[5] General Aptitude Test Battery
[6] Strong Vocational Interest Blank

mation are needed and bandwidth must increase. Counseling, diagnosis, remedial teaching, and supervision of professional workers generally involve multifaceted decisions. The testing effort should be balanced to obtain relatively dependable information on the most important questions or those which are most likely to arise. It is better to ignore minor questions than to spread one's inquiry too thin (Cronbach and Gleser, 1957, p. 96).

Bandwidth can be greatly increased when it is possible to confirm or reverse judgments at a later time. Lack of fidelity does no harm unless it leads to costly errors. Narrowband instruments are desired for making final, irreversible decisions about important matters (e.g., scholarship awards). The wideband technique, on the other hand, serves well as the first stage in a sequential measuring operation. As a first stage, the wideband test scans superficially a range of important variables, pointing out significant possibilities for further study. In this use the wideband procedure is used for *hypothesis formation*, not for final decisions.

This is the proper function of the Strong blank, for example. It is not a highly valid basis for career choice. It is an inexpensive pencil-and-paper interview which gives an excellent preliminary mapping of the vocational field. Its ease of administration, objective scoring, and norms make it superior to the unconstrained interview (which has even greater bandwidth). Following the test, the counselor uses a more focused interview to confirm high scores and to determine their implications. Even this discussion should not lead to a final decision. It is better to narrow the choice to two or three areas; these hypotheses can be tested by enrolling in suitable courses and by trying relevant summer jobs.

Comparable opportunities for follow-up and confirmation of assessments or score interpretations exist in virtually every decision except selection. Fallible tests can suggest assignments for an employee, treatments for a patient, teaching techniques for a student. Even if the test is little better than a guess, it has some value when there is no sounder basis for choice. Since trying out the hypothesis permits verification, and change when the hypothesis was wrong, little has been lost. We may say, in sum, that the fallibility of wideband procedures does no harm unless the hypotheses and suggestions they offer are regarded as verified conclusions about the individual. And of course some degree of skepticism is required in interpreting the score from any psychological test, however precise and narrowly focused it may be.

Impressionistic procedures, and psychometric procedures in clinical settings, are chiefly used for hypothesis formation. Clinicians bring a Rorschach interpretation or a Wechsler IQ to a case conference, where it is considered along with other data, and this conference concludes that it is better to try one therapy than another. Only where the decision is irreversible, as when surgery is prescribed or where the patient once classified is forever left in the same pigeonhole, is this use of impressions and imperfectly valid scores dangerous. Likewise in executive appraisal or school psychology, the recommendations of the tester are recommendations about experiments to be tried. Unfortunately, assessors (and psychometric testers) have far too often claimed that their methods give valid final conclusions. This has two bad consequences; nonpsychologists expect more than the assessor can deliver, and the psychologist tries to live up to his claim by giving one description or recommendation instead of outlining the reasonable alternatives.

## ADAPTATION TO THE INDIVIDUAL

Closely related to the foregoing comments are the advantages of assessment procedures for shaping the testing to the individual. The psychometric tester standardizes his test to answer a question presumed to be important for everyone. The impressionistic tester may vary the problems and topics covered by the testing to fit the individual. The psychometric tester tries to standardize every aspect of his measuring procedure, so that precisely the same information is obtained about each subject. The impressionistic tester wishes to obtain whatever information is most significant regarding a particular individual, even if this means asking different questions of each person. The flexibly administered interview, the individualized Rep test, and the unstructured projective technique elicit idiosyncratic, personally significant responses for which there is no counterpart in psychometric methodology. These responses can only be interpreted impressionistically.

Meehl (1954) gives several examples of such interpretations, which he properly regards as the essence of the clinical art. One is from the psychoanalyst Reik (1948, p. 263):

Our session at this time took the following course. After a few sentences about the uneventful day, the patient fell into a long silence. She assured me that nothing was in her thoughts. Silence from me. After many minutes she complained about a toothache.

She told me that she had been to the dentist yesterday. He had given her an injection and then had pulled a wisdom tooth. The spot was hurting again. New and longer silence. She pointed to my bookcase in the corner and said, "There's a book standing on its head." Without the slightest hesitation and in a reproachful voice I said, "But why did you not tell me that you had had an abortion?"

How Reik made this correct inference from the patient's chain of associations and silences is not our concern here. The skill is compounded of theory, imagination, experience, and willingness to make (and verify or discard) rash guesses. The important point is that this interpretation, which might accelerate appreciably the therapy, could not possibly have been reached by a formal testing procedure. In the first place, such a procedure would be unlikely to touch upon the particular topic of abortion. Even if it did, there is no "trait" on which the response could be scored, unless one envisions keying the MMPI to distinguish ex-abortion patients from other women—and similarly for every other group having conceivable clinical interest. Secondly, the response cannot possibly be interpreted by any multiple-regression or other formal procedure. How could one establish frequency tables to give the meaning of associations-about-a-dental-extraction-plus-silence-plus-observation-about-an-inverted-book? This is a unique datum to be interpreted only by a creative act of applying such a theory as the psychoanalytic hypothesis that tooth extraction is a disguised symbol of birth. This extreme example of symbolic communication shows clinical idiographic interpretation in its purest form, but unique content is interpreted by every assessor.

The interpreter must likewise deal with the unprecedented when he predicts response to a specific situation. "Should this child be sent back to his mother or placed in a foster home?" is a decision in which statistics cannot aid. No experience table can predict from IQ, anxiety level, or anything else whether he will adjust well to his mother. This can be estimated only from her particular character, the child's character, and the precise home situation. Any decision about this problem is likely to be wrong, but that is beside the point. The decision must be made, and insofar as psychological study of the child can improve the decision, the risk of error is reduced. In this case, impressionistic appraisal is the best available basis for decision. All the "little" decisions that take place from minute to minute in therapy and teaching are similarly resistant to measurement and statistics. In these judgments, where the psychometric tester would have nothing to say, the hints from the TAT or a case history may provide valuable guidance (Meehl, 1954, p. 120).

The difference between psychometric and impressionistic assessment, we find, is not that one uses multiple-choice questions and one uses inkblots, or that one is compulsively cautious, the other erratically overambitious. The two approaches to observation and interpretation are suited to different purposes. When clinical testers answer questions for which their methods and theory are badly suited, their answers are next to worthless or at best are costly beyond their value. When psychometric testers are faced with a clinical problem calling for understanding rather than simple evaluation (e.g., what lies behind a given child's anxious withdrawal?) they are unable to give any answer at all. Each in his own proper province will surpass the other and each outside his province is nearly impotent. Assessment methods have earned a bad name for themselves by trying to compete with measurement techniques on their own ground. In the absence of excellent research to guide the combination of information, the wideband technique should not be advanced as a means of predicting specific, recurring criteria. The precisely focused instrument, on the other hand, should not be exalted into the sole approved technique for gathering information. It is efficient only when the decision maker asks the particular question for which it has been designed and validated. Even the TMC [7] must be interpreted impressionistically when one wants to explain a low score, or to predict performance in a new training program.

---

[7] Test of Mechanical Comprehension

---

## 6.4   Why a Taxonomy of Affective Learning?

*David W. Darling*

The terms "interests" and "attitudes" appear frequently in the stated objectives of schools and other institutions devoted to behavioral change. Unfortunately, such important traits continuously resist the best attempts to measure them.

Reprinted with permission of the author and *Educational Leadership*, **22**, April 1965, 473–75, 522.

Perhaps one principal explanation for this refractory state of affairs is the lack of clear definition in observed response terms of the attainment of such objectives.

The author of the following article attempts to point out areas in which the teacher, the curriculum worker, and the researcher each in turn can immediately begin to use the Taxonomy.

As you read this, see if you can generate an evaluative situation in which the Taxonomy could assist you to measure some affective outcome.


Why a taxonomy of affective learning? [1] How does one go about answering such a question? What a task! I submit that this very important question, posed in its present form, cannot be directly answered. It is my intent to develop a rationale which justifies and helps explain the affective taxonomy by exploring the following questions:

1. Are the schools responsible for the development of qualities of character and conscience in learners as expressed in their interests, attitudes, appreciations, values, and emotional sets or biases?

2. Does the taxonomy of affective learning have any practical value in designing and evaluating learning experiences or in curriculum building?

3. Does the affective taxonomy have research potential which will contribute to our growing science of education?

If the answer to the first question is yes, then the affective taxonomy clearly has a contribution to make. The taxonomy represents an intelligent and rational synthesis of much thought and research in psychology and personality theory and gives this synthesis a structure heretofore not visible and hence not communicable. The taxonomy takes the old triad of "interests, attitudes, and val-

---

[1] Much of the structure of this article is based on the following sources: Benjamin S. Bloom, editor. *Taxonomy of Educational Objectives; The Classification of Educational Goals. Handbook I: Cognitive Domain.* New York: Longmans, Green and Co., 1956. David R. Krathwohl, Benjamin S. Bloom, Bertram B. Masia. *Taxonomy of Educational Objectives; The Classification of Educational Goals: Handbook II: Affective Domain.* New York: David McKay Co., Inc., 1964.

ues," redefines them in more specific terms (and more categories) and gives a rational ordering to their occurrence.

The reader may recall that there are five levels in the hierarchy of the affective taxonomy: (1) Receiving, (2) Responding, (3) Valuing, (4) Organizing, and (5) Characterization. All the behaviors of Level 1 (Receiving), i.e., *awareness, willingness to receive,* and *selective attention,* are indicators of a progression of interest. Likewise the first step of Level 2 (Responding), *acquiescence in responding,* is the highest level of interest before attitudes are affected. Both interest and attitude are at play when a child exhibits a *willingness to respond* and then derives some *satisfaction from his response* (the two remaining steps in Responding).

Interests, attitudes, and values are all apparent when a child indicates the *acceptance of a value* and then, through his behavior, indicates a *preference for a value.* These behaviors are the first two steps of Level 3, Valuing. When a child indicates a *commitment* to a value, he has moved beyond mere interest but attitudes and values are still of concern. Also in the attitude-value overlap is the *conceptualization of a value,* a step beyond *commitment,* and the first step of Level 4, Organizing. Finally, the child (or adult) moves beyond mere attitudes to the highest levels of value formation when he reaches the highest step of Level 4, *organization of a value system,* and then moves through Characterization by *formulating a generalized value set,* and then he is able to relate this set to the larger world in which he lives; there the set becomes the *Characterization of the individual.* The latter two behaviors compose Level 5, Characterization.

Are not the steps indicated in the taxonomy more specific and indicative of corresponding behaviors than are "interests, attitudes, and values"? Is there not a clear taxonomical progression of behavior that is completely lacking in the triad of "interests, attitudes, and values"? The answers to these questions are obvious. Yet are the schools responsible for the interests, attitudes, and values of students?

Certainly the terms "interests" and "attitudes" appear in the stated objectives of schools often enough to be considered within the province of the school. What about values? If schools are responsible only for "interests" and "attitudes" and not "values," what is the highest step in the taxonomy for which the school has a charge? Can the school ignore the other steps of affective learning indicated in the taxonomy? These questions are left for the reader to ponder.

## PRACTICAL UTILITY

It will be some time before any definitive answers to question 2 are forthcoming; the affective taxonomy is too new for any conclusive argument. The writers of the taxonomy are hopeful that the domain will permit curriculum workers to produce a systematic and comprehensive set of affective objectives which are stated clearly and in specific terms. The writers of the taxonomy are also hopeful that the taxonomy will aid in refining methods of measurement in this area and will provide a common vocabulary which will assist the communication process among people working in education. The writers of the taxonomy say little or nothing about how the teachers might use the work. The inference is that the taxonomy is for curriculum workers as such. I would like to pose the notion that a portion of the taxonomy is clearly the domain of the teacher and a portion is clearly the domain of the curriculum worker and that there is an area in which both have a concern—the vital link which gives direction to both ends of the affective continuum.

The daily interaction between pupil and teacher continuously involves the behaviors of Receiving and Responding. It is a long term objective of a teacher that the children develop an *acceptance of a value, preference for a value,* and *commitment to a value.* For instance, it takes time for a student to develop an acceptance of reading as something valued; then a preference for reading over some other activity; and finally, a real commitment to reading.

The curriculum worker's task probably *begins* at this Level 3, Valuing. The curriculum worker should state specifically what the valuing objectives are, *i.e.,* what values a child ought to accept, prefer, and develop a commitment for. The curriculum worker must then fit the value objectives into the continuum of higher affective objectives (Organizing and Characterization). The top three levels are very complex and can be realized only over a considerable period of time and after endeavors have produced many values that may be ordered and placed into a master configuration which becomes the characterization set of an individual. The vital link is the posing of Valuing objectives by curriculum workers and the achievement of these objectives by learners through activities provided by teachers.

At another level, a thorough knowledge of the taxonomy by persons who prepare materials for instruction, notably textbooks and programmed materials, might give these productions a significantly different flavor. Or stated in a different way, "What kinds of materials are likely to be produced by persons who lack a knowledge of the affective domain?"

Yet perhaps the most significant "practical use" of the taxonomy lies in whether or not it can be used for research purposes; for, if it is to have any long term effect on the curriculum, it must survive the test of researchability. Educators are looking more and more to research findings when deciding what is to be taught, to whom, by whom, and in what kind of environment. Laymen are becoming more aware of research activity in education and are more accepting of decisions "based on research." Cognitive behavior is clearly more observable and amenable to research. Conscious efforts to promote cognitive learning may crowd out conscious efforts to develop affective learning simply because research answers will be available in the former domain.

## RESEARCH POTENTIAL

By their own admission, the writers of the two taxonomies indicate that the separation of objectives into cognitive and affective domains is artificial and cite research which shows that cognition and affect can never be completely separated. Nevertheless, the two taxonomies do permit us to classify observably different kinds of behavior. The writers of the taxonomy indicate very intelligently and rationally what relationships they *believe* exist between the categories of the cognitive and affective domains. What is clearly missing is what the two taxonomies may now make possible; that is, a comprehensive controlled study which ferrets out any relationships that may actually exist.

Such questions as the following may now be posed: "Is the relation between growth at the various levels of cognitive and affective learning positive, negative, or zero?" "When a child is engaged in learning *knowledge of terminology* (Level 1.11, cognitive domain), is there a positive, negative, or zero relation with his *willingness to receive* (Level 1.2, affective domain)?" "At what level of the cognitive domain is the *willingness to receive* most positive?" It should be clear that the two domains (cognition and affect) give us a more definite structure in which to determine specific relationships and their nature. Perhaps the two domains have given us a systematic way to begin studying the vast implications of concomitant learnings.

As demonstrated earlier in this article, the research question is of paramount importance. Clearly, the affective taxonomy serves to generate significant and worthwhile questions which need resolving. The question is, can they be resolved? The authors of the taxonomy claim that the central research problem is how to measure affective behavior with greater validity, reliability, and objectivity.

What behavior will serve as evidence that a child is showing *commitment to a value* rather than merely a *preference for a value?* How does a researcher determine when a child is achieving the *conceptualization of a value* which is affective behavior rather than only cognitive conceptualization? There are many big problems to be solved in order that the affective taxonomy be made researchable.

This is the task of researchers. The writers of the taxonomy have done their task. Now it is up to researchers and practitioners to do the necessary changing and refining.

Why a taxonomy of affective learning? The taxonomy can serve as an aid in clarifying the school's responsibility for promoting learning in the affective realm. The taxonomy may provide practical help to teachers and curriculum workers. Finally, it may further the study of education.

If schools are to meet the needs of an ever changing society, the schools must be in a position periodically to change their educational objectives. The two taxonomies lend themselves well to this task because they give visibility, structure, and definition to objectives which represent current thinking. As the purposes of the schools change, so ought the taxonomies *or* their replacements.

# 7 Decision-Making and Prediction

## 7.1 Educational Decisions and Human Assessment

*Robert L. Thorndike*

Decision-making is ever present in every human enterprise, education not excepted. Professor Thorndike attempts to make his audience aware that they indulge in decision-making and do so often from ill-conceived knowledge about six principles. He explains these six "facts of life" and explores the limits associated with them. The reader ought to be able to recall easily occasions on which he has made decisions which ignored the principles described in this article. Hopefully, he will ignore these facts less often after reading it.

Of special importance is the author's desire to encourage caution on the part of educators who use psychological tests. In addition, he indicates the usefulness of both the "clinical" and "actuarial" approaches to the understanding of human behavior. What implications does this idea of balance between the two approaches have for classroom teachers who seek data for purposes of pupil evaluation?

When we speak of "measurement" in education, we can elect to use the term narrowly and rigorously in the way that the physical scientist and philosopher of science do when they speak of "fundamental measurement." We then must restrict ourselves to those attributes where we can establish both a zero point, meaning "exactly none of," and the equality of units, so that we can show in some meaningful way how X units of intelligence could be added to Y units of intelligence to yield Z units of intelligence. But a really rigorous definition of this sort would exclude all of the procedures

Reprinted with permission of the author and *Teachers College Record*, **66**, 2, Nov. 1964.

and devices that we have developed in psychology and education. We have no way of identifying exactly zero intelligence, and we can't add one moron IQ of 70 to another moron IQ of 70 and get a genius IQ of 140. Our zero points and our units in educational and psychological measurement are at best arbitrary and somewhat elastic. So both by necessity and by choice, we shall accept a much looser and more inclusive definition of measurement.

Going to the other extreme, we can mean by measurement any procedure that permits us to group specimens into distinct categories or arrange them in an ordered series with respect to some attribute, a procedure which permits us to say "Peter and Paul are alike, but Mary is different," or "Peter has the most; Mary is next, and Paul has the least." Of course, we would certainly welcome refinements that permitted us to assign numerical values to Peter, Paul, and Mary in a somewhat more discriminating way, but we recognize the usefulness of even rough classifications. The point is that this broader definition does not restrict us to formal tests, formally constructed and formally administered, but permits us to accept, with whatever weight and confidence it may deserve, any procedure by which we can make meaningful and consistent distinctions between persons. Teacher judgments, anecdotal observations, peer nominations, and evaluations of individual pupil products are all measurements in this sense, differing from formally planned, standardized, and distributed measurement devices only in degree of refinement and precision. For much of our thinking about educational measurement and evaluation, this is the most serviceable and appropriate definition. It is serviceable just because it emphasizes that the formal structure of educational and psychological testing differs from the broader foundation of pupil evaluation only in degree of refinement and not basically in kind.

## DECISION FROM PREDICTION

Decisions imply predictions. The decision to admit Jack Smith to Patchoula College is based upon the prediction that he is likely to be successful there. Depending upon our value system, success may mean that he will get all A's or that he will be all-Conference high scorer on the basketball team; but in either event, a prediction is involved. In the final analysis, a decision results from a complex and not always rational calculus, involving the interaction of predictions about facts and an existing framework of values. The values are numerous, though not always clear and explicit. Should Johnny take algebra in the ninth grade, or should he take general mathematics? A fact, which we would like to predict as accurately as we can, is how successful he will be in algebra. But the decision depends equally heavily upon the value that we place on algebra—as preparation for later mathematics courses, as a requirement for college admission, as a tool in various professions, as a component of our intellectual heritage. These values will enter into the picture with different weights depending upon all that we know about Johnny—his family setting, his educational goals, and his vocational aspirations.

Should Henry apply for admission to Wigwam University? One basic fact is his likelihood of being admitted, and a second is his probability of maintaining the required academic average once he is there. But a complex of values is also involved. Henry's rich Uncle Henry, for whom he was named, is an alumnus of Wigwam. Wigwam has a good program in forestry, in which Henry has expressed interest. Wigwam is over a thousand miles from Henry's home. Henry prefers a small college to a big university. The list of considerations which lend valence, positive or negative, to college in general and Wigwam in particular as Henry views them could be extended without limit. Whether Henry should apply is a resultant on the one hand of these values, and on the other hand, a best prediction of the facts concerning his acceptance and success.

Where measurement has a role is in making the predictions of fact more accurate. If measures are worth their salt, it is because they enable us to predict within a smaller margin of error that Jack Smith will achieve a C average, or that Mary Jones will improve in reading if put in a remedial section, or that the students in Indianapolis will learn more algebra if they work through a specific sequence of programed instruction, each at his own rate, or that Henry Schute will be happier as an electrician than as a bank clerk.

Let us see what some of the facts of life are about making predictions, and try to draw from a contemplation of these facts some principles to guide us on how best to use measurement in the decision-making process.

## OF PROBABILITY AND TIME

The first, the most fundamental and the most disheartening fact is that *all* predictions are fallible. All have a component of error. Even if the prediction is only from how well Johnny reads today to how well he will read tomorrow, there is still an element of indeterminacy. Changes in vocabulary and structure from one passage to another, changes in Johnny, and an element of sheer chance combine to produce unpredictable shifts from day to day, from one measurement to another. So all predictions must have an element of tentativeness about them, be couched in terms of probabilities rather than in absolutes! "If we were to give him the Gateford Reading Test, there are 2 chances in 3 that Johnny would fall between the 65th and 85th percentile."

Unfortunately, it is the nature of decisions that they *cannot* always or even usually be tentative. There comes a time when we must act. But many decisions *do* have an element of tentativeness. They are decisions to explore, decisions to try. They are revocable. The inescapable fact of the standard error of estimate in any prediction points out to us that we should cherish this tentativeness, where it is admissible, and view as many as possible of our decisions as hypotheses to be pursued and tested further, but to be abandoned if further evidence points to abandonment as desirable.

A second general point is that our predictions will typically become less accurate the greater the time span over which we attempt to extend them. The effect of increasing the time interval is marked when the time interval includes a large part, or the crucial part, of the growth span. Thus, if made at the pre-school level, even two- or three-year predictions of intellectual level are quite fallible, whereas in adult life, predictions of intellectual level can be made over 20 to 30 years with a fairly high degree of accuracy.

The decreasing accuracy of predictions with increasing time span has implications both for decision-making and information-seeking. On the one hand, especially at the earlier school ages, we should try to schedule our measuring so that the evidence will be as current as possible at those points at which crucial decisions are likely to be made. From another point of view, we should give relatively less weight to old than to recent information in the decision process. And thirdly, we should be more tentative about those decisions that have implications for the more remote future than about those whose reference is immediate. Thus, we might be quite ready to assign a pupil to the accelerated ninth-grade algebra section on the basis of an eighth-grade mathematics achievement test, but be quite unwilling to decide on that basis that this pupil should continue math through the twelfth grade.

## DETERMINERS OF THE PREDICTED

Principle number three states that predictions will, in general, be less accurate the more difference there is between the predictor and what is being predicted. In the 10-year-old, the best predictor of 12-year-old reading ability will be present reading ability. Prediction from a measure of verbal intelligence will be somewhat less good; prediction from a measure of nonverbal intelligence will be still less good, and prediction from the size of the pupil's head will be no good at all.

There are times when this principle does not hold. Thus, at the first-grade level, a good individual intelligence test will give a better long-range forecast of reading ability than will a beginning reading test. At this point, there has been so little development of reading, and the patterns are so unstable and rapidly changing, that they do not provide a solid basis on which to make extended forecasts. Other instances come easily to mind in which a particular ability has not yet been developed or is in so formative a stage that a direct measure of it provides little basis for extended predictions. But it is still a good working strategy to base educational predictions, and consequently decisions, on performances as much like the one in which we are ultimately interested as possible. Thus, achievement in arithmetic on the one hand and a miniature algebra-learning test on the other provide good bases for predicting achievement in algebra. High school rank in class remains the best single forecaster of college freshman grade-point average. A biographical inventory covering past mechanical or selling activities provides as good a basis as an ability test for judging future choice of a mechanical or sales occupation. It will, then, usually pay us, as educational decision-makers to analyze presently available information with an eye to how closely it resembles that which we wish to forecast, and to start, at least, by "doing what comes naturally"—by using that present information which has the most evident relationship to the relevant outcomes.

A fourth principle asserts that all behavior is multiply determined. The progress that a six-year-old will make in learning to read depends not only upon his mental age, but also upon his specific stock of language experiences, the level and type of his home support, the security of his relationships with parent and teacher, the manner in which reading is taught, the skill with which his initial difficulties are identified and corrected, and a host of other components of him and his environment. The grade-point average that is made by a college freshman reflects his verbal and quantitative abilities as they have developed up to the time of college entrance, his background of educational skills and knowledge, his techniques of study and preparation, his level of interest and effort, his freedom from emotional stresses and strains that prevent him from mobilizing his resources for academic work, the courses he takes, and the instructors who teach them—to mention only a few of the components in an involved complex. The more of these determinants we can include in our prediction, the more accurate, in theory at least, our prediction can be and, consequently, the more informed our decision. Thus, as a general strategy of decision-making, we should recommend the measurement of a multitude of the factors that contribute to our prediction and are therefore relevant to our decision.

The simplest application of this principle would say, "The more we know about the individual, the better; and if we know enough, our predictions will approach perfection." This is the faith underlying the detailed, intensive case history as well as the multi-test aptitude battery. To what extent is it sound? What are its shortcomings? What factors limit the accuracy of our prediction even as we accumulate vast amounts of information about the individual? Let us examine four such factors.

### LIMITS ON FAITH

The first limiting factor is overlapping or redundancy in the various items of information. Take the prediction of freshman grade-point average as an example. Suppose we start with high school grades, which have generally appeared to be our most valid single predictor. Then we decide to add on a scholastic aptitude test because we have evidence that such tests correlate with grades in college. But only a part of the information that the scholastic aptitude test adds is really new information because scholastic aptitude also correlates with and is strongly represented in high school grades. So we try out a self-report inventory of study skills and attitudes. But the same thing is true here, for good or poor study skills and habits helped the pupil to get those good or poor marks in high school. All right then, let's have a go at measuring motivation to achieve, as best we can, by inventory or by projective device; and we find that such motivational measures *do* give some modest prediction of freshman GPA, but, alas, we also find that they too add little if anything new to the prediction from high school grades because grades are themselves indicators of level of academic motivation.

The situation is not *quite* as gloomy as I have pictured it, but it is certainly true that increments in predictive accuracy from the addition of predictors come only slowly and grudgingly because of the overlapping in the information that different predictors provide. Two or three predictor measures, chosen because they are each good predictors when taken singly and because they are as independent of one another as possible, each yielding new and different information, will usually do about as much for us as the most elaborate and extensive battery.

Increments in accuracy of prediction are held down, in the second place, because each additional fact that we consider about an individual introduces irrelevant information into the picture along with any new and relevant information. Thus, the aptitude test may place a premium on a type of facileness and a range of superficial acquaintance that is different from and does not contribute to ability to master college work. The report of study techniques may indicate what the individual thinks he *ought* to do, rather than what he does do. The motivational measure may be distorted by anxiety about being away from home or by last night's fight with the girl friend. The determinants of *test behavior* are also multiple, and only a fraction of these determiners are relevant to the life behavior that we are trying to predict. This is another way of saying that *all* tests fall short of perfection so far as validity and reliability are concerned, and that our tests and other indicators for some of the factors that we would like to measure are woefully imperfect.

The increment in accuracy of prediction from a complex of information may be held down, thirdly, by inappropriate weighting of the different component facts. In trying to understand Johnny's poor reading and thereby to predict what remedial steps are likely to be effective, we may be overly influenced by his rivalry with his little sister and give inadequate attention to a shift in schools and a change in the philosophy of instruction that took place at the second grade. We may be over-influenced by a low group-test IQ and insufficiently impressed by specific incapacities shown by a test of word-analysis skills. If a complex array of facts is to enable us to make the best possible prediction, each of the facts must enter into our awareness with the proper emphasis and weight. How is this to be achieved?

## ACTUARY VS. CLINICIAN

Basically, there are two ways in which a number of facts about an individual can be combined to yield a prediction relating to him. They may be combined actuarially, or they may be combined clinically. When we combine data actuarially, we combine them in accordance with a formula or table based upon extensive previous experience. Thus, experience accumulated over previous years may have indicated that in order to predict achievement in ninth-grade algebra, we should give a weight of three to achievement in eighth-grade arithmetic, a weight of two to the Orleans Algebra Prognosis Test, and a weight of one to the Numerical Ability test of the Differential Aptitude Tests. Proceeding actuarially, we would apply this formula to past records and prepare an expectancy table, showing what the probabilities are of different levels of success in algebra for any given composite score on the weighted team of predictors. To make our prediction concerning Johnny, we would apply the 3-2-1 formula to his grades and test scores, find the composite score, and look up the probabilities in our expectancy table. Our prediction for Johnny would be taken directly from this actuarial table of past experience.

Proceeding by the clinical approach, we would get the same three facts about Johnny—eighth-grade arithmetic grades, prognostic test score, and numerical ability test score—but we might also give some consideration, intentionally or inadvertently, to a variety of other facts about Johnny. We might know that his father is an engineer, that Johnny is tall for his age, that Johnny is an Eagle Scout, that Johnny is the oldest of four children, that Johnny won second prize in physical science in the school Science Fair, that Johnny is an engaging redhead. Programming this complex of data through that original electronic computer, the human brain, we would come out with a judgment as to how good a bet Johnny is for the algebra class.

Note that the "clinician," if we can apply this designation to any person who is called upon to digest a set of facts about a person and arrive at a decision about him, typically has a much larger number and wider range of data available than could be incorporated into an actuarial prediction equation. At the same time, the only weighting system that the clinician has is that somewhat unstable and untested one represented by his own fluctuating judgment. Theoretically, in view of the relative wealth of information available to him, it should be possible for the clinician to make much more accurate and discriminating predictions than can result from the mechanical combining of two or three measures into an actuarial prediction, but this potentiality can only be realized if he picks out the *right* components from the mass of available information and gives them the *right* weight. Those comparative studies that we have of clinical and actuarial prediction tend, by and large, to find more accurate results for actuarial than for clinical predictions. I hasten, however, to add that the conditions in these studies have generally been somewhat artificial, not giving full scope to the talents of the skilled clinician. The studies nevertheless point out that there is no guarantee that human judgment will use data optimally, and that even though it is possible to feed both more data and a wider variety of data into a human judge than into a prediction equation, the judge may process his information inappropriately or inefficiently and come out with generally inaccurate predictions.

## RECURRENCE AND UNIQUENESS

Of course, we can only use an actuarial approach to prediction and decision-making successfully if we have systematically accumulated the type of actuarial data that will permit us to select the most efficient team of predictors and determine the optimum weights to assign to each. This is possible only where the event to be predicted is a frequently occurring one—success in college, success in a particular course or program, or some such tangible and recurring item. The roles and settings under which this can occur are unfortunately limited. If we are in charge of admissions for a college, freshman grade-point averages at our institution can be accumulated in quantity, and expectancy tables for prediction can be developed if we wish. In the same way, a school or school system can develop expectancy tables for success in any of its own courses or programs. There are also possibilities for making such material more broadly available. Thus, in the state of Georgia, expectancy tables are published and made available to high school counselors, showing the probability of a grade-point average of C, of B, and of A at each of the colleges within the state for individuals with any given combination of high school grades and College Board Scholastic Aptitude

Test scores. Again, hidden in the College Board's *Manual of Fresh-man Class Profiles*, there is material that would permit development of at least crude expectancy tables showing chance of admission to some hundreds of different colleges in relation to SAT scores and high school grades, and these tables should be quite useful to high school counselors.

But many events are relatively unique in the experience of the decision-maker. As a high school counselor, you have never before had a student who wanted to go to Williwaw Tech, and you must synthesize as best you can any available information about the college and the student in order to arrive at an estimate of his prospects of success. No remedial reading teacher works with enough pupils, or with pupils enough alike in age, reading level, and type of difficulty, to have the possibility of assembling formal expectancy tables that could be applied in making a forecast about a new case. The range and individuality of the problems encountered by a school psychologist in working with the problems of individual pupils defy any accumulation of evidence of a formal actuarial nature. Research studies may have pointed out the factors that are relevant and the strength of general relationships that exist, but these general findings must be interpreted and applied in new combinations with the individual case.

For the vast numbers of situations in which we must make predictions concerning events that are of infrequent occurrence or that represent a new and somewhat different combination of familiar components, we necessarily rely upon the informal prediction equations that have accumulated in the neurones of the school psychologist, the remedial reading teacher, the guidance counselor, or the principal, based upon their knowledge of previous research and their background of experience. And then prediction is inaccurate to the extent that these prediction equations are inappropriate or unstable or both.

To recapitulate, (a) all events are multiply determined, so (b) our predictions can be improved by taking account of a number of determiners, but (c) the gain from adding on additional predictors is held down by the fact that our different predictors are redundant or overlapping and (d) by the difficulty of giving optimum weight to each component, especially (e) when the weighting is done intuitively on the basis of the fluctuating judgment of an individual "clinician." Thus, the accuracy of our predictions is limited in part by the information available to us and in part by our techniques for processing that information.

## PREDICTING CHANGE

A fifth fact of life, or principle underlying educational decision-making, is that change is much more difficult to predict than status. As I suggested earlier, we can make a very good forecast of where pupils will be in reading a year from now just by knowing where they are at the present time. Present educational status is the best single predictor of future educational status. But just in proportion as this is true, predicting who will gain most from initial test and who will gain least becomes impossible. To the extent that today's performance forecasts next year's performance, we are saying that gains will be uniform or differ only by chance and in unpredictable ways from one pupil to the next, and that individual differences in gain are essentially unpredictable. It is my impression that this is not far from the fact of the matter, at least in those educational achievements that have a continuous history of development through the school years.

I'm not certain how often educational decisions are based on the type of prediction that states that Mary can be expected to make rapid progress in reading this next year, but Helen can be expected to show less than average progress. I hope not too often, because I am sure that the batting average on such predictions is really low. But I suspect that we often have a feeling that we are predicting differential growth when we are really just predicting differences in future status from differences in present status.

A sixth principle, related to the one that I have just presented, but of more fundamental importance, is that differential prediction is more difficult and less accurate than absolute prediction. An example of absolute prediction is the assertion that Joe's freshman grade-point average will be C or lower. One type of differential prediction, on the other hand, asserts that Joe will do better in freshman math than in freshman English. Another type of differential prediction states that Joe will learn more English if he is put in a remedial section than if put in a regular section. Thus, differenital predictions are of two somewhat different kinds, one referring to a difference between areas and the other to a difference between treatments. Differential predictions are at the heart of most educational decisions, because most decisions represent choices between different actions. Thus, they are based on predictions of differences associated with the different possible choices that the individual or school faces.

Why are differential predictions relatively undependable? Primarily, it is because many of the predictive factors bear a similar relationship to both alternatives. A high level of general abstract ability, a supportive and culturally rich home environment, motivation to achieve in academic pursuits, a conscientious disposition, patterns of organizing one's time and doing one's work systematically are all predictive of good achievement, be it in English or in mathematics, and account in considerable measure for our ability to predict in either direction. Thus, the remaining components that are different—*specific* talent in numerical thinking *vs specific* fluency with words, or preference for devoting time to reading or writing *vs* preference for working on quantitative problems—account for only a modest fraction of final performance.

In the same way, the facts about an individual that determine whether he will do well or poorly in freshman English are in large part the same without regard to the treatment he receives. If he comes to us with a large vocabulary, effective skills in expressing himself, and the ability to read rapidly and with understanding, he is likely to show good achievement at the end of the year no matter what kind of an instructor or curriculum he is exposed to; and if he falls at the other end of the scale on these predictive measures, he can be expected to do relatively poorly. This is not to say that differential treatments for different kinds of individuals are of no importance, or that we are completely blind in our estimations of who will benefit most from which treatment. But it is to say that judgments of these matters are far from precise and much more difficult to make than a simple judgment of who will do well or poorly.

## SALVATION VIA HUMILITY

Recognizing the difficulty and fallibility of differential predictions, what are the practical implications of this state of affairs for administrators, counselors, and individual pupils? One implication is to reinforce even more strongly the humility and tentativeness with which we make choices and plans for and with students. When we have a low level of certainty that occupation A or course A or section A or method A will work out better for Roger than will occupation or course or section or method B, we can ill afford to be dogmatic and rigid in our effort to bring about or enforce the choice of A. And we need, so far as possible, to maintain the doorways open for shifting to B or C or D if further developments suggest that A is not working out well.

Secondly, we need to recognize that there are many roads to salvation for each individual and that a number of them may be almost equally satisfactory. That is, there is no *one* best job, no *one* best curriculum for each pupil. In many of the choices that must be made, where the basis for differential prediction is inadequate, the choice may actually not make much real difference in the long run. Whether to take French or Latin, whether to be in the advanced math section or the regular section, whether to enter college X or college Y, the important thing may be less which choice is made than that some choice is made and is followed up wholeheartedly once a commitment has been made to it.

Thirdly, when we lack any clear indication from the objective evidence as to which choice is likely to be more successful, as may often be the case, we may find it wise to be guided by the subjective preferences of the individual. Where we have little basis for affirming a difference from without, it may be wise to be guided from within.

Let me try to recapitulate the points I have tried to make, first about the facts of the case and then about the strategy for using measurement in educational decision-making. As basic facts or principles, I would affirm these points:

Decisions are based jointly on judgments of fact as to what would occur and judgments of value as to what should occur.

Educational and psychological measurements have their function in making more accurate our judgments of what would occur if a certain action were taken.

The information most likely to permit accurate judgments is information on past behavior most similar to that which we are trying to predict in the future.

The information most likely to permit accurate judgments is recent information, especially when the function being studied is undergoing rapid change.

Joint prediction from several measures can be more accurate than prediction from any one taken singly.

The gain from adding on additional measures, however, is sharply limited by overlapping of the measures and by our difficulty in weighting them properly.

It is much more difficult to make sound judgments about growth and change than about status.

It is more difficult to make sound judgments about differences—of area or of treatment—than about status in a single role or dimension.

The elements of decision-making strategy that seem to me to flow from these considerations are as follows:

So far as possible, think of decisions as hypotheses to be made tentatively, subject to review and revision in the light of further data and events.

Do not force decisions in advance of the time that they need to be made, but take each decisive step as the time for it arrives.

Since there are many differential decisions for which measurement data provide meager evidence on which to make a choice, be relaxed about the whole affair and at the same time give scope for subjective evaluations.

Finally, clarify the values involved first; only as you know what you are seeking can measurement be of any help to you in finding it.

---

## 7.2   The Prediction of Vocational Success
### *Robert L. Thorndike*

Questions about reliability and predictive validity are usually discussed in the literature in necessarily isolated and abstract terms. In this article, which was presented as a paper delivered at the 1963 American Personnel and Guidance Association Convention in Boston,

Reprinted with permission of the author and *Vocational Guidance Quarterly*, **11**, 3, 1963, 179–187.

Professor Thorndike describes a rare type of study. Rare because it is seldom that an investigator deliberately chooses to do the painstaking work needed in order to follow up several thousands of subjects twelve years after they were tested in order to obtain predictive validity on the instruments.

This article is particularly valuable because it constitutes *empirical* evidence on the predictive power of highly respected measurement instruments. And quite sobering it is to learn that when one tries to predict "success" in an occupation, he can do as well by flipping a coin as by giving a battery of aptitude tests!

The author offers cogent reasons why tests given at about age 20 cannot predict occupational success 12 years later. His reasoning will be equally valuable for other decision-making and prediction situations of the individual kind.

Some four years ago, with Dr. Elizabeth Hagen, I brought out a little volume entitled *10,000 Careers*. This was a report of the follow up of a group of men who had taken a uniform battery of tests as applicants for aircrew training in the Army Air Force during World War II. As the results of this study got spread around, and received some slight comment in the public prints, my psychometric friends started to hurry by me with averted eyes and without speaking. I seemed on the way to becoming, in my own small way, a psychotechnical pariah. And so naturally I started to brood about the whole thing. Today I plan to share with you some of my soul-searching, for such light as it may throw on the psychological, or more specifically the psychometric bases for vocational guidance.

As I said, *10,000 Careers* was a study of men who were tested with a uniform aptitude battery as applicants for aircrew training during World War II. The group of 17,000 that we undertook to study was an approximately random sample of the 75,000 men tested on one uniform battery that was in operational use during the last half of 1943. Testing for a given individual required a day and a half, one day for paper-and-pencil group tests and half a day for six different psychomotor tests administered to squads of four men at a time. The day and a half of testing yielded 20 separate scores measuring various combinations of verbal-intellectual, numerical, spatial, perceptual, and motor abilities. These test results formed the primary basis for the decision as to the type of Aviation Cadet training a given man should be assigned to—pilot, navigator, or bombardier—subsequently to be commissioned as an officer, or whether he should revert to enlisted status and become a radio operator, tail gunner, or some other enlisted member of the bomber crew.

Fortunately, results from the testing were retained in Air Force files, and in 1955, with funds from the Grant Foundation, it was possible for us to get a roster of names, serial numbers, and test scores and begin our search. To carry out this search, we sought and received the help of many governmental agencies. The Veterans Administration was our primary resource for locating men, and their comprehensive locator file gave us some sort of lead on all but eight of our 17,000 cases. Among other things this file immediately identified for us some 1500 of the men who were deceased, and whose careers we could no longer follow with the limited resources available to us. Current military files identified another group of about the same size who were still on active military duty, and who became the subjects of a separate special study. The Air Force Reserve personnel records and the Army Demobilized Personnel Records gave us leads to many others. We salvaged a substantial number of lost souls—or bodies, in any event—through the services of the Retail Credit Company, a resource worth remembering by those interested in longitudinal research.

The hunt was a fascinating one, and we abandoned some of the more interesting trails only reluctantly as it became necessary to get on with the job and analyze our data. In all, we got records on some 10,000 of the men. This represented about a 70% rate of return of those who were alive and in civilian life. We found them every-where—at home and abroad, wielding the gavel in the board room of a corporation or the broom in the locker room of a country club, in a university teaching psychology, or in a penitentiary serving time for forgery. (Incidentally, the forger became quite a favorite around our shop. We immediately looked up his scores, and found that he had been very low in finger dexterity. We like to think that if he had come to us for vocational guidance we could have told him that forgery was not the career for him.)

In our follow up of each man, we tried to get as much information as we could, within the limits of a one-page mail questionnaire, on all aspects of his post-war occupational history. We inquired about education, about jobs held, about earned income, about self-perceived work satisfaction and success. Using the information, and drawing upon the experience and wisdom of our colleague, Donald Super, and of Sidney Fine of the U. S. Employment Service, we sorted the men into some 120 occupational groupings, trying to make each grouping as homogeneous as we could in terms of the occupations that we grouped together within it. Then we computed the average score and the spread of scores on each test for each group. Furthermore, we tried to extract from our data any indicators we could find that might serve to represent success in the different occupations. We used such indicators as reported earned income, self-rated success and satisfaction, vertical and horizontal job mobility, as judged by a research worker examining the work record, number supervised, and length on the job. Within each occupational grouping, we correlated each of these indicators with score on each of the 20 tests.

So far as differences within and between occupational groups were concerned, we found a good many. Some were quite substantial, and most of them were sensible and reasonable. Thus, we not only found that those who had become accountants had done better on number tests than those who had become writers; we also found that those who had become accountants had done better on the numerical tests than they had on any of the other tests. We found company presidents highest on intellectual ability, company treasurers highest on numerical fluency, draftsmen highest on visual perception, foremen highest on mechanical ability, and machinists highest on psychomotor coordination. We found that embryo professors were highly verbal, whereas embryo plumbers were not. We found some surprises, due probably to the initial pre-screening of our group, for example, a rather surprising level of intellectual ability in our few day laborers, who scored higher in this respect than our high school English and social studies teachers, but most of the patterning was consistent with what you or I would have predicted. Occupational groups did differ in significant and sensible ways on the tests.

However, it is easy to overstate these group differences. Along with differences in mean, it is also true that there was a very wide range of test performance represented within any group. The variability within a single occupation was typically almost as great as the variability in the total group of 10,000. There were accountants whose scores on tests of mathematics, arithmetic reasoning, or computational speed fell almost as far down as the lowest carpenter or truckdriver. There were college teachers—I won't say where or of what—whose verbal comprehension would not have been impressive in our group of auto mechanics. Overlapping was just as real and as impressive as difference.

We turn now to the 12,000 correlations of test scores with indicators of job success. What of these?

I think the simplest and most honest way of summarizing these results would be to say that they clustered around zero—almost as many negative as positive—with the number "significant at the 5 per cent level" making up perhaps 6 per cent of the whole. Of those presumably "significant" correlations, about as many were in the "silly" direction as in the sensible one. Applying these results, taken at face value to the question, "Can tests given at about age 20 predict occupational success 12 years later?" the answer is clearly, "No."

So now you know what has made my friends turn away, and why I have been brooding. Now you can join me as I try to dig behind these results, to see what they really mean, and what message they have for guidance. Why were differences between occupational groups no sharper than they were? Why did we fail essentially completely to predict our indicators of occupational success? Let me present a series of propositions that might be offered to account for these results and examine each one with you in turn.

**PROPOSITION 1**

*The groups had been pre-screened, and so were too homogeneous to yield significant differences and relationships.*

It is true that the groups we studied had been pre-screened by a qualifying examination roughly resembling a scholastic aptitude test, with a cutting score set somewhere near the average of high school seniors. There were few below-average individuals in the group who took the classification test battery. This certainly reduced the sharpness of the differentiation among different occupational groups. That we found a difference of only six-tenths of a standard deviation in reading comprehension between our group of lawyers and our group of truck-drivers stems from the fact that we had a pretty verbal group of truck-drivers. Any others could not have passed the screening test. The effects of pre-screening were certainly most sharply felt in our unskilled and semi-skilled groups, and our samples in these groups are clearly unrepresentative of the total occupational groups to which they belong.

Curtailment is much less likely to have distorted our findings on test validities—especially in the professional and managerial categories that comprised a large proportion of our sample. One feels with some conviction that in these occupations most of the persons excluded by the pre-screening would have fallen by the wayside anyhow in the course of trying to gain entry to or to complete the higher education required for the occupation. At least, it seems to me that any effects of curtailment would have been quite minor, and could not have accounted for the essentially complete lack of significant relationships with the indicators of success.

And I should point out in passing that counselors will often have occasion to deal with groups at least as homogeneous in their abilities as this Air Force group. This would be the case for the counselor in almost any college counseling bureau, and even for one working in a selective high school or with a college preparatory school clientele. So that it would seem reasonable to expect as much difficulty in making long range predictions within many of the groups with which a counselor must work as within ours.

## PROPOSITION 2

*The tests were inappropriate for civilian jobs.*

The tests were, of course, designed for use in a military context. Some concessions to this military context can be found in the content of certain items—for example, an arithmetic rate and distance problem involving an airplane rather than a train or car, a mechanical comprehension item involving the trussed roof of an airplane hangar rather than a bridge truss. But the basic functions covered were in large measure the same ones that appear in current widely-used civilian guidance batteries—verbal ability, numerical ability, mechanical knowledge and understanding, perceptual speed and accuracy, finger dexterity, and eye-hand coordination. A factor analysis of the Air Force battery together with the DAT or the GATB would show that in large part the factors that appear in one also appear in the other. I doubt that we can charge much of the outcome to inadequate tests or testing. If the Air Force battery failed to predict, it seems unlikely that we could expect current commercial aptitude batteries to do so.

## PROPOSITION 3

*Ability tests picked because they have predicted success in training are of no value for predicting success on the job.*

The Air Force battery was initially validated against training school criteria, and those tests were retained in the battery that aided in predicting training school success for some one of the aircrew specialties. Even during the war, there was no convincing evidence that these same tests would predict criteria of combat performance or evaluations by superior officers. Furthermore, predictions of promotions or of proficiency ratings in the military for those of our original 17,000 who stayed in the service were no better than predictions of success in civilian occupations—that is to say, no good at all.

But of course, these findings are consistent with much that we already know concerning the gap between training and job performance. Thus, Ghiselli made an extensive survey of the literature on test predictors of training success and job success, and found that there was essentially no correspondence between the tests that were valid for training criteria and the ones that were valid for job criteria.

It seems likely that much of the distinctiveness in the profiles that we find, especially for the professional occupations, is due to the selection that operated at entry into and during the process of professional education. Thus, the generally high mathematics scores of engineers are probably more a reflection of the hurdle imposed by engineering school than of any further selection that has taken place on engineering jobs. Realistically, it may be that the most helpful counseling that can be given with respect to many occupations will deal with the individuals' prospects of successfully gaining entry to and completing the program of training set as a requirement, either legal or conventional, for entry into the occupation. Perhaps we should be content to estimate Johnny's chances of getting through law school, or medical school, or engineering school, not concerning ourselves with what will happen thereafter.

## PROPOSITION 4

*The tests were not sufficiently pure and homogeneous measures to bring out occupational differences.*

There is a school of thought among test theorists that says that each aptitude test should be a pure measure of some single ability factor, and that each of these pure factor measures should be uncorrelated with all the other tests in a battery. Without question such a test battery has a good deal of appeal to the theoretician. Since each test is measuring a distinct, independent factor, each will give entirely new information; there will be no overlapping or redundance. Each will be able to make a maximum contribution of new validity to whatever validity is possessed by the others, and specific ones of the tests will differentiate specific occupations. The prospects for *different* profiles or *different* patterns of validity for different occupations is a maximum.

But in practice, it has more often been the complex tests that have shown high validity as predictors. The Army General Classification Test, for example, was a hodge-podge of verbal, quantitative and spatial material, but this potpourri showed validity quite generally for all sorts of military training programs. It didn't show much *differential* validity but its general validity for many military jobs compared very favorably with that of narrower and more specialized tests.

The Air Force battery, like all others that are known to me, was composed of somewhat impure and somewhat correlated tests. Its ability to differentiate among different occupations may well have suffered somewhat from this fact. However, we can hardly account for its failure to predict *within* occupations on this basis. The battery covered a number of the common ability factors, combined in varying ways and amounts. If these combinations of factors failed to show any signs of validity, it is unlikely that purer measures of the component factors would have done so. Factor purity in the tests of a battery may permit better differentiation between occupations, but it is unlikely to yield validity where none has existed before.

## PROPOSITION 5

*The tests were too limited in the range of attributes that they covered, and missed the really crucial ones.*

The Air Force battery was limited largely to a range of cognitive and motor abilities. The cognitive tests dealt primarily with symbols of one sort or another—words, numbers, maps, diagrams. There was very limited appraisal of the individual's ability to deal with things, and essentially none of his ability to deal with people. Appraisal of interest or temperament aspects was limited to what may have been revealed in a biographical data blank.

Evidence has been accumulating that, at least in college level groups, differences in interests may be fully as important as differences in abilities in determining curricular and occupational choices. Thus, Berdie found interest test scores to be the most differentiating and aptitude test scores the least differentiating for curricular groups at the University of Minnesota. McCully found large differences by type of job in Kuder interest scores of veterans tested in the VA and followed up several years later—differences that I would estimate were fully as marked as those reported in the Kuder manual. Even in our data, the biographical items seemed to differentiate occupational groups about as well as did the tests. Better interest measures might have sharpened the differentiation still further.

Evidence on temperamental differences between occupational groups is rather less convincing at the present time. Cattell reports some occupational profiles for the 16 Personality Factor Inventory, but these are concurrent rather than predictive data, and most of the groups are distressingly small. Data for occupational groups are reported here and there in the literature, but the material is scrappy, there is rarely any genuine prediction over time, and almost never are there any data on occupational success. My guess at the present time is that most of the useful discrimination between occupations that might be achieved through personality measures is already built into the interest inventories—but I may be wrong.

The evidence concerning interests and temperament relates largely to differences among occupational groups. I am not aware of any convincing evidence that these measures predict success within an occupation, and until we see such evidence we should remain very skeptical that they do so.

How about other sorts of ability measures, beyond those that were included in the Air Force battery? Were there any noteworthy gaps, so far as predicting occupational success is concerned? I would like to call your attention to two areas that seem at least possibilities.

One is the region that Guilford and others have spoken of as divergent thinking, or sometimes more loosely and optimistically as "creativity." These traits are tested with tasks in which the individual is called upon to produce responses, and in which his productions are evaluated with respect to one or more of the attributes of fluency, flexibility, originality, or appropriateness to the demands of the situation. Tests of divergent thinking show only a limited overlap with our conventional ability tests, and in fact they show only a limited overlap with each other. Here is a loosely-knit and as yet poorly-explored area of testing. The plausibility of tests calling for fluency and originality of intellectual production as predictors of occupational success in at least some kinds of jobs is high, so the area is one of promise for future exploration.

A second area that we have long recognized as being important is ability in manipulating people. No tests of such an ability were included in the Air Force battery, nor are any included, so far as I know, in other published aptitude batteries. And perhaps this is because no satisfactory tests of these abilities exist. Certainly, the paper-and-pencil devices that try to use verbal responses to verbal descriptions of interpersonal situations as a way of appraising what the individual will actually do in the real situation have been most unconvincing. Such analyses as we have of them show that they are plausible measures of ability to handle words, but suggest that they are very indifferent indicators of ability to deal with people. After 50 years and more of tests and testing, the development of effective methods of appraising talent for dealing with people is still one of our most obvious and urgent needs.

So in response to Proposition #5, we must cheerfully agree that there were large gaps in our Air Force battery, and that measures which would have filled these gaps *might* have improved our differentiation among occupations, and *might* have even enabled us to predict success within certain of the occupations. And at the same time, we must also admit that measurement procedures for filling some of the most interesting of these gaps are still lacking or at best in an early stage of development.

## PROPOSITION 6

*Specific abilities of the type included in the Air Force battery show too little stability over time to permit useful prediction.*

We know that the individual changes. Particularly in the case of young children, we know that the correlation between ability tests drops as the interval between tests increases, and that in the case of very young children the correlation may drop to substantially zero after a lapse of only a few years. However, we also know that with adults a general measure of intellectual ability is likely to show marked stability over even a long time span. The longest span for which I know of data is the period of about 30 years that was involved in Owens' retest study of men who had taken the Army Alpha as freshmen at Iowa State. For this period, Owens found the rather striking correlation of 0.77 between test and retest. Terman and Oden report a correlation of 0.88 for the original Terman highly gifted group and 0.92 for their somewhat more variable spouses on the Concept Mastery Test over a 12-year span from age 30 to age 42.

But we face a stickier problem when we seek for stability in the *pattern* of *specific* abilities. The reliability of difference scores is typically somewhat low even for immediate retesting. Part of the stability of ability test scores stems from the general factor or factors that they share in common. When we work with score differences, we are typically dealing with a less stable phenomenon —a fact that every guidance worker should keep continually within the fringe of his awareness. So perhaps these differences or patterns don't maintain themselves from one year to the next.

Evidence on the stability of patterns of ability over a period of time is pretty limited, and we sorely need follow-up studies in which a battery such as the GATB is readministered to a group after an interval of 10, 15, or 20 years. Evidence from groups of secondary school age tested after an interval of about 3½ years, in one case with the DAT and in another with PMA, suggests that the reliabilites of differences between pairs of tests (i.e., numerical ability minus verbal ability) is about as high after several years as it is after a few days or weeks. Correlations of score differences on the one occasion with score differences between the same pair of tests three years later averaged about 0.50, and though this is not impressively high, it is about as high as the reliability of those same difference-scores with no time lapse. So far as evidence is available on the point, it appears that we must reject instability of aptitudes over time as a significant component of our failure to predict—but I would like to see more and better evidence on this point.

## PROPOSITION 7

*The occupational groups were so heterogeneous that no differentiation or prediction was possible.*

It must be admitted that a certain number of our 124 occupational groupings contained a wide range of specific occupations and probably some rather strange bedfellows. It is amazing how meager a sample of even 10,000 becomes when one wishes to identify adequate-sized samples of homogeneous occupational groups. And so we put all our machine operators into two groups—one of fabricating machine operators and one of processing machine operators. We had a single inclusive grouping for laborers, and four groups included all the handicraftsmen. However, at the upper occupational levels, where our yield was better, the groups were generally much narrower, in many cases corresponding to only one or two specific codes in the Dictionary of Occupational Titles. These were such groups as accountant and auditor, architect, airplane pilot, insurance claim adjuster, chemical engineer, civil engineer, electrical engineer, sales manager, and so on. In these cases, the classification is about as homogeneous and restricted as one could hope for in terms of occupations included in a single category. If there is a difficulty, it lies not in our grouping procedure, but in the conception of an occupation as a uniform and homogeneous entity.

Our experience in the conduct of the project gave us a lively sense of the diversity of the specific jobs that are included within even quite a fine occupational code. Thus, the category "lawyer" included trial lawyers and tax lawyers, assistant district attorneys and small town magistrates, individuals whose position was primarily political and individuals who were "organization men" in a large corporation. In activities and setting, they varied widely. Similarly, "college professor" included persons professing speech, physical education, psychology, agriculture, and so on for the full gamut of interests and competence.

The diversity of individuals in a single occupation has been documented more than once. For example, Strong and Tucker's analysis showed the distinctive interest patterns in different medical specialties. Preparing special Vocational Interest Blank keys for pathologists, internists, psychiatrists, and surgeons, they found that these groups could be separated so that there was only a moderate amount of overlapping—though all groups were alike in scoring high on the general "physician" key. And psychiatrists had interest patterns more like those of psychologists than those of surgeons.

Thus, we may suggest that the range of specializations within many occupations that the layman, and perhaps the guidance worker, thinks of in a unitary way is quite wide. People of quite different talents may then be able to find an appropriate niche within the gallery of possibilities. The sharpness of difference *between* occupations may be considerably blurred by this variability *within*. And the task of the counselor may be as much to make a client aware of how he can best achieve fulfillment within a chosen occupation as to identify the occupational category for which he is uniquely best fitted.

## PROPOSITION 8

*Occupational success was not adequately evaluated, and so could not possibly be predicted.*

The evidences of success that we obtained were only those that could be obtained by mail from the respondent. Job satisfaction was rated only crudely. Adequacy of performance was indicated only by increases in pay and in responsibility, and by final level of salary reached. The accuracy of this report could not be checked against independent records, and no performance evaluations could be obtained from associates or supervisors. Our feeling from the flavor of the responses themselves was that when income was reported—and the frequency varied, depending upon the occupation—it was seriously and accurately reported. However, no external verification was possible.

One can argue that the proof of the pudding is in the paying, and that the objective standard of success, at least within a homogeneous occupational category, is the income the person receives from his work. At least to a first approximation, the more successful professors are the better paid professors, the more successful clergymen the better paid clergymen, the more successful accountants the better paid accountants. One can argue that this criterion is more "operational," and consequently more meaningful than any rating or other expression of opinion by an associate or superior. One can argue with somewhat greater force and conviction that ratings obtained from hundreds of different associates and supervisors in hundreds of different companies, regions, and settings would be so lacking in any common point of reference as to be almost completely devoid of meaning.

So though one can quarrel with the self-reported and incomplete measures of success that we were able to obtain, one finds it hard to visualize anything much better as a basis for comparing individuals who have scattered out over the country into hundreds of different work settings. We had wanted to take one or two of our largest groups, our 900 engineers, for example, to work intensively to develop the best possible criterion information on each one, and then to see whether any more meaningful predictions could be obtained from our tests. However, we never found the wherewithal to do this. And frankly, I am not convinced that we would do much better. "Success" is a rather slippery concept, to which it is difficult to give a form and a shape. Perhaps we make a mistake to concern ourselves with it. Let me offer you, instead of Proposition #8, Proposition #8a.

## PROPOSITION 8A

*Beyond survival in an occupation, "success" is a meaningless concept, which we might as well abandon.*

I have pointed out some of the difficulties that we had with appraisals of success. Let me now point to a few others. The one to which I want to give primary attention is what we might call the institutionalization of rewards in certain occupations. Thus, in those occupations in which rates of pay (and sometimes of work) are set by union contract, individual differences in competence beyond the minimum necessary to survive are irrelevant to success in the occupation. In a large other group of occupations, we find pay scales set by civil service schedules, and salary increments coming largely automatically with seniority. It is hard to estimate to what fraction of the total world of work these conditions apply. They are certainly widespread as one drops below the professional and managerial categories, and even these are not entirely exempt. It appears to me that within many occupational categories, it is realistic to say that degree of success has largely ceased to have a meaning, and that success is evidenced only by a shift to another occupation, i.e., from the ranks of worker into the ranks of management, and failure by dropping out of the occupation. If this be so, success must be evidenced primarily by the occupation reached, rather than by indicators within an occupation.

## PROPOSITION 9

*Long range "success" depends so heavily upon contingency factors that one can never hope to predict it from what can be known about the individual in advance.*

As used here, "contingency factors" refer to the whole gamut of things that can happen *to* a person, and that are not known or knowable from any information about him that we could obtain at the time we might be testing or counseling him. On the morbid side, he might be hit by a car or by polio and lose the use of his legs. More happily, his college fraternity brother might be able to get him started in the family business or might introduce him to the boss's daughter. Less dramatically, the jobs that happened to be open the day he started looking for work, the ad he happened to see as he was looking through the paper, the foreman who happened to take over his training as a green hand, the vacancy that happened to become available at the point when he was a candidate for promotion—all of these and many more interact to shape his occupational career.

Nobody knows the extent to which occupational histories are truly dependent upon such external events. Their impact is certainly real. There are certain instances in which they are the swamping influence—as, for example, in the case of our most financially successful farmer, who was making an excellent living leasing out the grazing rights to 20,000 acres of Texas landscape which his wife had inherited from her forbears. The longer the period over which we wish to make our vocational predictions, and the more major choice-points in the vocational career that are included, the more chance there is for these outside factors to come in as determining factors. To the extent that these contingency factors determine success, any attempt to predict it is futile.

## SUMMARY

I have tried to share with you some of the thoughts that have come to me as I have pondered over the large regions of negative result in our study of 10,000 civilian careers. Some part of the reason for such negative results may lie in our somewhat curtailed group, and more of it may be found in the incomplete coverage of possibly significant domains of interest, temperament, and ability. But I suspect that most of it resides in the heterogeneity of many occupations, the differences between training and work, the limited meaning of success in occupations in which pay and promotions have become institutionalized, and the impact of contingency factors upon the vocational careers of individuals. These are factors that set a fairly low ceiling on *any* predictions of occupational success by *any* means. So far as they are determining, they suggest that we may need to focus our attention upon more immediate and more limited objectives—both for our testing and for our counseling.

---

## 7.3 The Tester and Decision Theory
### Lee J. Cronbach and Goldine C. Gleser

Nearly every time a person takes a test and a score is computed a decision follows. The decision may be easy or difficult, short term or long range, trivial or momentous. In every case, however, some action is taken, even if it is to postpone an overt action as a consequence to testing.

The following excerpt is taken from an important book aimed at those who must design and choose methods for making decisions about the choice of treatments for people. It should give you some notion about an aspect of test construction and utilization which only recently has begun to come under the control of educational and psychological practitioners. Indeed, the wish to arrive at qualitative decisions based on quantitative data is more and more often yielding to techniques sketched out in this reading.

Our society continually confronts people with decisions for which they have inadequate information. It is for this reason that psychological and educational tests exist. Some of the problems on which tests are brought to bear are purely individual: the uncertainties of a boy trying to choose a career, or of a young couple trying to decide whether they are suited for marriage. Equally numerous are the occasions on which an administrator, teacher, or clinician turns to tests for assistance in making decisions about many people. The personnel manager wishes to know whom to hire; the military psychologist determines which men are adequately trained and

From *Psychological Tests and Personnel Decisions*, 2nd ed., 1965, 1–6. Reprinted with permission of University of Illinois Press.

ready for duty; the teacher inquires whether his class should be taught at a rapid or a slow pace. There is no end to such examples of the role of tests in decision making.

It is therefore desirable that a theory of test construction and use consider how tests can best serve in making decisions. Little of present test theory, however, takes this view. Instead the test is conceived as a measuring instrument, and test theory is directed primarily toward the study of accuracy of measurement on a continuous scale. Hull (1928, p. 268) voiced a principle that has been the root of nearly all work on test theory: "The ultimate purpose of using aptitude tests is to estimate or forecast aptitudes from test scores." It is this view that we propose to abandon. We acknowledge the usefulness of accurate estimation—but we maintain that the *ultimate* purpose of any personnel testing is to arrive at qualitative decisions such as those illustrated in the preceding paragraph.

The value of a test depends on many qualities in addition to its accuracy. Especially to be considered are the relevance of the measurement to the particular decision being made, and the loss resulting from an erroneous decision. Recommendations regarding the design, selection, and interpretation of a test must take into account the characteristics of the decisions for which the test will be used, since the test that is maximally effective for one decision will not necessarily be most effective elsewhere.

An appropriate test theory can evolve from a general and systematic examination of the decision problems for which tests are used and of the demands these problems place upon the test. In such a study of decision making and its implications for testing, we are fortunately able to draw on extensive mathematical contributions, many of them recent.

The following comment by a leading contributor to decision theory, M. A. Girshick (1954, pp. 448, 464), indicates the need for study of this sort and the difficulties:

> Statistical decision theory was originated some 15 years ago by Abraham Wald. In the past decade, great strides have been made in the field by Wald and others. However, so far these developments have had but little impact on experimental research in the social and physical sciences. There appear to be two basic reasons for this: one is the natural lag between theory and practice which so often occurs in science; the other, which in the present case

may be more fundamental, is that decision theory to date has been too much concerned with the mathematical foundations of the subject and less with its immediate application. Curiously enough, here is a situation in which the foundational development, difficult as it is, is easier than the application to actual problems. . . .

. . . Decision theory is in the process of development and is not yet a completed science. It takes for its domain the problem of rational behavior in the face of unknown states of nature. It gives a logical foundation and framework to mathematical statistics which it has never had before. It grapples with the problem of design of experiments in a manner never before attempted in statistics. It insists that cost considerations and consequences of decisions be taken into account in every statistical investigation. In doing so, it has brought sequential theory into the general framework and has made sequential decision procedures the rule rather than the exception. It bridges the gap existing in classical statistics between testing hypotheses and estimation by showing that the distinction lies mainly in [the collection of alternative actions that may be taken] . . . , which in one case is finite and in the other infinite. In its attempt to clarify the nature of the statistical decision process, it exposes the limitations as to what is attainable in the face of ignorance, and raises serious problems concerning rational behavior. . . . Finally because decision theory deals with the problem of decision making in its greatest generality, every particular statistical problem can be immediately placed in a general framework and thus exhibit its ramifications and implications.

## ORIGINS OF DECISION THEORY

Despite the recency of its development, decision theory is closely related to long-standing problems in the social sciences, and is being used to some extent by psychologists, economists, and sociologists. Within psychology alone, the theory has been brought to bear on problems ranging from learning experiments to studies of attitude measurement.

Economists have been concerned with decision processes for a long time. Businesses are continually faced with choices among alternative courses of action. Principles are needed that will assist managers in making the most profitable or most beneficial choices among products, among investments, etc. Serious limitations have been found in the theories of classical economics which emphasize the welfare of the individual entrepreneur. Most conspicuously, they fail to consider how decisions are reached by coalitions of individuals with different interests. This criticism led von Neumann and Morgenstern (1947) to study how an individual should make decisions when he is one of a group of participants in a game or a market. The resulting "Theory of Games" proved to have a great interest not only for economists, but also for military planners.

The work of Wald (1950), who extended the statistical theory of testing hypotheses into a general "statistical decision theory," paralleled and has merged with game theory. Wald's interest was partly instigated by problems of inspection and quality control in industrial production, where decisions to accept or reject manufactured articles are required. (Such inspection has an obvious similarity to one variety of personnel testing.) Both the statistician and the game theorist are concerned with decisions in the face of an uncertain future, but in game theory the uncertainty comes from the prospective selfish actions of competitors, while in statistical decisions the uncertainty comes from random variation in events.

Studies of decisions take into account the benefit or "utility" of various courses of action. Much thought has been given to problems of defining or estimating such utilities. Economists and mathematicians have tried, for example, to estimate what hypothetical utilities, attached to various consequences, could account for a person's decision to gamble even though he knows that the "house percentage" prevents his winning over the long term. Experimental psychologists have recently begun to study how people actually choose between courses of action, that is, what utilities are consistent with their actions.

Even where it is possible to determine what benefit each individual will receive from various courses of action, the best decision is hard to select if the interests of many individuals are at stake as, for example, in economic decisions of government (Arrow, 1963). One might assess the total effect of a decision by combining the benefits received by all individuals, but this can scarcely be done unless we can measure all persons' utilities on the same scale. Is the benefit rendered by reducing a rich man's taxes by $100 equal to the benefit when a poor man's taxes are reduced by $100? A whole body of theory referred to as "welfare economics" has tried to resolve dilemmas encountered in balancing the welfare of many persons affected by a decision.

A tremendous amount of knowledge has been developed around the general topic of decision problems. Since the tester is concerned with decision making, it is reasonable to expect significant understandings to result from restating testing problems in such a way that this knowledge can be brought to bear.

## CHARACTER OF THIS REPORT

Our study did not begin as an attempt to translate utility and decision theories into psychometric terms. Rather, it began with recognition of certain questions about tests which we could not answer adequately under then existing formulations. One question, for instance, was how one might evaluate a test battery which measures several aptitude dimensions. Hitherto, testers have discussed only the validity of each single score or of the combined test against any single criterion. Except for Horst's recent work (1954), no effort has been made to consider the total contribution of the test in making decisions over all criteria. In trying to formulate theoretical models which would permit study of such questions, we were led inevitably to examine the utility of personnel decisions. It was at this point that we recognized our approach as a case within Wald's more general decision model. This comprehensive model, we found, clarified a wide variety of testing problems.

We have not drawn all possible inferences from decision theory. Indeed, we barely touch on some issues that patently lead to deeper and deeper inquiries. Furthermore, decision theory has been growing at a rate which has quite prevented us from exploring the significance for the tester of all new developments.

We have confined our own study to the simplest and most definite mathematical methods. No doubt some person with greater mathematical competence than ours can extract much further material for the tester from the mathematical literature.

The conceptual tools of decision theory make the tester aware of problems that have hitherto been minimized or overlooked. We believe that our restatement of testing problems in these new terms will assist all users of tests to understand what assumptions they are making and how adequate their procedures are.

At a more technical level, this report examines specific principles of test development and use. Some of the generalizations are restatements of results already in the psychometric literature, which take on new importance, new interrelations, and new meaning in the decision framework. Others are new developments entirely. . . . Since the topics include efficient design of tests, construction of selection batteries, interpretation of validity coefficients, and use of tests for individual assessment, we anticipate that the results will concern a large and diverse audience of test users.

The reasoning of this report is mathematical rather than empirical. A mathematical treatment has both advantages and hazards. The advantages lie in the precision with which conclusions can be stated, the finality with which they can be established, and the wide range of circumstances to which a derivation can apply. In contrast, an empirical study covers only a few particular circumstances and obtains results which are perturbed by various sorts of sampling error.

The disadvantage of the mathematical attack is that it involves assumptions that may not adequately describe real conditions. At times it is even necessary to make assumptions about postulated variables that have never been observed. In our model, for example, it is assumed that the contribution of a person to an institution, and the costs of testing, can be evaluated in some tangible, countable unit. Girshick's comments on this difficulty (1954, p. 463) are worth quoting:

> Here again we see that decision theory demands a great deal of the decision maker. It demands that he be in a position to evaluate numerically for every possible state of nature in the situation under consideration the consequences of any of the actions he might take. It has been argued by many that no human being possesses the ability so to evaluate the utility of the various actions in all possible states. . . . The inability of the decision maker to formulate clearly the loss function is, in fact, a stumbling block in determining what a rational mode of behavior is for him. More bluntly, it is impossible to tell a person what is an optimal way for him to behave if he is unable to formulate clearly what he is after. . . . Decision theory acts as a gadfly to the research worker. It says to him: You cannot solve your problem unless you more clearly define your goal and the consequences of your decisions. Such a prodding is likely to be healthy.

Possibly a major contribution of the approach through decision theory is that it points clearly toward a variety of needed empirical studies. Thus our argument indicates that many *present* personnel procedures are based on assumptions regarding the interaction of the characteristics of the individual and the nature of the treatment to which he is assigned. These implicit, widely employed assumptions have been tested sketchily if at all. A similar finding is that tests used for placement of individuals (e.g., among various levels of instruction) should be validated in ways quite different from those in general use.

To provide the general reader with an overall grasp of concepts and results, the main body of this report contains a minimum of technical detail and mathematical reasoning. The detailed mathematical argument is found in a series of technical appendices.

This report does not attempt to present decision theory *per se*. A mathematical presentation of decision theory may be found in *Theory of games and statistical decisions* (Blackwell and Girshick, 1954). Girshick (1954) has presented an elementary survey of basic concepts in the field, and a popularized treatment is offered in Bross's *Design for decision* (1953). The subject of utility analysis has been reviewed by Adams (1960) and Edwards (1954), the latter review being particularly directed toward psychologists.

Decision theory is provocative, and forces one to alter his accustomed thought patterns. We anticipate that each reader will find a different facet of our argument important for him, and often his thoughts will veer off into pathways not covered by this investigation. The intended contribution of this monograph is, in a word, to stir up the reader's thoughts.

**REFERENCES**

ADAMS, E. W. (1960), "A survey of Bernoullian utilities and applications." In H. Solomon, ed., *Mathematical thinking in the measurement of behavior*. Glencoe, Ill.: Free Press, pp. 151–268.

BLACKWELL, D., and GIRSHICK, M. A. (1954), *Theory of games and statistical decisions*. New York: Wiley.

BROSS, I. D. J. (1953), *Design for Decision*. New York: Macmillan.

EDWARDS, W. (1954), "The theory of decision making," *Psychol. Bull.*, 51, 380–418.

GIRSHICK, M. A. (1954), "An elementary survey of statistical decision theory," *Rev. educ. Res.*, **24**, 448–466.

HORST, P. (1954), "A technique for the development of a differential prediction battery," *Psychol. Monogr.*, **68**, 9.

HULL, C. L. (1928), *Aptitude testing*. Yonkers: World Book.

VON NEUMANN, J., and MORGANSTERN, O. (1947), *Theory of games and economic behavior*. Princeton: Princeton Univ. Press.

WALD, A. (1950), *Statistical decision functions*. New York: Wiley.

# 8 Teacher-Made Tests

## 8.1 Improving the Competence of Teachers in Educational Measurement

*Robert L. Ebel*

This article identifies seven serious errors commonly made by teachers in constructing tests. It is virtually impossible to separate effective teaching and accurate assessment techniques. Unless the teacher develops a sound foundation upon which to base evaluative instruments, his effectiveness as a teacher is seriously jeopardized. What might be done to help reduce the occurrence of these common errors? Are they primarily a consequence of training or attitude? The author describes in this article a practical technique which should very quickly improve teacher test-making skills.

It is of the utmost importance to educational progress that the competence of teachers to measure educational attainments be improved. Far more harm, perhaps ten times as much harm, is currently being done to student learning as a result of the shortcomings of the classroom tests by which a student's educational efforts are largely stimulated, directed, and evaluated, than is being done by all the faults of external testing programs. Let us concede that some faults do exist in external testing programs—faults of coercion, of duplication, and of misuse of test results. Let us also concede that these faults detract from the great service that external testing programs can render to education. But let us not allow the recognition of this mote to distract our attention from the beam. I am fully persuaded that the current problem in testing which most urgently requires the attention of all professional educators is that of improving the tests made and used by the classroom teacher.

Reprinted with permission of the author and *The Clearing House*, 36, 2, Oct. 1961.

To establish the importance of improving teacher competence in measurement, it is necessary to show not only that measurement of educational attainments is needed and possible but also that teachers are currently deficient in getting this job done. I know of little objective data which would confirm this critical view of teacher competence in measurement. It does, however, seem to be quite generally supported by the opinions of all concerned—measurement specialists, school administrators, students, parents, even by teachers themselves.

What are these deficiencies? What are the most serious errors teachers commonly make in measuring educational attainments? A review of the comments of competent educators who can also claim competence in educational measurement leads to this list of seven prevalent errors.

First, teachers tend to rely too much on their own subjective, but presumably absolute, standards in judging educational attainments. The essential relativity of educational attainments, and the unreliability of subjective judgments, have been demonstrated over and over again. Yet few teachers have been persuaded to use pooled judgments in co-operative test construction and markings or to recognize their inevitable use of relative standards in evaluating student attainments.

Second, teachers tend to put off test preparation to the last minute, and then to do it on a catch-as-catch-can basis. Not only is a last-minute test likely to be a bad test, but also it cannot possibly have the kind of motivating and guiding influence on student study and learning that a test planned, developed, and described to the students early in the course could have.

Third, many teachers use tests which are too poorly planned, too short, or too inefficient in form to sample adequately all the essential knowledge and abilities in the area of educational attainment covered by the tests. Essay tests have many virtues, but neither adequacy of sampling nor reliability of scoring can ordinarily be attributed to them.

Fourth, teachers often place too much emphasis on trivial or ephemeral details in their tests, to the neglect of basic principles, understandings, and applications. It is, for example, far less important to know the year in which the Articles of Confederation were drawn up than to know what proved to be their basic weaknesses, yet many teachers are inclined to ask about the date rather than about the weaknesses.

Fifth, teachers often write test questions, both essay and objective, whose effectiveness is lowered by ambiguity, or by irrelevant clues to the correct response. Too seldom do they seek even one independent review of their questions by a competent colleague.

Sixth, many teachers overlook, or underestimate, the magnitude of the sampling errors which afflict test scores. If no error has been made in scoring individual responses or in adding these to obtain the test score, they presume that the score is absolutely accurate. Differences as small as one score unit are considered to reflect significant differences in attainment.

Seventh, most teachers fail to test the effectiveness of their tests by even a simple statistical analysis of the results from the test. They do not even calculate a mean, to see if the test was appropriate in difficulty, or a standard deviation, to see if it differentiated well among the students, to say nothing of calculating the reliability of the scores. Yet calculations of these statistics can be quite simple. There is no better way to develop skill in testing than to analyze systematically the results of previous efforts, and to compare the findings of these analyses with ideal standards.

Let us now approach the matter more positively by considering what a teacher needs to know or to be able to do if he is to be competent in measurement. A detailed consideration of all aspects of this kind of competence cannot be presented here, but some of the major elements can be outlined.

A teacher who is competent in educational measurement should:

1) Know the educational uses, as well as the limitation, of educational tests.

2) Know the criteria by which the quality of a test should be judged and how to secure evidence relating to these criteria.

3) Know how to plan a test and write the test questions to be included in it.

4) Know how to select a standardized test that will be effective in a particular situation.

5) Know how to administer a test properly, efficiently, and fairly.

6) Know how to interpret test scores correctly and fully, but with recognition of their limitations.

This constitutes a fairly large order, but not one beyond the capabilities of most teachers. How can we go about developing this kind of competence?

While a great variety of things might be done to foster improvements in teacher competence in measurement, special emphasis may be focused on only three: increased attention to educational measurement in teacher-training programs; provision of special testing services to teachers in school systems; and special organization of in-service-training programs in measurement for teachers.

The first suggestion, increased emphasis on educational measurement in programs of teacher preparation, seems so obvious as to call for little elaboration or defense, once the importance of measurement in education and the current deficiencies of teachers are granted. Yet this emphasis will surely be opposed by those outside the profession who seek more stress on content and less on methods, and by those inside the profession who have other axes to grind. If, to make room for a solid course in measurement, it is necessary to eliminate some other professional courses, room can be made. In almost all programs for teacher preparation, some courses are so barren of practical value, so duplicative of the content of other courses, or so concerned with formalizing the obvious, that elimination of them would pain only those professors whose livelihood depends on having the colleges continue to require courses of all students.

Some of my professional colleagues have urged legislative requirement of credit in educational measurement as a condition for certification to teach. I would oppose this suggestion on the ground that such legislative requirements tend to be both unduly restrictive and practically ineffective. But an alternative suggestion which strikes me as highly reasonable is that teacher competence in general, and in special areas such as educational measurement, be judged not only from credit in courses taken but also, in part, from performance on appropriate examinations.

The second suggestion would require a school system to employ a staff member with special competence in testing. The main function of this person would be to generate concern over inadequate educational measurements and to offer assistance in improving them. I know of no other way in which a professionally competent superintendent, serving an educationally alert and sympathetic community, could move more quickly and surely, at less cost, to improve the educational program of his district. Concern with the quality of tests inevitably involves concern with the appropriateness of objectives and curriculums and with the quality of teaching. And concern is an essential prerequisite of change and improvement.

A number of the larger and better school systems have made effective use of such test specialists for years. There appears to be an accelerating trend for other school districts to follow their example. Given reasonable freedom of action and sympathetic administrative support, a good specialist in educational measurement can do many things for the school and the community. He can help them to define their educational objectives specifically and meaningfully. He can help staff and students to maintain high motivation. He can help to provide information on the capabilities and achievements of students, information which makes efficient teaching easier for the staff and effective leadership easier for the administration. Above all, he can help teachers improve their competence in the essential task of measuring educational achievement in the classroom.

Schools exist to educate children, but it is the exceptional teacher or school administrator who can say precisely or meaningfully how much education his pupils are getting. Administrators can discuss per pupil costs, pupil-teacher ratios, and average daily attendance with specificity and assurance, but not the educational achievement of the pupils. Teachers can speak fluently of objectives and methods, plans and resources, but ordinarily they find it difficult to say definitely how much education has been achieved. If tests can help to supply this information, and indeed they can, what valid excuse is there for our failure to use them more competently?

My final suggestion of a means for improving the competence of teachers in measurement grows out of experience with a variety of in-service programs intended to help teachers solve measurement problems. These programs, variously referred to as conferences, seminars, institutes, or workshops, have ranged from an afternoon lecture to a three-day preschool program with several follow-up meetings later in the year. Some of these programs were sponsored by a single school system and involved the teachers of that school in all subject areas and at all levels. Others reflected the interest of a single professional group, such as engineers or nurses.

Two main weaknesses have been apparent in the in-service training programs of this type with which I have been acquainted. One is their brevity. While an hour or two a year spent in considering measurement problems under the guidance of a specialist is far better than nothing at all, it is unreasonable to suppose that satisfying, enduring progress in solving the manifold problems of educational measurement, or in developing the requisite knowledge, understanding, and skills, can be made in so short a time.

The second weakness of many of these programs is that they involve too much talking and too little doing. For the cultivation of a practical art like educational measurement, sound pedagogy requires a mingling of theory and practice. A means by which theory and practice can be combined conveniently and effectively is what I would propose.

During the past four years I have watched hundreds of skilled teachers at work on committees charged with the development of new tests for the College Entrance Examination Board and for the Educational Testing Service. (There have been thousands of others whose work I was not able to observe.) Over and over, from the teachers themselves and from our own staff members, have come testimonies as to the educative values of the experience. I am strongly persuaded that the best way to learn how to make good educational tests and how to use them skillfully is to co-operate with other teachers, under expert supervision, in the construction and use of some important tests.

Something along these lines is what I would propose as the ideal program of inservice training for improving the competence of teachers in measurement. Suppose that a school administrator and his staff have decided to focus attention for a year on the improvement of classroom testing. Suppose they engage a specialist in educational testing to meet with them five times during the year, at intervals of six weeks or so, for a day or two. Participation in the initial program might well be limited to five, six, or seven groups of four to six teachers each.

The goal of each group would be to make, to use, and to analyze a quality test in a subject which all members of the particular group were teaching. Examples of subject areas in which these tests might be developed are: fourth-grade mathematics; sixth-grade geography; eighth-grade English; or high-school history, chemistry, or economics.

The first meeting of each participating group would be devoted to a description of the entire project, with special consideration of the first step—the preparation of specifications for the test to be developed. Sample specifications would be presented for study and analysis. Between the first and second sessions each teacher group would work out the specifications for its test. These could be reviewed at the second meeting, and work on item writing would be launched. The third meeting would be devoted to item review and test assembly, the fourth to test administration and analysis, and the fifth to a review of the test developed and of the entire project as a learning experience.

    While I have never participated in a project exactly like this, the most successful ones I know about have much in common with it. I have no doubt that it would produce not only a handful of excellent tests but also a sizable group of teachers whose competence in measurement was vastly improved and, by current standards, highly respectable.

---

## 8.2  *Making* and *Using* Tests
### Paul B. Diederich

Some experts in measurement suggest that a test include only one type of question: objective or essay. In this article, Dr. Diederich outlines a test that includes various types of forms. Which type of test do you feel would be most generally effective? What consideration must be made to ensure that the score on the type of test preferred by the author accurately reflects a student's test performance level?

    *Warning:* Doctor Diederich here presents in a most persuasive manner a measurement technique which can have a powerful influence on student motivation. If you try it in your own classroom, guard against overdoing it, for the technique can easily become a substitute for other important teaching methods.

The topic, "New Methods of Evaluation in the Language Arts," permits several kinds of treatment. I suppose that what you really want me to discuss is, "What should we do about testing?" Another way of putting this question is, "What would you do, Mr. Diederich, if, after twenty years in testing, you returned to your classroom and resumed teaching?" I shall try to give a definite answer to that

From *English Journal*, March 1955. Reprinted with permission of the author and the National Council of Teachers of English.

question no matter how dogmatic it may sound, for I have no fear that any of you will do exactly what I recommend.

I would have started, of course, three months ago when students first came to class, but you can start preparing that test next week with a view to using it during the first week of school next year. It is well to allow such a "cooling off" period for all the tests you write. Put them aside for a time; and about a week before you give them, take them yourself. After that lapse of time you will find that some of the questions have either no defensible answer or several. These items can be either touched up or eliminated.

The purpose of this test will be to find out how well students read and write when they come to you, partly to find out what you will have to teach, and partly to find out what, if anything, you *have* taught after nine months have elapsed. Say nothing about this to the students, but plan to give the same test again during the last month of the school year. I recommend using the same test again rather than a parallel form. The so-called "practice effect" will make no difference after so long an interval, especially if the students have no way of finding out which of their earlier answers were correct.

## MEASURING PROGRESS

You can compare scores on the *objective* portions of this test and find out whether the later scores were higher *if* you can find the first set of papers by the time you collect the second. That is by no means easy. Time after time I have seen retesting spoiled because someone lost the initial papers. Wrap them up, label them clearly, put a curse on whoever removes them, and have the principal lock them up in his vault. That will lend an air of importance to the undertaking, and the extra trouble may enable either you or the principal to remember where the papers are when you want them.

Comparing grades on the initial and final *essays* requires a bit of ingenuity to detect real differences in a convincing manner. If you simply grade the first essays when you receive them and the second essays later, there is likely to be no difference in average grades, for you will adjust unconsciously to the general level of the essays you are grading. That is to say, the best papers in the first set will get A's, and so will the best papers in the second set, regardless of the fact that the second A's are better than the first. On the other hand, if you compensate for this tendency and find striking differences between initial and final papers, no one will believe you. They will think, "He marked the first papers severely, as English teachers usually do, and gave the final papers the benefit of every doubt." You yourself will never know whether you applied the same standards to the second set as to the first.

The correct precedure, I am sure, is this. Have both essays written on the same topic and on the same kind of paper. Threaten students with annihilation if they give any hint in the second essay that they have written on this same topic before. If you find such hints, discard those papers from the comparison. Have names and dates written only in the top corner of the first page of each essay. Make no marks of any kind on either set of essays. You will want to read them, of course, but keep your comments, corrections, and grades on a separate sheet of paper. After the ink on the second set of papers has dried sufficiently so that you can no longer distinguish initial from final papers by the mere fact that the first are black and the second blue, shuffle them and number them in the order in which they happen to fall, putting the same number on the face of each essay and on the corner in which the name and date are written. Then clip these corners off and hand both sets of paper, mixed together in random order, to the head of your department or to some other colleague whose judgment you trust. Ask him to grade all the papers by the same standards without knowing which papers were written first or last, or by what students. You may offer to do the same for him whenever he has the courage to try the experiment.

When he returns the papers with a letter-grade written on each, sort them into initial and final sets for each of your classes by referring to the numbered name-slips that you have kept in your possession. For example, suppose the top paper is numbered 17. Name-slip 17 tells you that this paper was written by John Jones in your first-period class in September. The next paper may be numbered 91, and the corresponding name-slip tells you that it was written by Mary Smith in your fourth-period class in June. After you have sorted out the initial and final papers for each of your classes, add up the number of grade-points each set was awarded, counting any variety of A, plus or minus, as 4, B as 3, C as 2, D as 1, and F as 0. Then divide by the number of students to get the initial and final average grades. If there is no difference, after you have checked the arithmetic, only two conclusions are possible: either your teaching made no difference or a colleague whose judgment you trust was unable to detect it.

The fear of this result will probably deter you from trying this experiment. The hope I offer you is that it almost never happens. We English teachers are a lot better than anyone else knows, and even better than we think. Whenever I have seen this experiment tried, the result has been extremely gratifying to the teacher concerned. I remember one class in which only 14% of the initial papers received any grade higher than D, while of the final papers, 70% received grades higher than D. There was absolutely no way under heaven to fake this result. The person grading the papers had not taught these students, did not know which student had written any paper, did not know which papers were written by the same students, and did not know which papers were written first or last. The result was as solidly established as any fact in science. We could even apply a rigorous statistical technique, known as chi-square, to the significance of the difference and prove that such a difference could occur by chance less than once in a thousand times. I should like to see a physical scientist prove that his students had gained that much in one year in any ability of comparable importance.

## BUILDING THE TESTS

Now let us consider what kind of test to build for this pre- and post-testing. Since I cannot propose a test that will be equally appropriate for all grade levels, I shall use a senior high school test as an example. The same principles apply at lower and higher levels, but of course one has to modify the content. I believe that I tested the same mental functions by the questions I used to ask my daughter about the long series of Cinderella stories that I used to improvise for her at bedtime when she was three years old. It is worthy of note that she enjoyed answering the questions as much as she enjoyed the stories.

I like to find a passage or two that will pose a good problem for the essay and to build the whole examination around them (or it). Take this passage from the New Testament as an example:

> Therefore I say unto you, Take no thought for your life, what ye shall eat, or what ye shall drink; nor yet for your body, what ye shall put on. Is not the life more than meat, and the body than raiment? Behold the fowls of the air: for they sow not, neither do they reap, nor gather into barns; yet your heavenly Father

feedeth them. Are ye not much better than they? Which of you by taking thought can add one cubit unto his stature? And why take ye thought for raiment? Consider the lilies of the field, how they grow; they toil not, neither do they spin; and yet I say unto you that even Solomon in all his glory was not arrayed like one of these.

Wherefore, if God so clothe the grass of the field, which today is, and to-morrow is cast into the oven, shall he not much more clothe you, O ye of little faith? Therefore take no thought, saying, "What shall we eat?" or, "What shall we drink?" or, "Wherewithal shall we be clothed?" (For after all these things do the Gentiles seek): for your heavenly Father knoweth that ye have need for all these things. But seek ye first the kingdom of God, and his righteousness; and all these things shall be added unto you. Take therefore no thought for the morrow: for the morrow shall take thought for the things of itself. Sufficient unto the day is the evil thereof.

Compare this with the following passage from the Old Testament:

Go to the ant, thou sluggard;
Consider her ways, and be wise:
Which, having no chief,
Overseer, or ruler,
Provideth her meat in the summer,
And gathereth her food in the harvest.
How long wilt thou sleep, O sluggard?
When wilt thou arise out of thy sleep?
Yet a little sleep, a little slumber,
A little folding of the hands to sleep:
So shall thy poverty come as a robber,
And thy want as an armed man.

The writing assignment may be worded as follows:

1. These passages seem to contradict one another, yet both are from the Bible. In your introduction, explain what the apparent contradiction is, and support your explanation by quoting the words, phrases, or sentences that express the contradiction most clearly. Show as vividly as you can the dilemma in which a devout believer in the Bible is placed. What is a good Christian to do?

2. In the next section of your paper, write a careful interpretation of the two passages. Do not merely substitute other words for the words of the original but tell as clearly as you can what important ideas or doctrines these passages express. Support your interpretation with relevant quotations.

3. In the next section, examine the case for the birds and lilies, then the case for the ant. Give the most compelling reasons you can think of for acting in accordance with each of these positions and show what difficulties or losses an extreme adherence to either position would entail.

4. Finally, try to work out some resolution of this conflict: either a way of reconciling the two passages with one another or some middle ground that you regard as a tenable position. Remember that both passages are translations. These words are not the words of the original speaker or writer, and even in this English version they may be taken in several different senses.

You will probably regard this assignment as too hard. Everybody regards my assignments as too hard—except the students. This one worked quite well in an eleventh-grade remedial-English class—at least in terms of interest, if not of accomplishment. I could hear students arguing about it all the way home. I did not expect them to write a definitive interpretation of these texts that would satisfy a theologian. I only wanted them to be moved to think hard and to write as well as they could. I also wanted the problem to be hard enough so that they could show improvement in their treatment of it nine months later.

You may also think that this assignment would get me into trouble with devout parents. It might, if I were a village atheist and chose these passages maliciously in order to show that the Bible contradicts itself. But since I love both passages and see no contradiction that cannot be resolved by liberal interpretation, I am immune.

I like the writing problem to be set by reading passages because then the essays will give me insight both into how well the students write and how well they read. For purposes of measuring growth in both skills, you may assign one grade for reading comprehension and another for writing, but they are usually so highly correlated with one another that I have never found it profitable to distinguish between them.

## THE OBJECTIVE SECTIONS

The writing assignment normally comes at the end of the test. We work up to it first by objective questions on readings, second by an objective or semi-objective exercise on a student paper on the same topic, based on the same readings.

While the reading items may be extremely varied, I find it useful in most tests to think of four main types. The first I call "words in context." I pick out all the words and phrases in the passages that might cause difficulty and ask students whether—in the context— they mean A, B, C, or D. The crucial phrase in the parable, for example, is "take no thought." It can be reconciled with the story of the ant only if it means something like "do not worry," "have no anxiety," or "do not make it your primary concern." You put down one of these as the preferred interpretation and give two or three other answers, such as "make no plans," "put off thinking," and "do not accept anyone else's ideas." The chief point to remember is not to look just for hard or unusual words, like "cubit" in this passage. It makes little difference whether "cubit" means one inch or eighteen inches, although I think students ought to recognize it as a measure of length. But it makes a lot of difference how they interpret "take no thought," and that is a hard intellectual problem, even though the words are in Basic English. You may also have trouble framing acceptable answers for the meaning of "the kingdom of God" and "sufficient unto the day is the evil thereof."

The second section I call "interpretation," even though all four sections require interpretation. It is a series of statements to be marked: "A—The Passage agrees," "B—The passage disagrees," or "C—The passage neither agrees nor disagrees." For example, the statement, "Providing for our future needs should concern us deeply" would be keyed as "disagree" for the first passage and "agree" for the second.

The third section is called "analysis" and consists of multiple-choice questions on such matters as the author's purposes and attitudes, main ideas, arguments, assumptions, definitions, figures of speech, organization, soundness, and literary merit. For example, we might ask, "What course of action is the chief concern of Passage 1?" Clearly it is "seeking the kingdom of God and his righteousness." "What is the opposite of this course of action?" "Anxiety over making ends meet" might be an acceptable answer.

The last section, which I call "Comparison," is a special favorite of mine, for I regard the power of seeing likenesses and differences as one of the highest intellectual functions. Coleridge calls it "the sunshine comparative power." I quote a number of additional short passages and ask whether the point of view expressed is similar to that of Passage 1, Passage 2, both, or neither. For example, the passage,

"The world is too much with us; late and soon,
Getting and spending we lay waste our powers,"

would be keyed as agreeing with the point of view of Passage 1.

For the objective writing exercise, I like to use a short but complete paper written by a student on the problem posed by the readings. To get enough of these papers early in the year so that I may have time to prepare tests, I get all my reading passages and writing assignments ready during the first month of school and have from five to ten students write on each assignment. The very worst papers are of little use, for there is not a firm enough underlying structure to show what parts are out of line: they are all out of line. I usually pick about a C paper that has some interesting faults and duplicate it in the left-hand column of a divided page with certain portions underlined and numbered. These portions may or may not contain errors. In the right-hand column I offer four ways of writing, arranging, or punctuating each marked portion, and students indicate which they prefer. There are also some general questions on the writer's purpose, organization, reasoning, rhetorical effectiveness, and the like. Even though you may call this a proofreading exercise rather than a writing exercise, I have known scores on successful exercises of this type to correlate above .70 with grades on essays written in the same examination. This is higher than the correlations usually found between grades on successive essays written by the same students. The abilities tested may be different, but students who have one usually have the other also.

If you object to calling attention to possible errors by underlining, you may simply print the essay triple-spaced and have students insert corrections and comments. In scoring such exercises, concentrate on points at which something needs to be corrected; never mind what happens in between. First read a sample of papers to find out what students have done at these points and make a list of unacceptable corrections to which you will give zero credit, improvements that will get one point, and completely acceptable corrections that will get two points. Some corrections are either acceptable or unacceptable: for example, either there is a comma or there is not. Other corrections admit the two degrees of credit. It has been shown repeatedly in College Board examinations that exercises of this sort can be scored by different readers with almost perfect agreement.

## THEIR EFFECT UPON TEACHING

I have now outlined a test, consisting of a reading exercise, a writing exercise, and an essay assignment, all based on a problem posed by the reading passages, that can be used for pre- and post-testing. It is my firm conviction that similar tests should be given about once a month as homework, followed by class discussion of items that gave trouble. In such discussions I try to restrain myself from simply giving the right answer and defending it; I let students argue out their differences and try to reach a conclusion themselves. An important point for them to learn is that one student may have five arguments to support his answer while another may have only two and yet be right. They have to learn not only to recognize contextual clues but to evaluate them properly.

Although I have a book of tests of this sort in press, I strongly urge you to make your own: first, because it is great fun; second, because your own tests always look better and mean more to you than tests prepared by anyone else; and third, because after you have made a year's supply of these tests and studied the results, you will be a better teacher. You will know better what kinds of questions to ask about a text or a student paper in order to develop sensitivity and insight. By such questions you will give daily practice in the many complex skills of interpretation and expression.

You will probably give up trying to annotate every paper you receive with handbook symbols and illegible comments. Instead, you will write a sentence or two of praise or blame at the end of most papers and select one or two out of each batch to duplicate triple-spaced, asking students to take them home, insert corrections, and argue with one another about their corrections the following day in class. It will do them more good, I believe, to argue strenuously with one another about how to correct someone else's paper than to correct their own. For one thing, they will do it and enjoy it, while you know perfectly well that it is like pulling teeth to get them to correct their own. For another, they will approach the problem more objectively. Their author's pride will not be involved, and their judgment will not be clouded by defensive reactions.

## THE SIGNIFICANCE OF SUCH TESTS

Tests of verbal reasoning are better general predictors of how well students will do in school, college, graduate school, or professional school than any other kind of test so far devised. I refuse to believe that they have attained these results in hundreds of studies over the past thirty years simply because they get at innate powers that are independent of instruction. It takes more than the intelligence of a new-born babe to recognize that "have no anxiety" is a better paraphrase of "take no thought" in the parable than something like "make no plans," if you want to reconcile it with the story of the ant. Every developed trait of an organism is the product of *both* nature and nurture. While I do not deny or overlook the part played by nature in what these tests measure, we can do nothing about that, but we *can* do something about the part played by nurture. I have good reason to believe that practice and discussion of the kinds of exercises I have described will improve verbal reasoning and hence the ability to learn. The evidence is that students who have had such practice fail fewer examinations in all their courses than equally able students who have not. For this reason I believe that the ultimate objective of our work goes beyond the improvement of reading and writing, although they are very important as means. The ultimate objective is to sharpen man's most precious tool, his mind, on the whetstone of language. There is no more important task in which a teacher can be engaged.

---

## 8.3    Teacher-made Tests: Models to Serve Specific Needs
*William J. Laidlaw*

Generally, there are two broad purposes in testing in an educational program: (1) testing for mastery of minimum essentials, and (2) measuring the extent of *each* student's attainments or proficiency.

Reprinted with permission of *The Clearing House*, Feb. 1965.

The author of this article suggests that teachers keep the two models clearly in mind. He particularly points out the utility for the student and teacher of the first (criterion) model as a direct, clear, motivating and guiding device. The second (prediction) model is explained as appropriate when the aim is to display the *relative* competence of each student compared to his classmates. As he shows, quite logically, combining the two in a single test is potentially the teacher's most powerful evaluation device.

Most teachers have had instruction in making and using tests, but many have gotten lost in a haze of statistical and technical detail: validity, reliability, norms, item indices, and more. In frustration and confusion, they sometimes relegate testing to the status of an onerous clerical chore. They label it a low-level bookkeeping procedure and throw together last-minute tests in which they have little pride or confidence. In so doing, they increase their own frustration and add to the anxiety of their students. Most importantly, they deny their students valuable knowledge about the progress they are making in learning, and they deny themselves invaluable information about how well they are teaching and how much they can assume their students know as they move on to new teaching goals. These teachers are unable to see the forest for the trees, the tests for the techniques. They could do a better job of testing if they had a clear idea of what they were trying to accomplish with their tests and if they knew the models or types of tests that could aid them in achieving their purposes.

Teachers' tests can be usefully classified by the purposes for which they are used. These are (1) to see whether a student has learned the essentials of a unit of instruction, and (2) to see how much or how well he has learned in comparison to his classmates. Tests designed for one or the other of these purposes, or for both at once, represent distinctly different test models.

## CRITERION-LEVEL MODEL

When the teacher wants to see whether students have mastered the essential content of a unit of instruction, whether it be facts, concepts, principles, or skills, a criterion-level test is appropriate. Tests of essentials are referred to as criterion-level tests, because when using such tests the teacher is interested in seeing whether the student has achieved the minimum acceptable level of competence in dealing with the content of a unit of instruction. The essentials and the level of acceptable competence are determined by the teacher in terms of his instructional objectives. Ideally, every student who completes a unit of instruction that leads to such a test scores 100 per cent. This is true because only those things stressed by the teacher are tested. Practically, a class average of 90 per cent, with a range from 80 to 100 per cent, might be considered a sign that the teaching and learning of a unit have been adequate.

Every teacher knows that it is important to state clearly what his instructional objectives are before he teaches a unit. This is particularly important if criterion-level tests are used, because only attainment of essential objectives is tested. For these objectives to be useful, they must state what a student does to show that he has reached them; otherwise, it is difficult or impossible to judge whether a goal has been achieved. For example, if it were essential that students learn about hypothetical "wing-bangs" the following objective would not help much: "The student will know about wing-bangs." Knowing what about wing-bangs shows minimum acceptable accomplishment? The following statement is more helpful: "The student will identify the three distinctive characteristics of wing-bangs and select the three wing-bangs from a group of 12 bangs." In this case the teacher knows what he must teach about wing-bangs and exactly what the student must do to show that he has learned. Achievement of such an objective can be readily tested with either essay or objective test items.[1]

The most obvious of the uses for the criterion-level test, as defined above, is as a post-test. However, another important use for the criterion-level test is as a pre-test to see whether students have the minimum prerequisite competencies to profit from a new unit of instruction or if they already know some of the things the teacher considers essential in the new unit. This information lets the teacher judge more effectively where to begin instruction to accomplish the objectives of the new unit. Actually, the best use of the criterion-level test combines the pre- and post-test benefits. Criterion-level tests given at the end of lessons, as weekly quizzes, or at the end of other short instructional units provide a continuous audit on the teaching-learning process. The results of the tests let the teacher

---

[1] To learn more about stating instructional objectives, see Mager, R. F. *Preparing Objectives for Programmed Instruction.* San Francisco: Fenron, 1962.

know whether the objectives of a unit have been accomplished and whether he can proceed on the assumption that students have the prerequisites for subsequent units. Criterion-level tests also keep students continuously informed about their progress. Because such tests get at a limited set of precisely stated essential objectives, they are typically short and take little time from teaching, but they provide both teacher and students with valuable information.

Tests representing the criterion-level model are very useful, but they provide no basis for assigning grades. Only pass-fail ratings make sense when most students get 90 per cent or better, because no range of performance is provided to make possible discriminations with respect to competence among those who pass. Therefore, teachers need an additional model for tests that will provide information upon which to base grades.

## PREDICTION MODEL

In order to assign grades, a teacher must see how much or how well each student has learned, in comparison to his classmates. Tests that sort out students in a class according to competence are similar to standardized tests of aptitudes and abilities used to predict future school or job performances. The purpose of these standardized tests is to see how well individuals handle test tasks as compared to members of some appropriate group. Concern is with a student's relative performance, not his absolute achievement of specific objectives. Performances on these tests are used to predict some future event such as course grade, school graduation, or vocational success. Students who perform well on the tests typically get A's, graduate, or are successful; conversely, F's, dropouts, and failures have done poorly on the tests. The majority of students fall between these extremes.

Teachers who have taken a course in tests and measurements are familiar with the prediction model. It incorporates the normal probability distribution, and the statistics of testing are concerned with it. The concepts of reliability, validity, and norms are most appropriate to it. And most test construction techniques seek to assure correspondence of tests with this model.[2]

When a test is developed that is based on the prediction model, it is usually assumed that the behaviors being tested and the situations

[2] A good traditional treatment of test construction for teachers that is based on the prediction model is Wood, Dorothy A. *Test Construction.* Columbus, Ohio: Merrill, 1960.

in which they are expected to occur are so complex that only representative aspects of them can be tested within practical limits of time and student endurance. To assure that what is tested is representative, the situations (e.g., content or subject matter) and the relevant student behaviors (e.g., concepts, principles, or skills) are carefully outlined. Test items are then selected because they represent appropriate situation-behavior combinations. Only items that good students consistently get right and poor students consistently get wrong are used. To assure optimum discrimination and spread of test performances, very easy and very hard items are not used. Instead, items that have mid-range difficulty are preferred. Enough items are used to give the weight to each area of content and kind of behavior that the test builder judges it should have to assure that the whole test will be a balanced representation of the situations and behaviors that are its object. Because there are usually numerous items in the test, the more efficient objective-type test items are favored.

When the purpose of a test is solely to sort people in a group according to relative competence with tasks that represent a fairly large area of subject matter, the prediction model is appropriate. Teachers can use tests of this type at the end of large units of instruction: at the end of marking periods, as midterm or final examinations, and as comprehensive examinations. They provide a basis for assigning grades and for making predictions about the future relative performances of students when faced with similar tasks. However, while prediction tests give the teacher essential information, the information is no more sufficient than that provided by criterion-level tests. Prediction tests seldom make it possible to determine whether essential objectives have been achieved or what the particular strengths and weaknesses of an individual or group are. These tests are used to get a stable estimate of relative performance with representative tasks; specific instructional objectives do not usually form a basis for their design and development. Therefore, an adequate testing program should probably include criterion-level tests and predictions tests, or perhaps tests that combine the criterion-level and prediction models.

## COMBINATION MODEL

Tests that combine the criterion-level and prediction models are potentially the teacher's most powerful evaluation devices. They make it possible to assess accomplishment of essential objectives and at the same time to sort students according to competency so that grades can be assigned and future performances predicted.

The procedure for developing a combination test is straightforward. First, a criterion-level test is developed to include all the essential objectives of a unit of instruction. This test serves as the framework for the larger test; its items provide anchor points of minimum acceptable competence on the dimensions defined by the objectives. These items are the easiest items in the combination test, being answered correctly by about 90 per cent of the students. Second, several test items are selected or written to assess level of attainment of each objective beyond the acceptable minimum. These items represent situations in which it is increasingly difficult for the student to make discriminations or generalizations and to perform operations or apply procedures that are the behavioral manifestations of the instructional objectives. They range in difficulty for each objective from about 80 per cent to 20 per cent, and they should be passed by good students more frequently than by poor students, just as with any prediction test. In fact, a combination test is a prediction test superimposed on a criterion-level test.

All forms of test items can be used in a combination test, true-false to essay. It is advisable, however, to use objective items or short, structured essays, because many items will be required to assess the several points of competency on each of the instructional objective dimensions. Other item forms take too much time to administer and are cumbersome and time-consuming to evaluate.

Combination tests can be scored in the same way as either criterion-level or prediction tests, but it is usually worth the effort to derive subscores. First, the items that represent minimum acceptable competence with essential objectives are scored to get information about the effectiveness of teaching and learning. Second, the discriminating items are scored to form the basis for predictions about future relative performance in related situations. Last, the subscores are combined to form a basis for assigning grades. They may be simply summed, or different judgmental weights may be given to each before summing. However, it is possible, and more reasonable, for the teacher to make pass-fail decisions with the criterion-level subscores and to assign grades to those who pass on the basis of the distribution of prediction subscores. This procedure uses more of the information provided by the combination test.

Tests combining the two test models are appropriate whenever the prediction model is appropriate. Actually, it is hard to justify preference for the prediction model over the combination of models for teacher-made achievement tests. Some teachers express preference for the prediction model, because they think it allows them to get a broad sample of student ability to cope with larger bodies of subject matter. However, general information and general abilities, while important, are difficult to relate to specific learning and instructional objectives. Too often the argument in favor of general tests of the prediction type masks a lack of clear behavioral definition and statement of objectives, a condition which is not desirable for a higher order of evaluation.

Teachers who understand the basic test models and who use them to accomplish the purposes of their achievement tests should become more confident about their tests and attach more value to the information provided by them. They will be in a good position to improve their teaching, because they will have stated their instructional objectives in precise behavioral terms, and their tests will let them know how well they have accomplished their objectives. They will be able to provide their students with useful guidance for their learning and reliable evaluation of their accomplishment. Their testing can be a professional task, rather than a clerical chore.

## 8.4   The ABC's of Test Construction
### Julian C. Stanley

Professor Stanley, in this article, offers some concrete suggestions on how to make the classroom test. You will not be able, from a mere reading of this article, to produce a commendable achievement or diagnostic instrument. That was not the author's aim. Rather, what we have here is a condensed summary of the basic principles of test construction. It is necessary to acquire many details from a more extensive study in order to profit adequately from this meaty article.

Reprinted with permission of the author and *NEA Journal*, April, 1958.

For example, Dr. Stanley speaks about a "table of specifications." If the design of such a table is not familiar to you it might be advisable to read about the topic in a measurement text. A review of this article at some later time, before you expect to prepare a test, should prove most helpful as a refresher and handy guide.

Constructing a good test is one of the teacher's most difficult duties. Good tests do not just happen. Actual test construction, therefore, requires much thought and careful planning.

## PLANNING THE TEST

A well-planned test will provide the means for evaluating progress toward the expected outcomes of instruction, as expressed in the educational philosophy of the particular school and as defined in the objectives of the particular course.

If the school hopes to produce "good citizens" with "integrated personalities," for example, tests must measure the development of good social attitudes and a widening range of significant interests.

For any given course, instructional objectives must be expressed in terms of the specific changes in pupil behavior or growth which the teacher hopes to bring about.

A teacher, for instance, should be conscious that such an objective as the development of an appreciation of literature may express itself in various forms of student reaction. He sets out then to phrase test questions which will determine whether a particular piece of writing gave individual students a sense of satisfaction and enthusiasm, made them want to read more by the same author, stimulated their own creative expression.

The well-planned test will reflect the relative amount of emphasis each objective has received in the actual teaching of the course. The same test might not be equally valid for two teachers of general science if one has emphasized the memorizing of isolated facts, while the other was more concerned with the interrelation of facts. Each teacher would be helped by drawing up in outline form a kind of table of specifications to indicate not only the objectives of the course, but also the relative amount of time spent on each.

The content of the test should show a similar proportion in regard to the number of items to be included but not the type, for the type of item depends upon the nature of the objective to be measured.

The well-planned test must be designed to accomplish the purpose it is to serve. If the purpose is to give the basis for school marks or classification, it will attempt to rank the pupils in order of their total achievement. But if the purpose is diagnosis, its value will depend upon its ability to reveal specific weaknesses in the achievement of individual pupils.

Diagnostic tests would cover a limited scope, but in much greater detail than a test of general achievement, and would be arranged to give scores on the separate parts. The range of difficulty of items is relatively less important, also, in diagnostic tests. This is true, too, of mastery tests administered at the end of a teaching unit to see whether minimum essentials have been achieved.

The well-planned test will also fit the conditions under which it is to be administered, such as the time available for testing, facilities for duplicating the test copies, and cost of materials, as well as the age and experience of the pupils being tested.

## PREPARING THE TEST

In actual construction of a test, these suggestions have helped:

1. Prepare a rough draft of the test as soon as possible. Many teachers jot down items day by day for possible inclusion to help ensure that no important points will be omitted, particularly those appearing in supplementary material that might be overlooked if the textbook itself is the chief basis of the test.

2. Do not make the test items too easy. Many teacher-constructed tests fail to make the items difficult enough. This, no doubt, is due in part to the influence of the "70% should be the passing grade" tradition. However, the test that is too easy is not an efficient instrument for measuring pupil progress.

3. Include more items in the first draft than will be needed in the final form. This will permit culling out of weak items and those not needed to produce proper balance.

4. Subject the test to critical revision some time after it is drafted by checking items against the table of specifications to see if they show the desired emphasis on various topics. If tests are submitted for criticism to other teachers of the subject, points of doubtful importance can be weeded out and ambiguous wording corrected.

5. Include more than one type of item in the test. A variety of test types is more interesting to students. The test situation may also require that three or four forms of objective items be used, or that these be combined with discussion or essay-type questions.

6. Place all items of one kind together in the test. Sometimes completion, true-false, and multiple-choice questions are thrown together in random order. This arrangement is rarely, if ever, desirable. When like items are grouped the pupil can take full advantage of the mind-set imposed by a particular form, and the teacher will find scoring and interpretation of scores easier.

7. Arrange test items in an ascending order of difficulty. The placing of very difficult items at the beginning is likely to produce needless discouragement for the average or below-average student.

8. Avoid a regular sequence in the pattern of responses. If items are arranged alternately true and false, or two true and two false, pupils are likely to catch on and answer correctly without considering the content of the item at all.

9. Make directions to the pupil clear, concise, and complete. Instructions should be so clear that the weakest pupil knows what he is expected to do, though he may be unable to do it.

It is better to tell young children to "draw a line under" than to "underline." In lower grades, teachers find it helpful to read instructions aloud while the class follows silently the written instructions. If the form of the test is unfamiliar or complicated, a generous use of samples correctly marked, or practice tests, is recommended.

Regardless of how carefully a test is planned and edited, it is impossible to know solely by inspection exactly how good it is, or which are the weak items. If possible, therefore, the test should be given some advance tryout which will approximate the conditions under which the real test will be given, know the actual time it will require, and indicate what scoring difficulties may result.

Because various studies have shown that a majority of teachers, especially at the high-school level, use a combination of essay and objective questions, the uses and limitations of both will be briefly examined here.

## THE ESSAY TEST

The essay test has both unique advantages and serious disadvantages. Some authorities claim that it calls forth less than half the knowledge the average pupil possesses on a subject, compared with results from an objective test, and takes twice the time to do it; that it overrates the importance of knowing how to say a thing and underrates the importance of having something to say; and that the score resulting from an essay test depends more upon who reads it and when than upon the student who wrote it.

Offsetting the serious scoring difficulties connected with essay tests and their frequently low degrees of validity, reliability, and usability, there is much to indicate that such tests have a legitimate place in the modern school.

Specifically, they are useful for measuring functional information, certain aspects of thinking, study skill and work habits, and an active social philosophy. These are educational objectives which emphasize the functioning of knowledge rather than its mere possession.

Such tests are especially valuable in courses in English composition and journalism, where the student's ability to express himself is a major instructional objective, and in advanced courses in other subjects where critical evaluation and the ability to assimilate and organize large amounts of material are important.

Essay tests have at least one other general merit: When pupils expect the test to be of that type, in whole or in part, they seem more likely to employ such desirable study techniques as outlining and summarizing, and to make a greater effort to recognize trends and relationships.

Despite popular opinion to the contrary, a high-quality essay test is more difficult to construct than is a good objective test. These three rules, however, should be helpful in improving the construction and use of essay tests:

1. Restrict such a test to those functions for which it is best adapted.

2. Increase the number of questions asked and decrease the amount of discussion required for each.

3. Make definite provisions for teaching pupils how to take such examinations.

## TYPES OF OBJECTIVE TESTS

The simple *recall test* item employs a direct question, a stimulus word or phrase, or a specific direction to elicit from the pupil a response based on his previous experience. The typical response is short—hence its other name, the short-answer question.

The main problem is to phrase these test items so that they will call forth responses from a higher level than mere memory, and so that they can be readily scored.

*Example:* Eight is what percent of 64?

The *completion test* consists of a series of sentences in which certain important words or phrases have been replaced by blanks to be filled in by the students. This test has wide applicability, but unless very carefully prepared, it is likely to measure rote memory rather than real understanding, or to measure general intelligence or linguistic aptitude rather than school achievement.

Scoring is also more subjective, and complicated by the fact that the missing words are written in blanks scattered all over the page, rather than in a column. This difficulty can be avoided by a form such as this:

1. The man who headed the first expedition to circumnavigate the globe was _____ .

2. The Articles of Confederation were in force from 1781 to _____ .

An *alternative-response test* is made of items each of which permits only two possible responses. The usual form is the familiar true-false item and its cousins, the right-wrong, yes-no, same-opposite, and multiple-choice questions.

While the true-false type of question is popularly considered easy to prepare, experienced test-makers point out that this type of test requires great skill, and care must be taken in wording so that the content rather than the form of the statement will determine the response. The following suggestions may be useful in constructing such tests:

1. Avoid specific determiners, that is, strongly worded statements containing words such as "always," "all," or "none," which may indicate to pupils that the statement is likely to be false.

2. Avoid using the exact language of the textbook, with only minor changes to give the true-false pattern, because this puts too great a premium on rote memory.

3. Avoid trick statements which appear to be true but which are really false because of some inconspicuous word or phrase, such as "The Battle of Hastings was fought in 1066 B.C."

4. Avoid "double-headed" statements, especially if partly true and partly false, as in this sentence: "Poe wrote *The Gold Bug* and *The Scarlet Letter.*"

5. Avoid double negatives lest pupils versed in grammar conclude that two negatives equal an affirmative, while others think such statements are emphatic negatives.

6. Avoid unfamiliar, figurative, or literary language and long statements with complex sentence structure—for reasons which should be obvious.

7. Avoid words that may have different meanings for different students. "Often" may mean once a week to one child; three times a year to another.

A *multiple choice test* is composed of items which require the student to select a correct or definitely better response from two or more alternatives (at least four whenever possible). This is one of the most useful test forms. It may be used to ascertain the ability to give definitions, identify purposes and causes, similarities and differences, or to ask many other varieties of questions.

In phrasing multiple-choice questions, it is essential to avoid giving irrelevant or superficial clues, and to assure that the question measures more than memory. The diagnostic value of this type of item depends as much on the skillful wording of the incorrect choices presented as upon correct statement of the right choice.

Scoring may be facilitated by arranging the items in groups, putting together all items with the same number of choices, and requiring the simplest possible method of recording the response.

Other useful rules are:

1. Make all responses grammatically consistent. For example, if the verb is singular, avoid plural responses.

2. Use direct questions rather than incomplete statements whenever possible. This helps eliminate irrelevant clues.

3. Arrange the responses so that the correct choice occurs about equally in all positions, and do not consistently make the correct answer longer or shorter than the others.

4. Make all the responses plausible, and when testing at higher levels, increase the similarity in the choices under each item in order to better test the powers of discrimination.

A *matching test* involves the association of two things in the mind of the learner by requiring him to pair the items in two columns; events and dates, events and persons, terms and definitions, laws and illustrations, and the like. Matching exercises are well adapted to testing in who, what, where, and when areas but not to measuring understanding as distinguished from mere memory.

Since most of the tests used in classrooms are teacher-made, it is highly important that teachers develop proficiency in the building of tests by discriminating use of what is now known, by keeping themselves informed on new studies of testing techniques and methods, and by careful evaluation of their own testing, day by day.

# 9 School Testing Programs

## 9.1 Testing Programs—Misconceptions, Misuse, Overuse

*Frank B. Womer*

Testing in the schools is the most visible measurement activity. Everyone, including parents, is aware that some sort of formal appraisal procedure has taken place and this same "everyone" wonders what the findings have been.

Dr. Womer, in this widely distributed article, exposes some of the more common misconceptions about test scores and the frequent misuses to which they are put.

Are you surprised, for instance, that exactly half of all pupils are "below average" on tests they take as members of a "norms" group? Or that two counselors will often disagree on the meaning of the same set of pupil scores? If so, you are not too different from most nonexperts. Read this article with the expectation that when you have finished studying what it contains, you will be more expert about educational and psychological measurement than you are now. Also, you will be better prepared to tackle some of the more technical material contained in upper division textbooks on measurement.

We are in a boom period of standardized testing in elementary and secondary schools. To pupils at all grade-levels, millions of tests are administered each year—achievement tests, mental ability tests, aptitude tests, and interest inventories, as well as several types of tests and inventories. Some of these tests are given for college scholarship purposes and some for college admissions purposes. Title V of the National Defense Education Act has stimulated, and in some instances, required, additions to testing programs at the secondary

Reprinted with permission of the author and *Michigan Journal of Secondary Education*, Spring 1961.

level. In general, however, these external influences account for a relatively small percentage of the total standardized testing undertaken by a school system.

There are at least two factors which have had a greater impact upon the amount of testing done in the schools than NDEA or college requirements. First, there has been and continues to be a natural growth of standardized testing at all grade levels. Second, the rapid growth of the guidance movement has meant a corresponding rapid growth in testing. This latter influence may well be the most influential one operating, for in many schools the testing program is developed by and operated by guidance personnel.

Inauguration or expansion of a testing program is relatively easy. Decisions made one day can be implemented within a week or two. The only time lag is that of the United States mail in delivering orders for tests and getting test materials from the publisher to the school. Machine methods for test scoring have reduced, and in many cases eliminated, objections that a testing program is a burden upon individual teachers. The school budget and allocation of time for testing are the only real problems to face if an administrator or faculty decides to enlarge the testing program. Thus it is relatively easy to test.

The values of standardized testing, however, cannot be dismissed so quickly. Such values are dependent upon two processes: (1) establishment of proper goals of testing and the development of a testing program to meet those goals, and (2) proper use of test results. Both of these processes are essential to the operation of a successful testing program. Most educators feel, and rightfully so, that the major weakness of testing today is in the area of test use.

Many writers have made this point, and most school administrators are acutely aware of the fact that the ultimate criterion for judging the effectiveness of their testing programs is the correct use of test results. Accumulating test scores in cumulative files is not evidence of test use. Correct use depends upon getting test results into the hands of counselors, teachers, administrators, pupils, and parents and of being sure that each consumer of these results is made knowledgeable enough to interpret them. In this latter statement—"made knowledgeable enough to interpret them"—lies the key to proper test use.

There are a number of ways that test scores are misused or overused, and a number of misconceptions about tests and test scores that are common enough to warrant special attention. While one could think of innumerable examples of specific errors in test interpretation, the purpose of this article is to point up some of the more common mistakes, in order to help increase the knowledgeable use of test results. Ten points have been selected for discussion; others could have been added.

### CATEGORIZING A PUPIL AT A SPECIFIC LEVEL OF ACHIEVEMENT OR ABILITY

One of the most common mistakes made by persons unskilled in interpreting test results is the assumption of perfect reliability of a test score. Too often it is assumed that an IQ of 105 represents performance definitely superior to that represented by an IQ of 104 and definitely inferior to that represented by 106. Too often we fail to realize that a test score is best interpreted as a good estimate of the general level of performance, and that it will vary from test to test and from time to time. Test users must accept the concept of variability of test scores over time and over tests. The assessment of human traits and abilities is not at the same level of accuracy as that found in a physics laboratory. It probably is closer to the level of accuracy found in the predictions of weather, in which temperature predictions are generally within a few degrees of actual temperatures, but in which differences of ten or more degrees are common enough to be remembered vividly by critics.

Another aspect of this assumption of greater accuracy than actually prevails is the use of a single estimate (test score) to predict human performance. It is generally wise to insist on having two or three reading scores, or two or three aptitude scores, before putting much confidence in them. This is a direct result of the unreliability present in all test scores. If a pupil receives percentiles of 35 to 40 on arithmetic tests given in two different years, one can have greater confidence that his level of achievement in arithmetic is in the average range than if only one of these scores is available.

### CONFUSION OF NORMS AND STANDARDS

Norms are test scores which tell us the level of performance attained by an average or typical group of pupils. Standards represent human judgments of the level of performance that "should be" attained by a group of pupils. A test user should not assume that "typical" pupil performance is automatically the "proper" level of performance for pupils in a particular school system. It is reasonable, of course, to assume that pupils in many school systems will tend to perform at a level close to the level of test norms. In others, however, it is reasonable to assume that pupils will perform at a higher level or at a lower level.

One occasionally finds a test user who completely fails to grasp the conception of what a test norm is. Since a test norm represents "typical" performance, then, of necessity, half of the pupils in a typical or average group will have scores at or below the average score. If a teacher of a typical group of pupils finds that 40 per cent of his pupils are below grade level in reading, he is to be congratulated. In the norm group for whatever test is being used, 50 per cent of all the pupils were at or below grade level. The assumption that all pupils in a class should be at grade level is patently impossible, unless one knows that the poorest achieving pupil in one's class is in the top 50 per cent of all pupils his own age or grade.

## ASSUMPTION THAT TEST SCORES PREDICT SUCCESS OR FAILURE FOR INDIVIDUAL PUPILS

One way that test results often are overused is the assumption that a particular score or series of scores does in fact predict success or failure with unfailing accuracy. It is well established that students who succeed in colleges of engineering generally make high scores on numerical ability tests. Yet it is not correct to conclude from such data that Johnny with a 50th percentile rank on a test of numerical ability, will not succeed in an engineering course. It is correct to conclude that of every 100 students with numerical ability scores the same as Johnny's, only a small percentage will succeed in an engineering curriculum. The test score does provide information of a probability type; it enables a student or parent or counselor to know the odds for success or failure. It is a well-known fact that long shots occasionally win the Kentucky Derby, but year in, year out, the favorites generally win.

It is not unusual for two counselors to look at the same test scores for an individual pupil and to come to somewhat different conclusions. For this reason, it is well to face the fact that while test scores do provide information that can be helpful in decision making, the decisions for courses of action are made by human beings, not by the scores.

Added to this overuse of test scores is the failure of some people to utilize all pertinent data available about a student when test scores are known. To allow test scores to outweigh all other judgmental data is a misuse of these scores; to ignore test scores in favor of other judgmental data also is a misuse of these scores.

## DETERMINATION OF VOCATIONAL GOALS

"Mary's scores from a clerical speed and accuracy test and from a spelling test are only average. Therefore, Mary should not consider secretarial work as a career possibility." Or, "Since Jim's interest profile shows high scores in 'Scientific' and 'Social Service' he should elect a premed course in college." How often can vocational counseling be summed up in just such simple statements? It is so easy to make the jump from test score to occupation, and it seems so logical that this type of interpretation should be accurate. Unfortunately, the predictive validity of test scores in high school for success in specific occupations is not good enough to permit such interpretations. Most evidence of the predictive efficiency of test scores relates those scores to academic curricula. We can say with a fair degree of accuracy that certain patterns of test scores predict fairly well in different curricula. That is the type of validity data that is generally available.

The use of test scores in vocational counseling should tend to open doors of possible occupations rather than close them. Again, presenting the relationship between test scores and occupational areas on a probability basis can be helpful, and is certainly more accurate than making the assumption that certain test scores assure success in one field and failure in another.

## ASSUMPTION THAT INTELLIGENCE AND ACHIEVEMENT ARE SEPARATE AND DISTINCT

Here are two sample questions from standardized tests:

1. Extraneous
   a. extra   b. foreign   c. transparent   d. noisy
2. Make indelible means
   a. indistinct   b. permanent   c. purple   d. identical

Both are vocabulary items. One of them is taken from a widely-used intelligence test (California Test of Mental Maturity) and the other from a widely used achievement battery (Iowa Tests of Educational Development). Vocabulary items measure the learned meanings of words; vocabulary items are our best single measure of general intelligence or scholastic aptitude. Arithmetic items and general information items are also found in both achievement tests and intelligence tests. It is true, of course, that some items suitable for an intelligence test (number series, verbal analogies) are not good measures of achievement. It also is true that many direct measures of achievement (capitalization, punctuation, spelling) are not good measures of intellectual potential.

There is considerable overlap between standardized tests of achievement and standardized intelligence tests. One of the important differences between the two is the way the results are used. When analyzing achievement test scores, one is generally considering past performance, what has been accomplished. When analyzing intelligence test scores, one is generally looking forward to the future; predicting performance.

It is well to keep in mind the fact that intelligence is inferred from achievement. We have no direct measures of intelligence completely divorced from achievement.

### ASSUMPTION THAT INTERESTS AND APTITUDES ARE SYNONYMOUS

Probably few users of standardized tests would acknowledge a belief that interests and aptitudes are the same thing. Webster defines the terms in different domains. Yet how many users of standardized interest inventories can truthfully say that they have never made the jump from a high percentile score in "Persuasive" to the suggestion that Bill probably could succeed in sales activities? To say that Bill seems to be interested in many of the same things that are of interest to people who work in occupations that require influencing other people may be accurate. But to say that Bill will likely succeed in one of these occupations is to make the unwarranted jump from interest to aptitude.

There is evidence that interests and aptitudes are correlated, but not at a level that allows us to predict one from the other with a high degree of accuracy. This is not to say that interest inventories are useless, but their use might well center on their motivational attributes, on their power to stimulate pupil concern over long range planning.

## MISCONCEPTION OF THE MEANINGS OF
## CERTAIN TYPES OF DERIVED SCORES

Students of education have been and are continuing to be taught that an intelligence quotient is obtained by dividing mental age by chronological age, and that mental age is determined by the test performance of students at different levels. Yet, as a matter of fact, very few of the IQ's to be found in the cumulative folders of elementary and secondary schools today are quotient scores at all. IQ's are standard scores, just as are the z scores, T scores, stanines, College Board scores, and others for almost every widely-used intelligence test.

It is true that IQ's originally were quotient scores. But, primarily for statistical reasons, the deviation IQ was developed some years ago and has since met with almost universal adoption. Even the Stanford-Binet test switched to a deviation IQ in 1959. The change from a quotient score to a standard score has not necessitated any drastic change in interpretation. Yet it seems to the writer that test users would be well advised to stop paying lip service to a type of score that no longer exists, and to become familiar with standard scores, the type of scores actually being used with our intelligence tests.

The grade placement or grade equivalent score is another type of derived score that is frequently misinterpreted or overused. All too often it is assumed that a grade placement score is an indication of the grade to which a pupil should be assigned. It does not provide that type of information; it simply tells a user whether a pupil is doing high, average, or low quality work. A percentile rank also provides the same assessment of level of work, yet avoids the danger of overinterpretation. If one wishes to compare a pupil's achievement on two different tests in an achievement battery (e.g., reading level versus arithmetic level), a grade equivalent score may lead one to an important misinterpretation. Because of the variability (standard deviation) of grade placement scores from test to test it is possible for a sixth grade pupil to be at the 90th percentile in both reading and arithmetic, yet receive grade placement scores of 8.8 in reading and 8.0 in arithmetic.* If a teacher sees only the grade placement scores of 8.8 and 8.0 he may assume superiority in read-

---

*Iowa Tests of Basic Skills, end-of-year percentile norms for sixth grade pupils.

ing, whereas the two scores represent *equivalent* performance. For test-by-test comparisons in elementary level achievement batteries, percentile scores should be used.

## GRADING OR PROMOTING PUPILS

Standardized achievement tests are designed with certain purposes in mind. In general, test authors attempt to identify those skills and understandings that are common to most educational programs. They look for the common denominators; they make no attempt to cover those unique aspects of content that a particular school system may incorporate in its curricular offering. They cannot attempt to reflect a particular teacher's goals for his own pupils. Thus, while achievement test results represent very useful assessment of certain skills and understandings that are common to many classrooms, they should not be used to replace a teacher's own assessment devices.

In many schools standardized achievement tests are given toward the beginning of the school year. They are used to look ahead rather than to look back, to diagnose rather than to evaluate or grade. In those schools that use standardized achievement tests at the end of the year, it may be interesting for a teacher to compare the results with his own judgments. It is not wise for the test results to be used to replace his judgments, in either grading or promotion.

## JUDGING EFFECTIVENESS OF INSTRUCTION

Just as standardized tests are not designed to be used for grading pupils, they are not designed to be used for grading teachers. Many of the outcomes of classroom instruction cannot be programmed in standardized tests. Those that can be programmed in tests may not be meaningful because of different emphases, different content, and different grade placement in a particular school.

Of special concern is the attitude engendered in teachers in a school attempting to assess instruction through achievement tests. When test results are used to judge teachers, teachers soon learn to teach for the tests.

It is interesting to note that in some instances teachers even feel compelled to "teach for" ability tests. They somehow feel that it isn't respectable to turn in a set of IQ scores for filing in a cumulative record unless all or almost all of them are at least 100. Such a feeling, of course, is based on a misconception of the meaning of intelligence. A teacher may be cutting his own throat with such high scores, for if his pupils are all above average in ability they may be expected to show equally high achievement levels.

## COMPARING RESULTS FROM DIFFERENT TESTS

There is a very natural tendency for test users to assume that a language usage score from one test is directly comparable to a language usage score from another test, that an IQ from one test means the same thing as an IQ from another. When making such assumptions one tends to forget two very important characteristics of standardized tests:

1. Test authors do not build their tests on the same specifications, following the same blueprints. Each one develops his own specifications for test construction. There usually is considerable overlap between the plans for a language usage test developed by one author and the plans developed by another. However, there is never a complete overlap. Scores from two tests measuring the same attribute vary to a certain extent because the test designs vary.

2. The norms for different tests are based upon different groups of pupils. Each test author aims at securing a truly random population of pupils for use in standardizing his test. Each author falls somewhat short of his goal. While it is correct to assume that test norms for two different arithmetic tests are based on groups with considerable overlap in achievement, it is not correct to assume 100-per cent overlap.

Thus, two IQ's derived from two different intelligence tests are not exactly equivalent. It has been demonstrated that IQ's can vary as much as 5 or 10 points between different tests for no other reason than that they are different tests.

Sometimes one hears this objection: "But how can IQ's be different from different tests? I thought that all good intelligence tests correlated well with each other." It is true that the correlation between different intelligence tests are generally sizable, and many times are almost as high as the reliability of the separate tests. Such correlations do not guarantee comparability of norms. Such correlations simply say that pupils taking the different tests will tend to get scores putting them in the same relative rank order but not with the same scores. For example, suppose one were to take a set of IQ's (or any other test score) and add 50 points to each score. The correlation between the original IQ's and the new scores would be perfect, yet the two sets of scores would be 50 points apart.

As we mentioned earlier, we are in the middle of a boom period of testing. If the users of tests do a good job of interpreting the results for the improvement of our understanding of boys and girls and for the improvement of instruction, the boom will level off on a satisfactory plateau of test use. If the users of test results fall into the various misuses, overuses, and misconceptions that are possible, the boom will most certainly be followed by a "bust."

It is the thesis of this article that the consumers of test scores must be thoroughly conversant with proper methods of test use and must studiously avoid misuses, overuses, and misconceptions.

"A little knowledge is a dangerous thing."

---

## 9.2   The Teacher's Role in Evaluating Pupil Achievement
### D. Welty Lefever

Preservice teachers wonder about their role in school testing programs. Professor Lefever presents a survey of general national practices along with some excellent guides to individual action for teachers and administrators.

Particularly important is his effort to foster a desirable *attitude* toward the formal testing program. What effect do you think his idea of the "submerged sample" technique might have on teacher morale versus system-wide testing? It is intended to reduce the tendency to "teach for the test." Also, it is expected to allay, somewhat, the suspicion by some teachers that achievement testing constitutes an administrative undercover operation.

The testing program as it operates in many school systems contains some elements which are determined by the central office; other

Reprinted from the Dec. 1950 issue of *Education* by permission of The Bobbs-Merrill Company, Inc., Indianapolis, Ind.

aspects of the program may differ from school to school. The appropriate part and function of the classroom teacher in the total program of measurement is not always easily defined. The range of practice with respect to the amount of participation by the teacher in setting up the total pattern of testing is considerable. In some school systems, especially the larger ones, the total plan for testing is determined by the staff at headquarters and detailed instructions are passed down the line to the rank and file of teachers and building administrators. On the other hand some schools take a completely *laissez-faire* attitude toward all forms of testing. Whatever measurement is carried on will be a matter for each principal or teacher to decide. Somewhere on the continuum between over-planning and under-planning is the democratic procedure which provides an opportunity for the classroom teacher to assume an important role in setting up the over-all design for evaluation.

No doubt much can be said regarding the advantages of detailed central planning and of uniform system-wide testing. The staff at the central office usually includes one or more specialists in research and measurement. Much time is saved by the fact that a single pattern is applied to all schools. Duplication and inconsistency are prevented. A picture of achievement for all aspects of the curriculum is made available for every classroom in the system. Because the measuring devices are uniformly applied, the comparative status of the several schools can be clearly seen and a minimum base for testing every pupil definitely established.

The system-wide survey of achievement may involve certain hazards. The teaching staff may feel that the whole testing program has been imposed from above; they may regard it as someone else's business and not a matter for deep personal concern. Remote planning often fails to elicit whole-hearted cooperation.

Teachers have been known to chafe under the extra burden of the testing program, especially scoring the tests and recording the results. Some have resented the loss of time from the scheduled routine of the classroom. These attitudes appear to be most prevalent when the instructor has not been sold on the value of measurement as a direct aid to better teaching and when he has not been assigned an active part in defining the purposes and determining the general nature of the program.

When the data from an achievement survey are summarized for the administration by individual classrooms and schools, it is very likely that some, if not all, of the teachers and principals will feel that they have been put "on the spot." That is, they may feel that their professional competence is being judged from the test scores when many other facts about the school and classroom would need to be considered to guarantee a really fair judgment. This effect will be intensified if the test results are made available generally to the professional group. Even if the standings for each school are reported to that school only, principals and teachers have been known to compare average scores in such a way as to produce an unwholesome rivalry. Whenever the central office knows where each teacher stands in the table of survey results that teacher may well believe that his status in the eyes of the administration is more or less directly affected. Benevolent statements to the contrary by the superintendent may well be discounted by the staff.

A more subtle danger that may carry unfortunate consequences for the over-all effectiveness of education, is the possibility that the achievement tests employed may determine what will be taught in the classroom. If the results of these tests are interpreted in any way, directly or indirectly, by the administration as an index of successful instruction, the teacher may well endeavor to produce higher test scores. The greater the emphasis placed on test findings the stronger will be the teacher's desire to conform to the curriculum pattern set by the test. An important question arises: are the test makers qualified to set the curriculum for the school? And if they should be, does such an indirect and remote plan of curriculum making represent a wholesome educational policy? The school system that believes in using democratic process in developing its educational program will certainly find that it is essential to provide for teacher participation in the development of measurement policies and program.

Many school systems have found it possible to develop a balanced program of measurement and evaluation to which specialists and teachers, as well as administrative and supervisory staff, can all make their unique contributions. When each member of the educational team is given an opportunity to participate in setting the general policy, individual initiative is encouraged and many, if not all, show an intelligent interest in evaluating the effectiveness of their professional activities.

Some specialists in measurement, knowing the increasing complexity of the technical aspects of testing, will seriously question whether any considerable number of instructors are able to offer worthwhile assistance in planning the testing program. The average teacher is not an expert in testing and would certainly lay no claim to such distinction. On the other hand, he is well acquainted with the objectives of the curriculum and with the activities designed to aid each pupil progress toward these goals. The modern concept of evaluation recognizes that the aims of the course of study must determine the scope and character of the measuring devices used. Achievement cannot be adequately measured until a working definition of the nature of what is to be achieved has been clearly stated, recognized by the teacher and incorporated into the daily work of the classroom.

When it is understood that the approach to evaluation must reflect what has actually been accomplished in the classroom, the teacher's part in the program of achievement testing stands out more clearly. Many educators believe that it is essential for the classroom teacher to participate in determining the general nature of the curriculum, and in selecting the specific activities through which its goals will be realized. It should be equally important for the classroom teacher to assist in determining the general character or flavor of the testing program and to help in deciding the *kinds* of measuring devices to be used. The services of a specialist will probably be needed in determining *which* instruments are most likely to do best the work required of them.

Perhaps the total program of measurement can be divided into two major phases: (1) the day to day evaluation of many aspects of classroom activity and (2) the general survey administered uniformly throughout the school system.

In planning the first phase, the frequent measurement of a variety of pupil activities, the teacher must certainly play the leading role. Outlining the general character of these activities and determining how they will be evaluated are parallel responsibilities. Published test materials are available for testing some aspects of pupil achievement. Perhaps the skill subjects are most satisfactorily measured by tests developed and standardized for nationwide use. Satisfactory "content" samplings in such areas as history, biology, literature or geography are much more difficult to produce. Curriculum emphases are more nearly constant from school to school and from region to region in the skill subjects than in the other phases of the program. No doubt most teachers can profit by some expert help in selecting standard achievement tests and particularly in interpreting the results for the maximum benefit to all. If the assistance from specialists in measurement is to be most effective, it should endeavor to make the teacher less dependent on such help as the years go by. The in-service training of the teaching staff in the art of skillful evaluation should be a major objective of all supervisory and administrative workers.

Teacher-made tests should be considered essential tools for checking pupil achievement. They are especially important on the secondary level where courses of study differ widely among the school systems of the country. Published tests cannot do justice to so wide a range of subject matter emphasis. It should be kept in mind that valid instruments of evaluation must represent faithfully the objectives and activities which constitute the functioning curriculum of the school. This means that home-designed tests will be needed for the "content" areas and for measuring the less tangible phases of education.

There is much reason to believe that teachers grow in professional competence as they participate in test construction. Well-constructed tests require that the teacher analyze thoughtfully the exact goals of instruction as well as the nature of the pupil activity through which these aims are to be realized. By participating in evaluation the classroom teacher will learn to observe and interpret the evidences of pupil growth as shown in specific instances of pupil behavior. When these observations are made regularly and according to an orderly plan they contribute not only to more adequate evaluation but they also form a vital part of an in-service training program for the faculty of the school.

Specialists in measurement can contribute vitally to the effectiveness of education in their communities by encouraging and assisting teachers to plan their instruments and techniques of evaluation while they develop their courses of study and their classroom procedures.

A survey of educational accomplishment for the entire school system makes possible a much needed general assessment of the strengths and weaknesses of the curriculum and of the instructional effectiveness of the school program. The plan of measurement may focus on a single grade level or on selected grades; it may deal with all curriculum areas or with a limited number of subjects. Such a system-wide achievement survey usually possesses the advantages of careful design, expert test administration, machine scoring, complete statistical analysis and painstaking interpretation.

Since the major purpose of a general survey is to evaluate the educational program and not to pass judgment on the individual teacher, certain precautions can insure better faculty morale. The evils of direct appraisal of the skill of an individual teacher from achievement test scores are widely recognized. In milder form they include a reduced sense of teacher security, a tendency to slant instruction in harmony with the curricular emphasis of the test, and a desire to rationalize away any weaknesses the test may reveal. Direct coaching for the test, or a strongly antagonistic attitude toward all testing on part of the faculty, represent some of the more serious hazards. Few administrators plan to judge the professional competence of their instructors from class averages, but the availability of survey data which has been summarized for individual teachers and schools suggests that such judgments may be an incidental outcome of the survey. *Unwelcome and unnecessary comparisons among teachers and schools can be prevented and any possible form of appraisal of particular teachers from the survey results can be completely eliminated by the use of a "submerged sample."* (Italics ours, Eds.)

The simplest procedure is to omit teacher and school identification from the final summary sheets so that the survey outcomes are expressed in terms of grade level averages for the entire system or, in large urban centers, for neighborhood areas. Since most surveys would be more comprehensive in the sense of including more evaluative devices if time and cost would permit, a sampling procedure can be employed which will extend the scope of the survey. In one such survey in which the writer participated, four random samples of pupils were selected by the use of code numbers and a table of random numbers. Each random group of pupils was given a different set of tests. Separate teacher rating forms, observation schedules, and evaluative devices were used with each of the four groups. Since each of the four random groups was relatively large, it was felt that no serious loss of validity resulted from the use of a sampling procedure. Perhaps the most difficult part of the planning arose from the necessity for providing four test administrators to test simultaneously the four groups from a particular grade level within each school. A team of qualified testing personnel moved from school to school as the survey progressed. Teacher cooperation was exceptionally good because the demand for time beyond the regular school day was reduced to a minimum and because class groups were so thoroughly submerged by the sampling procedure as to make the identification of the individual instructor very difficult.

There are many important ways in which classroom teachers can and should participate in the functioning of a system-wide survey of achievement. They certainly ought to be well represented on committees assigned the task of designing the survey. Again, valuable in-service education can be a major by-product of such planning when it is thoroughly done. After the measuring devices have been administered, scored, tabulated and analyzed, there is still much significant thinking to be done. What are the implications of the survey findings? Are important changes in the curriculum indicated? Should the character of the teaching methods be altered? What other improvements in the educational program ought to be made? The maximum amount of cooperative thinking by the largest number of teachers under skillful leadership should produce the most successful overall evaluation.

The findings from a general achievement survey can provide excellent subject matter for discussion by teacher committees, faculty meetings, summer workshops, in-service training seminars and supervisory staff sessions. The classroom teacher can contribute to improved public relations by bringing the survey results and their attendant problems to the attention of parent groups for their consideration and suggestions. No doubt certain selected aspects of the survey could be discussed with profit by student groups, particularly in the secondary school, under competent teacher leadership.

By way of summary, the role of the teacher in the measurement of pupil achievement may be described in terms of the following list of specific activities. In relation to the evaluation of achievement, the classroom teacher will need to:

1. Participate in planning the appraisal of the educational program. When achievement testing is considered to be an integral part of curriculum design, the teacher's role is clarified. He will work closely with the administration in setting up behavioral objectives, in developing curricular patterns, in devising evaluative instruments and in selecting appropriate measuring tools from those already available. Through such cooperation he will grow in professional competence and perspective.

2. Provide important kinds of assistance in the actual operation of the testing program. Such cooperation would probably include:

a) Administering many of the achievement tests under the supervision of specialists. Whether the teacher takes full charge of giving the tests or not, he can do much to aid in establishing class rapport. How pupils feel about the test has much to do with the validity of the results. If the class understands the purposes of the measurement and if they see that they will benefit personally from the findings, they are more likely to cooperate wholeheartedly and to make good use of whatever scores are made available to them. Naturally all teacher-made tests will be administered by their designers.

b) Scoring some, if not all, achievement tests. Where IBM machines are available, the tests can be constructed for ease of handling by such scoring devices. Some tests, at least, could be corrected by the class through exchange of papers or by pupils scoring their own examinations.

c) Recording the results in some form of cumulative system so that the necessary evidence for the systematic study of pupil growth will be available.

3. Examine test scores carefully in order to understand the needs of his pupils more adequately. While measures other than those of achievement are probably of greatest importance in understanding each pupil, achievement tests may throw much valuable light on interests, special skills, serious deficiencies, and on the general nature of pupil growth in school learnings. By comparing these scores with measures of aptitude for learning, the overachievers and underachievers in the class may be located. The former may be compensating for personality difficulties or weaknesses by an unhealthy concentration on certain narrow aspects of school success. The latter are more generally recognized as belonging to a relatively large group who fall considerably short of their potential levels of accomplishment.

4. Study the errors made by each pupil in order to discover learning difficulties and to plan a remedial campaign when necessary. More effective teaching should be the result of such a diagnostic analysis of pupil strengths and weaknesses. Shooting with a rifle at specific targets will usually produce superior results to firing a shot gun in the general direction of a rather vague objective.

5. Utilize the test outcomes as a basis for more skillful guidance. Whether employed as aids to a group guidance approach or in counseling the individual pupil, achievement test scores can assist in

a)  Developing suitable educational goals,
b)  Improving the techniques of study, and in
c)  Selecting vocational areas in which success seems probable.

6. Marshal the outcomes from the evaluation of each pupil's growth so that a meaningful report of his progress can be made to his parents. An accurate and objective picture of his achievement will aid his parents in cooperating more intelligently with the school and will increase their respect for the program of education.

7. Appraise his own teaching success in light of test results. Even though self-appraisal is accompanied by a greater sense of personal and professional security for the teacher than is possible when class averages are judged by the central administration, there is still some danger that the test scores will be taken too seriously by the teacher as direct evidence of teaching skill. Teacher success must be evaluated in terms of many factors only a few of which are measured by the achievement scores.

8. Cooperate with the superintendent and his staff in thinking out an overall interpretation of system-wide achievement surveys and in presenting many of the findings to groups of parents.

---

## 9.3   Testing: Bond *or* Barrier between Pupil *and* Teacher?

*Roger T. Lennon*

Not only can school testing programs supply dependable information for use by administrators, counselors, and teachers, but they can also serve to strengthen the commitment of the pupil to his own growth. However, it is unfortunately true that testing in the schools often fails to serve as a positive influence but rather is viewed as some sort of diabolical instrument of pupil punishment.

Reprinted from the Sept. 1954 issue of *Education* by permission of the author and The Bobbs-Merrill Company, Inc., Indianapolis, Ind.

Dr. Lennon discusses and describes in this fine article some excellent techniques which the classroom teacher can use to ensure that the school testing program will tend to promote positive attitudes in children toward themselves as students and toward the school experience generally.

"Children, tomorrow we are going to have a test in arithmetic." When you make an announcement like this to your class, how do your pupils react? If you are Miss Average Teacher, and your class is a typical one, it is a good bet that such an announcement is not greeted with shouts of approval, or expressions of enthusiastic anticipation. More likely moans, groans, and other signs of dismay are forthcoming. To be sure, a good deal of the children's reaction may be discounted as spurious, intended to impress fellow pupils and perhaps to soften the teacher's heart; but even after allowance is made for the counterfeit character of some expressed distaste for testing, it still remains true that the announcement of impending testing, to say nothing of the testing itself, is an occasion of some uneasiness, tension, or anxiety to pupils. This is true whether the tests be the teacher's own or standardized ones, though the latter, coming less frequently, clothed in the impressiveness of a printed booklet, and perhaps administered by a stranger or by the teacher in an unaccustomed role, may be especially disturbing.

## WORRY ABOUT TESTS

Parents and teachers are well aware that the anticipation as well as the actual experience of test-taking can be an upsetting experience for children. In a survey (1) among a large representative sample of high school students, 43% indicated that worry about tests was a problem to them; it is not likely that the figure would be any lower for elementary school pupils—rather the contrary. It is safe to assume that these feelings of anxiety as a rule are inimical to the development of ideal pupil-teacher relationships and a healthy learning environment, for underlying such attitudes on the pupil's part is generally the notion that in testing the teacher is doing something to him, rather than for him. The purpose of this article is to consider why testing has these disturbing characteristics and what may be done to have pupils acquire more positive attitudes toward tests, so that the tests may serve as a helpful bond between pupils and teacher, rather than as a barrier between them.

## TOWARD COMMON GOALS

The development of sound pupil-teacher relationships rests, in the final analysis, on recognition by pupil and teacher that they are working toward common goals. It calls for confidence on the pupil's part that all of the teacher's activities are directed only to the pupil's own good, difficult or distasteful though some of these activities may seem at any given moment. The pupil must believe of his teacher what Goldsmith wrote of the schoolmaster in *The Deserted Village:*

> "Yet he was kind, or,
>                     if severe in aught,
> The love he bore to learning
>                     was at fault."

The teacher, for her part, must have the welfare of each of the pupils, as her primary concern, and be possessed of a reasonable sensitivity to the requirements of adequate human relations in the classroom. Failure to apply these elementary mental-hygiene principles to the testing and evaluating aspects of the instructional process is usually responsible for whatever undesirable feelings children may entertain toward tests.

We talk much about testing as being fundamentally for the good of the pupils and no doubt, in the final analysis, it is generally the good of the pupils that the administrator or teacher has in mind in giving tests. But how well is this fact communicated to the pupils? How often does the teacher, by word or action, indicate to the pupil the ways in which testing is related to the pupil's own purposes, helps meet his own needs? All too often the pupil perceives testing as an instrument utilized by the teacher primarily, or even exclusively, for checking up on his mastery of certain assigned tasks, and as a basis for assigning grades or determining promotion. Such applications of test results are not improper; but where these appear to the pupil to be the only reasons for which tests are given, it is not likely that testing will serve to strengthen the relationship between pupil and teacher.

Very few persons, children or adults, feel so secure that they can contemplate taking tests, of whatever kind, with equanimity. The thought that we may not do well on a test, either absolutely or relative to our fellows, poses a threat to our egos. When, in addition to loss of self-esteem, poor performance on a test may incur the displeasure of parents and teachers and a lessening of prestige among peers, it is not hard to understand the anxiety that testing may produce. This type of danger is well stated in a recent book (2, page 121.):

"To the extent that evaluation involves a large amount of introspection and self-criticism, it is potentially a destructive influence on the child. Such a danger may seem remote; but parents, particularly those in privileged groups, are frequently overanxious about the progress of their children and often communicate their anxieties to them. Because it is possible to probe and prod more than is conducive to healthy growth, those who do evaluation should always take into consideration its effect on the child."

### SOME CAUSES OF TENSION

We may say, therefore, that improper use of tests, producing uneasiness and tension among pupils and harmful to healthy pupil-teacher relations, stems largely from (1) lack of understanding of the proper role of tests, often accompanied by some insecurity on the part of the teacher herself; and (2) failure to appreciate the emotional problems posed for some children by any ego-threatening evaluation procedure.

To be specific:—

1. If a teacher looks upon the norm on a standardized test as a goal to be reached by all children, and criticizes those who fail to meet this rigid standard, the pupils will quite naturally come to think of tests as hurdles rather than as stepping stones to development.

2. If a teacher in interpreting test results fails to take into account other relevant information—ability differences, health status, home background, and the like—she is likely to render an unjust appraisal of a child's work, which may well have the effect of discouraging or antagonizing the child.

3. If a teacher overemphasizes tests in her evaluation program, and fails to realize that they cover only a part of the desired outcomes, she runs the risk of placing undue emphasis on certain objectives and of confusing the pupil as to what he is supposed to be learning.

4. If a teacher habitually uses test results as bases for invidious comparisons among pupils, not only is the pupil-teacher relationship damaged, but also the relationships among the pupils.

5. If a teacher berates or scolds a child because of poor performance on a test, she may be building up unfavorable attitudes toward future testing.

6. If a teacher fails to let a pupil know how he did on a test, or give him any indication of how the testing is related to his purposes, it is hard for the pupil to make sense of the procedure.

7. If a teacher is herself insecure, and feels threatened by the tests, it is almost certain that her attitude will be communicated to the children. If a school or system-wide program is in operation, in the planning of which the teacher has had no part, and the purposes of which she does not understand, she is obviously in no position to make clear to the pupils how the testing is likely to do them any good. If the test results are used as a means of appraising teacher competence, the temptation becomes very strong for the teacher to teach for the tests.

8. If a teacher is unsympathetic to a testing program in which she must participate, and makes slighting or sarcastic reference to "these tests that we have to give again," she is certainly engendering a poor attitude on the pupils' part; even young pupils are shrewd enough to sense, however vaguely, that by such behavior the teacher is abdicating her rightful position.

## TO STRENGTHEN THE BOND

Need testing and evaluation, such important phases of instruction, have adverse reactions of this kind on pupil attitudes and pupil-teacher relations? Not at all. A great deal of testing, both of the ordinary classroom variety and in connection with large-scale programs, is conducted in such a way as to elicit willing and interested cooperation from pupils. Where tests are being used for legitimate instructional or administrative purposes, where pupils appreciate why the tests are used and how they contribute to their self-understanding and improvement, and where the teacher interprets and utilizes results in accordance with sound mental hygiene principles, testing serves to strengthen the bond between pupil and teacher.

How can teachers carry on testing and evaluation procedures so as to minimize pupil feelings of tension or hostility to these activities? It goes without saying that the first essential is that the teacher herself must be persuaded of the value of these activities, and understand how they are to contribute to the improvement of the child's learning. Assuming that the teacher is genuinely interested in testing as a means to the improvement of the learning process, the task is then one of communicating to the pupil a realization of how test results contribute to and serve the pupils' own interests.

It is unrealistic to expect pupils to have a voice in planning testing and evaluation, for as a rule they do not have the information, skills, or judgment to contribute effectively to such planning. It is not unreasonable, however, to propose that prior to the administration of any test the teacher say a few words to the pupils, to indicate why she needs information about each pupil's level of attainment if she is to be able to help them, to point out the essential fairness of tests as impartial yardsticks by which all pupils' attainments are measured, and to point out why it is helpful for the pupils to know their own strengths and weaknesses so that they may capitalize on the former and work to overcome the latter.

### AFTER TESTING WHAT?

What the teacher says before testing, however, is much less important than what she does after testing in creating proper attitudes. It is in her actual use of the test results that the teacher reveals her real purposes and it is here that she must convince the pupils that the testing is being done for their benefit. Here are a few suggestions that may help demonstrate the beneficial outcomes of testing to pupils:

1. Return test papers to pupils after they are marked, and go over the test in class so that each pupil can quickly see what mistakes he made and have a chance to ask questions about them. For tests whose results are not to be used for marking or grading pupils—and there should be numerous such tests—it is well to let the pupils correct their own papers. Under these circumstances the tests are free of any threatening aspect; the pupils realize that the only purposes the tests serve are the pupils' own learning needs.

2. Do not disclose individual pupil's results in such a way as to permit comparisons among pupils. It is a good practice to show on the blackboard a distribution of the scores for an entire class, thus letting each pupil know where he stands in relation to the class but

not revealing to the entire group the standing of any individual pupil. The writer is not one of those who would discourage all competition in school activities, but he believes that, in general, this competitive aspect is best divorced from routine use of test results.

3. Indicate by notations on test papers or otherwise that you have given individual consideration to each pupil's results. Thus a given test score might be the occasion for a word of special commendation for one pupil, but fall below expectation in the case of another. The important thing is that the teacher demonstrate in each case that she is interested in the test results only insofar as they help her to understand the pupil and to do a better job of instructing him.

4. Guard against the temptation to view the children as collections of test scores. Accurate information such as tests provide about pupil characteristics is important, even essential; but every pupil has a worth that is not measured by any test score.

The development of proper attitudes toward testing not only contributes to the building of sound pupil-teacher relationships; it may also have character-building consequences of enduring value. The taking of tests is a lifelong experience for everyone: On the job and in the home, life presents a series of tests, very often under circumstances much less friendly than those the pupil encounters in school. If the child learns to meet these challenges, to face up realistically to his own limitations, to accept success without complacency or smugness, and to accept failure without undue distress or bitterness, he will be that much farther along on the way to becoming a well-adjusted adult.

**REFERENCES**

1. REMMERS, H. H., and SHIMBERG, B. *SRA Youth Inventory*. Manual of Directions. Chicago: Science Research Associates, 1949.
2. GANS, ROMA, *et al. Teaching Young Children*. New York: World Book Company, 1952.

# 10 Measurement in Research

## 10.1 The Evaluation of Learning under Differing Systems of Instruction

### William A. Brownell

In today's schools more and more attention is given to research which shows increasingly sophisticated design. Two or more methods of instruction, kinds of materials or other manipulations are incorporated into a school program for the purpose of determining which variable more effectively produces a desired outcome.

Quite frequently, much of this effort leads to uninterpretable, meaningless results because insufficient thought was given to all conditions which might affect the outcome.

Professor Brownell, in this recipient's address for the E. L. Thorndike Award, attempts to share some of the wisdom with regard to evaluative research which he has managed to acquire during a long and fertile career as an educational psychologist. After reading what he says here, you should have a somewhat better appreciation for the complexity inherent in a masterfully executed evaluative procedure and perhaps be better able to design and execute a meaningful educational or psychological study of your own.

Some of you who are present can recall the time when the possible uses of the silent motion picture for instructional purposes attracted wide attention. As is regularly true on the appearance of a new educational medium, opinions ranged through the whole gamut from expressions of doubt and opposition to extreme claims such as that we might soon be able to dispense with much that teachers do in the classroom. Naturally, some brave souls saw in the controversy

Reprinted with permission of the author and *Educational Psychologist*, 3, 1, Nov. 1965.

the need to undertake research in order to evaluate the effectiveness of the silent film in comparison with traditional procedures.

I shall describe only one of these studies. The investigator was fortunate in finding a film which pictured substantially the same small body of biological phenomena as were covered in a textbook lesson. One group of high school subjects saw the film while another group read the parallel written account. On the test given afterward, the motion picture subjects considerably outscored the textbook subjects. On the basis of his comparative findings, the investigator recommended the wholesale substitution of the motion picture for the form of instruction then prevalent.

Many reasons will occur to you, to question the soundness of this proposal, which, nevertheless, as far as I can ascertain, was criticized in but a single article. The investigator had, in his data, little to support his sweeping generalization, especially when one notes that the test given for evaluation was based solely on the captions in the film. These captions, as such, were seen only by the film subjects, and they identified for them facts which, if present at all in the text assignment, were not so clearly marked for learning on the part of the reading subjects.

You may wonder why I cite so superficial a study, and particularly one made nearly four decades ago. Your wonder may be motivated by the conviction that improvement in experimental design in the intervening years makes it improbable that evaluative research so deficient at many points is still being done. If so, I assure you that we are far from having attained the millenium and that, on the contrary, evaluative research seriously lacking in crucial respects is even now being reported and—worse yet—being accepted at face value.

Had I the time, I could support my last statement by citing several instances of comparatively current studies which are faulty; but I must content myself with a single one. Within the past five years an investigator attempted to assess the relative effectiveness of two unlike programs for teaching a certain school subject, one which was of recent origin; the other, of long standing. He selected a part of a test battery, the part having to do with the subject in question, and administered it to large samples of children taught according to the conventional or traditional system, or according to the relatively new system.

The results of the testing could have been safely predicted. While the instrument chosen deservedly enjoys an excellent reputation, it was designed for a purpose quite different from that for which it was used. Furthermore, it seriously prejudiced the case against the more novel program. That is to say, it was devoted to the content and objectives of the conventional program, and it disregarded certain important content and objectives peculiar to the more recent program. Hence, the achievement of the traditionally taught children was measured precisely with respect to what they had been taught. By contrast, the achievement of the children in the rival program was measured with respect only to what they had been taught in common with their counterparts. They therefore had no chance to show what they had learned with regard to those aspects of the subject unique to their program of instruction.

On this account one can accept the reported superior rating of the traditional program only on the assumption that the content and the objectives represented therein *should* constitute the curriculum of the subject in question. Moreover, when we follow the pattern of research typified by this study, our reasoning becomes circular, and our research becomes pointless. As a consequence, we may merely confirm current practice and block educational progress in favor of the *status quo*.

### COMPLEXITY OF EVALUATIVE RESEARCH

So much for this particular investigation, which serves to bring me to the first of the three major points I wish to consider with you at some length. This point is that we tend to minimize the complexity of evaluative research.

It is not strange that this is so. At first glance, nothing would seem to be simpler. We teach a segment of subject matter to two or more groups of children, these groups being exposed to dissimilar systems of instruction. After a period of time, by means of tests or in some other way, we assess the learning which has taken place in all the groups, compare their test scores, and rank the instructional systems for effectiveness in terms of the relative standings of the groups taught. Program B may be found to be most effective, and both B and C more effective than A; or, A and C may be found to be more effective than is B, but with little to choose between the first two; or, all three systems may be found to produce about the same results, one being as effective as is each of the other two.

Not uncommonly the final rankings of programs are presented without qualification. The implication, stated or not, is that Program B, for example, is the way to teach the subject under any conceivable set of conditions. Yet a moment's reflection should warn us against agreeing to a conclusion so categorical.

In the first place, we are able to do no more than to sample a fraction of the content taught. However, if we should test on a different sample, the findings might reveal an unlike array of ranks.

In the second place, the assumption that, as planned, the same content has been taught to all groups is very probably in error. For instance, it may be necessary, in keeping with the theory basic to Program C, to introduce subject matter not essential to the other two programs, or, by the same token, to omit phases of subject matter taught in the other two. And again, the relative emphases given to *parts* of the common content may be so different as to make the programs in actuality quite unlike each other as wholes in this respect.

In the third place, the effect of differences among the systems in the objectives stressed may not be taken into account. And these differences can obtain even on the unlikely chance of uniformly taught content. Thus, one system may be preferable to the other two when the main objective is creative thinking but less desirable when it is the mastery of information.

In connection with this matter of objectives, significant types of learning data, seldom collected, could *if* collected materially affect the relative rankings of programs. Prominent among these are the kinds of thought process used by children, and differences in this respect may vary all the way from parroted verbalizations to meaningful and logical ways of thinking. Our concern too often is confined exclusively to measures of correctness of final responses. Hence, we may be unable to state which, if any, of the rival systems of teaching procedures produces the greatest amount of movement toward maturity of thought process.

In the fourth place—and again closely associated with the matter of objectives—is the possibility of marked dissimilarities in the pacing of instruction. Thus, programs may agree in assigning high priority to learning Outcome M, but the realization of this outcome may be set as a goal by Program A at one time, but by Program B a year or two later. Tested too soon, children in the latter program may seem to be inferior to those in Program A. But if the testing is delayed a year or so, the apparent superiority of that program may disappear.

In the fifth place, a system of instruction represents no more than a paper organization. In the best of circumstances it cannot be truly prescriptive, in the sense that all teachers who agree to teach according to that program will do the same things in the same way and will refrain from doing anything not specifically required by that system. Variations in teaching practice within each of the competing systems can be such as to reduce considerably the supposed differences between or among them and make them more alike than was expected or intended. When this happens, the programs involved become myths. That is to say, they are "impure," being contaminated one by another; and disparities in findings for the programs are bound to be lessened in amount, and they may actually be reported as nonexistent. Yet, were it possible to establish and maintain model or "pure" systems of instruction, different degrees of effectiveness might obtain.

Finally, in the sixth place, it is almost, if not actually, impossible to control quality of teaching. Program C may be reported as more effective than Program A when the seeming superiority is attributable to differences in excellence of teaching the two programs. This possibility proved to be the fact in research which I recently completed, using children in Scottish and in English schools.

In the cooperating Scottish schools, Program A was found to be more effective than was Program B on the basis of the criterion I employed, whereas in the cooperating English schools Program B was the more effective. In both countries Program B was a traditional system of instruction while Program A was relatively new and highly controversial.

How was I to reconcile these divergent findings? At first I had to rely on inference from my observations of classroom practice and from secondary sources—teaching materials, conversations with knowledgeable educators, and the like. Later on, just five months ago as a matter of fact, I was able to check the validity of my interpretation with experts in the teaching of the subject in Great Britain. Fortunately, they agreed with me that the conflicts in ratings of the programs were explicable in terms of quality of teaching.

In the schools of Scotland for a long period of time practically the only system of teaching was what I am calling the conventional program. It went with few changes and without challenge until about ten or twelve years ago when Program A was introduced and tried out here and there. Many of the teachers who experimented informally with the new program became convinced of its special merits, under direction from experts learned how to teach it well, and at the time of my study warmly and vigorously advocated its general adoption. Hence, my Program A subjects had been taught skillfully and enthusiastically. The same statement cannot be made about my Program B subjects in Scottish schools, for their teachers, for the most part, had continued to teach about as they always had.

In England, on the other hand, teachers in general had been exposed to one new system of instruction after another, and they tended to view Program A as just another scheme in a long series. Of course with conspicuous exceptions, the teachers of this program in my study were not genuinely convinced of its advantages and had not mastered the requisite techniques. By contrast, the cooperating Program B teachers believed that their system of instruction had held up very well indeed in competition with the various new programs and taught their system with considerable confidence.

If my interpretation is correct, it follows that my investigation, supposedly of the comparative worth of unlike systems of instruction, turned out to be something quite different. It showed that the significant variable in my research was not the two programs, as was intended, but quality of teaching. If so, it bore out the by-no-means new fact that an instructional program is one thing in the hands of expert, interested teachers, and another thing in the hands of teachers not possessed of these characteristics.

And yet, in evaluating rival systems of instruction how can we assure comparable quality of teaching or allow for the effect of differences in this factor? And in how many instances of evaluative research have the findings and subsequent recommendations been determined by differences in this factor rather than by differences in instructional programs?

I have mentioned only six sources of difficulty in evaluative research, and my analysis is certainly incomplete. Nevertheless, these six are enough to confirm the statement that this kind of research is far from being simple. Moreover, they warrant the belief that we cannot hope to evaluate programs of instruction *as wholes*. Instead, we must settle for evaluating them only in part, on this basis or that; and we need to describe fully the conditions which impose restrictions on the extent to which our findings can be generalized.

## INSUFFICIENCY OF "OBJECTIVE" DATA ALONE

My second major point is not readily expressed in a sentence. It has to do with the role of judgment in the process of evaluation. There seems to be the notion that in evaluative research there is little place for subjective decisions,—that on this account the aim should be to collect an abundance of objective measures and that the thorough manipulation of these measures will in itself produce a dependable ranking of systems of instruction.

This position I intend to attack; but, as I have just said, it is difficult in a few words to state just what that position is. I am not at all happy with my attempt to do so. One reason is inherent in the problem of defining "objective." For example, does the observation of behavior yield objective measures, and do interviews with children and teachers' estimates of children's ability or achievement? Certainly these procedures supply data that are quantitative or can be made so; but are they objective? This is hardly the place to debate the issue, and the easiest (if most cowardly) way for me to extricate myself from the dilemma is to define "objective" in an utterly arbitrary manner. In this paper I shall use the term to refer to measures obtained from so-called new-type paper and pencil tests, as well as measures closely allied to them in their apparent finality.

There is a second reason for my embarrassment in trying to state simply what it is that I plan to attack. I face the likelihood of misinterpretation, in seeming to set up a dichotomy: judgment vs objective data, one or the other; and the inference may be that I have constructed a straw man to demolish.

Of course, any such dichotomy would be unreal. In this day when quantitative research is so highly regarded, few persons indeed will claim to have truly evaluated the relative merits of rival programs of instruction when they have done no more than to engage in conjecture, weighing one guess or opinion against another. They know full well that others will properly demand a reasonable amount of empirical evidence, no matter how educated their guesses and how sophisticated their opinions. On the other hand, those who work primarily with objective measures must know that now and then they have had to make decisions on subjective grounds. Pure judgment and pure use of objective data may be thought of as representing the theoretical extremes of a continuum; but very, very few evaluators can properly be assigned to either extreme. Rather, each evaluator occupies a position more or less close to the midpoint of the continuum.

Be all this as it may, it is still possible to say that some evaluators depreciate—if they do not deprecate—the place of judgment in evaluative research. In the reports of their investigations—could it be because of their unawareness of their reliance on judgment?— they make no mention of such instances; or, if they do, they cite them hurriedly and without comment, or they appear to apologize for them.

Yet, judgment, recognized or not, is perhaps the determinative factor in organizing and in conducting evaluative research; and there is no reason for us to hide or to decry this fact. Following are some of the places where judgment *must* play a more or less prominent role because basic objective data may not be available or, if available, are none too trustworthy:

a. the decision to make an evaluative study;

b. the determination of the grade level at which to make it;

c. the selection of appropriate subjects;

d. the decision concerning the length of the period of time to be included;

e. the analysis of the content and of the objectives in rival programs, for the purpose of selecting only what is common to them or of determining what is to be done about unlike content and objectives;

f. the decision regarding the kinds of data to be collected; e.g., correct answers on tests or levels of thought process;

g. the choice of available tests or other instruments, or the making of original tests or other instruments;

h. the determination of measures to assure equal quality of teaching or of means to allow for differences;

i. the selection of the statistical methods best suited for the treatment of data, and

j. the final interpretation of the findings.

What is the investigator to do about these ten sources of subjectivity and about others not mentioned? He may do nothing at all so far as the reader of his report knows, and merely tell in a factual manner just what he did and what he found. And I fear that relatively few readers will even notice his silence at crucial points, having self-hypnotized themselves into the ready acceptance of anything that appears in print. For example, whatever test, if any, is used, it will be satisfactory to them; and, in the absence of comment, they will assume that all of the dissimilar programs have been equally well taught. They may be disturbed, however, if in the end the investigator rates systems of instruction in a manner counter to their biases. In this case they have only to reject the investigation out of hand as being just another instance of wasted effort.

Nevertheless, uncritical as many readers of research may be, it would seem to be the part of wisdom and honesty for the evaluator to disclose his judgments frankly,—to disclose them and to justify them to the degree possible. For instance, if he chose a particular standard test, readers are entitled to know why he did so in preference to others. If he rejected paper and pencil tests and elected to observe and interview his subjects, why did he do so, and what did he hope to achieve by his decision?

I realize that it requires considerable space to put in print not only the essential experimental data, but also the judgments made and the reasons therefor, to say nothing of an account of what actually happened in competing classrooms. Indeed the inability of periodicals to allot the requisite number of pages for adequate reporting may in some measure account for the omission of significant information. If this be so, then the alternative would seem to be the more careful selection of manuscripts and publication, in the space saved, of longer analytic descriptions of studies that can satisfy higher standards. Certainly there is little to justify the appearance of so many reports of evaluative studies, limited to three or four pages and stripped of the details which alone enable one to tell whether to agree or to disagree with the investigator's conclusions.

To end this digression: permit me to summarize what I have said on my second major point. I certainly have not argued for leaving evaluation to guesswork and the exclusive use of personal opinion, however expert. Rather, I have suggested that we should seek to base evaluation as fully as possible upon objective evidence, but that we should not deceive ourselves into thinking that we can reduce to zero the need for judgment. If this is so—if decisions on subjective grounds are inevitable—then we should report and discuss them as openly and freely as we do our strictly quantitative data.

## "COMMON SENSE" IN EVALUATIVE RESEARCH

Much that I shall want to say with respect to my third major point has already been foreshadowed in what I have already said.

It is, I think, highly doubtful that the quality of evaluative research will be enhanced as much by new technical improvements as by something else. This is not to say that we should call a moratorium on efforts directed to technical advances. Quite the contrary: the search for new and better means of controlling experimental factors and of treating quantitative data should certainly be encouraged; and the evaluator will do well to employ all proved improvements in his own investigations. Even so, such gains provide no guarantee that his research will consequently be much sounder and more fruitful.

Let me illustrate what I have in mind. Over the years there has been commendable progress in statistical methods of ascertaining the reliability of differences between the means of test scores of experimental groups. This progress, however, has not been matched by equal progress in our methods of procuring valid and relevant data to start with or by our methods of determining the *educational* significance of differences that stand up statistically. Thus, even the most refined formula for determining the reliability of differences does not eliminate the possibility of drawing conclusions that are false or otherwise indefensible as far as educational practice is concerned.

Some years ago an investigator sought to discover the relative effectiveness of three methods of teaching simple subtraction in arithmetic, methods which, for the sake of variety, I shall label X, Y, and Z. I shall not go into the details of his procedure other than to say that his study involved measures of errors and of rate of work on subtraction tests and the use of large groups of subjects, one set of the groups being about two years older than the other. I shall not be distorting his findings as a whole if I mention only those for the younger group, for those findings are typical.

On the end test, the means of these subjects in terms of errors were 21, 14, and 13, respectively, for Groups X, Y, and Z. To determine the reliability of differences between pairs of means he employed a formula acceptable at the time, and he found that Method X was definitely the least effective of the three, with a slight but unreliable advantage for Z over Y. He therefore recommended the adoption of Method Z.

Now, this investigator neglected *opportunity* for error, with the result that he inflated the differences among the programs with respect to effectiveness. Each child took two tests and had a chance to make a total of 224 errors. On the average, the X subjects, who made a mean of 21 errors, were accurate in 203, or in 91%, of their chances. The corresponding average percents of accuracy for the Y and Z groups were both 94. In a word, the least accurate group differed in this aspect of skill from the two more accurate groups by three chances in 100, a margin so small as properly to be disregarded in classroom practice and to justify the conclusion that one method of teaching subtraction was about as good as were the other two.

Now, what would have happened had the investigator had available to him the best and most refined formula for determining the reliabilities of differences among the pairs of means? He might have found the measures of reliability to be greater or less in magnitude than were those he reported. Regardless of whether he submitted to this test his averages of errors or his average percents of accuracy, the differences found to be reliable would still have been of dubious educational significance. Rarely indeed are choices made among instructional practices on the basis of differences so small as three percentage points; and rightly so. Along with questions concerning the dependability of such small differences are, in this instance, other questions not answered by the data. For example, might not the procedure reported as poorest (namely, X) have been easier to teach meaningfully and might it not have yielded learning with greater potential transfer value?

What this investigator overlooked—and what some other investigators overlook—is that programs of instruction are supposedly evaluated, not to provide opportunities to demonstrate mastery of sophisticated niceties of research methodology (though they are important), but to obtain facts with which to improve the conditions of school learning. In a word, by hypothesis such research has a *practical* purpose, and this purpose should not be lost sight of at any stage of an inquiry. I have already insisted that evaluative research must be competently done; that is, it must be planned and conducted with due regard for approved technical requirements. But this is not enough: it should be oriented toward the possible usefulness of the results in managing the processes of teaching and learning. When this last condition is met, as well as the first, negative findings may be as valuable as are positive findings. For example, it is useful to disclose the hollowness of exaggerated claim of excellence for some new or old organization of content and for an instructional plan for teaching it.

In my manuscript I have entitled this last section of my paper " 'Common Sense' in Evaluative Research," but I have been careful to place quotation marks around the first two words, and for two reasons: a. "common sense" usually means "my sense," and b. "my sense" does not seem to be exhibited often enough to make the term "common" appropriate. Nevertheless, the caption may serve to turn attention in a neglected direction, but perhaps little more so than I have endeavored to do in the first two sections of this paper.

## CONCLUDING STATEMENT

In conclusion, do I seem to have presented a gloomy picture of the status and the prospects of the kind of research about which I have been speaking? As I have dealt, first, with the great complexity of evaluative research, then with the insufficiency of objective data alone to furnish trustworthy answers and with the corresponding and unavoidable need for sound judgment, and finally with the necessity for "common sense" at every point in doing evaluative research,—as I have done these things, have I appeared to imply through my strictures and criticisms that it is time to abandon this kind of endeavor?

Certainly this has not been my intention. On the contrary, I have sought to offer several positive suggestions, however much they represent the personal opinion of a single individual. Moreover, I have done so because of my firm faith in the worth of evaluation through research and because of my steadfast hope that we can make this research steadily better. In my view we cannot escape this responsibility. After all, we are *educational* psychologists, and by definition, I think, we must assign high priority to the psychological study, in one way or another, of the pressing problems relating to the practical enterprise of educating children and youth. If we do not accept this obligation, who will? Who else is technically as well equipped as we are to plan and execute investigations that will increase our understanding of the optimal conditions of teaching and learning in the classroom? And, finally, who should be more dedicated than we are to the continuous improvement of education?

I face the future with confidence, and I join you optimistically in meeting the challenge of a never-ending but a critically important task.

---

10.2    Traits Revisited

*Gordon W. Allport*

The following reprint is from a paper given by Professor Allport in response to the American Psychological Association for having given him its highest award for outstanding contributions to psychology.

This paper is almost epic in its breadth and depth. For readers new to educational and psychological studies, the author's purpose in arguing for a belief in the existence of traits or even of personality may seem curiously unnecessary. It must be understood that many educational and psychological researchers in their enthusiastic adoption of what philosophers of science call "logical positivism" have so successfully "explained" away the components of human behavior that only an "empty organism" remains.

One might say that Professor Allport is imploring certain psychologists to regain a balanced perspective when they regard human behavior. It would seem that the narrowed focus on refining mathematical tools and techniques of assessment is leading some to the point of denying the reality of the very *people* who are doing the behaving.

Perhaps this article will be worth "revisiting" as your knowledge of the field enlarges.

Years ago I ventured to present a paper before the Ninth International Congress at New Haven (G. W. Allport, 1931). It was entitled "What Is a Trait of Personality?" For me to return to the same topic on this honorific occasion is partly a sentimental indulgence, but partly too it is a self-imposed task to discover whether

Reprinted with permission of the author and *American Psychologist*, 21, 1, Jan. 1966.

during the past 36 years I have learned anything new about this central problem in personality theory.

In my earlier paper I made eight bold assertions. A trait, I said,

1. Has more than nominal existence.

2. Is more generalized than a habit.

3. Is dynamic, or at least determinative, in behavior.

4. May be established empirically.

5. Is only relatively independent of other traits.

6. Is not synonymous with moral or social judgment.

7. May be viewed either in the light of the personality which contains it, or in the light of its distribution in the population at large.

To these criteria I added one more:

8. Acts, and even habits, that are inconsistent with a trait are not proof of the nonexistence of the trait.

While these propositions still seem to me defensible they were originally framed in an age of psychological innocence. They now need reexamination in the light of subsequent criticism and research.

## CRITICISM OF THE CONCEPT OF TRAIT

Some critics have challenged the whole concept of trait. Carr and Kingsbury (1938) point out the danger of reification. Our initial observation of behavior is only in terms of adverbs of action: John behaves aggressively. Then an adjective creeps in: John has an aggressive disposition. Soon a heavy substantive arrives, like William James' cow on the doormat: John has a trait of aggression. The result is the fallacy of misplaced concreteness.

The general positivist cleanup starting in the 1930's went even further. It swept out (or tried to sweep out) all entities, regarding them as question-begging redundancies. Thus Skinner (1953) writes:

> When we say that a man eats *because* he is hungry, smokes a great deal *because* he has the tobacco habit, fights *because* of the instinct of pugnacity, behaves brilliantly *because* of his intelligence, or plays the piano well *because* of his musical ability, we seem to be referring to causes. But on analysis these phrases prove to be merely redundant descriptions (p. 31).

It is clear that this line of attack is an assault not only upon the concept of trait, but upon all intervening variables, whether they be conceived in terms of expectancies, attitudes, motives, capacities, sentiments, or traits. The resulting postulate of the "empty organism" is by now familiar to us all, and is the scientific credo of some. Carried to its logical extreme this reasoning would scrap the concept of personality itself—an eventuality that seems merely absurd to me.

More serious, to my mind, is the argument against what Block and Bennett (1955) called "traitology" arising from many studies of the variability of a person's behavior as it changes from situation to situation. Every parent knows that an offspring may be a hellion at home and an angel when he goes visiting. A businessman may be hardheaded in the office and a mere marshmallow in the hands of his pretty daughter.

Years ago the famous experiment by La Piere (1934) demonstrated that an innkeeper's prejudice seems to come and go according to the situation confronting him.

In recent months Hunt (1965) has listed various theories of personality that to his mind require revision in the light of recent evidence. Among them he questions the belief that personality traits are the major sources of behavior variance. He, like Miller (1963), advocates that we shift attention from traits to interactions among people, and look for consistency in behavior chiefly in situationally defined roles. Helson (1964) regards trait as the residual effect of previous stimulation, and thus subordinates it to the organism's present adaptation level.

Scepticism is likewise reflected in many investigations of "person perception." To try to discover the traits residing within a personality is regarded as either naive or impossible. Studies, therefore, concentrate only on the *process* of perceiving or judging, and reject the problem of validating the perception and judgment. (Cf. Tagiuri & Petrullo, 1958.)

Studies too numerous to list have ascribed chief variance in behavior to situational factors, leaving only a mild residue to be accounted for in terms of idiosyncratic attitudes and traits. A prime example is Stouffer's study of *The American Soldier* (Stouffer et al., 1949). Differing opinions and preferences are ascribed so far as possible to the GI's age, martial status, educational level, location of residence, length of service, and the like. What remains is ascribed to "attitude." By this procedure personality becomes an appendage to demography (see G. W. Allport, 1950). It is not the integrated structure within the skin that determines behavior, but membership in a group, the person's assigned roles—in short, the prevailing situation. It is especially the sociologists and anthropologists who have this preference for explanations in terms of the "outside structure" rather than the "inside structure" (cf. F. H. Allport, 1955, Ch. 21).

I have mentioned only a few of the many varieties of situationism that flourish today. While not denying any of the evidence adduced I would point to their common error of interpretation. If a child is a hellion at home, an angel outside, he obviously has two contradictory tendencies in his nature, or perhaps a deeper genotype that would explain the opposing phenotypes. If in studies of person perception the process turns out to be complex and subtle, still there would be no perception at all unless there were something out there to perceive and to judge. If, as in Stouffer's studies, soldiers' opinions vary with their martial status or length of service, these opinions are still their own. The fact that my age, sex, social status help form my outlook on life does not change the fact that the outlook is a functioning part of me. Demography deals with distal forces—personality study with proximal forces. The fact that the innkeeper's behavior varies according to whether he is, or is not, physically confronted with Chinese applicants for hospitality tells nothing about his attitude structure, except that it is complex, and that several attitudes may converge into a given act of behavior.

Nor does it solve the problem to explain the variance in terms of statistical interaction effects. Whatever tendencies exist reside in a person, for a person is the sole possessor of the energy that leads to action. Admittedly different situations elicit differing tendencies from my repertoire. I do not perspire except in the heat, nor shiver except in the cold; but the outside temperature is not the mechanism of perspiring or shivering. My capacities and my tendencies lie within.

To the situationist I concede that our theory of traits cannot be so simpleminded as it once was. We are now challenged to untangle the complex web of tendencies that constitute a person, however contradictory they may seem to be when activated differentially in various situations.

## ON THE OTHER HAND

In spite of gunfire from positivism and situationism, traits are still very much alive. Gibson (1941) has pointed out that the "concept of set or attitude is nearly universal in psychological thinking." And in an important but neglected paper—perhaps the last he ever wrote —McDougall (1937) argued that *tendencies* are the "indispensable postulates of all psychology." The concept of *trait* falls into this genre. As Walker (1964) says trait, however else defined, always connotes an enduring tendency of some sort. It is the structural counterpart of such functional concepts as "expectancy," and "goal-directedness."

After facing all the difficulties of situational and mood variations, also many of the methodological hazards such as response set, halo, and social desirability, Vernon (1964) concludes, "We could go a long way towards predicting behavior if we could assess these stable features in which people differ from one another (p. 181)." The powerful contributions of Thurstone, Guilford, Cattell, and Eysenck, based on factor analysis, agree that the search for traits should provide eventually a satisfactory taxonomy of personality and of its hierarchical structure. The witness of these and other thoughtful writers helps us withstand the pessimistic attacks of positivism and situationism.

It is clear that I am using "trait" as a generic term, to cover all the "permanent possibilities for action" of a generalized order. Traits are cortical, subcortical, or postural dispositions having the capacity to gate or guide specific phasic reactions. It is only the phasic aspect that is visible; the tonic is carried somehow in the still mysterious realm of neurodynamic structure. Traits, as I am here using the term, include long-range sets and attitudes, as well as such variables as "perceptual response dispositions," "personal constructs," and "cognitive styles."

Unlike McClelland (1951) I myself would regard traits (i.e., some traits) as motivational (others being merely stylistic). I would also insist that traits may be studied at two levels: (a) dimensionally, that is as an aspect of the psychology of individual differences, and (b) individually, in terms of *personal dispositions*. (Cf. G. W. Allport, 1961, Ch. 15.) It is the latter approach that brings us closest to the person we are studying.

As for factors, I regard them as a mixed blessing. In the investigations I shall soon report, factorial analysis, I find, has proved both helpful and unhelpful. My principal question is whether the factorial unit is idiomatic enough to reflect the structure of personality as the clinician, the counselor, or the man in the street apprehends it. Or are factorial dimensions screened so extensively and so widely attenuated—through item selection, correlation, axis manipulation, homogenization, and alphabetical labeling—that they impose an artifact of method upon the personal neural network as it exists in nature?

## A HEURISTIC REALISM

This question leads me to propose an epistemological position for research in personality. Most of us, I suspect, hold this position although we seldom formulate it even to ourselves. It can be called a *heuristic realism*.

Heuristic realism, as applied to our problem, holds that the person who confronts us possesses inside his skin generalized action tendencies (or traits) and that it is our job scientifically to discover what they are. Any form of realism assumes the existence of an external structure ("out there") regardless of our shortcomings in comprehending it. Since traits, like all intervening variables, are never directly observed but only inferred, we must expect difficulties and errors in the process of discovering their nature.

The incredible complexity of the structure we seek to understand is enough to discourage the realist, and to tempt him to play some form of positivistic gamesmanship. He is tempted to settle for such elusive formulations as: "If we knew enough about the situation we wouldn't need the concept of personality"; or "One's personality is merely the way other people see one"; or "There is no structure in personality but only varying degrees of consistency in the environment."

Yet the truly persistent realist prefers not to abandon his commitment to find out what the other fellow is really like. He knows that his attempt will not wholly succeed, owing partly to the complexity of the object studied, and partly to the inadequacy of present methods. But unlike Kant who held that the *Ding an Sich* is doomed to remain unknowable, he prefers to believe that it is at least partly or approximately knowable.

I have chosen to speak of *heuristic* realism, because to me special emphasis should be placed on empirical methods of discovery. In this respect heuristic realism goes beyond naive realism.

Taking this epistemological point of view, the psychologist first focuses his attention on some limited slice of personality that he wishes to study. He then selects or creates methods appropriate to the empirical testing of his hypothesis that the cleavage he has in mind is a trait (either a dimensional trait or a personal disposition). He knows that his present purposes and the methods chosen will set limitations upon his discovery. If, however, the investigation achieves acceptable standards of validation he will have progressed far toward his identification of traits. Please note, as with any heuristic procedure the process of discovery may lead to important corrections of the hypothesis as originally stated.

Empirical testing is thus an important aspect of heuristic realism, but it is an empiricism restrained throughout by rational considerations. Galloping empiricism, which is our present occupational disease, dashes forth like a headless horseman. It has no rational objective; uses no rational method other than mathematical; reaches no rational conclusion. It lets the discordant data sing for themselves. By contrast heuristic realism says, "While we are willing to rest our case for traits on empirical evidence, the area we carve out for study should be rationally conceived, tested by rational methods; and the findings should be rationally interpreted."

## THREE ILLUSTRATIVE STUDIES

It is now time for me to illustrate my argument with sample studies. I have chosen three in which I myself have been involved. They differ in the areas of personality carved out for study, in the methods employed, and in the type of traits established. They are alike, however, in proceeding from the standpoint of heuristic realism. The presentation of each study must of necessity be woefully brief. The first illustrates what might be called *meaningful dimensionalism;* the second *meaningful covariation;* the third *meaningful morphogenesis.*

### Dimensions of Values

The first illustration is drawn from a familiar instrument, dating almost from the stone age, *The Study of Values* (Allport & Vernon,

1931). While some of you have approved it over the years, and some disapproved, I use it to illustrate two important points of my argument.

First, the instrument rests on an a priori analysis of one large region of human personality, namely, the region of generic evaluative tendencies. It seemed to me 40 years ago, and seems to me now, that Eduard Spranger (1922) made a persuasive case for the existence of six fundamental types of subjective evaluation or *Lebensformen*. Adopting this rational starting point we ourselves took the second step, to put the hypothesis to empirical test. We asked: Are the six dimensions proposed—the *theoretic*, the *economic*, the *esthetic*, *social*, *political*, and *religious*—measurable on a multidimensional scale? Are they reliable and valid? Spranger defined the six ways of looking at life in terms of separate and distinct ideal types, although he did not imply that a given person belongs exclusively to one and only one type.

It did not take long to discover that when confronted with a forced-choice technique people do in fact subscribe to all six values, but in widely varying degrees. Within any pair of values, or any quartet of values, their forced choices indicate a reliable pattern. Viewed then as empirical continua, rather than as types, the six value directions prove to be measurable, reproducible, and consistent. But are they valid? Can we obtain external validation for this particular a priori conception of traits? The test's *Manual* (Allport & Vernon, 1931) contains much such evidence. Here I would add a bit more, drawn from occupational studies with women subjects. (The evidence for men is equally good.) The data in Table 1 are derived partly from the *Manual*, partly from Guthrie and McKendry (1963) and partly from an unpublished study by Elizabeth Moses.

For present purposes it is sufficient to glance at the last three columns. For the *theoretic* value we note that the two groups of teachers or teachers in preparation select this value significantly more often than do graduate students of business administration. Conversely the young ladies of business are relatively more *economic* in their choices. The results for the *esthetic* value probably reflect the higher level of liberal arts background for the last two groups. The *social* (philanthropic) value is relatively low for the business group, whereas the *political* (power) value is relatively high. Just why nurses should more often endorse the *religious* value is not immediately clear.

TABLE 1     MEAN SCORES FOR OCCUPATIONAL GROUPS OF
WOMEN: STUDY OF VALUES

|  | Female collegiate norms N = 2.475 | Graduate nurses training for teaching N = 328 | Graduate students of business administration N = 77 | Peace Corps teachers N = 131 |
|---|---|---|---|---|
| Theoretical | 36.5 | 40.2 | 37.3 | 40.6 |
| Economic | 36.8 | 32.9 | 40.4 | 29.9 |
| Esthetic | 43.7 | 43.1 | 46.8 | 49.3 |
| Social | 41.6 | 40.9 | 35.0 | 41.2 |
| Political | 38.0 | 37.2 | 41.8 | 39.7 |
| Religious | 43.1 | 45.7 | 38.7 | 39.2 |

Another study of external validation, showing the long-range predictive power of the test is an unpublished investigation by Betty Mawardi. It is based on a follow-up of Wellesley graduates 15 years after taking the Study of Values.

Table 2 reports the significant deviations (at the 5% level or better) of various occupational groups from the mean scores of Wellesley students. In virtually every case we find the deviation meaningful (even necessary) for the occupation in question. Thus women in business are significantly high in *economic* interests; medical, government, and scientific workers in *theoretical;* literary and artistic workers in *esthetic;* social workers in *social;* and religious workers in *religious* values.

One must remember that to achieve a relatively high score on one value, one must deliberately slight others. For this reason it is interesting to note in the table the values that are systematically slighted in order to achieve a higher score on the occupationally relevant value. (In the case of social workers it appears that they "take away" more or less uniformly from other values in order to achieve a high social value.)

Thus, even at the college age it is possible to forecast in a general way modal vocational activity 15 years hence. As Newcomb, Turner, and Converse (1965) say, this test clearly deals with "inclusive values" or with "basic value postures" whose generality is strikingly broad. An evaluative posture toward life saturates, or guides, or gates (choose your own metaphor) specific daily choices over a long expanse of years.

TABLE 2  SIGNIFICANT DEVIATIONS OF SCORES ON THE STUDY OF VALUES FOR OCCUPATIONAL GROUPS OF WELLESLEY ALUMNI FROM WELLESLEY MEAN SCORES

| Occupational groups | N | Theoretical | Economic | Esthetic | Social | Political | Religious |
|---|---|---|---|---|---|---|---|
| Business workers | 64 | Lower | Higher | | | | |
| Medical workers | 42 | Higher | Lower | | | Lower | |
| Literary workers | 40 | Higher | Lower | Higher | | | |
| Artistic workers | 37 | | | Higher | Lower | | |
| Scientific workers | 28 | Higher | | Lower | | | |
| Government workers | 24 | Higher | | | Lower | | Lower |
| Social workers | 26 | | | | Higher | Lower | |
| Religious workers | 11 | | | | | | Higher |

One reason I have used this illustration of trait research is to raise an important methodological issue. The six values are not wholly independent. There is a slight tendency for theoretic and esthetic value to covary; likewise for economic and political values; and so too with social and religious. Immediately the thought arises, "Let's factor the whole matrix and see what orthogonal dimensions emerge." This step has been taken several times (see *Manual*); but always with confusing results. Some investigators discover that fewer than six factors are needed—some that we need more. And in all cases the clusters that emerge seem strange and unnamable. Here is a case, I believe, where our empiricism should submit to rational restraint. The traits as defined are meaningful, reliably measured, and validated. Why sacrifice them to galloping gamesmanship?

## Covariation: Religion and Prejudice

Speaking of covariation I do not mean to imply that in restraining our empirical excesses we should fail to explore the patterns that underlie covariation when it seems reasonable to do so.

Take, for example, the following problem. Many investigations show conclusively that on the broad average church attenders harbor more ethnic prejudice than nonattenders. (Some of the relevant studies are listed by Argyle, 1959, and by Wilson, 1960.) At the same time many ardent workers for civil rights are religiously motivated. From Christ to Gandhi and to Martin Luther King we note that equimindedness has been associated with religious devoutness. Here then is a paradox: Religion makes prejudice; it also unmakes prejudice.

First we tackle the problem rationally and form a hypothesis to account for what seems to be a curvilinear relation. A hint for the needed hypothesis comes from *The Authoritarian Personality* (Adorno, Frenkel-Brunswik, Levinson, & Sanford, 1950) which suggests that acceptance of institutional religion is not as important as the *way* in which it is accepted. Argyle (1959) sharpens the hypothesis. He says, "It is not the genuinely devout who are prejudiced but the conventionally religious (p. 84)."

In our own studies we have tentatively assumed that two contrasting but measurable forms of religious orientation exist. The first form we call the *extrinsic* orientation, meaning that for the churchgoer religious devotion is not a value in its own right, but is an instrumental value serving the motives of personal comfort, security, or social status. (One man said he went to church because it was the best place to sell insurance.) Elsewhere I have defined this utilitarian orientation toward religion more fully (G. W. Allport, 1960, 1963). Here I shall simply mention two items from our scale, agreement with which we assume indicates the extrinsic attitude:

What religion offers me most is comfort when sorrows and misfortune strike.

One reason for my being a church member is that such membership helps to establish a person in the community.

By contract the *intrinsic* orientation regards faith as a supreme value in its own right. Such faith strives to transcend self-centered needs, takes seriously the commandment of brotherhood that is found in all religions, and seeks a unification of being. Agreement with the following items indicates an intrinsic orientation:

My religious beliefs are what really lie behind my whole approach to life.

If not prevented by unavoidable circumstances, I attend church, on the average (more than once a week) (once a week) (two or three times a month) (less than once a month).

This second item is of considerable interest, for many studies have found that it is the irregular attenders who are by far the most prejudiced (e.g., Holtzmann, 1956; Williams, 1964). They take their religion in convenient doses and do not let it regulate their lives.

Now for a few illustrative results in Table 3. If we correlate the extrinsicness of orientation with various prejudice scales we find the hypothesis confirmed. Likewise, as predicted, intrinsicness of orientation is negatively correlated with prejudice.

In view of the difficulty of tapping the two complex traits in question, it is clear from these studies that our rationally derived hypothesis gains strong support. We note that the trend is the same when different denominations are studied in relation to differing targets for prejudice.

Previously I have said that empirical testing has the ability to correct or extend our rational analysis of pattern. In this particular research the following unexpected fact emerges. While those who approach the intrinsic pole of our continuum are on the average less prejudiced than those who approach the extrinsic pole, a number of

TABLE 3    CORRELATIONS BETWEEN MEASURES OF RELI-
GIOUS ORIENTATION AMONG CHURCHGOERS AND VARIOUS
PREJUDICE SCALES

| Denominational sample | N | r |
|---|---|---|
| Unitarian | 50 | |
| Extrinsic—anti-Catholicism | | .56 |
| Intrinsic—anti-Catholicism | | −.36 |
| Extrinsic—anti-Mexican | | .54 |
| Intrinsic—anti-Mexican | | −.42 |
| Catholic | 66 | |
| Extrinsic—anti-Negro | | .36 |
| Intrinsic—anti-Negro | | −.49 |
| Nazarene | 39 | |
| Extrinsic—anti-Negro | | .41 |
| Intrinsic—anti-Negro | | −.44 |
| Mixed [a] | 207 | |
| Extrinsic—anti-semitic | | .65 |

[a] From Wilson (1960).

subjects show themselves to be disconcertingly illogical. They accept both intrinsically worded items and extrinsically worded items,
even when these are contradictory, such as:

My religious beliefs are what really lie behind my whole approach to life.

Though I believe in my religion, I feel there are many more
important things in my life.

It is necessary, therefore, to inspect this sizable group of muddle-
heads who refuse to conform to our neat religious logic. We call
them "inconsistently proreligious." They simply like religion; for
them it has "social desirability" (cf. Edwards, 1957).

The importance of recognizing this third mode of religious
orientation is seen by comparing the prejudice scores for the groups
presented in Table 4. In the instruments employed the lowest possible prejudice score is 12, the highest possible, 48. We note that the
mean prejudice score rises steadily and significantly from the intrin-

TABLE 4     TYPES OF RELIGIOUS ORIENTATION AND MEAN
PREJUDICE SCORES

| | Mean prejudice scores | | | |
|---|---|---|---|---|
| | Consistently intrinsic | Consistently extrinsic | Moderately inconsistent (proreligion) | Extremely inconsistent (proreligion) |
| Anti-Negro | 28.7 | 33.0 | 35.4 | 37.9 |
| Anti-Semitic | 22.6 | 24.6 | 28.0 | 30.1 |

Note.—N = 309, mixed denominations. All differences significant at .01 level.

sically consistent to the inconsistently proreligious. Thus subjects with an undiscriminated proreligious response set are on the average most prejudiced of all.

Having discovered the covariation of prejudice with both the extrinsic orientation and the "pro" response set, we are faced with the task of rational explanation. One may, I think, properly argue that these particular religious attitudes are instrumental in nature; they provide safety, security, and status—all within a self-serving frame. Prejudice, we know, performs much the same function within some personalities. The needs for status, security, comfort, and a feeling of self-rightness are served by both ethnic hostility and by tailoring one's religious orientation to one's convenience. The economy of other lives is precisely the reverse: It is their religion that centers their existence, and the only ethnic attitude compatible with this intrinsic orientation is one of brotherhood, not of bigotry.

This work, along with the related investigations of Lenski (1963), Williams (1964), and others, signifies that we gain important insights when we refine our conception of the nature of the religious sentiment and its functions. Its patterning properties in the economy of a life are diverse. It can fuse with bigotry or with brotherhood according to its nature.

As unfinished business I must leave the problem of nonattenders. From data available it seems that the unchurched are less prejudiced on the average than either the extrinsic or the inconsistent churchgoers, although apparently more prejudiced on the average than those whose religious orientation is intrinsic. Why this should be so must form the topic of future research.

## Personal Dispositions: An Idiomorphic Approach

The final illustration of heuristic realism has to do with the search for the natural cleavages that mark an individual life. In this procedure there is no reference to common dimensions, no comparison with other people, except as is implied by the use of the English language. If, as Allport and Odbert (1936) have found, there are over 17,000 available trait names, and if these may be used in combinations, there is no real point in arguing that the use of the available lexicon of a language necessarily makes all trait studies purely nomothetic (dimensional).

A series of 172 published *Letters from Jenny* (G. W. Allport, 1965) contains enough material for a rather close clinical characterization of Jenny's personality, as well as for careful quantitative and computational analysis. While there is no possibility in this case of obtaining external validation for the diagnosis reached by either method, still by employing both procedures an internal agreement is found which constitutes a type of empirical validation for the traits that emerge.

The *clinical* method in this case is close to common sense. Thirty-nine judges listed the essential characteristics of Jenny as they saw them. The result was a series of descriptive adjectives, 198 in number. Many of the selected trait names were obviously synonymous; and nearly all fell readily into eight clusters.

The *quantitative* analysis consisted of coding the letters in terms of 99 tag words provided by the lexicon of the General Inquirer (Stone, Bales, Namenwirth, & Ogilvie, 1962). The frequency with which these basic tag words are associated with one another in each letter forms the basis for a factor analysis (see G. W. Allport, 1965, p. 200).

Table 5 lists in parallel fashion the clusters obtained by clinical judgment based on a careful reading of the series, along with the factors obtained by Jeffrey Paige in his unpublished factorial study.

In spite of the differences in terminology the general paralleling of the two lists establishes some degree of empirical check on both of them. We can say that the direct common-sense perception of Jenny's nature is validated by quantification, coding, and factoring. (Please note that in this case factor analysis does not stand alone, but is tied to a parallel rational analysis.)

TABLE 5      CENTRAL TRAITS IN JENNY'S PER-
SONALITY AS DETERMINED BY TWO METHODS

| Common-sense traits | Factorial traits |
|---|---|
| Quarrelsome-suspicious⎤ | |
| Aggressive            ⎦ | Aggression |
| Self-centered (possessive) | Possessiveness |
| Sentimental | ⎡Need for affiliation |
| | ⎣Need for family acceptance |
| Independent-autonomous | Need for autonomy |
| Esthetic-artistic | Sentience |
| Self-centered (self-pitying) | Martyrdom |
| (No parallel) | Sexuality |
| Cynical-Morbid | (No parallel) |
| Dramatic-intense | ("Overstate") |

While this meaningful validation is clearly present, we gain (as almost always) additional insights from our attempts at empirical validation of the traits we initially hypothesize. I shall point to one instance of such serendipity. The tag words (i.e., the particular coding system employed) are chiefly substantives. For this reason, I suspect, *sexuality* can be identified by coding as a minor factor; but it is not perceived as an independent quality by the clinical judges. On the other hand, the judges, it seems, gain much from the running style of the letters. Since the style is constant it would not appear in a factorial analysis which deals only with variance within the whole. Thus the common-sense traits *cynical-morbid* and *dramatic-intense* are judgments of a pervading expressive style in Jenny's personality and seem to be missed by factoring procedure.

Here, however, the computer partially redeems itself. Its program assigns the tag "overstate" to strong words such as *always, never, impossible*, etc., while words tagged by "understate" indicate reserve, caution, qualification. Jenny's letters score exceedingly high on overstate and exceedingly low on understate, and so in a skeletonized way the method does in part detect the trait of dramatic intensity.

One final observation concerning this essentially idiomorphic trait study. Elsewhere I have reported a small investigation (G. W. Allport, 1958) showing that when asked to list the "essential characteristics" of some friend, 90% of the judges employ between 3 and 10 trait names, the average number being 7.2. An "essential characteristic" is defined as "any trait, quality, tendency, interest, that you regard as of major importance to a description of the person you select." There is, I submit, food for thought in the fact that in these two separate studies of Jenny, the common-sense and the factorial, only 8 or 9 central traits appear. May it not be that the essential traits of a person are few in number if only we can identify them?

The case of Jenny has another important bearing on theory. In general our besetting sin in personality study is irrelevance, by which I mean that we frequently impose dimensions upon persons when the dimensions fail to apply. (I am reminded of the student who was told to interview women patients concerning their mothers. One patient said that her mother had no part in her problem and no influence on her life; but that her aunt was very important. The student answered, "I'm sorry, but our method requires that you tell about your mother." The *method* required it, but the *life* did not.)

In ascribing a list of traits to Jenny we may seem to have used a dimensional method, but such is not the case. Jenny's traits emerge from her own personal structure. They are not imposed by predetermined but largely irrelevant schedules.

**CONCLUSION**

What then have I learned about traits in the last 4 decades? Well, I have learned that the problem cannot be avoided—neither by escape through positivism or situationism, nor through statistical interaction effects. Tendencies, as McDougall (1937) insisted, remain the "indispensable postulates of all psychology."

Further, I have learned that much of our research on traits is overweighted with methodological preoccupation; and that we have too few restraints holding us to the structure of a life as it is lived. We find ourselves confused by our intemperate empiricism which often yields unnamable factors, arbitrary codes, unintelligible interaction effects, and sheer flatulence from our computors.

As a safeguard I propose the restraints of "heuristic realism" which accepts the common-sense assumption that persons are real beings, that each has a real neuropsychic organization, and that our job is to comprehend this organization as well as we can. At the same time our profession uniquely demands that we go beyond common-sense data and either establish their validity or else—more frequently—correct their errors. To do so requires that we be guided by theory in selecting our trait slices for study, that we employ rationally relevant methods, and be strictly bound by empirical verification. In the end we return to fit our findings to an improved view of the person. Along the way we regard him as an objectively real being whose tendencies we can succeed in knowing —at least in part—beyond the level of unaided common sense. In some respects this recommended procedure resembles what Cronbach and Meehl (1955) call "construct validation," with perhaps a dash more stress on external validation.

I have also learned that while the major foci of organization in a life may be few in number, the network of organization, which includes both minor and contradictory tendencies, is still elusively complex.

One reason for the complexity, of course, is the need for the "inside" system to mesh with the "outside" system—in other words, with the situation. While I do not believe that traits can be defined in terms of interaction effects (since all tendencies draw their energy from within the person), still the vast variability of behavior cannot be overlooked. In this respect I have learned that my earlier views seemed to neglect the variability induced by ecological, social, and situational factors. This oversight needs to be repaired through an adequate theory that will relate the inside and outside systems more accurately.

The fact that my three illustrative studies are so diverse in type leads me to a second concession: that trait studies depend in part upon the investigator's own purposes. He himself constitutes a situation for his respondents, and what he obtains from them will be limited by his purpose and his method. But this fact need not destroy our belief that, so far as our method and purpose allow, we can elicit real tendencies.

Finally, there are several problems connected with traits that I have not here attempted to revisit. There are, for example, refinements of difference between trait, attitude, habit, sentiment, need, etc. Since these are all inside tendencies of some sort, they are for the present occasion all "traits" to me. Nor am I here exploring the question to what extent traits are motivational, cognitive, affective, or expressive. Last of all, and with special restraint, I avoid hammering on the distinction between common (dimensional, nomothetic) traits such as we find in any standard profile, and individual traits (personal dispositions) such as we find in single lives, e.g., Jenny's. (Cf. G. W. Allport, 1961, Ch. 15, also 1962.) Nevitt Sanford (1963) has written that by and large psychologists are "unimpressed" by my insisting on this distinction. Well, if this is so in spite of 4 decades of labor on my part, and in spite of my efforts in the present paper—I suppose I should in all decency cry "uncle" and retire to my corner.

## REFERENCES

ADORNO, T. W., FRENKEL-BRUNSWIK, ELSE, LEVINSON, D. J., and SANFORD R. N., *The authoritarian personality*. New York: Harpers, 1950.

ALLPORT, F. H., *Theories of perception and the concept of structure*. New York: Wiley, 1955.

ALLPORT, G. W., "What is a trait of personality?" *Journal of Abnormal and Social Psychology*, 1931, **25**, 368–372.

ALLPORT, G. W. (Review of S. A. Stouffer *et al.*), "The American Soldier," *Journal of Abnormal and Social Psychology*, 1950, **45**, 168–172.

ALLPORT, G. W., "What units shall we employ?" In G. Lindzey (Ed.), *Assessment of human motives*. New York: Rinehart, 1958.

ALLPORT, G. W., "Religion and prejudice." In *Personality and Social Encounter*. Boston: Beacon Press, 1960. Ch. 16.

ALLPORT, G. W., *Pattern and growth in personality*. New York: Holt, Rinehart & Winston, 1961.

ALLPORT, G. W., "The general and the unique in psychological science," *Journal of Personality*, 1962, **30**, 405–422.

ALLPORT, G. W., "Behavioral science, religion and mental health," *Journal of Religion and Health*, 1963, **2**, 187–197.

ALLPORT, G. W. (Ed.), *Letters from Jenny*. New York: Harcourt, Brace & World, 1965.

ALLPORT, G. W., and ODBERT, H. S., "Trait-names: A psycholexical study." *Psychological Monographs*, 1936, **47** (1, Whole No. 211).

ALLPORT, G. W., and VERNON, P. E., *A study of values*. Boston: Houghton-Mifflin, 1931. (Reprinted: With G. Lindzey, 3rd ed., 1960.)

ARGYLE, M., *Religious behavior*. Glencoe, Ill.: Free Press, 1959.

BLOCK, J., and BENNETT, LILLIAN, "The assessment of communication," *Human Relations*, 1955, **8**, 317–325.

CARR, H. A., and KINGSBURY, F. A., "The concept of trait," *Psychological Review*, 1938, **45**, 497–524.

CRONBACH, L. J., and MEEHL, P. E., "Construct validity in psychological tests," *Psychological Bulletin*, 1955, **52**, 281–302.

EDWARDS, A. L., *The social desirability variable in personality assessment and research*. New York: Dryden Press, 1957.

GIBSON, J. J., "A critical review of the concept of set in contemporary experimental psychology," *Psychological Bulletin*, 1941, **38**, 781–817.

GUTHRIE, G. M. and McKENDRY, MARGARET S., "Interest patterns of Peace Corps volunteers in a teaching project," *Journal of Educational Psychology*, 1963, **54**, 261–267.

HELSON, H., *Adaptation-level theory*. New York: Harper & Row, 1964.

HOLTZMANN, W. H., "Attitudes of college men toward non-segregation in Texas schools," *Public Opinion Quarterly*, 1956, **20**, 559–569.

HUNT, J. McV., "Traditional personality theory in the light of recent evidence," *American Scientist*, 1965, **53**, 80–96.

LA PIERE, R., "Attitudes vs. actions," *Social Forces*, 1934, 230–237.

LENSKI, G., *The religious factor*. Garden City, N. Y.: Doubleday, 1961.

McCLELLAND, D. C., *Personality*. New York: Dryden Press, 1951.

McDOUGALL, W., "Tendencies as indispensable postulates of all psychology." In *Proceedings of the XI International Congress on Psychology: 1937*. Paris: Alcan, 1938, pp. 157–170.

MILLER, D. R., "The study of social relationships: Situation, identity, and social interaction." In S. Koch (Ed.), *Psychology: A study of a science*. Vol. 5. *The process areas, the person, and some applied fields: Their place in psychology and the social sciences*. New York: McGraw-Hill, 1963, pp. 639–737.

NEWCOMB, T. M., TURNER, N. H., and CONVERSE, P. E., *Social psychology: The study of human interaction*. New York: Holt, Rinehart & Winston, 1965.

SANFORD, N., "Personality: Its place in psychology." In S. Koch (Ed.), *Psychology: A study of a science*. Vol. 5. *The process areas, the person, and some applied fields: Their place in psychology and in science*. New York: McGraw-Hill, 1963, pp. 448–592.

SKINNER, B. F., *Science and human behavior*. New York: Macmillan, 1953.

SPRANGER, E., *Lebensformen*. (3d ed.) Halle: Niemeyer, 1922. (Translated: P. Pigors, *Types of men*. Halle: Niemeyer, 1928.)

STONE, P. J., BALES, R. F., NAMENWIRTH, J. Z., and OGILVIE, D. M., "The general inquirer: A computer system for content analysis and retrieval based on the sentence as a unit of information," *Behavioral Science*, 1962. 7(4), 484–498.

STOUFFER, S. A., *et al.*, *The American Soldier*. Princeton: Princeton Univer. Press, 1949. 2 vols.

TAGIURI, R., and PETRULLO, L., *Person perception and interpersonal behavior*. Stanford: Stanford Univer. Press, 1958.

VERNON, P. E., *Personality assessment: A critical survey*. London: Methuen, 1964.

WALKER, E. L., "Psychological complexity as a basis for a theory of motivation and choice." In D. Levine (Ed.), *Nebraska symposium on motivation: 1964*. Lincoln: Univer. Nebraska Press, 1964.

WILLIAMS, R. M., JR., *Strangers next door*. Englewood Cliffs, N. J.: Prentice-Hall, 1964.

WILSON, W. C., "Extrinsic religious values and prejudice," *Journal of Abnormal and Social Psychology*, 1960, **60**, 286-288.

---

## 10.3    Mental Testing and the Logic of Measurement

*Andrew L. Comrey*

Professor Dingle's article (Chapter 1) put alongside this piece seems to present a conflict. The former maintains that no science measures the *real* world, the latter that any true science does measure real events and objects. The issue of what is real is a persistent problem not only for professional logicians and philosophers but for educators and psychologists engaged in practice and research. The reader would be well warned to keep in mind that measurement in psychology is still quite indirect (observation of performance) as Professor Comrey makes clear; yet, with all its faults, known and unknown, mental testing manages, to an impressive extent, to predict future behavior. Is the mental variable being measured really real or does it only behave as though it were? Does it matter which answer is chosen so long as the researcher takes account of possible nonadditivity of variables? The author stands on the side which says "No" to

Reprinted with permission of the author and *Educational and Psychological Measurement*, 11, 1951, 323–334.

this question. In other words, it is just as meaningful to measure by rather indirect methods as it would be, if we could, to utilize electric meter readings of direct neurological changes accompanying mental activity. Possibly mental testing is more meaningful.

By comparison with measurement in the physical sciences, psychological measurement has always enjoyed a somewhat unsavory reputation and has even been called by some the "queen of the inexact sciences." Many writers have pointed out deficiencies in the techniques employed in psychology; some have based their criticisms upon alleged violations of the traditional "laws of measurement." In a previous article (Comrey, 1950) certain implications of the logic behind measurement were given some attention. The traditional requirements were stated, criticisms of psychological measurement were discussed, and an interpretation of the position of psychological measurement with respect to these requirements was offered.

In the present paper, some of the general problems of psychological measurement will be discussed as they apply to the mental-test field. A brief review of the requirements of fundamental measurement will be given, together with a discussion of some difficulties in applying this model to mental testing. Some of the consequences of these difficulties for measurement practice will be mentioned and, finally, some suggestions regarding criteria for evaluating mental-test methods will be made which depart from the customary criteria of conformity to the pattern of fundamental measurement. The point of view will be expressed that the excellence of measurement methods in mental testing may be judged by the practical validity of those methods for the purposes at hand, in addition to comparing them with the model of measurement in the physical sciences. Reasons for giving greater emphasis to the former criterion will be offered.

### CRITICISMS OF MENTAL TESTING

Perhaps the most comprehensive treatment of the requirements for fundamental measurement has been given by Campbell. Some of the more important requirements will be summarized with respect to ordinal characteristics, the relation of equality, and the operation of addition. The requirements for order specify that a class of elements must be defined unambiguously so that the elements vary with respect to some particular property. To be measurable with respect to that property, the elements must vary only in degree, not in kind. Furthermore, a relation "greater," which is transitive and asymmetrical, must be physically defined. That is, if Stimulus A is greater than Stimulus B, and B is greater than C, then A should be greater than C; also, if A is greater than B, B cannot be greater than A.

To satisfy the requirements for equality, a physical definition of the relation "equals" is needed. This definition must be such that physical equality is transitive and symmetrical, i.e., if A = B, and B = C, then A = C; also, if A = B, then B = A. And finally, the requirements for addition state, among other things, that some experimental operation must be found whereby two elements possessing the measurable property can be added together to get an element containing an amount of this property greater than that of either element added. For properties which satisfy these requirements, a complete, or *fundamental* measurement is possible. Numbers assigned to elements of such classes of measurables can be manipulated in accordance with the rule of arithmetic. Furthermore, such measurements are made on scales with equal-unit and ratio properties. A few properties so measurable are weight, length, period of time, and electrical resistance.

It is fairly well known that certain difficulties are involved in trying to apply the model of fundamental measurement to the mental-test area. One of the first criticisms laid at the doorstep of mental testing is that classes of measurables are not even defined, i.e., the class of degrees of some property supposedly indicated by different scores on some test do not represent merely differences in degree but differences in kind as well. A Gestalt interpretation of mental organization would tend to contradict the notion that merely a quantitative difference is reflected by different test scores. Furthermore, the relation of equality does not meet the necessary conditions. It is stated that equal test scores do not mean identity with respect to some ability. Individuals may get the same test scores by solving correctly different combinations of items. Furthermore, by this line of reasoning, if A = B (i.e., equal test scores), and B = C, there is no reason to suppose that the underlying ability organizations of A and C are the same, even though their numerical test scores are identical.

Interesting as these objections may be, the psychologist can minimize their importance on operational grounds. He can state that by the only measuring instrument available to him, i.e., the test, $A = B$ if they have the same test score. Aside from the question of differences in kind represented by different test scores, no contradiction in the actual numbers assigned can occur with respect to the relations "greater" and "equals." The fact that different combinations of items add up to the same score does not bother him too much because he feels that if the items themselves are of the same sort, the total score should be fairly indicative of the person's level of achievement.

That mental testing has no suitable operation of addition is quite apparent, and critics have not failed to mention this point. There seems to be no way to add physically one psychological magnitude to another to get a third even greater in amount. With fundamentally measurable variables, such as weight, length, resistance, and so on, this can be accomplished easily and, from such an operation, numbers can be assigned such that differences and ratios are endowed with the desired experimental meaning. The fact that the operation of addition is not defined in mental testing leads to considerable difficulty, since this operation is employed in fundamental measurement to endow measurement scales with equal-unit and ratio properties. Thus, it would appear that mental-test workers may not be able to develop test scales with equal units and ratio properties.

Let us consider, for a moment, two opposed points of view which might be adopted with respect to the nature of measurement involved in a mental test. First, it might be assumed that the human mind is composed of an undetermined number of abilities. A test may tap, so to speak, a few of these abilities which inhere basically in the physiological structure of the organism, but the test can be only an indirect measurement in terms of certain behavioral manifestations. A direct measurement is out of the question, at the present state of our knowledge of physiology, for there is no way that variations in these abilities can be directly observed. Behavioral products represent the only available indicators of such underlying variables at the present time.

Taking a simple case, suppose there were such an underlying ability and a test which measured this variable alone, plus some error variance. What is the functional relationship between the performance variable and the underlying ability? If a performance variable is to be used to yield a measure of ability in this sense, it is obvious that such functional relationships must either be determined experimentally, or assumed to follow a certain form. This functional relationship must be known before the task of securing equal-unit scales, with respect to the underlying variable, can be accomplished, for the equality of units must be in terms of the underlying ability, not the performance.

Unfortunately, it is not now possible to determine the nature of such functional relationships. An independent measure of the underlying ability would be necessary before the relationship of such measures to scores on the performance test could be found. Since no independent measurements (e.g., physiological determinations) for the underlying variable can be taken, this method of proceeding is impractical. It should be mentioned at this point that an approach to this problem can be made through the use of certain types of judgments. For example, one might employ fractionation and equal-appearing-interval methods for the scaling of the subjective difficulty of digit series and words in a vocabulary test. These methods do not comprise an experimental verification of unit equality on an underlying mental-ability variable, however. They do allow an operational meaning to be attached to unit differences on the subjective scale, but such units do not represent those of a fundamental type for the underlying variable.

From this analysis, it appears evident that one cannot prove that a performance or behavior test yields equal units along the scale of some basic underlying ability which in itself is not directly observable. It should be emphasized that the task of disproving an assumption of equal units in such cases is equally difficult, for this, too, would require experimental checks of the relationship between the performance variable and independent measurements of the underlying ability.

An opposite position which might be assumed by some persons with respect to the nature of measurement involved in a mental test is the point of view that a test measures a variable of some kind, or variables, and these behavioral products themselves are what concern us. It amounts to behavioristic approach, so to speak, which denies the necessity of dealing in terms of concepts which have no basis in observation. The extreme behaviorist might ask, "What is the point of assuming an underlying ability which cannot be measured, observed, or proved to exist?"

If the second approach is taken, what are the consequences? First, the matter of a functional relationship between the behavior variable and a hypothetical underlying variable is no longer of importance. The behavior itself is the variable, as determined by the performance on some test. The emphasis with this approach is switched from a consideration of whether the test measures the underlying variable properly to that of whether the variable measured is a useful one. It is assumed that the measures obtained from a test represent some variable in a one-to-one fashion. Since the variable is defined by the test scores, there can be no question as to whether the units on such a test are equal, because that is implicit in the assumptions. It follows from the general approach involved that the units of such tests are equal by definition. It is not the intention of the writer to advance either of these positions as his own. These points of view are considered as represented opposed positions which may flank most observers rather than represent them. The point of importance in this discussion is merely that, regardless of what systematic position one adopts, we do not have equal units of the fundamental type with any mental test and we will not have them until means are devised for direct observation of underlying physiological phenomena.

### Some Possible Consequences of the Difficulties

It has already been suggested that the objections raised against mental-test methods with respect to the requirements for order and equality are crucial. The issues raised by the failure to achieve an operational definition of addition in mental testing are more serious, however. Since equal-unit and ratio properties of measurement scales are based upon addition, mental testing faces the task of evaluating the effects of this deficiency.

The most obvious conclusion which might be drawn is that measurement in this area is confined to the ordinal level. That is, numbers assigned by means of mental tests can indicate only the rank-order positions of performances to which those numbers have been given. This is the sort of conclusion which is often made by critics of psychological measurement.

Now, it is quite clear that many of the statistical procedures which are applied to mental-test results demand something in the way of a unit of measurement. (1) Means, standard deviations, product-moment correlations, and all the statistical procedures based upon these must necessarily depend upon interval sizes along the scale of measurement. This is no less true of the rank-difference correlation method, which is derived from the product-moment formula, and hence involves the same concepts. (Ratio characteristics of measurement scales do not constitute as much of a loss to mental testing as the lack of equal units, for most purposes, since the typical statistical treatments need not involve such relations between test scores.)

These considerations suggest that one of two courses of action must be taken by those attempting to use mental tests for measurement purposes. First, they may show that using methods involving unit assumptions does not introduce serious errors or that certain procedures can be employed to minimize such error in spite of the absence of fundamentally equal units. Secondly, they may avoid the use of methods of analysis which depend upon interval interpretations. The multiple cutting-score methods, for example, do not demand such assumptions. Further, non-parametric methods may be used for statistical tests of hypothesis.

It is likely that further development of measurement techniques in mental testing will proceed along both these lines. Certainly, there is a vast unexplored territory in the area of the second procedure suggested above. With respect to the first program, it can be stated that insufficient attention has been given to the problem of determining the degree and kind of error introduced into the results of measurement by virtue of the fact that such measurements lack certain characteristics they are presumed to have. In the next section, criteria for judging the work of measurement methods will be treated in the light of the discussion to this point.

### Criteria for Evaluating Mental Test Methods

The fundamental-measurement model has typically been used as a criterion by which measurement procedures should be evaluated. Those procedures which fit this scheme are termed "good" methods, and procedures which fail to do so are held to be primitive and unsatisfactory as scientific instruments. Mental tests fall in this latter category, for they certainly fail to fit the fundamental-measurement model in at least one important respect, namely, in their defection with respect to the operation of addition. Are there other criteria by which mental tests can be evaluated which may be more useful? Under the first criterion mentioned above, all mental tests are unsatisfactory, and no discrimination among them is provided. Certainly, some tests are better and more useful than others.

The obvious answer to this question is that other criteria are available for judging the value of procedures in mental testing. These criteria are to be found in the validity of such instruments for the practical purposes of assessing and predicting status under a variety of conditions. Lest some misunderstanding on this point arise, it should be hastily added that the logic of fundamental measurement should not be forgotten or ignored. It is a good thing to know where one's methods fail to meet this more exacting pattern in order to avoid the errors which are likely to occur in the absence of this knowledge. The fact that mental-test methods do not satisfy such criteria need not blind us to the possibility and usefulness of evaluation in terms of these other more practical criteria.

Whereas many difficulties are involved in the use of mental tests for the purpose of establishing scientific laws, there seems to be little doubt as to their value for certain practical purposes. It seems reasonable to assert that mental testing is and will be for some time essentially an empirical science with certain rather well-defined practical objectives, rather than primarily a theoretical scientific enterprise. At least, in terms of relative proportion of activity in this area, such a position could scarcely be questioned. Some individuals may object to this point of view, since personal preferences in matters of emphasis are involved. Be that as it may, this position will be adopted with respect to the objectives of mental testing.

These considerations lead to certain conclusions regarding the attitude which practical mental-test workers should adopt toward the logic of measurement. In the first place, they should abandon attempts to manipulate their test scores for the purpose of making their measurements approximate fundamental measurement. It is quite clear that such objectives can never be attained in this manner; they can be attained only through experimental operations upon the underlying physiological determiners of behavior. The practical test worker is not in a position to engage in the type of research activity which might conceivably succeed in reaching such ends. This fact would be evident to anyone familiar with the logic of fundamental measurement, so mental-test workers should by all means be acquainted with measurement theory.

It should be pointed out in this connection that scaling procedures which are apparently designed for obtaining measurement properties beyond rank order are not necessarily bad. What is not defensible is to assume that such procedures can stand on their own because they appear to resemble, in the end result, measurement in the physical sciences. Whether such methods are good or bad can be assessed in terms of their capacity to help achieve the practical objectives of mental tests. Ultimately, methods may become available for checking the claims of such procedures with respect to measurement properties beyond rank-order but, for the present, such claims must rest upon assumptions for which there is insufficient experimental evidence.

Attempts to improve quantification techniques in mental testing should not be confined to the pattern of fundamental measurement but should be spread over a much wider area. Any and all techniques should be explored which might conceivably lead to better predictions or assessments of status, even though such techniques do not appear to have any possibility of making mental-test measurement more like fundamental measurement.

As a matter of fact, some such successful techniques may appear to be in contradiction to a goal in terms of the fundamental-measurement pattern. An article by Richardson (1936), for example, emphasizes the importance of considering the effects of test difficulty on validity. Richardson states that the validity of a test depends in large measure upon whether the test is properly tailored to the job with respect to difficulty. He states:

> Suppose, for example, that a test of clerical aptitude is meant to sort out the best 15 per cent of all applicants. This is on the assumption that the labor market is such that one hundred persons will apply for 15 positions. It is then clear that the optimal difficulty of test elements should be in the neighborhood of plus 1 sigma and that easier tasks would give us discriminations between individuals in whom we are not interested. . . . Under any circumstances involving educational or psychological measurement, the distribution of difficulty of the elements to tasks can be arranged to fulfill more accurately the purposes of measurement.

If, by some procedure, it were possible to develop a test of clerical aptitude which would represent truly a fundamental-measurement scale with a given number of items, the scale would be the same whether 15 per cent or 85 per cent of the applicants were being selected. Under conditions where error variance is not present in the test, success would probably be equal for any cutting score. However, under the conditions of testing existing, this fixed scale could not do the measuring job at a given level as well as a test tailored for that level, although this fixed scale might conceivably be the best general-purpose scale. Thus, the approach to better measurement through meeting the requirements for fundamental measurement, were it possible, would not necessarily give the best practical methods, since it ignores at least one of the important factors affecting test validity.

The methods to be employed in mental testing, then, have a definite purpose and they can be evaluated in terms of that purpose. From the standpoint of the ideas presented here, the primary value of item analysis and factor analysis, for example, lies in the possibility of using such techniques to increase predictive efficiency. Developing batteries of pure tests to predict some criterion through factor analysis of tests and criteria, constitutes a method the value of which can definitely be assessed in terms of higher validity coefficients. The same criteria can be applied to other methods introduced into the mental-test field. Where such good means are available for evaluating measurement methods it seems inappropriate to rely principally on comparisons with abstract logical criteria that were designed for a different context.

## SUMMARY

1. Many difficulties lie in the path of securing for mental-test measurement the type of rigor found in the fundamental type of measurement. Among these, one of the most serious is the impossibility of obtaining equal units without independent physiological assessment of the variables under consideration.

2. This failure brings up many important problems with respect to the treatment of mental-test data by statistical methods, since many of these methods presume that a unit of measurement has been established. Some justification for the use of such methods should be offered.

3. It would be desirable to attain a fundamental type of measurement for mental testing but, at present, such a goal seems out of reach. If fundamental measurement is made the sole yardstick by which the excellence of measurement procedures are to be judged,

mental-test methods are automatically classed as primitive and virtually without prospect of substantial improvement.

4. The objectives of mental testing are held to be primarily empirical in nature. Testing techniques are designed mainly for the prediction and assessment of status. These objectives provide additional criteria by which mental-test methods can be judged, namely, the practical validity determinations for the purposes at hand.

5. Mental-test workers should certainly be aware of what is involved in fundamental measurement, but they should devote their major efforts toward developing measurement techniques which give some hope for better satisfying the practical validity criteria rather than the fundamental-measurement criteria. This position is taken because (a) the fundamental-measurement criteria cannot be attained by the methods available to the mental-test worker, if at all, and (b) the practical-validity criteria and the fundamental-measurement criteria may sometimes be contradictory objectives in the practical situation.

---

## 10.4    On the Meaning of Intelligence
### *George D. Stoddard*

Among other suggestions about the questions needing exploration under the heading of intelligence, Professor Stoddard urges attention to creativity, sex differences in mental ability, and the design of test items which reveal the manner in which sensation transforms thinking. The author presents one of the clearest cases for defining intelligence in terms of developed ability (a theme which permeates many of the readings in this book). He brings together evidence from fields as diverse as anthropology and neurology, to offer the reader a hint as to the kind of measurement tools which researchers will need to begin to design and validate very shortly.

---

From *Proceedings: 1965 Invitational Conference on Testing Problems*, 3–11. Reprinted with permission of the author and Educational Testing Service, Princeton, N. J.

In measuring intelligence, we perceive an accumulative phenomenon in which learning not only affects the mental age and I.Q. at the time but also, through memory, mental skill, and cognitive structure, progressively affects the scores obtained. If we add to this overlap a measure of environmental constancy, let us say through the impact of speech habits, a planned curriculum, and television, we can expect I.Q. constancy to a mild degree. Until recent years, tens of millions of potentially bright children in Asia, Africa, and Latin America remained illiterate and therefore consistently test-dull. At the same time we may postulate that in advanced countries millions of potentially dull children, under favorable conditions, went up the mental ladder faster and farther thus altering our concept of the norm.

Intelligence is as intelligence does; it is no secret pocket hidden away in the brain like a pituitary gland. Intelligence is indeed based on the brain—on the brain as reconstituted by experience. Childhood education is in part a name for organized experience that is designed to develop intelligence, along with other desirable attributes in personality and behavior, to an optimum degree. At the root of all experience and all education is *the mind as consequence.*

What it has come down to, ever since the first Binet-Simon tryouts, is the identification of behavior deemed intelligent with rather simple cognitive matters—with geared-in information, speech, and problem solving. I have long felt that in the total pattern we need to insert two additional factors, namely 1) creativity and 2) resistance to emotional or other forces that distort the process of reasoning. The memorizer, the computer, the plodder simply should not be given the highest rank in the field of *general intelligence.* The tested and scored operations exhaust his talent; his assorted mental skills can be measured and totalized. Beyond the standardized test lies open-ended testing not *of* but *for* the emergence of original ideas. Case histories help but do not suffice. Likewise, a merger of mental testing with personality testing will give us clues as to why individual "A" remains intelligent under social, political, or religious pressure while "B", his mental-test equal, becomes confused, misled, or ridiculous.

Of course, creativity cannot be guaranteed. Creativity is no sure outcome of the mastery of even the far reaches of what is known or surmised. Thus in science a solid jumping-off place is needed; intuition does not serve there unless it is intellectually allied to previous knowledge or theory. Jerome B. Wiesner postulates a condition for creativity in the sciences:

> The term "creativity" is principally used to mean activity resulting in contributions that have novelty and value in the intellectual sphere of human experience, including the sciences, as well as literature, music, and the visual arts. In all such contexts, "creativity" universally implies a departure from, and advance beyond, what is conventionally attainable. However, there is an important characteristic of creative contributions in science that is not significantly present in many other fields, namely, quantitatively definable logical relationships to pre-existing scientific knowledge.

Along with studies of what's what in the environment, I should place reliable measures of creativity and intellectual integrity at the top of the heap for new research.

Perhaps two or three additional suggestions are worth considering.

The young girl, further along physiologically and presumably mentally, learns to read sooner and better than the boy. For a time, she holds her own in mathematical and other abstractions, but the boy catches up. He keeps growing for a longer time. It may be that the so-called genius rating—a precarious label—is achieved by a child who starts fast like a girl and perseveres like a boy. In any case, sex-related differences should be reexamined in relation to cognitive theory and test standardization. As long as scores are computed with chronological age as a denominator, we need separate male and female norms.

Doubtless, intelligence tests for the adolescent and the mature adult should break up into branches that reach out from the main stem of general intelligence. In these later stages, intelligent behavior needs to be differentiated in terms of the ability to solve abstract problems that involve acquired formulas and methods, together with certain cognitive tools such as may be found in logic, science, or music. Concrete tools like the telescope, the microscope, the camera, hearing devices, and other detectors may be regarded as extensions of the sensory organs whose contribution to cortical power is indirect. The skills involved in their use are akin to those that the race developed long ago—to cutting and pounding devices and agricultural implements. They help the technician, but they are not necessarily a part of his intellectual structure. Hence, for our purposes we need not measure the motor skills they call for, but only the way in which their sensory revelations transform thinking.

General intelligence becomes a base for special development that may be measured more meaningfully than that afforded by adding discrete items that are validated on the percent passing in a given sampling. It is a profound error in mental measurement to derive the abilities of the "superior adult" from an aggregation of simple tasks. With new test items of the kind Jerome S. Bruner and his colleagues are working on we could carry the concept of general intelligence to more advanced levels before reaching the rational outcome in the branching I have referred to.

For adults it is scarcely a matter of predicting a future mental state. What counts is the ability to perform immediate mental tasks that embody the essence of whole families of tasks. There is a change-over point from interest in the child's present and future levels of accomplishment to what the adult does or is able to do *now*. How shall we test this? After all, for adults we do not predict anything except a decline—not so much a decline in the basic skills but in mental power that may be applied to real situations. By this time, through heredity and long experience, the intellectual structure is characterized by observable potentials, limits, and stable achievements. While the general trend is downward, as with a river, the immediate capabilities may hold steady or at times surge upward. There can be a late-blooming intelligence as long as the nervous system has not suffered damage or deterioration. Of course, no new brain cells are involved in this phenomenon—there aren't any—only a better coordination of those that remain functional.

Whether intelligence be viewed in terms of current behaviorism or of cognitive psychology, there is postulated a sufficient chemical, physical, and neurological base. Neurological studies are of interest to the psychologist just as cellular studies are to the nutritionist or the physiologist. Nevertheless, psychology is essentially a social science. Men think in man-made symbols or they do not think at all. Intelligence, as an ability that grows through the interaction of nervous structures and mediated social events, may be regarded as our most purely psychological phenomenon. In studying early education that may be designated effective or good, we turn to the significance of images, concepts, formulations, and experiences rather than to actual changes in nervous tissue or in physiological function. Actually, when we find a gain in measured intelligence that is correlated with age or experience, we postulate either a temporary or long-range improvement in the nervous system. Let the biochemist, the physiologist, the neurologist, and the nutritionist discover what they can. It may or may not have discernible psychological outcomes, but it makes sense to improve our knowledge of the substrata of behavior. In fact, therapeutic principles of great importance to an individual or to a whole population may emerge. Consider, for example, the operational difference between brain $X_1$ that is optimally supplied with oxygen and twin-brain $X_2$ whose oxygen supply is deficient or in excess.

The brain is not a dead tool or chest of tools. It is not a machine. Its stores of remembered items are not lined up on a shelf or imbedded in an automatic circuit. They are chosen in the first place and once chosen, their quality depends upon their availability on demand for abstract thinking, problem solving, and creativity. That, in turn, depends upon a prior process of coding and integrating. Without the early intervention of speech this whole series of events would be encumbered. In the words of Neal E. Miller:

> We no longer view the brain as merely an enormously complicated telephone switchboard which is passive unless excited from without. The brain is a device for sorting, processing, and analyzing information. The brain contains sense organs which respond to states of internal environment, such as osmotic pressure, temperature and many others. The brain is a gland which secretes chemical messengers, and it also responds to such messengers, as well as to various types of feedback, both central and peripheral.

So much for the inside. In regard to the outside we have, as one example, the flat statement of Harold G. Wolff, a neurologist at the Cornell University School of Medicine: "I am prepared now to say, after four years of inquiry, that the brain may be damaged in the process of attempting to make adaptations to situations that the individual cannot meet."

Language is the great stimulator and the basis of most logical thought. Illiteracy imposes a massive mental defect. A neurosis is a partial mental defect; if our tests do not discover it and negatively incorporate it into the total score of mental ability, so much the worse for the tests. Similarly a psychotic involvement carries a corresponding mental defect, for it rains down intellectual corruption upon the trivial discrete responses which are superficially intact. To decimate activity deemed intelligent is one way of reducing mental ability, although the condition is different from the overall defectiveness of a congenital imbecile. If the psychosis develops relatively late in life, the harmful social effects are compounded. By that time the person may be able to wield power over others.

Granted that each of us is a unique bundle of cellular units, we *learn* to be intelligent, or not to be, and some persons learn faster than others. In fact, for some children such learning is so hard to come by, even under conditions of expert instruction, that we are justified in applying a low I.Q. rating, and in retaining it if the learning difficulties persist, but not otherwise. At times, neurological conditions permit us to predict a permanent mental defect. Lacking such physical evidence, we should be cautious about applying restrictive labels. A functional defect not traceable to brain deficiency or damage may or may not endure; we have to find out by repeated measurements based on differentiated educational stimuli. These, in turn, may call into play novel forms of stimulation, motivation, and achievement. At the other end of the stick, we have to be cautious about predicting an abiding mental superiority. Brains deemed neurologically intact may become addled. In your own community look about you!

J. McV. Hunt has pinpointed a semantic error that runs through much mental testing:

> The application of such terms as *dimension* and *scale* may at once tend to carry their meaning in the physical world over to the world of organismic behavior and to imply that the constancy of dimensions is being generalized from static objects to non-static persons and their behavior . . . Fixed intelligence is a conception like the pre-formationistic notion that the bodily structure of a species is to be found within the egg or the sperm . . . Calling intelligence a *dimension* and speaking of tests as *scales* may be unfortunate.

Hunt develops in some detail "the notion of intelligence as central processes developing as a function of the child's interactions with the environment." Here the key word is *interactions*, and its significance for education is emphasized by Hunt: "Inasmuch as development rates are most rapid, in absolute terms, during the early months and first couple of years, this is probably the period of most importance for maximizing intellectual potential."

Since the reliability of infant tests may reach r = .90, their failure to predict later or final mental standing is another way of saying that we do not know what the subsequent environmental encounters will consist of; in fact, we have poor measures of such influences at any stage of development. The studies of S. A. Kirk and others, comparing I.Q. changes in retarded children, indicate the fruitfulness of such an attack even when the precise forces at work are, to say the least, homogenized. Whatever the events, learnings, and situations may be, it appears that the essence of a fruitful interaction is to get beyond repetitions or aggregations to a spiraling integration. This means a putting away of childish things in the later portions of any mental test. Even to test the hereditary component as a *potential*, we need to give full play to hierarchical experiences and to relate them in time sequences to the intellectual demands of a particular growing child.

So, let us stop worrying about how much of intelligence is due to heredity and how much to environment. It never was a good question. There can be a hereditary or congenital defect so severe as to make an environmental influence negligible. I have myself seen an adult inmate of an institution whose I.Q. might be placed at 1; she could smile, period. On the other hand, potential geniuses who "waste their sweetness on the desert air," for all we know, may be rather numerous. Illiteracy in a society reaching toward literacy not only stamps out genius; it obscures all objective measurement of what is or might have been.

We observe three action worlds: 1) the preconception world of eugenics; 2) the prenatal world of nutrition and protection; and 3) the postnatal world of education. The prenatal condition is really a special case: by informing the mother, you safeguard the fetus. Thus Ashley Montagu has shown that the heavy smoking of cigarettes by pregnant women may damage the unborn child. By maximizing beneficent environment, early and late, but especially early, we are in a sound position. With or without formal schooling, the first six years are the most important—logically because all of life follows, and psychologically because this is a period of rapid mental growth. Far in advance of scientific knowledge, we have done rather well, by law, to keep children away from tobacco, alcohol, and narcotics, but we are just beginning to give economic and educational aid on behalf of children below the age of five.

Consider this educational dilemma:

Allowing 182 out of 365 days to formal schooling and noting that one-half of the waking time of each child during this formal schooling period is spent out of school, we come abruptly upon a sobering thought: in the preschool years, the family and neighborhood carry 100 percent of the educational load; during school years they still carry 75 percent of the load, as they say on Madison Avenue, "timewise." Hence the need for a sound education of the child at home by parents who are soundly educated is urgent. And this is not all. If Benjamin Bloom is right in his hypotheses, this preschool period accounts for as much variance in tested intelligence as all the remaining years of childhood and adolescence. While the kind of testing advocated in this brief paper will search out new cognitive structures and will give scope to emerging factors less appropriate to early childhood, the principle remains: to neglect the young child is to invite a progressive slowdown in intellectual attainment.

To turn a phrase, we can discern the three forces of intellect, namely, home education, school education, and self-education. Technically self-education is all. No one of these simply works *upon*, none directly *impinges* on the child's inherited nervous system —rather, all unite in a vastly complicated interaction between what the child was born with (and has grown into) and the determiners, overt or obscure, in the environment.

The national educational program carried on last summer on behalf of over 500,000 underprivileged preschool children is indeed a *Head Start*. (The new crop of underprivileged children, by the way, will be those who do not get such attention before the age of five.) If the movement spreads, I predict a lifting of the fog that has settled over so many discussions of inferiority due to race, nationality, or parental status. Children differ from one another in their inherited structures, but this cannot be determined by extrapolation from external categories.

We learn in order to make better decisions now and in the future —in order to safeguard and enrich our lives. The aim of education is life fulfillment through learning. It is true that a small amount of learning may produce a vast amount of thinking, but such "thinking" tends to become repetitive and self-defeating. In our culture pattern, the Dark Ages furnish the supreme example; the people were terribly short of knowledge, or of the scientific method. Who knows but today, with all our vast array of science and technology, we may be judged as being terribly short of *thinking*, that is, of problem solving directed toward viable and humane political structures.

Has not the worldwide drift up to now been on the side of the dysgenic? We have the well-documented population "explosion." We have the prospect of wars which, in the future, will disproportionately kill city people and wipe out their cultural achievements. Still, if education from nursery school to college becomes endemic, social competition will operate as an effective eugenic moderator. We can then forget about large families versus small. Also, except for extremes which rarely run in families, we can forget about "good stock" and "poor stock." Man's ancestry is so unlike the incestuous breeding lines that produce good dogs and horses as to make such comparisons hilarious. In a world of love-at-first-sight, or perhaps on-second-thought, the crossing gene lines are as invisible as the genes themselves.

All animals evolve by natural selection and a responsiveness to the environment. A family group, a tradition, a language, a space ship is as much a part of the environment as a seashore or a tree. Our ancestors climbed down out of trees, made use of sticks and stones, and gradually were changed. Now we climb up into the sky. Since *change* is the universal condition of life, and of sublife for that matter, who can say what human forms will evolve? While a centrifuged, irradiated, weightless person may not expect to see any special effects in his offspring, if we put enough of the breeding segment of the human race in space contraptions, generation after generation, mutations might appear. Perhaps in a hundred thousand years the computer men who never get off the ground will develop so differently from astronauts that a demand for desegregation will arise!

Clearly, the stage is set for interchange, interaction, interdependence. The brain responds to internal and external events. In responding, it changes. Of course it would change anyway through the mechanics of growth and decline, but we like to think we can prevent or postpone deleterious happenings and accentuate what is organismically and behaviorally sound. Therein lies the foundation of the good life for the individual. It is, I suppose, an article of faith that a reliance on actions and experiences deemed favorable *for this child today*, if they are constantly modified by new insights, will also be of long-range value to the human race. The fearful alternative is to lose sight of *this child*, or of *all children*, by poisoning the materials or events that interact with cortical functioning. A sustained indifference to the inroads of disease, injury, ignorance, frustration, or superstition will lower the intelligence level of a given generation and lend a gloomy outlook to the future of man.

---

## 10.5   The Digital Computer Simulates Human Rating Behavior
### *Herbert Garber*

The following was written especially for this publication and is based largely on a paper delivered as part of the Symposium "Essay Grading by Computer: Measurement Frontier?" at the 73rd Annual Convention of the American Psychological Association, Chicago, 1965.

Although routine automatic data processing by digital computer is becoming less mysterious, to workers involved in educational and psychological measurement the use of the computer as a research tool for studying human behavior by simulation is infrequently well understood.

In this article, the author describes the strategy followed in a research aimed at developing a system for analyzing and marking written compositions by computers.

With the steady growth in computer availability, the educator and psychologist will turn, naturally and readily, to so powerful and accessible a tool for swift answers and labor-saving efficiency on hosts of practical problems.

Project Essay Grade (PEG), later known as Analysis of Essays by Computer, is a research effort designed to see if a digital computer can assign grades to student compositions which agree with the grades assigned to them by well-qualified human raters. It can.

The rationale is fairly simple. When a teacher, editor, or other critical reader reads a piece of writing effort he is at the very least encountering and attending to certain conventionalized visual stimuli. Words and punctuation signals probably occupy the first order of discriminations. A skilled reader never pauses over such discriminations except when the handwriting or typescript is atrociously distorted. At successive levels, we may postulate that sound values such as rhythm, alliteration, rhyme, and pitch and meaning values such as imagery, mood, tone, and other semantic properties are responded to. Associated with these variables *in the minds of readers* are sets of values for such things as word fluency, spacing of commas, etc.

The meaning or content interpretation of a prose passage is utterly dependent upon the previous experiences of the reader well beyond his mere lexical and grammatical sophistication. For instance, although one may understand perfectly the words and sentence structure in a political paper written by someone of an opposing point of view, the meaning obtained will be more a function of the reader's values than his skill in reading. For this and similar reasons, it was decided to initiate the study by choosing from the opinions of experts in English composition and teaching a list of elements of "good writing style," rather than looking for components denoting "knowledge of subject."

These stylistic elements such as "use of subordination," "use of apt words," "avoidance of overuse of subject-verb sentence openings," etc. next were studied to determine what aspects of them could be stored in computer memory so that some sort of count could be made of the frequency with which they occurred in each essay.

If it is true that when a human judge of writing ability reads an essay rapidly, trying to gain an overall impression of writing ability that he notes only such gross visual properties which he can grasp quickly then the evaluation or judgment he makes is probably based on such items as: presence of unusual words, varied sentence structure, few spelling errors, and in general a suitable length of essay. Also, if these are what he notes he probably evaluates them in an interrelated way. That is, his final judgment of the whole composition is not a simple sum of discrete, independent sets of scores for each variable. Each variable, rather, bears a particular weight in the final judgment which to some degree is modified by the weights given to all the other variables. Thus, an essay which contains many unusual words will possibly be more highly valued if it *also* shows variety in sentence length and type of sentence used. In other words, one should be able to count the relative frequency with which the several variables occur within a composition, assign a specific weight to each which was derived from its correlations with both a criterion and with the other variables in the passage, add up all the weighted scores and arrive at the overall score. This corresponds, more or less, to a description of the statistic known as multiple regression or multiple correlation. And this is exactly what the computer was made to do for PEG.

What was needed at once, in addition to computer facilities and a good plan, was some appropriate, analyzable data. This was one point at which Lady Luck played a significant role in hastening the early trial of the strategy. Fortunately, excellent data were made available from a study in composition at the University of Wisconsin. The project was supplied two typewritten essays from each of 276 secondary students, Grades 8 through 12. Each essay had been graded independently on a four point scale by four teachers of English who had been carefully coached to minimize idiosyncratic values and to read each essay with the prescribed purpose of gaining for themselves an overall, general impression of writing ability. The procedure was carefully planned and conditions were so arranged, as to conform to strict standards of acceptable research practice. That the Wisconsin study succeeded in achieving a high degree of control over rating behavior is confirmed by the rather solid .83 reliability coefficient on the pooled raters' judgments. The average interjudge agreement was about .5. (The reader will recall that essay grading is notoriously unreliable.)

The essays were key-punched into IBM cards for input, *just* as written by the students with all mistakes intact.

The first phase of this program, in general, performs the two operations of word recognition and selective counter incrementing, and the second phase inserts the first numerical output into the statistical multiple regression program.

What was involved was a looking for and enumerating of the occurrence within each essay of 31 selected variables. The choice of each variable was reasoned from the principles of English composi-

TABLE 1.    VARIABLES USED IN PROJECT ESSAY GRADE

| A. Variable | B. Transformation for Processing | C. Correl. with Pooled Human Judgments | D. Beta Weight |
|---|---|---|---|
| 1. Title present | 1 or 0 | .04 | .095 |
| 2. Av. sentence length | × 100 | .04 | −.108 |
| 3. Number of paragraphs | | .06 | −.114 |
| 4. #Subject-verb openings | (Div. by # sent.) × 100 | −.17 * | −.004 |
| 5. *Length of essay in words* | | .31 * | .320 |
| 6. Number of parentheses | (Div. by # wds.) × 1000 | .05 | −.009 |
| 7. Number of apostrophes | Same | −.24 * | −.067 |
| 8. *Number of commas* | Same | .34 * | .090 |
| 9. Number of periods | Same | −.04 | −.021 |
| 10. Number of percentage marks | Same | .00 | .000 |
| 11. Number of underlined words | Same | .00 | .001 |
| 12. No. dashes | Same | .22 * | .103 |
| 13. No. colons | Same | .02 | −.036 |
| 14. No. semi-colons | Same | .08 | .066 |
| 15. No. quotation marks | (Div. by # sents.) × 1000 | .11 | .044 |
| 16. No. exclamation marks | Same | −.05 | .038 |
| 17. No. question marks | Same | −.14 | −.085 |
| 18. No. prepositions | (Div. by # wds.) × 100 | .26 * | .109 |
| 19. No. connective words | Same | .18 * | −.016 |
| 20. No. spelling errors | Same | −.20 * | −.129 |
| 21. No. relative pronouns | Same | .10 | .103 |
| 22. No. subordinating conjunctions | Same | −.12 | .068 |
| 23. *No. wds. on Dale common wd. list* | Same | −.48* | −.046 |

TABLE 1.    (*Continued*)

| A.<br>Variable | B.<br>Transformation for<br>Processing | C.<br>Correl.<br>with Pooled<br>Human<br>Judgments | D.<br>Beta<br>Weight |
|---|---|---|---|
| 24. No. sents. with end punct. present | (Div. by # sent.) ×<br>100 | −.01 | −.039 |
| 25. No. declar. sents. type "A" | Same | .12 | .004 |
| 26. No. declar. sents. type "B" | Same | .02 | −.021 |
| 27. No. hyphens | (Div. by # wds.) ×<br>100 | .18 * | .063 |
| 28. No. slashes | Same | −.06 | −.016 |
| 29. *Av. word length* | × 100 | .51 * | .128 |
| 30. *Stan. dev. of word length* | × 100 | .54 * | .315 |
| 31. Stan. dev. of sent. length | | −.07 | .019 |

Multiple R is .71.
Number of student essays judged is 276.
 F ratio for Multiple R is 7.99 (very significant).
* Significant at or beyond the .01 level.

tion and the suppositions concerning the human judgment of these principles.

In Table One, you will find these variables listed in Column A. As can be seen, *none* of them can be construed as anything more than possible *correlates* of writing style, certainly not the intrinsic variables which may be believed to be the components that make the difference between good, bad, or indifferent prose. But as it turns out they are quite adequate for the job.

The PEG analysis produced, during the first computer pass, a series of counts. In order to eliminate the effect of essay length and other components on each such count, most of them were transformed to a ratio. The nature of each transformation is indicated in Table One in Column B. For example, certain punctuation marks, variables 6 through 14, were divided by essay length in words and this quotient was multiplied by 1,000. Thus the use of a comma correlate to adequate use of punctuation in a short essay would not be hidden, so to speak, by the possible fact that a mediocre but longer paper had had an identical number of commas. Incidentally, as you may note, this particular variable, number eight, yielded the fourth from highest first-order correlation with the criterion.

On pass two, the transformed counts served as the input predictor data for a standard multiple regression computer program. The pooled ratings from the four teacher-raters from the Wisconsin study were the criterion to be predicted. The computer predicted the human ratings very impressively. Its scores correlated with those of the human raters with a coefficient of .71. The F test of significance for that coefficient was, of course very significant, well beyond the .01 level.

Even in this first crude test, therefore, the ability of the computer to simulate the expert human group was remarkable to say the least. It was in the range of accuracy expected from the single expert English teacher, coached to do his reliable best.

In addition to this demonstration that the strategy and procedures were viable the first order correlations and computed beta weights, which are listed in columns C and D, began at once to serve a valuable heuristic function. One can say some things with assurance now about how a judged good essay written by one of these high school students will look. Variables five, eight, twenty-three, twenty-nine, and thirty, which are underlined in column A, permit one to describe such an essay as a bit over 400 words long, sprinkled with commas (probably a sign that complex sentence structure is prevalent), with subordination, and employing more unusual and longer words.

PEG thus far indeed had met with most encouraging success. It had delivered improved knowledge of the correlates of essay ratings, demonstrated that the machine can simulate a highly complex human activity, and, perhaps most exciting of all, provided clues to what additional strategies to follow in pursuit of future objectives. But, after all, any predictive power remained only a statistical inference. A valuable addition would be a true attempt at cross-validation. This was immediately done by utilizing a random split-half of the present group of subjects. In the first trial 138 subjects produced beta weights which predicted, now in the *generic* sense of the term, the human judgments on the other 138 subjects with a .62 correlation. This is a coefficient based on a random validating sample and is therefore presumably lower than it would be if all 276 subjects had been employed.

TABLE 2.        WHICH ONE IS THE COMPUTER?

Below is the intercorrelation matrix generated by the cross validation of PEG in the following fashion:

All "judges" graded the overall quality of a set of 138 essays written by high-school students in Grades 8–12. One "judge" was a computer, the other four were independent human experts. The correlations in this table show the extent to which each "judge" tended to agree with each other in grading essays. The computer-assigned grades were based upon beta weightings generated from the multiple prediction of human judgments on 138 essays by *other* students randomly drawn from the same population. Which one, A, B, C, D, or E is the computer vector?

| Judges | | | | |
|---|---|---|---|---|
| A | B | C | D | E |
| | 51 | 51 | 44 | 57 |
| 51 | | 53 | 56 | 61 |
| 51 | 53 | | 48 | 49 |
| 44 | 56 | 48 | | 59 |
| 57 | 61 | 49 | 59 | |

Now in Table Two is a display which rather dramatically illustrates the degree to which the computer behaved as the human raters did. The column and row headings of this intercorrelation matrix designate the four human judges and the computer. A mere visual inspection of these numbers does not permit a ready certainty as to which column represents the machine "who thinks he is a people." Since these numbers indicate to what extent each human rater and the automaton agreed on writing ability with the other "judges" and since no single one is markedly different from the other four, the conclusion that they behaved in approximately the same way becomes logically persuasive. We must conclude then that for the specified task which all five performed, they were doing substantially the same thing. The computer, by the way, is designated by C.

The computer is simulating the products of human rating behavior in a controlled fashion. What new areas of knowledge this has made accessible can scarcely be conceived save by the most imaginative.

| Judges |   |   |   |   |   |
|---|---|---|---|---|---|
|   | A | B | C | D | E |
| A |   | 51 | 51 | 44 | 57 |
| B | 51 |   | 53 | 56 | 61 |
| C | 51 | 53 |   | 48 | 49 |
| D | 44 | 56 | 48 |   | 59 |
| E | 57 | 61 | 49 | 59 |   |

## 10.6   The Adjective Check List, a Device to Assess
## Perceived Self

*John T. Flynn*

The difficulties involved in the accurate assessment of human behavior are numerous. Psychologists recognize that most individuals are reluctant to reveal certain aspects of their personality. To account for this reluctance, which is related to the idea of social acceptability of responses to personality tests, elaborate attempts have been made to develop tests yielding reliable and accurate behavioral descriptions that keep threats to the self at a minimum. The Edwards Personal Preference Schedule is such an instrument. This study suggests that such elaborate attempts might not be warranted. Gordon Allport suggests that the best way to know an individual is to question him directly about himself. What are your feelings on this matter? Do you feel people are threatened to the extent they will deliberately alter personality test responses? This article suggests one possible approach to the area of educational research that utilizes some measurement concepts.

The purpose of this study was to investigate the relationship between performances upon two different approaches to the assessment of personality, an objective personality instrument and an adjective check list. Four tests of the *Edwards Personal Preference Schedule* (EPPS) were selected: (1) Achievement, (2) Dominance, (3) Change, and (4) Heterosexuality. In addition, the *Gough Adjective Check List* (GACL) was used. This is an instrument comprised of 300 personal human adjectives, and subjects are instructed to indicate which of them could be used to describe themselves.

The study was designed to test the hypothesis that graduate students in education who scored high on the four dimensions of the EPPS would ascribe a greater number of human adjectives to themselves than students who scored low on the EPPS subtests. In addition, it was hypothesized that a significant correlation would exist between scores on the EPPS subtests and positive adjectives selected on the GACL.

The EPPS was administered to 50 graduate students at Indiana University during the summer of 1965. The following week the

Reprinted with permission of the author and *Journal of Teacher Education*, **XVII**, 2, Summer 1966.

*Gough Adjective Check List* (2) was administered to the same sample. The GACL was scored by simply counting the total number of items each subject had checked and the number of positive and negative adjectives he had selected. Some interesting findings were: (1) The correlation between total number of adjectives checked and achievement scores was not significant, r = .21. (2) The correlation between total number of adjectives checked and dominance scores was not significant, r = .11. (3) The correlation between total number of adjectives checked and change scores was not significant, r = .23. (4) The correlation between total number of adjectives checked and heterosexuality scores was not significant, r = .22.

An analysis of the correlations between total number of adjectives checked and subtest scores for males and females revealed no significant relationship within sexes or between sexes.

No significant relationship was found between total number of positive adjectives selected and the dimensions of achievement (males, r = .20; females, r = .13) and change (males, r = .17; females, r = .05).

A significant correlation was also noted between number of positive adjectives checked and performance on the dominance subtest (males, r = .61; females, r = −.57).

A significant correlation was also noted between number of positive adjectives checked and performance on the heterosexuality subtest (males, r = .67; females, r = .53).

On the basis of the limited data revealed by this study, it appears that persons who see themselves as dominant also perceive themselves as possessing a significant number of negative traits, such as talkative, aggressive, severe, and headstrong. Logically this appears reasonable, and apparently both the dominance subtest of the EPPS and the GACL instruments are refined enough to detect this phenomenon to the same degree.

The desire and ability to relate successfully to members of the opposite sex seems to be directly related to a perception of such persons that they possess a significant number of positive characteristics. Again, the heterosexuality subtest of the EPPS and the GACL seem to detect this in a similar fashion.

One important, although tentative, implication of these data is that some aspects of heterosexual behavior and dominant behavior may be susceptible to measurement in a simple manner: a count of the number and type of adjectives that individuals would choose to describe themselves.

# CORRELATION CHART OF READINGS AND POPULAR MEASUREMENT TEXTS

| Author and Text | Text Chapter (Cell entries contain suggested *Readings* chapters.) | | | | | | | | |
|---|---|---|---|---|---|---|---|---|---|
| | 1 | 2 | 3 | 4 | 5 | 6 | 7 | 8 | 9 |
| Adams, Georgia S., *Measurement and Evaluation*, Holt, 1965 | 1.2<br>1.3<br>1.4 | 4.4 | 2.1<br>3.4<br>4.3 | 1.1<br>2.2<br>7.1<br>7.3 | 1.3<br>2.3 | 3.2<br>3.3<br>5.1<br>7.2 | 6.1 | 5.2<br>6.3<br>6.4<br>10.6 | 6.2<br>6.4 |
| Anastasi, Anne, *Psychological Testing*, 2nd ed., Macmillan, 1961 | 1.4<br>4.1<br>5.1<br>5.2 | 1.1<br>10.3 | 3.1<br>3.3<br>8.2<br>9.3 | 1.2<br>3.2<br>10.3 | 3.3<br>3.4 | 3.2<br>3.4<br>7.2 | 7.1<br>7.2<br>7.3 | 3.4<br>5.3<br>10.4 | 4.2<br>5.2<br>10.2 |
| Cronbach, L. J., *Essentials of Psychological Testing*, Harper, 1960 | 1.3<br>9.1 | 1.4<br>4.1 | 3.1<br>9.3 | 4.1<br>4.3<br>4.4 | 3.4<br>7.1 | 2.1<br>3.3 | 3.2<br>5.1<br>5.2 | 4.2<br>5.3<br>7.2 | |
| Davis, F. B., *Educational Measurements and Their Interpretation*, Wadsworth, 1964 | 1.1<br>1.3 | 2.1<br>2.3<br>3.4<br>4.1 | 1.3<br>2.3 | 4.3<br>8.2 | 1.2 | 3.2<br>5.1<br>5.3 | 7.2<br>10.6 | 4.1 | 4.3<br>4.4<br>9.1 |
| Ebel, R. L., *Measuring Educational Achievement*, Prentice, 1965 | 1.2<br>1.3<br>2.3<br>8.4 | 7.1<br>10.3 | 8.1<br>9.3 | 8.2<br>10.5 | | 8.2 | 3.1 | | 3.4 |
| Gronlund, N. E., *Measurement and Evaluation in Teaching*, Macmillan, 1965 | 1.4<br>1.3 | 6.1<br>8.4<br>9.2 | 1.2<br>6.4 | 2.3<br>4.1<br>8.3 | 2.1<br>3.4 | 8.2<br>8.3<br>9.1 | | 1.3<br>5.3 | |
| Noll, V. H., *Introduction to Educational Measurement*, 2nd ed., Houghton-Mifflin, 1965 | 1.3 | | | 2.1<br>3.4 | 1.2<br>1.4<br>6.1 | 8.1<br>8.2<br>10.5 | 2.1<br>3.4<br>10.1 | 1.2<br>8.2 | 1.2<br>8.2 |
| Remmers, H. H., Gage, N. L., Rummel, J. F., *A Practical Introduction to Measurement and Evaluation*, Harper, 1960 | | 1.4<br>9.1 | 1.1<br>10.3 | 5.2<br>8.1<br>9.2 | 3.2<br>3.4<br>4.1 | 3.2<br>5.3<br>9.3 | 6.1<br>6.4 | 5.1<br>8.1<br>8.2<br>8.3 | 9.2<br>9.3 |
| Stanley, J. C., *Measurement in Today's Schools*, 4th ed., Prentice, 1964 | 8.1 | 1.3<br>10.2 | 1.1<br>2.1<br>7.3 | 4.1<br>4.4 | 2.1<br>3.4<br>4.1<br>5.2 | 2.3<br>3.1<br>6.1 | 8.4 | 8.2<br>10.2<br>10.5 | 6.3<br>6.4 |
| Thorndike, R. L. and Hagen, Elizabeth, *Measurement and Evaluation in Psychology and Education*, Wiley, 1955 | 1.1<br>1.4<br>4.2 | 1.2<br>5.2 | 8.1<br>8.2<br>9.1 | 1.2<br>8.4 | 4.3 | 2.1<br>3.4<br>4.1<br>7.2 | 4.3<br>4.4 | | 3.2<br>5.2<br>10.4 |

| 10 | 11 | 12 | 13 | 14 | 15 | 16 | 17 | 18 | 19 | 20 | 21 |
|---|---|---|---|---|---|---|---|---|---|---|---|
| 8.1<br>8.2<br>9.3<br>0.5 | 5.3<br>8.2<br>8.4 | 7.1<br>7.3<br>10.1 | 1.4<br>7.1 | 6.2<br>7.3<br>8.3 | 7.2<br>9.1<br>9.2 | 4.3<br>4.4 | 5.3<br>7.2 | | | | |
| 4.1<br>5.3<br>9.1<br>0.1 | 1.4<br>4.1 | 6.3 | 10.1<br>10.2<br>10.3 | 7.2 | | 1.2<br>3.4<br>8.3 | 1.4<br>3.2<br>10.2 | 4.1<br>10.2 | 6.1<br>6.3<br>6.4<br>10.2 | 6.2<br>7.3<br>10.2 | 6.2<br>6.3<br>10.2<br>10.6 |
| 7.1 | 7.2 | 7.3 | 1.2<br>5.3 | 7.2 | 6.2<br>6.3 | 6.2<br>10.2<br>10.6 | 7.1 | 6.2 | 6.1<br>6.4 | | |
| 7.1<br>0.1 | 10.4 | 8.4 | 9.2<br>9.3<br>10.5 | | | | | | | | |
| 2.1<br>3.4 | | 1.1<br>4.1<br>10.3 | 9.3 | | | | | | | | |
| 0.5 | 3.1<br>9.3 | 3.2<br>5.1 | 9.1<br>9.2 | 4.3<br>4.4<br>10.3 | 6.2<br>6.3 | 6.3 | 7.3<br>9.3 | | | | |
| 3.2<br>5.1<br>5.3<br>0.4 | 7.1<br>7.2 | 10.6 | 6.3 | 9.1<br>9.2 | 4.1<br>7.3<br>10.1 | | | | | | |
| 5.3<br>0.2 | 6.2<br>6.3<br>10.2 | | | | | | | | | | |
| 7.3<br>8.1<br>8.3 | 1.2<br>9.2<br>9.3 | | | | | | | | | | |
| .3<br>.2 | 1.2<br>3.3<br>4.3 | 6.3<br>7.1 | 6.1<br>6.2<br>6.4 | 6.3<br>10.6 | 6.2 | 9.1<br>9.2 | 9.3 | 7.1<br>7.2<br>7.3 | 2.2<br>3.3 | 6.2 | |